Consciousness, Reality, and the Spiritual Journey of the Wayward Soul

A Reality of Consciousness Pervades the Cosmos
The Consciousness of Reality Redeems the Soul

Jeffrey L. Imes

Consciousness, Reality, and the Spiritual Journey of the Wayward Soul
A Reality of Consciousness Pervades the Cosmos.
The Consciousness of Reality Redeems the Soul

Quoted scriptures and Scripture references marked as KJV or unmarked are from the authorized (King James) version of the Holy Bible. Rights in the authorized version in the United Kingdom are vested in the Crown. Reproduced by permission of the Crown's patentee, Cambridge University Press.

Quoted scriptures and Scripture references marked NIV are from New International Version of the Holy Bible. Copyright © 1973, 1978, 1984, 2011 by Biblica, Inc.™ Used by permission of Zondervan. All rights reserved worldwide www.zondervan.com The NIV and New International Version are trademarks registered in the United States Patent and Trademark Office by Biblica, Inc. ™

Edgar Cayce readings © 1971, 1993–2007
The Edgar Cayce Foundation.
All Rights Reserved.

Print ISBN: 979-8-99307-162-6
eBook ISBN: 979-8-99307-163-3

Contents

The Search for the Mind and the Source of Consciousness

What is the nature of the mind and consciousness? The standard dictionary definition of the mind is that part of us that reasons and thinks, our intellect and intelligence, that part of us that contains our memories and that gives us the ability to perceive and analyze, and which allows us to feel and comprehend. Consciousness is defined as a state of self-awareness, of being cognizant of one's independent existence with the ability to comprehend one's surroundings during the normal waking state of the body. Consciousness involves interactions with external forces and events that allow us to assess our relation to our environment and reveals the certainty that our identity is separate from and unique with regards to all other humans and the world in which we live. There has been a tremendous advance in scientific knowledge during the past hundred years, but there are still many unanswered questions about the nature of the human beings who so diligently seek those answers. Do the plants of the world have minds and consciousness, or is the ability to have thoughts and feelings limited to the animal world and to humans? We often speak of the human mind and marvel at its intellectual capacity and resilience in the face of highly stressful life situations, but do we really understand what that term means and implies?

The mind gives humans the capacity to process the sensory information that constantly reminds us of the existence of a vast outer world beyond our human bodies, a world of non-living physical matter and living biological organisms. Matter is apparently devoid of any level of thought and awareness. Living biological organisms display various levels of awareness of their surroundings. Are the minds that we humans use to make decisions and choices as we navigate our complex society simply highly evolved animal minds, or something different? Human brains interface with the world outside of our bodies via a complex neural network and detect, store and analyze the incredible amount of sensory information received by the sensory organs of the body. Do our minds arise out of the electrical activity of the billions of neurons and synaptic junctions that makeup the human brain? This idea drives much of the current scientific research that is directed at discovering the nature and origin of the human mind, but perhaps the underlying assumption that the brain is the source of the mind constrains and limits our concept of the mind and inhibits our ability to really understand its true origin. Perhaps this widely held idea prevents us from imagining the possibility that the mind might exist as an independent agent and persist even in the absence of the body. All of us habitually use the phrase "human mind," which reinforces the idea that a mind exists only as an extension of a human being, but why should a human body be a necessary component of the mind?

The mind is a source of incredible strength. Our mind gives us the ability to face many life challenges with stamina and bravery as we navigate this world of matter. It gives us the ability to express a wide range of emotions, from love, patience, and kindness to anger, hate, jealousy, and frustration as we interact with our fellow human beings. But our mind has its limitations, is fragile, and under some circumstances can easily break. Humans can, and too frequently do, descend into mental-health disorders characterized by unbalanced states of consciousness, such as depression, anxiety disorder, schizophrenia, obsessive-compulsive disorder (OCD), post-traumatic stress disorder (PTSD), and autism spectrum disorder (ASD). Depression brings feelings of sadness and loss of interest in life activities; anxiety disorder brings chronic fear or worry that negatively effects daily life; schizophrenia includes symptoms like hallucinations and delusions; obsessive-compulsive disorder is characterized by repetitive behavior and obsession; post-traumatic stress disorder is triggered by horrific events that cause flashbacks, nightmares, and severe anxiety; and autism spectrum disorder interferes with the ability to communicate, learn, and behave normally in society. If the mind is a product of the human brain, then medical researchers should find a corresponding physical, chemical, or genetic condition underlying these disorders. Some neurological disorders are caused by deterioration or injury of the human brain. They include Alzheimer's disease, an all-too-common illness brought on by the age-related destruction of nerve cells that leads to memory failure, personality changes, and problems carrying out daily activities. Some mental disorders such as Down syndrome are precipitated by a genetic abnormality. Mental disorders not only impair and destroy the lives of the affected individuals, but also severely stress and disrupt the lives of family members that at first contend with the developing symptoms of these individuals and later become their caretakers and source of financial support for extended periods of time.

Consciousness allows humans to physically interact with the world beyond the human body while retaining awareness that we are separate from that world. How well-defined is the boundary between the subjective consciousness of a human being and the objective reality of the physical world? How do humans acquire consciousness? As with the mind, there are theories that propose that consciousness is formed by brain activity, the result of the mind integrating the broad spectrum of information flow across the brain's neural network and emerging out of that neural electro-chemical activity. Mathematicians have even applied integrated information theory to the task of measuring levels of consciousness in plant and animal life, although the success of this approach has been questioned. Is consciousness reality? Does consciousness produce, in part or whole, the reality we navigate every day as life events, or does the reality in which life events play out help create consciousness? The answers to these questions are beyond the scope of current scientific methodology and may even be outside the purview of science, entering into the realms of meta-physics, philosophy, and religion. Unfortunately, the traditional scientific and mathematical approaches to developing a better understanding of the origin of the mind and consciousness do not even attempt to answer the most important questions that can be asked. These questions include whether the mind and consciousness are tethered to the human body and expire with the death of the human body, or whether they transcend the human body and can survive in a non-material realm independent of a human body. These questions should make us wonder whether reality can exist independently from the mind and consciousness, and whether our minds can perceive any other forms of reality than the physical world. If we answer these questions in the affirmative, we should also ask whether our minds have a greater purpose beyond allowing us to interact with our physical environment and our fellow human beings.

What about the universe of matter and energy? Have you ever wondered how the physical universe got its initial impetus to apparently emerge out of nothingness and evolve into a vast spectacular array of suns and galaxies, the immensity of which we can barely fathom? Did the physical universe spontaneously emerge out of nothingness, or is it the physical expression of some master plan conceived by a powerful creative intelligence? Is physical reality influenced by or precipitated by our conscious attempt to measure or observe the universe, and if it is, does that make physical reality a transient and ephemeral moment as opposed to a concrete and definite state of existence. In other words, does reality exist independently from that which we detect with our senses? Did you ever wonder how the random motion of clusters of unconnected organic molecules transformed into coordinated biological activity with a sense of self-preservation and survival skills? And how and why collections of primitive cellular units evolved into a complex human body? Did you ever wonder from a scientific perspective or even a theological perspective how a highly evolved biological organism could develop a mind capable of comprehending and applying the laws of electromagnetism and chemistry to create alloys and compounds that can never be produced by nature? Have you ever considered how human beings came to dominate the Earth or what gives humans the capacity to reason and solve problems? What is the source of the inner drive that urges humans to constantly search for answers about the existence and meaning of life beyond the physical universe? What drives this desire in humans to seek a greater understanding of their purpose in life and that allows them to believe they are connected to a higher power or are protected by and beholden to a higher power? It is so easy to ask questions and so difficult to come up with reasonable and correct answers.

The various methods we use to answer questions about human life and the world around us were developed by conscious minds in pursuit of knowledge from different perspectives. Philosophers, theologians, psychologists, and scientists bring different approaches and types of analysis to the search for answers to the perplexing questions about life and the universe in which we live. Philosophers and theologians usually concentrate on why we have minds and whether they are part of a greater cosmic consciousness, while psychologists and scientists are usually interested in the question of how the mind works. Philosophy gives us free rein to speculate on the origin, nature, purpose, and connectivity of life. Psychology allows trained professionals to explore the inner workings of the mind and consciousness through interviews with patients who are experiencing emotional trauma or various forms of mental illness. Religion attempts to understand the purpose and role of humanity in relation to a creator using the words of accepted scriptures and prophets. Scientists delve into the nitty-gritty details of energy and matter and the many ways in which they can interact to form our physical universe and study how biological organisms interact with the physical world and form interdependent societies. However, these methods of searching for answers about the material universe, biological life, and even the spiritual nature of man are limited by the finite nature of the conscious mind that is seeking those answers.

Philosophical Reflection and Psychological Deduction

The earliest recorded approach to the study of the mind, consciousness, and reality was the less-than-rigorous philosophical debates of scholars and notables such as the Greek philosophers Socrates (self-analysis, ethics, belief, opinion), Plato (ethics, the nature of reality), and Aristotle (perception, memory, the nature of the soul). More recently, P.D. Ouspensky (1878-1947), a Russian theoretical philosopher, explored various esoteric ideas as he attempted to understand the nature of the mind, consciousness, and the reality that the mind perceives. His most well-known book on consciousness, *Tertium Organum*, reveals the heavy influence of Eastern philosophies in his thinking and explores such topics as existence, the nature of reality, the nature of the soul and its perception of reality, and concepts of higher dimensionality. He considered the possibility of higher states of consciousness and the interconnectedness of all life (Ouspensky, 2022). The philosopher René Descartes (1596-1650) proposed the dual nature of man. The human body was perceived as being infused with "animal spirits," a nonphysical substance that pervades the nervous system of human bodies to activate muscles and give motility to the cells of the human body. This substance was identified as being an incorporeal soul (mind) that seeks expression in the material world. The soul or mind is the indivisible cognitive agent that is capable of thought and reason and the body is the divisible material object that is animated by the soul. Descartes coined the now famous phrase, "I think, therefore I am." He envisioned the brain as the biological agent that acts as the major interface between the soul and the body and that directs intentions of the soul toward the appropriate muscle to create the desired motor responses. The activity of this nonmaterial component of humans is limited to expression through human bodies and is not able to participate in earthly activities through animal bodies. Descartes speculated that the pineal gland, located at the base of the brain, serves as the primary interface between the physical body and soul. The spiritual philosophy we will explore herein supports that conclusion.

During the previous two centuries, many investigations of the human psyche were conducted by applying the newly established method of psychoanalysis. The practitioners of psychoanalysis interviewed people and studied their responses to various natural and contrived situations, often working with subjects who had various mental disorders or certain types of brain damage. These studies led to several concepts and hypotheses about the nature of mind which have been useful in the treatment of mental illness. Unfortunately, the results of psychoanalysis are difficult to quantify empirically and the investigative procedure generally did not lend itself to the rigorous repeatable experiments and quantitative analyses required for proper scientific validation of the ideas and conclusions that were gleaned from these thousands of excursions into the mind. Scientists can't measure the breadth of a thought, and there is no physical apparatus that can determine the magnitude of an emotion or track its growth from a psychological impulse. Also, psychoanalysis gives insight into the nature of the mind and the manner in which the mind perceives and interacts with human society and the world of matter, but doesn't reveal the source of the mind.

Sigmund Freud (1856-1939) used the results of his psychoanalytical studies to understand the mind as having three major structures: the ego, the id, and the superego, each having its separate function. The ego provides access to the sensory receptors of the body and is in charge of perception and analysis of the environment. It is the seat of self-awareness. In contrast, the id is a deep unconscious component of the mind controlled by thoughts of seeking pleasure and avoiding pain. The ego and the id are in a constant state of tension. The ego is undeveloped in an infant but matures as the child grows into adulthood, interacts with its environment, and accumulates and analyzes social experiences. The super ego holds the moral code and the ambitions of the individual (Freud, 2010).

The Swiss psychologist Carl Jung (1875-1961) was one of the most famous psychologists of the twentieth century. His interpretations of the mind and consciousness have some resemblance to the concepts of the mind and consciousness presented herein. In Jungian psychology, the human psyche or the mind is divided into the conscious and the unconscious mind. These two facets of the mind acquire their individual characteristic according to the source of knowledge and various experiences available to each. The conscious mind primarily accumulates, categorizes, and stores knowledge of the material world through the five types of sensory receptors in the human body. The interpretation of this data is greatly influenced by the way in which the mind perceives causality. The unconscious mind contains all the information that has passed through the conscious but is no longer remembered, plus all the knowledge inherited or instinctually present in the human species. It is the storehouse of all the memories that ever existed in the active conscious mind and all the memories that have been transmitted from the individual's ancestors. The totality of an individual psyche, called the Self, contains both conscious and unconscious elements and, therefore, cannot be realized in its entirety by conscious awareness. In its broader definition, the term "psyche" also includes the soul. Although Jung implies that the nature of the soul, and God's relation to man, cannot be arrived at by the psychological analysis of individuals, he nevertheless attempts to address these questions based on his own personal experiences, the religious content of the unconscious minds that he observed in his patients, and religious myths and images produced by different cultures over the centuries (Jung, 1971; Jung, 1989).

The development of consciousness begins with the acquisition of knowledge of the physical world through a gradual process whereby initial chaotic sensory stimuli are recorded by the psychological sense organs and relationships are perceived among the sensory stimuli and sensory data previously stored in memory. An infant is not consciously aware of its body or environment at the beginning of psychological sense perception. Awareness only begins to emerge after relationships among the various recorded sensations have been established. As more sensory data is collected and stored more relationships or groups of relationships become established in memory. The development of the ego begins when these groups or blocks of memory content involve the individual's self-perception. Conscious self-awareness becomes more pronounced over time, until the individual perceives himself as separate from the physical world. The persona, or mask, that each person presents to the world is a façade that covers the true self and ego, and is built by the individual as a method of coping with expectations and situations that arise in the daily interaction with other individuals in the physical environment.

Conscious awareness matures by apperception, the cooperative functioning of several mental processes to determine the nature of sensory stimuli. Apperception develops by the application of the separate processes of recognition (thinking), evaluation (feeling), and intuition. Recognition involves the comparison of sense perception with previously acquired memories and an assessment of the degree of similarity or difference between the sensation and memory images. Evaluation is the analysis of emotional reactions evoked by the sense perception or associated memory images. Jung uses the term "so-called free will" and rarely mentions free will in his descriptions of the psyche, which suggests that he believes that free will is not an especially important conscious process. We will discover that free will is paramount in the life of a human being. Intuition is the passive perception of the possibilities inherent in a situation independent from sensation, thinking, and feeling and is a separate but coequal function of the conscious mind. Intuition is a type of perception that is not entirely based in the senses and conscious mind, but has its roots in the unconscious mind. Sensation and intuition are means by which the conscious mind receives information, whereas thinking and feeling are means by which information is analyzed.

Jung concluded that the unconscious mind is divided into two parts based on the source of knowledge or material available to it. The personal unconscious mind consists of that part of the unconscious created from the accumulation of sensations and conscious processes that are no longer present in the conscious mind, having been forgotten or repressed. The collective unconscious mind is inherited knowledge that is not acquired by the individual but is an accumulation of the accessible memories of the individual's ancestors. The collective unconscious memories are more universal and include many elements in common with the collective unconscious of other individuals. This is the source of the similar mythological images that appear in diverse cultures, and is considered evidence of underlying universal forms in the unconscious mind. These universal forms or archetypes are closely related to instincts, which are defined as motive forces acting independent of the presence or degree of consciousness, and may be considered as imaged patterns of instinctual behavior. Although the conscious is considered finite because it receives only a small part of the sensory data from the outer world, the unconscious is considered infinite because it contains the entire, consciously unknown, contents of the inner world.

Dreams are the principal language of the unconscious mind in Jungian philosophy and offer a way to look into the deeper hidden aspects of consciousness. Through dreams the unconscious mind is revealed to and communicates with the conscious mind. Dreams are not a series of random events that result from a desire of the unconscious mind to manifest itself into the physical consciousness, but transmit specific information meant to guide the growth of the individual as it seeks to resolve personal conflicts. They strengthen the weaker and less-developed aspects of the conscious mind that need to be reinforced or redirected in the face of contradictory and unresolvable problems. The unconscious mind presents a dream to the conscious mind when the need to communicate with the conscious mind becomes strong enough to activate a force that propels the unconscious information above the threshold of conscious awareness.

Theological Insight

Various religious scholars have sought answers to the meaning of life in realms of thought that take them beyond the physical universe. However, their efforts to find answers about the nature of man through scriptures are often severely constrained by the self-imposed limited range of perception of their conscious minds because these scholars are unwilling to explore beyond the narrow confines of their particular religious scripture, doctrine, and traditions. This can severely constrain their ability to perceive truth and understand the mind in relation to human life. Theologians within a particular religious organization may be reluctant to explore or openly profess new ideas because of peer backlash, potential loss of a coveted position, or reduction of advancement possibilities within the organization. They issue anathemas by the dozens to rein in potentially disrupting thoughts in the minds of church members, declare without evidence that souls are created at conception, or profess that there is no such thing as a soul, only a breath of life that sustains the bodies of the faithful while they progress along the spiritual path to physical resurrection in a glorified body after death. They are more likely to parrot the party line than to be free thinkers who push the envelope. For example, despite a substantial body of strong circumstantial evidence that indicates the reality of reincarnation, certain biblical passages that strongly suggest it is true, the fact that it was and is a common belief in some Jewish sects, and the fact that it is a belief held by the majority of the world's population, mainline Christian theologians reject the idea out of hand.

Some Christian theologians are more interested in promoting a strict literal interpretation of Scripture than in pursuing and revealing the truth that unifies science and religion. They give the spiritual realm names like heaven and paradise without really knowing what those terms mean or where this mysterious place is located, and often lack a clear understanding of how to get there. Some religions teach that performing a certain indefinite number of good actions during a lifetime will earn a person a glorified body and a special place with God after death — a shortcut doctrine that ignores the soul's higher purpose of attaining a state of God consciousness, not merely moral goodness. Still, these efforts are not in vain. Theologians have developed some credible insight into the meaning of life and many correct or partly correct answers about spirituality and the spiritual realm. Most Christian theologians believe the soul is the spiritual essence of a human being, and that the mind and consciousness are faculties of the soul. The soul is the center of self-awareness and reason, and the soul consciousness survives the death of the body and exists eternally with God or separate from God. Its ultimate fate greatly depends upon the moral behavior of the person during life and whether that person has accepted Jesus as its savior. The various belief systems of Christian and non-Christian religions will not be discussed in this book, but the reader is encouraged to explore these concepts of human nature, perhaps with a focus on their similarities instead of their differences. Philosophers may be less constrained by the need to stay close to tradition and doctrine, but also may inject a considerable amount of supposition and conjecture into their philosophical ideas. Unless and until we are able and willing to set aside preconceived ideas in our conscious mind and shift away from our intense focus on materiality, personal prejudices, and self-centered personality, we will never clearly perceive reality in its fullness.

Scientific Investigation

Scientists have devised sophisticated electrical and mechanical instruments to detect and accurately measure physical phenomena. Their range of observation is constrained to the world of matter and energy by design and necessity. The scientific method that they use in investigations of the physical world effectively weeds out untenable theories and allows tenable theories to be adjusted to fit new evidence. This approach to material knowledge helps mankind better understand the basic facts and mathematics of physical, chemical, and biological processes but may not be suited to the pursuit of the answers to greater and more pertinent questions such as the purpose for the physical universe and human life, the source and role of the mind in our lives, and the reason we have consciousness and self-awareness. Will the scientific approach to the study of the mind, including the search for its source in the neural network of the human body, yield positive results or lead to a dead end? In the last few decades, biological scientists have made great strides in the study of the internal structure and mechanics of cells; the role of DNA in genetics; and the function and operation of organs, the vascular system, and the neural system in the human body. Recently, scientists have turned more and more of their attention to the neural network in their quest for the source of the mind. The human body contains a network of billions of neurons that extend throughout the body and serve the purpose of transmitting environmental and biological sensory information to and from the cognitive centers of the brain. These neural pathways transmit electrical signals from every square millimeter of the surface of the body, and every internal organ of the body, to various locations in the brain.

Current scientific research on human intelligence and the formation of the mind and consciousness is laser focused on the cumulative electrical activity in the estimated eighty-six billion neurons that are packed within a human brain, the anticipated source of mind. Scientists have delved deeply into the electrochemical activity of neurons and the biochemical processes that occur at the synaptic junctions that join neurons and now see more intensive analysis of the complex neural network of the human brain in relation to memory storage as the best hope for locating, defining, mapping, and understanding the mind (Kandel, 2006). The mind is visualized as a byproduct of bio-chemical processes and bio-electrical activity. The orderly transfer of information via electrical impulses through neurons, the chemical transfer of information across synaptic junctions, and the accumulation of stored information in working and long-term memory is believed to galvanize the creation of a conscious mind. The complexity of the mind varies greatly from animal to animal, and the mental capacity of any particular organism is related to the number of combinations and permutations of neural links that are formed in response to various types of sensory stimuli. This in turn depends upon the range and sophistication of the sensory organs that perceive our environment. There are many new technologies at the disposal of scientists, including magnetic resonance imaging (MRI), which uses a powerful magnetic field and radiofrequency wave pulses to visualize bone and tissue, and electroencephalography (EEG), which measures the electrical activity of neurons in the brain. Magnetic imaging can detect changes in the pattern of blood flow in the brain in response to various physical and mental stimuli and even to spiritual practices such as prayer and meditation (Newberg, 2012). The more traditional and invasive methods of studying the brain—such as inserting electrical probes into various regions of the brain—are becoming less necessary as skull masks with embedded highly sensitive electrical detectors linked to computers collect and collate faint electrical signals in the brain in real time. The historical transition from psychoanalytical descriptions of the mind to descriptions of the mind built around neural activity changed the understanding of the mind from a non-biological to a biological perspective. This was mainly driven by the fact that psychoanalysis as a method of finding the source of the mind was arriving at a dead end at the time when new technologies for imaging and studying the brain were being rapidly developed.

The two hypotheses of the mind and consciousness called Panpsychism and Gaia are briefly mentioned here, not because they are part of mainstream theories of mind, but because they introduce concepts of the mind and consciousness that have some superficial commonality with the information presented in this book. These ideas are still in a state of flux, are evolving from the original concepts, and do not have mainstream scientific support. Philosophers and scientists still debate their validity. These hypotheses reject the dual nature of humans and animals; that is, they are opposed to theories of consciousness that are based on the concept of a material body and a nonmaterial life force joining to form a conscious organism. They suffer from the same problem as the more mainstream scientific investigations that proceed from the idea that the mind and consciousness arise from matter alone. Both of these philosophies also suffer from the same problem as other speculative conjectures in that there is no clear path to a series of repeatable scientific experiments that can verify or reject specific material implications of the hypotheses.

The main thesis of Panpsychism is that all of physical reality—including all inorganic material and all living organisms, from the atoms of the periodic table to the elephants of the Serengeti plain—contain a form of mind and consciousness (Skrbina, 2017; Goff, 2017). Consciousness is a basic feature of the universe, present in both atoms and the cells of sentient life forms like animals and humans. Its presence in matter and the lowest life forms is not detected by human beings because it is only present in a rudimentary form. The rudimentary consciousness in the basic elements of matter (atoms) and the basic elements of biological life (cells) may lack full self-awareness or the ability to express thought, but the combined cellular consciousness forms the greater overall higher intellect of the organism. A major unresolved problem in Panpsychism is the question of exactly how these rudimentary states of consciousness combine and contribute to the overall consciousness of higher-order life forms. Any viable hypothesis would need to prove that each unit of rudimentary consciousness in a collection of cells can be synchronized in a manner that facilitates cooperation and a shared purpose.

The Gaia hypothesis gets its name from the Greek goddess of the Earth, mother of all life. The premise of this unproven idea is that a form of communal shared consciousness binds the biological world into a self-regulating organic system. It proposes that the Earth's ecosystem possesses a self-generated intelligence and shared consciousness that arises from the interconnected and interdependent biological activity of millions of different species of plants and animals (Lovelock, 1995; Boston, 2008). The individual consciousness of each biological organism that has evolved on the Earth, from cells to plants to animals, collectively form an integrated universal consciousness and the Earth's ecosystem is a single living organism. The Gaia hypothesis goes so far as to suggest that this biosphere consciousness manipulates the Earth's climate to generate an environment that is more conducive to a thriving biological community. This is posited to occur through a self-regulating feedback mechanism that constantly brings the biosphere—the bio-rich soil cover, oceans and atmosphere—back into an optimal environment for life to thrive and multiply.

A Different Approach: The Edgar Cayce Readings

Where will we begin our search for answers about the mind, consciousness and reality in this book? We will take a different approach than philosophy, science, and traditional religion. We will find a solution that provides a far richer perspective than that provided by current speculation and theories, and reveals a logical sequence of events that explains physical reality and the rise of human consciousness. We will use the Edgar Cayce readings (which we will refer to simply as the readings) to get a better understanding of reality, and to assess whether consciousness creates reality, reality creates consciousness, or whether both situations are possible depending on the circumstances. The readings will help us navigate the maze of possible answers to the most important questions about life and human existence and arrive at a reasonable, logical, and spiritually meaningful understanding of reality and consciousness as it applies to mankind and the physical universe in which man resides. We will see how the mind and consciousness are related to the physical world and to a spiritual realm not perceived by science. The answers to the many profound questions we can ask lie beyond the physical brain and behind the conscious mind in a vast nonmaterial realm where life exists without a physical body. The finite range of instruments used in scientific investigations and the exclusive focus of scientists on matter and energy prevents them from detecting the infinite cosmic realm that the readings assure us exists beyond the range of our human senses.

The readings will help us understand reality and consciousness from a perspective that includes answers to questions about the nature and purpose of the physical universe and the Earth's ecosystem, the true nature and source of the mind, and how and why humans acquired such complex analytical minds. They emphasize that there is a spiritual purpose behind the presence of human life on the Earth, the various activities that make up a human lifespan, and the many decisions and choices that the mind must make to successfully navigate the daunting and stressful events that we sometimes face during our lives. The readings will help us understand why the terms "human mind" and "human consciousness" can be inappropriate and misleading when describing the source of intelligence that reveals itself in human language and activity. We will use the term "physical conscious mind," or the shorter version "conscious mind" to refer to the mind that gives us our awareness of the world and that we use every day to navigate life as human beings. This will help us to avoid the pitfalls that might ensnare us when using the familiar, but less accurate, term "human mind" that can generate ideas that are inconsistent with the definition of "conscious mind" as presented in the readings. By looking at the origin of the soul, the universe and biological life, the human body, and the physical conscious mind from the perspective of the readings we will gain a much broader view of the mind and consciousness in general and will be in a better position to assess the role of consciousness in creation.

The Soul, the Mind, Consciousness, and the Edgar Cayce Readings

. . . the body, the mind, the soul are one. We see the body with those attributes. We can conceive of what the mind is, or see it in action, but never find the mind, in the body. (Edgar Cayce Reading 5254-1_12)

The readings are written records of the words spoken by Edgar Cayce (1877–1945) as he relaxed, set aside and suppressed his conscious mind and everyday concerns, and allowed his subconscious mind to answer questions submitted by those present during the readings. His answers were recorded by a stenographer, and when he awoke from the self-induced sleep or trance state he did not remember what he had said. The two major categories of readings are the physical readings and the life readings. The physical readings were given for individuals who requested advice about physical ailments, often after exhausting traditional medical options. Cayce only needed to be told where the person was located during the trance session to be able to diagnose their illness and give answers to their written questions. His subconscious mind was receptive to the subconscious mind of the individual who sought his help. His responses included suggestions for natural remedies and medical treatments to restore the physical health of the individuals who asked for his advice. During the last twenty years of his life, he answered many questions about the nature of God, the purpose of the universe and human life, and the relationship between God and mankind. These life readings on spiritual topics elucidate concepts of the nature of the mind, consciousness, and reality. They stress the existence of the soul and the fact of its recurring appearance on the Earth. During these readings, the subconscious mind of Cayce sought out and interpreted the records of stored memories and emotions left "on the skein of space and time" by the earthy activity of souls (2533-8_12; 1223-4_55; 378-13_7). The world view outlined in those life readings is of critical importance to anyone who wants to understand the destiny of the human body, the soul that animates every human being, and the true nature of the mind that we take for granted. The particulars of his conscious state during the readings and ability to access this subconscious information is well documented (Sugrue, 1997; Kirkpatrick, 2001; Millard, 2007; Bro, 2011). The period during which Cayce entered a self-induced sleep or trance state spanned at least forty years. The accuracy of his answers was to some degree dependent upon the sincerity of the person desiring the answers; the spiritual mindfulness of the persons present when the questions were submitted to Cayce; and the physical, mental, and spiritual attunement of Cayce himself. Along the way, Cayce learned that there needed to be a concerted effort by the individuals conducting the readings to adhere to high ethical standards to maintain the integrity and accuracy of the readings.

There is no logical order from one reading to the next, with a few exceptions in which a group of like-minded individuals would periodically come together to seek advice and answers about a particular topic. Christian theology is gleaned from the large body of prophetic and historical writings that form the Old Testament and the New Testament of the Christian Bible. The philosophy of the Cayce readings also is not spelled out in an orderly manner through a single comprehensive discourse, but must be coaxed out of thousands of readings given to people from all walks of life for their personal health and spiritual benefit, and the few discourses given to explain and clarify specific subjects. References to the Edgar Cayce readings given herein are from "The Complete Edgar Cayce

Readings" on CDROM (1993) and are denoted by a sequence of (usually) three numbers. For example, the number 5749-4_9 refers to Reading number 5749 (a number assigned to the person, or group, for whom the reading was conducted to ensure anonymity), the fourth reading in a series of readings for that person, and the ninth numbered paragraph in that reading. Occasionally, a reference may be a single number to indicate the individual or two numbers to indicate the individual and the particular reading. Reading 294-1_1 states that the subconscious mind of Cayce could converse with millions of other subconscious minds and was able to interpret the information he received so that it could be transmitted to his conscious mind and communicated to the stenographer or recorder who was present at the reading. The 262-series readings, the 281-series readings, and perhaps the 5749-series readings contain the most orderly discourses on specific topics of theological and spiritual interest. Many other readings contain information on a variety of medical and spiritual topics in a less organized structure based on the order in which the readings were given to satisfy the daily requests for help that came from people across the country. Embedded in the readings is a coherent philosophy of the existence and nature of God, the existence and nature of souls, the purpose of the physical universe, and the nature of man, but like many of the topics that were addressed, much of it is scattered through hundreds of readings and must be researched, compiled, organized, and interpreted to be useful. Much of that work has already been done and has been published in many books over the past eighty years.

The readings provide insight into many of the questions that we might ask about the origins of the universe, the origin and nature of biological life, and the origin and nature of the human beings that dominate life on the Earth. They reveal a common purpose that threads its way through these seemingly diverse subjects. The progression of physical and biological evolutionary activity that formed the material universe and the Earth's ecosystem was purposeful, as was the rise of the human-animal and its transformation into modern man. There is a spiritual purpose active in the universe that transcends ideas such as the formation of inorganic matter out of nothingness, the random transition of organic matter into living cells, and the purely biological and evolutionary explanation of the presence of modern man. This higher purpose gives unity to the four physical forces (the gravitational force, the strong nuclear force, the weak nuclear force, and the electromagnetic force) that control the movement and interaction of all physical matter and energy and the many forms and levels of consciousness that are active in the material world. The readings provide us with answers to philosophical and religious questions about why human beings exist in a state of disunity, disharmony, and absolute chaos with other life forms and with themselves. The answers that the readings provide to these complex scientific, theological, and metaphysical questions are quite consistent and logical, but don't always follow traditional science or traditional Christian religious doctrine in their description of the creation of the physical universe and man's appearance on the Earth. However, the unity between science and religion within the context of the readings is much deeper than between science and religion within the context of traditional Christianity and literal reading of Christian scripture. The profound ideas about our existence contained in the readings are certainly worthy of our open-minded consideration.

Have you ever wondered why the life force in animals is different from the life force in a human being and why human beings became the dominant life form on the Earth? There is a reason why the minds of human beings are far more advanced and intelligent than those of the other creatures that live on the Earth. There is a logical reason for the rapid increase in man's intellectual capacity relative to other animal species. Have you ever tried to resolve the confusion between the scientific explanation of the rise of human animals and the scriptural assertion that God created humans out of the dust of the Earth? One explanation implies that human consciousness arose out of biological evolution and that humans used that consciousness to imagine and build their concept of God. The other states that God created the first humans (à la Genesis) and injected them and their descendants with some seed of spiritual conscious awareness that can be awakened under certain circumstances? Can the two competing ideas, one derived from intellectual study of ancient remains and artifacts, human and animal fossils, and DNA evidence, and the other an expression of conviction and faith founded in Scripture ever be reconciled? The readings successfully and seamlessly reconcile these two competing theories of human existence to arrive at the origin of modern humans and the true nature and purpose of humanity in a manner that respects and honors both the scientific and religious understanding of the creation of man. The mind and consciousness are the most important factors in the development of humanity, but the true source of the mind lies outside of the purview of current scientific methodology and assumptions. It will take a fundamental change in the underlying scientific premise of the nature and source of the mind for scientists to begin to truly understand the mind. It will take a paradigm shift of the magnitude that opened the way for plate tectonics to replace continental drift in the geologic sciences, or that led to the Copernican description of the solar system that refuted the prevailing religious belief that the Earth is the center of the universe, or that gave rise to the movement from Newtonian physics to the theory of relativity and quantum physics.

We will use information from the readings to go where science cannot yet go and is unwilling to go, but we will not violate basic scientific principles of physics, biology, and anthropology. We will use the readings to describe the source and origin of consciousness to the extent possible, and will trace the evolution of consciousness and its connection to the evolution of the physical universe and biological life, especially as it pertains to the rise and destiny of human life on the Earth. The concepts of consciousness that are developed in the readings and the role of consciousness as it relates to the origin of the universe, the origin of biological life, and the animation and directed activity of human beings significantly advance our understanding of the human condition. The readings describe a human consciousness that reaches far beyond basic self-awareness and the decision-making process of human beings during their everyday lives. The readings describe a singular consciousness that is the source of and that partakes of all forms of consciousness that exist in all realms of activity. There is an underlying consciousness behind the universe, a thread of intentional purpose that wends its way through the universe, and a reason for the biological life that has evolved upon the Earth that transcends mere randomness and chance.

Cosmic Consciousness: The Basis of Reality

The readings, in agreement with the major religions, identify the source of all forms of consciousness as a cosmic intelligence, the mental creative force we call God. We will take particular interest in the intentional projection of that cosmic consciousness toward the manifestation of the three distinct and unique forms of consciousness that are most relevant to the human condition. The first and most important of these three forms of consciousness is souls, sentient beings with the ability to express love and other godly attributes. Souls are the main actors in this story and will ultimately be the only survivors of this grand play we call life (900-340_16). We will learn how souls fit into the overall scheme of human consciousness that allows us to interact in the physical world and the nature of the higher consciousness that hovers behind the human consciousness. The readings tell us how the desire of each soul to push at the boundaries of its new-found freedom, explore the nature of its mind and its capabilities, and test the limits of its creative abilities fractured the unity of consciousness in the spiritual realm. The descent into selfish thought patterns and the manifestation of various forms of selfishness was rampant among maturing souls. These thoughts and the desires that activated the thoughts were causing souls to lose awareness of their original intimate relationship with their creator. Souls were transforming into beings that could no longer remain in the presence of God. These delinquent souls are the behind-the-scenes puppet masters that motivate, stimulate and animate much of the human activity on the Earth. At their best, they are the driving force behind the goodness expressed by humans in the world and at their worst, they are the source of all of the evil that consumes and defiles humans as they go about their daily lives. These souls are the real us. If we are really souls that have been given life and existence in a spiritual realm, then what are we doing animating human bodies that are confined to one planet within the vast but finite physical realm? We will learn the answer to that question.

The second and third forms of consciousness are the structural reality of the universe and the cellular life that emerged and evolved into the biological ecosystem that flourishes on the Earth. These are independent and intentional acts of creation that followed long after the creation of souls. We will track the evolutionary rise of the human-animal, discuss the reason for the impressively rapid increase of the human intellect, and learn what sets apart modern man from the evolved human-animal. We will see why it is essential that humans live, have material experiences, and develop consciousness in this universe, and understand why we seem to have so little awareness of the truth that we are souls first and humans second. We will come to understand the purpose of human consciousness and its ultimate destiny. We will see how souls were spiritually compromised by the forces they unleashed when they chose to ignore their creator and reveled in various forms of selfish behavior without regard to the damage it inflicted on other souls. We will look at the role of human activity in the restoration and redemption of this greater soul consciousness and along the way identify a level of consciousness that has been seen only rarely, perhaps only once in the history of humankind, and recount the reason that this state of consciousness is the key to the survival of each soul that projects its thoughts into the world through human societal activity. It is a fascinating journey that links certain aspects of religious thought smoothly and seamlessly with current concepts of cosmology, archaeology, anthropology, and biology. This concept of unified and interconnected nonphysical and physical realms of activity is not accepted by science nor fully understood by traditional religions.

But it is possible that with an open mind and a willingness to make way for the new paradigm that will be required, scientists, religious scholars, and theologians, as well as the general public will enjoy the journey.

Like the paths that lead the strange but peaceful Silfen folk from world to world in the incredible universe that flows from the mind and pen of the British science-fiction author Peter Hamilton, the paths traveled by souls wend their way through many realms of reality and different periods of Earth history with their diverse cultures and civilizations. We don't travel from world to world like the Silfen folk but our souls have traveled from one moment to another in human history and are now part of the unfolding human history in which we participate. Our present activities contain the situations and events that will bring us face-to-face with similar situations that we failed to successfully navigate during previous life experiences. History repeats itself because we souls keep making the same mistakes. Along the way, souls might experience poverty, wealth, degradation, misery, elation, war, and peace in all of their possibilities and variations. As we souls incarnate in human form, we travel into a future of our own making where we study human history that we helped create, marvel that history seems to repeat itself so often, and try to comprehend why man is so thickheaded and dense that he continually fails to learn from the mistakes of the past. We are like Phil, the self-absorbed narcissistic weatherman who becomes trapped in a continual progression of groundhog days until he realizes that he can only escape this endless loop of life by being considerate and helpful to other lonely people like himself. He is only freed from his repetitious prison by engaging in loving service toward his fellow man.

Too many of us haven't yet realized the essential need to express love and service as part of life, and so we produce the same general pattern of behavior over and over again, with its repetitive wars and conflicts and the constant maneuvering for power and control over others. We keep repeating the same mistakes that lead us nowhere. We keep causing our soul to repeat life's lessons and add our latest contribution to the problems that future generations will face. The soul's journey is a journey from safety, security, and companionship in the presence of God, to spiritual decline brought about by pursuit of the rebellious beast of selfishness, to earthly lives of suffering and trials where, if it takes hold of offered opportunities in an attitude of love and selflessness, the soul can be freed from its self-imposed exile and return to a state of God consciousness. Our experiences in any one life time may be a bit like the adventures of Bilbo Baggins in The Hobbit, a "from here to there and back again" tale; a journey full of adventure and misadventure with the opportunity to slay the dragon of greed and selfishness, the beast that saw little to nothing of value beyond the acquisition of gold and treasure, an insatiable greed that consumed its every waking moment.

The future holds the promise of great scientific advances in the understanding of the nature of the world of matter and energy, the nature of humanity as a biological organism, the nature of the mind that finds expression through human beings, and even the nature of the minds that explore different modes of expression through living plants and animals. The physical universe and its plant and animal life are only a small drop in the ocean of existence that is ours to explore when we dare go in mind where few men and women are willing to tread. The challenge we face as human beings is to think outside of the material world in which our bodies are confined and the mundane and unimaginative mental boxes that we let confine our minds. The rewards we will receive when we are willing to expand our consciousness to embrace new possibilities of reality are enormous. We hold the power to fulfill our spiritual destiny or slide into conscious oblivion.

The title of this book could have referred to the journey of the human soul instead of the eternal soul, but the choice of that wording could easily cause readers to misconstrue the very specific definitions and meanings of soul and the mind presented in the readings. The terms "human mind" and "human soul," frequently used in literature, can be deceptive because of the potential for readers to form incorrect concepts based upon familiar but wrong connotations that follow in the wake of their ordinary use. These terms misrepresent the truth about our mind, our consciousness, and the nature of our soul. Humans do not have minds or souls. What? That can't be right! What is meant by that statement is that human bodies, physical flesh-and-bone beings, are not creatures that inherently possess a mind or a soul as part of, or as a consequence of, their biological structure or nature. Instead, souls, nonmaterial intelligent beings, animate human bodies through the intentional activity of the mind to carry out physical and social activity on the Earth. This is precisely why the efforts of neurobiologists to detect the origin of the mind in the intricate neural network of the human brain are doomed to fail. Their efforts may pay off in that they may unintentionally detect the physical influence of an outside force acting on the pineal, pituitary, hippocampus, amygdala, and/or other centers of nerve and hormonal activity. That would be a major achievement worthy of a Nobel prize, but seeking the source of mind in neurobiological activity is a lost cause. Whether mind-induced activity can be detected in neurons and can be correctly identified as being caused by an external nonphysical mental force is an open question. Such an experimental coup would electrify the scientific community, probably excite the religious community, and might be a major step toward unifying scientific and religious thought.

To avoid starting in the middle of the story, we will begin our study of the mind, consciousness, and reality, and trace the spiritual journey of the wayward soul, where it should start: with God. The readings assure us that God is the source of all that exists in all realms of mental and physical activity, and the Creative Force that instills life in all creatures, non-material or material. We will begin with the Creator and draw together the considerable background information to properly and definitively answer questions about human consciousness, human perception of reality, and the human experience in relation to the soul. God gives purpose and a sense of unity and cooperation to the many life forms within his infinite domain, and humans are no exception.

The Divine Consciousness We Call God

The divine consciousness of God is a universal, infinite, eternal, loving, creative force composed of an all-pervading omnipresent Spirit guided by an omniscient Mind that manifests his Will and creative desires.

How do we know there is a God? The truth is that many of us go about our busy lives on the Earth without any awareness of a God, or worse yet, without any desire to learn if there is a God. Unless we are looking for evidence of an Infinite Presence, there are few aspects of our daily activities that make us think about God or that point to his presence or existence. We may seek God for relief or diversion if our daily experiences are particularly harsh, but probably are less likely to seek him if we are comfortable in our wealth and social position. Many people attend church on a regular basis, but church can be a means of social interaction as much as a source of spiritual sustenance. When we feel the need to seek answers about life from a higher being, we can be pretty good at conjuring up one, or even more than one. Polytheism was a commonly accepted religious practice throughout the Near East before the New Testament historical period and persisted for several centuries after the birth of Jesus. Humans imagined an assortment of gods that they believed could protect them from enemies, bless their efforts to raise crops, help them engage in profitable commerce, and protect them when they traveled. They also believed the gods spent their idle hours observing, controlling, and interfering in the lives of humans. The base desires and impulses of humans were often manipulated or hijacked for the amusement of the gods. The pagan theological belief in a multiplicity of gods was held by most of the people who inhabited the Greek and Roman civilizations in the millennium before and the centuries after the birth of Jesus. And don't think these pagan beliefs arose because the people of these two ancient civilizations were all ignorant and uneducated. Although there was no formal public education system like the one we have today, wealthier families often gave their children the opportunity to study philosophy or law under well-known teachers or in private schools. The Roman and Greek civilizations were quite advanced and sophisticated, comprising many well-educated people and some of the world's most talented and famous philosophers.

Closer to home, the most rapidly growing religion in the Americas during the past two decades was the mixture of paganism and folk Catholicism called Our Lady of Holy Death (Nuestra Señora de la Santa Muerte). The prominently displayed visible symbol of the deity recognized by this religion is a female human skeleton clothed in a long robe holding a scythe and globe. The roots of Santa Muerte go back to the Aztec Empire. The first recognized modern-day followers of this religion conducted their occult practices at home in the 1940s, but in recent years the number of adherents in Mexico and the United States has exploded to twelve million after the word spread that miracles were being performed by the deity. It makes one wonder what would cause so many people to reject the prevailing Catholicism in favor of death worship. Part of the lure among poor workers, besides belief in the message that Santa Muerte produces miracles, may be the religion's promotion of the concept that death is universal. By placing emphasis on this concept, Santa Muerte may be bringing a form of equality among human beings at a basic human level, making it attractive for downtrodden and marginalized people. Even with the abundant presence of well-established religions in modern society, people continue to search for and satisfy their longing for spiritual answers in ancient ways.

The Near East may have been mostly polytheistic leading up to the New Testament historical period, but one group was decidedly monotheistic. The Jewish people of the occupied country of Israel were allowed to retain their long-held religious tenets proclaimed in the verses of the Jewish Torah and other religious literature. The core belief of Judaism is that there is only one God—a nonphysical, spiritual, and creative being. This emphasis on one singular God served to distinguish the ancient Jews from most of their neighbors (Deuteronomy 6:4). The concept of one God as a core tenet of religious belief was passed to Christianity and Islam, both of which are partly derived from Judaism (Mark 12:28-29; Surah 14:52). The Israelites held strongly to the idea that this unitary deity spoke to men through his prophets and would receive those who believed in him and held true to his laws as outlined in the Ten Commandments and the six-hundred and thirteen rules of the Mosaic Law regarding religious observances (mitzvot in Hebrew). These rules or laws instruct the Jewish people regarding the manner in which they are supposed to worship and conduct their lives. God is portrayed as an intelligent, loving being who is all-powerful, all-knowing, and eternal, and who is the creator of the universe and mankind. God rules his creations from a spiritual realm in which he resides and persistently encourages his human children to remain faithful to him so that in return he can grant them eternal residence in his realm after they leave the Earth. In the Jewish faith, actions are far more important than beliefs. This basic principle seems to have been reversed by modern fundamentalist Christians, who place an unduly strong emphasis on belief in Jesus as a personal savior. Many Christian churches require their members to believe in and strictly adhere to the doctrines and creeds espoused by their particular denomination. Some even demand that their members sign statements that they believe in and will abide by the authorized doctrines and specific interpretations of Scripture.

Why do human beings, perhaps especially those in the guise of theologians, feel the need to remake God in our image? Pastors and writers of Christian study guides promulgate the idea that God came down to Earth in the form of the man Jesus, and they mean that literally. Jesus was no doubt a special man, but was he the fullness and totality of God compressed into the form of a physical human? They pronounce that the Holy Spirit is really some nonmaterial person who looks like a human being and walks around in the heavenly sphere just like humans walk around on the Earth. They formulate descriptions of how God in some mysterious way is a continuous circular flow of love passing from "person to person" through the Father, the Holy Spirit, and Jesus, and state that these separate-but-one individuals are somehow the same but not the same. Some will read Genesis where it says God created man in his image and assume that God has a human-like body with facial features that are similar to ours. Are the facial features of God more Asian, African, or Caucasian? Many racist slaveholders connected the white race with moral superiority and divinity, suggesting Caucasian features. And down the rabbit hole we go, seeking to know if God looks more like us than the other racial groups because that would make us more special to him. We will discover the real and proper relationship among God, Jesus, and the Holy Spirit without resorting to these mental gymnastics. God is often referred to in the readings and will be referred to herein using the masculine personal pronouns *he/his/him*, but God does not have a gender, and the use of these masculine pronouns is only a matter of convenience.

Let's use the readings to better understand the nature of this one God proclaimed by the three major Western religions. The idea of a unitary God is wholeheartedly endorsed in the pages of the Edgar Cayce readings, often by using the phrase "The Lord thy God is One" (364-9_5; 262-32_10; 900-429_11). This concept of unity and oneness is stressed repeatedly to emphasize the truth and importance of the words and to reorient the thoughts of the individuals who received the readings. But it would be wrong for readers of these spiritually enlightening words to assume that the phrase "The Lord thy God is One" is used in the readings in precisely the same way as it is in the Torah and the Bible, or at least as it is generally interpreted from these scriptures. The Jewish and traditional Christian understanding of the concept of One God is narrower and more limited than the meaning of his Oneness as used in the readings. The meaning of the phrase "The Lord thy God is One" in the readings is all-inclusive; God is not only the One Consciousness that is the creator of all things spiritual and physical; God is also the source substance of all things spiritual and all inanimate physical objects, and the life force of all animate beings. He is the mental spark that gives consciousness and intelligence to all orders of life (391-4_23; 1299-1_27; 262-114_29). God is not separate from his creations. God does not sit in heaven overseeing his wondrous creations and influencing events so that they unfold to his will. The readings emphasize that God and his creations are a unified integrated Oneness.

God is the coordinated and harmonious activity of Spirit, Mind, and Will. Spirit is the substance of which God IS, not of which God is created because the eternal God is not a created being. Spirit is the essence of God himself. Spirit is the raw substance of every creation in every realm of activity. Spirit can be thought-shaped into manifested form by his desire. God is described as *I Am That I Am* in Scripture (Exodus 3:14) because there is nothing that precedes God and nothing that underpins God, and no words in any human language are adequate to describe God. He is what he is—nothing more and nothing less, a unique eternal presence, consciousness, and force in which all of his manifestations have their beginning and ending. We can learn far more about who God is by recognizing his moral, mental, and spiritual attributes than by contemplating his nonmaterial structure. The Mind of God gives rise to consciousness, his creative desires are manifested by the action of his Mind on Spirit, and his purposes and plans develop and evolve into maturity through the guiding intelligence of his Will. God is not only single and unitary—he is also the infinite consciousness that pervades every facet of his many creations and either directly or indirectly, overtly or covertly, guides the activity of all of his creations. The consciousness of God is ubiquitous.

God is the single Creative Force that conceived, designed, and brought into existence all that has ever existed in nonmaterial or material form. All reality, all realms of existence, all forms of life, are expressions of his creative thoughts. We will use this understanding of God and the purposes of God as identified in the readings to build a structure of reality that includes who and what we are, where we are and why we are here, and where our destiny lies.

Can the presence of this omnipresent consciousness be felt by humans? Can its effects be observed? How does this cosmic consciousness relate to our physical consciousness? Does its unimaginable immensity overwhelm and threaten us when we try to contemplate it and cause us to make God something or somebody to fear? Should we just laugh off the whole idea of such an abstract and esoteric being because the concept is too unbelievable and beyond our comprehension? What thoughts, feelings, and emotions might we rightly associate with an infinite non-physical sentient being? Many theologians quote Scripture to promote the idea of a static, unchangeable God who is the same now as he has always been, and the readings also say that "He is the same today, yesterday, and forever" (Hebrews 13:8; 1857-2_37). But does that mean we should think of God as a mentally rigid, emotionless, and unfeeling being that abhors change? God is a Creative Force and every act of creation brings change to the cosmic realm. The most important and overarching spiritual and mental quality that God radiates into all of his creations is love. God is Love. His love is completely unselfish and flows from him freely and without reservation and without restraint. Love is an emotion that can cause a wide range of feelings in humans, from anguish to contentment to euphoria. It is the most powerful force at work in human affairs. God's nature is unchanging, God's love is unchanging, and God's promises are unchanging, but God creates change and changes with every new creation he brings into existence.

There is no reason to believe that a God of love is immune to these same emotions. That doesn't mean he is excessively emotional or temperamental; it just means that he is capable of feeling intense emotions toward his creations. God is a perfect spiritual manifestation of love, and his creations reflect that loving nature. His love is the gold standard, the highest and purest form of love that can be imagined or expressed, and he freely and generously pours out that love into his many creations. Many attributes that man associates with God and goodness—such as patience, kindness, grace, and mercy—are the natural branches that sprout from the deep roots and sturdy trunk of divine love (2977-2_9). God's love is a force, a force of mind and emotion that flows through every sentient being in his domains. Humans are well aware of the power of love. It can give one person the desire and strength to sacrifice for another person, even to give up one's life so that another may have life or live in freedom. It is the power of a mother protecting her child even if that means running back into the burning building.

God is also described in the readings as Law and Life. We will see how God as passive law sets the rules that bring form to spirit and builds his structural creations. We will discover how God as active law manifests life in various creations. God as Life is expressed in his ability to project a combination of spirit and mind into certain nonmaterial and material substances to give them the ability to generate conscious activity that can mature into a quasi-independent sentient being capable of experiencing sensations, feeling emotions, being cognizant of one's surroundings, and having the ability to think rational thoughts (254-55_6). God's love is unconditional, but that does not mean that his creations have free rein to abuse that love without facing consequences. We will learn how God as spiritual law operates in tandem with God as love to set boundaries on the activities of the sentient beings that inhabit his created realms. Spiritual law does not constrain or prevent sentient creatures from engaging in certain modes of thought and activity, but ensures that irresponsible thought and activity does not unleash uncontrolled disruptive forces in the cosmos and cause unsustainable disharmony in the Whole that is God (3976-29_4; 900-20_5; 3350-1_18).

God is referred to as First Cause and Creative Force in the readings (262-52; 2012-1_24; 262-123). He is First Cause because his thoughts and ideas generated and initiated the foundational elements of the various expressions of reality. As Creative Force he is the motivating desire, power, and truth behind all forms of creative activity that manifest in various ways throughout the various realms of the infinite cosmos. This force of mind and consciousness has been called many names by people who seek to understand him and perceive his presence in their lives. He has been called God, Jehovah, Allah, Ahura Mazda, Brahman, the Lord, the Great Spirit, and other names by various people over the past centuries and millennia, but all of these names represent attempts to identify and understand one being. The consciousness of God molds Spirit into nonmaterial shapes and forms that defy our ability to understand them. The creative force that he wields and projects into manifested forms is an application of mind at the direction of his will in service of his purposes. God's creative endeavors, such as a desire to build a new universe or a new life form, are first conceived as unstructured ideas that evolve into more refined concepts that are eventually acted upon by the will. The will acts on the desire and commands the mind to mold spirit into a specific form or to formulate an appropriate system of rules or laws that will shape spirit into a complex creation. God is fulfilled by the act of creation and the satisfaction of seeing his ideas come into full bloom and fruition.

God is the repository of Truth (254-68_7). Not the truth of a biblical literalist, who is certain he perfectly understands God and vehemently insists that no one can really know God or be accepted into heaven unless they also believe the same myopic truth. Not the truth of the hard-core scientist, who, with blinders in place, peers at energy and matter interactions with an absolute certainty that nothing can possibly exist beyond that which can be probed and measured. Not the truth of the philosopher or theologian who with certainty has determined the number of angels that can stand on the head of a pin or who has accurately calculated the number of years and days and minutes since the creation of the Earth.

These actions may reflect sincere efforts to find truth, but too often these pundits build mental castles that stand as testaments to their own vanity and egos instead of spiritual truth. History is replete with people who constructed doctrine and creeds to corral the minds of the faithful and consolidate ecclesiastical power, rather than encourage the faithful to earnestly seek a personal truth through communion with God.

That is not to say that philosophies and religions do not contain moral and spiritual truth. When asked about the value of studying the teachings of organizations such as Unity, Rosicrucians, Spiritualists, or Indian Yogis, the sleeping Cayce stated that all have some truth within their areas of interest and activity, but that no finite mind has all of the truth (282-4_10). These and other philosophies and religious denominations can have value for the people who are seeking a deeper meaning to their lives than that which is apparent from their daily activity, but the readings declare that the highest material source of truth is to be found in the Word of God as made manifest in the life of Jesus (282-4_10). God is the ultimate and complete Truth because all things spiritual and physical flow forth from God and are part of God. The ultimate reason for every creative act, the particular application of Mind to Spirit that was required to initiate a certain law and creative action or to direct the progression of an ongoing creative activity is found in the Mind of the Creator and nowhere else. The Truth that answers all questions—whether they be in the scientist's quest for knowledge of the nature of a physical law, an anguished mother's need to know the reason for the birth of a deformed child, or the need of a child to understand the death of a parent—is only found fully and finally when answered by God within the context of his purposes. All other answers and perceived truths are preliminary, partial, and subject to revision. Are we privy to that pure, unadulterated knowledge untainted by our personal bias and the imperfect truths we use to construct our version of reality? Or do we believe such knowledge is so far above our pay grade that we will never be allowed access to it?

Is the question raised in the previous chapter as to whether consciousness is really reality already answered? Yes, the consciousness of God is directly or indirectly the ultimate source of all reality, nonmaterial or material, but this simple statement probably will not satisfy the scientifically minded discriminating seeker of truth, or those who might wish to understand some of the nitty-gritty details. It certainly won't satisfy anyone who leans toward agnosticism or atheism. God is certainly not the answer that researchers in theoretical and experimental quantum mechanics had in mind when they suspected and suggested the influence of the mind and consciousness in quantum experiments (Rosenblum and Kuttner, 2011). The religiously or spiritually motivated person may be completely happy to hear the short answer, but there are still far too many unanswered questions to make the short answer palatable and acceptable to the rational reasoning mind. How does the mind of man fit into this idea of an infinite cosmic consciousness and how does it relate to the concept of an all-pervading divine intelligence? If we accept that God consciousness is all pervasive, the obvious conclusion is that human consciousness is in some way derived from God consciousness; but how is that possible? Scientists are already convinced that the mind arises out of the neural network of the human brain and are devoting considerable research money and time into proving that hypothesis. To investigate the question of the origin and nature of mind, we must tackle some aspects of consciousness that are not obvious to most human beings and that cannot be or have not been detected by scientific experiments or biomedical research.

We will accept as a fundamental truth the principle that there is an omnipresent God of Spirit and Mind under the direction of a creative Will that is the living embodiment of love and patience and see how that premise unfolds in a series of logical steps to a conclusion that explains our current reality and our current state of consciousness as human beings. All that we see around us, all that we experience in our lives, the very nature of our personality—including our responses to the situations we encounter in life—can be explained or at least understood from this basic premise. If that sounds like wishful thinking or a gross extrapolation to the meaning of life from too few data points, then hang on for the ride and see how reality and consciousness evolve from the creative activity of Spirit and Mind, the essence of an Almighty God.

In the following chapters, we will look at various aspects of consciousness that arise from the creative desires of God and influence the structure of the physical universe, the plants and animals that populate the Earth, and the activity of human beings that walk upon its surface. We will approach the search for consciousness by following the trail that leads from cosmic consciousness to modern human consciousness from the perspective of the Edgar Cayce readings while respecting science and the core teachings of the major religions. The main thesis is that all reality arises from the application of God consciousness to fulfill his purposes and creative desires, but how does that thesis play out in the complex lives of human beings and the material universe where we make our home? Can we know the desires of God? It might be easy to just say no, but in reality we can and do know a lot about God's plans and his desires as they relate to the universe and humanity. To understand why and how that plan was developed and how it is unfolding, we need to understand why and how God set in motion a certain progression of spiritual and physical events that resulted in the creation of the universe, the Earth, and the life it supports. To begin to understand the purpose of that creation, the sequence of events that caused it to unfold, and the role of consciousness in bringing it all together, we must first look at an often unconsidered or overlooked emotion that God can feel: loneliness.

The Celestial Consciousness
of the Created Soul

The celestial consciousness of every soul is the gift of a portion of God that fulfills his desire for fully cognizant loving companions capable of sharing in his creative endeavors.

It is difficult to imagine that God could become lonely, but the readings state that God desired the companionship and company of other intelligent loving beings to share and enjoy in his creative endeavors (1230-1_8). The boundless love that radiates from God and that is a basic attribute of God remains unfulfilled if it is not appreciated and reflected back to him. God wanted change in his life! Love is not a feeling or emotion that can exist comfortably within the mind of a solitary individual, but is part of a relationship, an emotional interaction with another person that involves affection, commitment, and trust. God imagined the awe and joy of loving companionship and decided to act on that desire by creating the sentient beings we know as souls (262-115_21). Souls have the innate ability to express and receive love, and to reciprocate the love that God bestows upon them. The spiritual purpose embedded in the mind of each created soul is to seek companionship with God. It constantly and subtly urges the soul to engage in a loving relationship with its creator, share in the excitement and joy of his many creations, and participate in his creative endeavors (805-4_10-11). God is Love. He pours out his love to all of his creations, but for this love to be truly fulfilling for him, it must be received by a sentient intellectual being that is capable of feeling and reciprocating that love. Love is a two-way street, an emotion that is best fulfilled when it is shared. Love between a slave and master is possible, but the dependency of one on the other precludes the exercise of free choice by either party, which usually makes the relationship unhealthy and unfulfilling. To satisfy that longing for reciprocal love and to experience true companionship, it was necessary for God to create a reasoning being that could feel, understand and express love freely without coercion. God created souls as celestial beings made in his image with the potential to fulfill their intrinsic destiny to become his companions and cocreators (262-52_25).

Of all of his creations, the soul is most godlike and most closely resembles God in its nature. Spirit, the foundational eternal substance out of which souls were created, is the same substance that constitutes the essence of God. Reading 900-70_5 expresses the relation between soul, God, and the rest of his creations, "All souls were created in the beginning, all spirit of one spirit, Spirit of God, that spirit manifest in flesh, that spirit manifest in all creation, whether of earthly forces or Universal forces, all spirit being one spirit." Nonmaterial souls are real—just as real as any object in the material world. Every soul is a portion of God that he purposely set apart from himself so that each of his soul children would have an independent existence, only limited in that souls are bound by the force of spiritual law. Souls, like God, have the ability to create, to make their thoughts manifest in various desired forms. Souls also have an innate need to creatively express themselves, the natural tendency of any creature created in the image of God, the Master Creator. There is nothing that is absolutely independent of God or that is not part of God, but the soul is the nearest that any of God's creatures come to being independent of God (294-155_7). To be set apart as independent entities does not mean to be separated from him. The readings tell us a great deal about the soul from its creation to the ultimate fulfillment of its destiny as a companion of God and cocreator with God. It is largely up to the soul itself as to whether or not it will fulfill its destiny. To say that souls are created in the image of God is true, but we should not mistakenly construe that statement to mean that the countenance or appearance of a soul is similar to God. That conclusion would completely miss the real and far deeper meaning of the phrase. Because every soul is a portion of God, it has the same basic composition and structure as God. Each soul is an integrated unit of spirit, mind, and will; a quasi-independent self-contained entity formed out of the greater all-pervasive cosmic Spirit, Mind, and Will that is God. God literally set aside portions of himself so that each soul could develop a separate consciousness, identity, and individuality through the application of its own free will (263-13_19). The reality of the soul is a consequence of the reality of God. Every soul has the potential and the ability to become as much like God in mind as it desires, although no soul can become the totality of the divine God.

Souls have form, which is variously called the soul body, spiritual body, cosmic body, etheric body, and celestial body in the readings (900-348_4; 900-348_6; 5756-4_8). They all refer to the entirety of the soul including the mental-directed shape that spirit may take, its spiritual attributes, mental activity, conscious awareness, and individuality. Each soul has a single mind, but two distinct aspects or facets of the soul mind are specifically identified and mentioned in the readings. The aspect of the soul mind that serves as its primary seat of awareness out of which the individuality of the soul develops is called the subconscious mind. The aspect of the soul mind that forms a link or interface between the soul and the greater entirety of God is called the super conscious mind. The soul mind is a creative force that can manipulate and mold spirit into desired forms of expression. Spirit is the raw substance that the soul mind uses to manifest thoughts that have coalesced into ideas, concepts, and ideals. God is not only the creator and parent of every soul; he is also the life force that sustains every soul. The flow of life force into a soul is dependent upon the caliber of its kinship with the Whole of God, the willingness of the soul to remain in constant mental communion and communication with God, and the strength of its mental rapport with its creator. God is the singularity of Unity and Oneness (the Lord thy God is One). God is also the multiplicity of relationships among souls (each soul is intimately interconnected with every other soul). The intimate connection of the soul mind to the Mind of God brings an innate impelling need, a spiritual drive or impulse, that constantly and persistently, but subtly and softly, reminds the soul of its origin and urges the soul to seek its ultimate destiny, companionship with its creator. Peace of mind to the soul is secured only when the soul mind begins to realize and covet its oneness with God.

The ideal pattern of higher spiritual conduct that will lead a soul to fulfill its destiny as a companion of God is imprinted or embossed within the deepest recesses of every soul mind. This pattern contains knowledge of the soul's oneness with God and harbors knowledge of the qualities and attributes of God that have been conferred upon the soul by the fact of its creation in the image of God. These innate moral and spiritual values give rise to a higher and more spiritual sense of self within the soul when they are allowed to guide the activities of the soul and the interaction of the soul with other souls. Each soul mind in the spiritual realm can express itself through the transmission of thought to other soul minds (5753-1_22; 254-2_2) and can create in this nonphysical realm when the mental propensity to create is activated by will and desire. Souls are at their spiritual best when they reciprocate the love of God and apply the attributes of love, kindness, and patience when they interact with other souls. These godly attributes are inherited by the soul and are innate to the soul, but like any mental memories, they may be ignored, suppressed, or simply lie unused and forgotten for so long that they no longer register during normal activity.

Soul activity is guided by its mind at the behest of its will, a creative action that allows it to manifest thoughts and desires into various forms. This action mimics the way that God manipulates spirit into directed activity and creates shape and structure in all realms to bring his ideas and desires to fruition. In the words of the readings, the mind is the builder and that which the mind dwells upon, it becomes (364-10_6). When the soul mind remains attuned to thoughts that respect spiritual principles and spiritual law, the soul's activity is spiritualized and it manifests goodness, godliness, and love as it interacts with fellow souls. When the soul dwells upon self-centered thoughts that disrespect spiritual law, it brings destruction upon itself and becomes mentally and spiritually separated from God (23-1_14; 262-63_12; 262-78_11). Free will is a two-edged sword that brings both good and evil to the soul depending upon how it is used or abused. It allows the soul virtually unlimited freedom. It can be used to guide the soul toward perpetual awareness of the presence of its creator, a loving relationship with God, and eternal spiritual union with God, or it can be used to steer the soul toward an inflated sense of self-worth that leads to a destructive sense of self-centeredness that has serious spiritual consequences, including loss of God consciousness (5753-1_22).

In the nonphysical realm of its creation, the soul has ultimate control of the mind and determines the direction in which the mind will seek activity. The separate avenues of exploration that each soul selected, the particular choices and decisions it made as it sampled and investigated various aspects of its environment and interacted with fellow souls, was determined by its application of free will. All outward exertions and endeavors of the soul are manifested thoughts, and all thoughts are activated or suppressed according to the desire of the will. The soul can embrace a desire and follow it to its natural conclusion or reject a desire and let it expire without a trace. A thought or idea can be followed to the detriment of the soul's relationship with God if it lets the mind attach to or intently focus on a pleasurable activity that generates an excessive negative influence on others, an intense habitual sensation, or an exaggerated sense of self-worth in the mind. Choices that respect the soul's inherent godly attributes of love and patience draw the soul closer to God, and choices that disrespect those divine attributes drag the soul away from God. In a spiritually healthy soul, the will of the soul will be kept in check and be a positive influence and direct the mind away from these unhealthy attractions, and lead the mind into thoughts and activities that bring it toward a closer communion with God. In this way it will contribute to the fulfillment of the spiritual purpose of the soul and embark on a path that will ultimately lead the soul to its divine destiny. It is the responsibility of the soul to use its will to keep a tight rein on the mind, maximize virtuous thoughts and activities and minimize self-indulgence, and keep the soul on the path that fulfills its destiny.

When the soul fails to hold the will true to its spiritual purpose, the lure of selfishness, self-aggrandizement, and self-indulgence can seduce the mind and draw it away from its source of life and awareness of its destiny as a companion of God. The soul is capable of making course corrections by redirecting the will for the good of the soul, and can bring the soul mind back into alignment and attunement with God, but too often the soul allows the unwary and unfettered mind to be lured into unacceptable and immoral modes of thought and activity. The soul is subject to spiritual law. Spiritual law helps redirect the soul trajectory when the soul uses its will to engage in behavior that disrespects its purpose and destiny. God does not mete out punishment to souls that "break" spiritual law, but spiritual law urges the wayward soul toward companionship with God. Any thought and manifested action of a soul that is selfish constitutes spiritual rebellion against God, and places the soul on a trajectory that causes it to face consequences for that inappropriate behavior. The soul is required to again face the set of conditions that led to its poor choice and spiritual failure. It will be offered an opportunity to make a better choice under similar circumstances—a choice that ideally will be more spiritually correct. Repeated incorrect choices, especially those that involve harmful and hurtful interaction with other souls, lead the soul along a path toward more lessons on the failed subject and more opportunities to restore its spiritual character and move closer to companionship with God. The readings do not provide many details about the practical application of spiritual law in the nonmaterial realm, but do clearly explain it in relation to material soul activity, which we will discover in subsequent chapters.

The Maturing Soul

Souls were not created with a completely mature mind but had to grow in awareness and reasoning capability by compiling and processing information from their environment and from their original intimate connection with God. The newly minted souls had pure, undefiled, and unpolluted minds that were as close to God in consciousness as unsophisticated, immature, souls could be. As souls gained a greater sense of self-awareness and began exploring their creative powers, they developed a more mature understanding of their environment, their creative capabilities, and their neighbor souls. The reasoning skills and cognitive functions of the new soul minds expanded and developed as each soul used its maturing intellect to explore its nonphysical environment and made choices regarding the activities it would pursue and its method of interacting with fellow souls. All of this affected the degree to which each soul remembered and retained awareness of itself as a portion of God. This is how a soul mind learns, becomes able to more fully comprehend its environment, increases its intelligence and analytical abilities, and better understands the appropriate way to interact with other souls. Souls began creating mental patterns that reflected their experiences in the nonmaterial realm and a preferred manner of reaction and response to those experiences. They began to flex their creative powers like a human infant tests its ability to control the muscles of its body. They saw opportunities to use these creative abilities to fulfill selfish desires that, perhaps, belittled or demeaned their fellow souls and that relegated their creator to a distant past memory instead of embracing him as a close companion with whom they could share thoughts and feelings of camaraderie and love.

The created soul was like a newborn infant. Every new activity is a learning experience that is filed away for future reference and linked with information received from previous experiences to build a framework of thoughts and ideas that coalesce into the soul's individuality, the soul equivalent of the personality of a human being. The soul individuality is partly formed from the thoughts, experiences, observations, actions, deductions, and reasoning of the soul mind as it awakens to the reality of the nonphysical realm combined with the truth and love it absorbs through its link to the Mind of God. It contains the hopes and desires of the soul (5246-1_17). The analytical aspects of individuality are also blended with emotional aspects shaped by the intensity and degree to which the soul mind incorporates, integrates, and exercises the inherent godly attributes of love, patience, kindness, mercy, and grace it received at its creation. The less often souls rely on these inherited attributes in their activity; the less likely they are to retain an attitude of respect toward other souls. The mind of each of the billions of souls developed differently because every set of life experiences and responses is different, leading to a wide variation in the type and depth of selfishness harbored in the mind of each soul. Souls matured as they developed self-awareness and independence through different experiences in their realm of activity. Souls developed their own distinctive individuality based on these unique experiences, their responses, and the mental attitudes they held as they encountered and interacted with other souls. Each soul's individual nature was also affected by how closely it had attuned and aligned its will and mind with its creator, or how far it had distanced and separated itself from its creator as it pushed the outer limits of selfish expressions of free will. The unified consciousness of God and his soul children became fractured and divided as the gift of free will that gave souls self-expression was mis-applied and abused to satisfy the soul's selfish pleasures. God expected these individual points of consciousness to flourish, but had hoped that their use of creative powers would remain consistent with the primary purpose of souls, which was to become companions of God in the spiritual realm (5749-14_5).

The characteristic individuality associated with the subconscious mind of a soul is the mental representation of an amalgam of nonphysical experiences and expressions of the soul in relation to the desires that the soul has entertained and expressed. This acquired mental state embodies the standards or the criteria that the soul uses for judgment, mercy, and justice within its sphere of activity. It determines how the soul perceives other souls and how it interacts with other souls, and whether that interaction has a selfish dimension or whether love and kindness are paramount. The degree to which moral and spiritual values are integrated into the soul's individuality depends upon how well the soul has kept the lines of communication open between itself and God, and how often and how meaningfully the soul accesses and reciprocates the love that God wants to bestow on it. If the soul has set itself as the greater source of thought, desire, and knowledge and has effectively abandoned God by mentally shutting off all or most communication with the Mind of God, then the individuality of the soul easily becomes ruled by outside influences, self-centered thoughts, and a propensity to display selfish character traits such as an enhanced sense of self-entitlement and self-worth. The truth of the matter is that the eternal happiness and satisfaction of the soul lies in its willingness to embrace loving companionship with God, not in an excessively and unreasonably high sense of self-worth that usually is expressed in the nonphysical realm by lording itself over other souls or disrespecting the equality of other souls.

Many souls became enamored with their own creative abilities and allowed their minds to wander away from the knowledge of their creator. We see a reflection of this tendency in human society as young humans explore the limits of their abilities and drift away from an originally close relationship with their loving parents. It is subtle at first and not readily apparent or obvious to the soul that is pursuing its own self-interest and delights in the newly discovered ability to apply the mind to selfish creative pursuits instead of concentrating on improving and enriching its relationship with God. There are serious consequences to this loss of God consciousness. As that connection begins to weaken, a chain of events is set in motion that erodes the mental-spiritual connection that the soul originally had with God, causes it to lose the intimate communion with God that it originally valued, and eventually causes the soul to forget its spiritual heritage. Despite this undesirable weakening of the bond between creation and creator, God could not withhold this creative freedom and still remain faithful to his purpose for the creation of souls. If he would have restricted their ability to think and decide for themselves, then the companionship he was seeking would have taken the form of a slave-master or puppet-puppeteer relationship. There might have been a form of enforced companionship, but true loving companionship could never develop. The downside to the plan for soul companionship is that the soul has to realize of its own accord that its most fulfilling, rewarding and exciting life experiences are to be found within the context of a loving relationship with God, not within its own magnified egotistical sense of self-worth, and not in the many forms of self-gratification and self-indulgence that it can discover and act upon (531-3_23).

The act of rebellion against God, the willful disobedience or intentional decision to act in opposition to the purpose and plan for its creation, is the very definition of sin in the readings (262-52_25; 262-125_18). How does a soul sin in the nonmaterial realm? By indulging in any selfish expression or action that glorifies the soul instead of glorifying and serving its creator and that causes the soul mind to lose awareness of God. These include, but are not limited to, feelings of envy and jealousy toward others, pride and arrogance, an inflated ego and ambition that disrespects others, expressions of hatred and anger, lying and malicious gossip, and abusing any position of power over other souls. These sins are rooted in the mind and emotions. We don't understand the cosmic realm well enough to know if the soul environment contains nonmaterial equivalents of material objects, or whether the disincarnate soul perceives its environment through an analog of sensory organs. If it does, there might be other ways of sinning. The soul can have its own life and make its own choices as needed for survival or even pleasure, but these aspects of individual life must be balanced with selfless service and respect for spiritual law. The will of any soul can express a desire that is not consistent with the spiritual purpose of the soul as a companion of God. That in itself is not necessarily a spiritual disaster, and may not constitute sin, but when that idea is dwelled upon, entertained frequently, or—especially—when it is acted upon to produce an effect in the spiritual realm, it becomes sin. When ungodly thought patterns are repeatedly manifested, they can crystallize and metastasize into a habitual negative pattern of thought and behavior that generates serious spiritual consequences. There is no sense of shame or accountability reflected back to the mind of souls that engage in these inappropriate expressions of irresponsible individuality because time and space, which generate the perception of causality, are not properties of the cosmic realm (2560-1_24; 2925-1_45; 262-115_10-11).

The penchant many souls displayed toward excessive selfishness as they began to explore the limits of their mental abilities and the boundaries of acceptable behavior led to the degradation of God consciousness. The excitement and newness of life in the nonphysical realm distracted souls from their purpose and caused them to lose awareness of their oneness with God, which altered their consciousness into more ego-driven channels of thought and activity that pushed aside or suppressed memories of the imprinted spiritual pattern and their original awareness of God. The subconscious mind can always access the Mind of God through the super conscious aspect of the soul mind, as long as the soul keeps that channel open by not engaging in excessively selfish behavior or thoughts that obstruct or block the flow of love and spiritual guidance from God. But, as souls grew ever more independent, their subconscious minds developed a stronger sense of self and, too often, a sense of egotism and self-importance that led them to engage in behavior that was not in accord with the purpose of their creation. A soul that is self-absorbed can easily become self-indulgent, develop an inflated sense of self-worth, and open itself to the desire to indulge in activities that are pleasurable and gratifying in ways that move its center of attention far from its creator.

The soul is strongest when it routinely, frequently, and effortlessly communicates with God. This intimate sharing of thoughts and feelings coupled with a willingness to receive guidance and love from God through the reception of spiritual knowledge and exchange of ideas gives strength and security to the soul mind. The value of this mental relationship depends upon the attention that the soul mind gives to communion with God through the super conscious mind where the soul mind merges with the Mind of God. The super conscious mind is the gateway to the Mind of God and the fountain of life for the soul. When the soul mind is anchored to the Mind of God, it becomes the conduit through which love and truth replenish the spiritual strength of the soul. This is the key to eternal life and consciousness for the soul. If it is properly tended and cultivated, it will allow the soul to find and fulfill its spiritual purpose. The soul that allows this bond of communion to deteriorate or that ignores it out of an inflated sense of self-worth gradually loses its way because its spiritual rudder has been damaged. It gradually loses awareness of the true and pure source of spiritual sustenance for the soul. It is adrift in a realm of temptations while relying on dubious advice from a self-absorbed and selfish mind. Repeated sinfulness, i.e., spiritual rebellion against God, jeopardizes the ultimate destiny that God has in mind for the soul. The eternal nature of souls is not absolute, but is predicated on the soul mind remaining in a state of attunement with the Mind of God (2052-1_10-11). The permanence and immortality of souls are derived from their original creation from portions of God and sustained by the quality of their ongoing spiritual-mental connection to God. Souls do not die in the sense we humans understand death, but souls can cease to exist by being reabsorbed into the greater Whole of God with an attendant loss of individual identity and independent consciousness (826-8_9-10). God does not wish this fate on any soul and with every act of rebellion has provided a means for the soul to realize and rectify its spiritual errors and restore and redeem itself before God. This is the meaning of mercy and grace as granted by God to souls.

All souls were created with an unrealized potential for a higher, godlike consciousness. Some souls held true to the purpose and promise of their creation and developed a mature mind that retained spiritual union with God. Far too many souls squandered their inheritance and indulged too deeply in rebellious behavior that caused them to become separated in mind from God. When souls engage in cooperative activity that respects other souls, they bring harmony to the Whole of God, but when they act independently without regard to the needs and feelings of other souls, they create a state of disharmony and discord in the Whole of God (1776-1_19). Communication in the celestial realm, in which souls were created, does not require the intermediary of a human body analogue and is not constrained by the finite propagation speed of sound and light. The readings state that at the level of awareness of the subconscious mind, communication between souls is by transfer of thoughts (900-23_7) and that at the level of awareness of the super conscious mind, or cosmic consciousness, all minds begin to merge, and individual thoughts can become common knowledge and are no longer privately held. Souls have intelligence, emotions, and a sense of independence, but must learn to foster a sense of fellowship and brotherhood with fellow souls. The migration toward self-centeredness and self-gratification can easily overwhelm the ideal of brotherhood and community. An inflated sense of self-worth and a feeling of superiority over other souls caused soul-to-soul conflict that revealed itself in jealousy, anger, power struggles, and divisions among the created souls. Such continued activity was untenable and required a remedy, a way of bringing soul minds back into proper alignment with the mind and purposes of God. Community, as envisioned by God, is based on a sense of equality and service to others that lifts the spiritual consciousness of the society of souls in unison. Independent thinking, the development of individual talents, and the desire to grow intellectually and explore the environment are admirable traits in souls only as long as no soul activity is pursued at the expense of the well-being of other souls. Souls cannot behave in a manner that disregards the potential disruption and destruction of the soul community. Unfettered individualism leads to narcissistic behavior, a false sense of entitlement, and a willingness to pursue gain and pleasure at the expense of other souls without obvious repercussions. The ability of souls to perceive and understand the mental and spiritual damage that their ungodly manifested thoughts would eventually have on their relationship with God and fellow souls was rapidly diminishing as their behavior weakened their mental communion with God.

Souls were exploring thought patterns that were off limits and that were not consistent with beings designed to be companions of God. The ripples of disharmony produced by self-centered and rebellious soul behavior were propagating through the spiritual realm as selfish thought patterns were manifested in the society of souls. Because of the nature of the spiritual realm, there was no real accountability for the soul for the disunity and division produced by these thought patterns. This irresponsible pursuit of selfish experiences was dangerous for the soul's wellbeing. They needed a place where their exploration of selfish patterns of thought and behavior would reveal to them the damaging effects of that behavior. Errant souls were going to be introduced to a new, demanding environment that would cause them to face serious consequences for each and every decision that placed their selfish interests above all other interests and spiritual obligations. They would learn to release thoughts that engendered a sense of self-righteousness and replace them with thoughts of unselfish humbleness and an attitude of selfless service and commitment to generosity and support for less fortunate souls. In short, while immersed in this new realm, the soul would be forced to meet the consequences of its failure to remain faithful to the purpose for which it was created. To fulfill such an enormous undertaking God would design and create a realm of activity where the selfish thoughts and actions of souls would lead to specific consequences that would encourage them to change their unhealthy habitual thought patterns. Each action would generate a reaction, a future flow of events that would cause the soul to face situations and experiences that gave new opportunities to correct any tendency to harm other souls that were in the same realm of activity. Every selfish thought manifested as disrespect, disregard, or abuse of another soul in defiance of spiritual law would eventually come back to the soul as suffering and mental and spiritual anguish. God is supremely patient, but repeated refusal to return to a state of God consciousness and godly behavior, including respect for fellow souls, would soon have serious repercussions. Souls that chose to learn from their mistakes, engage in altruistic behavior toward fellow souls, and commit to the pursuit of spiritual perfection would naturally regain mental attunement with God and share in the glory of his creative endeavors.

A Soul Rehabilitation Facility

God arrived at the idea of constructing a realm for soul rehabilitation based upon the concept of experience in a dimension where soul thoughts are manifested into material activity and are subject to the principal of causality. Causality was determined to be the environmental factor that would best release the minds of souls from the desire to rebel against God and free them from attitudes of unrighteousness and self-serving behavior that can potentially lead to dissolution of the soul identity and individuality. A realm that incorporated the principle of causality would give souls that had separated themselves from God the opportunity to come to their senses and reestablish intimate contact with their creator. It would be a place where souls could continue exercising their new powers of mental creation with the difference that every thought that became activated or manifested in the new realm would create a material and spiritual response or consequence. The realm would include a region of matter and energy where souls would transform their thoughts into physical activity that would be subject to the concept of sow and reap, a spiritual principle that reflects back upon the soul the evil or goodness it has spread outward toward other souls. The companion principle of "like begets like" would draw like-minded souls together during their physical activity. Causality would ensure that every rebellious, evil, and ungodly thought that a soul dwelt and acted upon would precipitate an in-kind effect on the future activities of the soul in the physical realm. There were three major soul deficiencies to be addressed: the rebellion of souls against

God's authority as embodied in spiritual law; the willingness of souls to engage in self-gratification and self-indulgence to the detriment of their relationship with God; and the selfish, disrespectful, and uncooperative interaction of one soul with one another soul. The ultimate effect of this new realm would be nothing less than the rehabilitation and redemption of souls by the full restoration of God consciousness to the mind of every errant soul willing to make the effort to change.

Souls that had chosen to engage in sinful rebellious behavior in the celestial realm would be required to enter the material realm where they would come face-to-face with the ramifications of each and every spiritual misstep manifested through physical activity, particularly selfish words and actions directed toward their fellow souls. Activity that expressed goodness, love, and kindness would bring peace, security, and spiritual confidence to the soul mind and would attract like-minded individuals. Souls that continued to express activities that demonstrated self-centeredness, self-gratification, and expressions of anger, hate, and other inappropriate and ungodly emotions would bring discord and destruction upon themselves. The soul would be required to enter and reenter this rehabilitation facility until it learned that its eternal future, mental happiness, and spiritual satisfaction are only to be found in the mental and physical application of the spiritual attributes of love, patience, kindness, gentleness, grace, and mercy with regard to other souls (257-238_36). The soul was going to school, a work-study program where mental and spiritual education would be interwoven with practical application to determine how well it was absorbing the lessons. It would learn that, in the long run, its security and happiness are dependent upon its willingness to respect its spiritual purpose, adhere to the tenets of spiritual law, and project love and friendship toward its sibling souls. Souls would have to learn that as portions of God, they are no better, no more important, and no more deserving than any other soul. They would discover that at the super conscious level of the soul mind, all souls exist as a community in the body of God, not as totally individual and isolated beings. There are established rules of thought and behavior within the context of spiritual law that serve to maintain harmony in the body of God. Love is the supreme mental attribute of God and therefore a mental attribute of souls, but souls that are self-centered can suppress the expression of love to the point where it is difficult for them to remember and feel its power in their lives. When souls embrace love, they develop a more spiritual individuality, show themselves worthy of a restored relationship with God, and acquire the higher state of consciousness needed for a journey into eternity. They will rediscover their oneness with the greater Whole of God and will learn act accordingly.

Souls flourish when they maintain a sense of unified purpose and activity rooted in intimate friendship and companionship with God. The life of every soul depends upon an open and constant communion with its creator—a communion that gives the soul the freedom to become an independent entity while retaining awareness of the community of souls. The maintenance of peace and harmony in the spiritual realm requires that each soul respect fellow souls as equals and honor the oneness of souls, God, and all of his various creations. The readings describe souls as being corpuscles in the body of God (2724-1_8; 3333-1_13; 3395-2_8; 3481-2_9), an analogy with reference to the individual cells that make up the totality of a biological organism such as a human being. When each cell or soul goes its own way without regard to the whole, a cancer develops in the body. When each soul lives up to its spiritual purpose, the body of God remains in a peaceful and harmonious state instead of warring within itself. God is exceedingly patient with souls, but the disease and disharmony they were inflicting on the Whole of God could not be tolerated indefinitely.

The new realm would reward souls that initiated good and kind actions toward other souls and bring peace, happiness, and spiritual contentment and satisfaction into the society of souls that were active in the realm. The ensuing peace of mind would reignite awareness of the soul's true relationship with God. Activities consistently rooted in goodness and godliness would help the soul to regain knowledge of its oneness with God and teach it how to explore the limits of its mind while remaining within the appropriate arena of exploration and the type of thoughts that can be pursued and acted upon without negative consequences. Souls would be taught to control their manifested thoughts and emotions in a way that respected the spiritual law to which they were bound from the moment of their creation. They would learn that even the children of God must live within the boundaries defined by spiritual law and that there are serious consequences for failing to honor the law. Souls would gradually understand the necessity and value of acting in a manner that respected their elevated position in the greater cosmic scheme of things. This new realm with its physical universe of matter and energy would be the first of three major intercessions of God on behalf of and for the welfare of his soul children. How was such a realm to be constructed? How would souls interact with the new physical world and with each other in the new world? How would souls actually gain useful spiritual experience in a realm that would be completely foreign to them? The readings give us much information on these topics, which we will explore in some detail.

The Passive Consciousness
of Universal Physical Law

The passive consciousness we perceive as universal physical law, the unified forces of gravity, the strong force, the weak force, and the electromagnetic force emerges out of a Creative Mental Force of God that expresses his desire to create a causal physical universe.

The plan for a soul rehabilitation facility was formulated by God as he observed the misuse of creative powers and the glorification of self by his soul children and thought about possible methods to rectify the chaotic and dangerous situation. How was such a realm to be constructed? What form would this rehabilitation facility take and how would souls actually gain useful spiritual experiences in that realm? The facility that God created has a nonphysical component and a physical component. The nonphysical component is a group of mental-spiritual training centers or schools for soul education. The associated physical component is a physical universe where souls are periodically tested on their understanding of the spiritual principles they have been taught, sometimes referred to in the readings as the plane of application. How did God transform a portion of the cosmic realm into an alternate reality that would benefit the spiritual development of souls? To clarify terms and avoid confusion, the reader should be aware that the term "cosmic realm" as used in this chapter is consistent with its usage in previous chapters.

It does not mean the cosmos, which is the term commonly used to refer to the region of suns and galaxies beyond our solar system. The cosmic realm refers to the infinite spiritual realm where souls were created and whatever other realms that might exist beyond the physical universe and the closely associated nonmaterial surrounding regions that are part of the soul rehabilitation facility.

The creation of the physical universe was a conscious act by God (262-114_23), but its evolution into the form that we observe today was guided by a passive form of mind and consciousness that we recognize as the universal law of physics. This all-pervading physical law is a crystallization of the will and desire of God to initiate and set into motion his plan for soul rehabilitation. Universal physical law is a form of condensed consciousness, a divine plan of action congealed into a workable set of instructions to fulfill his purposes, a subsidiary law within the greater cosmic law that imposes constraints on the creation of manifested nonmaterial forms in the spiritual realm. Electromagnetic energy is accepted by science as the only component of the nascent physical universe (Whittle, 2008; Greene, 2005). The readings assure us that electromagnetic energy is a manifestation of God (1299-1), a form of spirit in motion, and a material expression of the foundational substance of which all physical things are made (262-78_6; 262-119_5). We will refer to this primordial energy of the nascent universe as spirit-energy. Matter is a compact form of electromagnetic energy and therefore a condensed form of spirit. There is only one force that guides and controls the motion and interactions of energy and matter, the Creative Force of God embodied in universal physical law (262-52_12; 3744-5_39; 4757-1_4).

God conceived universal physical law as the means to set the initial conditions needed for a physical universe to emerge as a unique finite and encapsulated portion of the infinite nonmaterial cosmic or spiritual realm and guide that universe through a multitude of physical interactions and chemical reactions. He provided the raw substance that would become energy and would be transformed into matter, and he established the rules that would guide that transformation. Various readings touch upon aspects of this creative process and describe it in words that are unique to the language of the readings, but which bring together the spiritual knowledge of the readings and the scientific knowledge of the field of cosmology. The spiritual philosophy of the readings is more in tune with the scientific knowledge of the universe than most interpretations of biblical Scripture. The doctrine of *creatio ex nihilo*, to which both Protestant and Catholic theologians subscribe, means to bring something out of nothing. It is promoted by theologians to explain the creation of the universe and their belief that God made the universe appear out of nothingness. It is fundamentally flawed. The concept of the universe arising out of nothing is inconsistent with the readings. As we have already seen, there is nothing that is not God, which also means that there is no such thing as nothingness because nothingness would be a region, space, or realm separate from the presence of God. Reading 3161-1_10 states that throughout any region or period of what we call space and time, it is impossible for a vacuum to form. This does not mean that there can be no region in which matter is totally absent, but means that there is no place in the universe where God as spirit-energy does not have a presence. Also, the united Spirit, Mind, and Will of God are the pervading presence and consciousness within all that exists. There is no need to force our minds into thinking that the universe was created out of nothing. The universe was created by encapsulating a region of Spirit, the nonmaterial precursor of energy, which then was allowed to morph into matter-antimatter pairs as the universe expanded under the guidance of physical law. Statements have been made in Christian study material that matter cannot be inhabited by God, but must somehow be external to God and made up of a different substance than God. Like the doctrine of *creatio ex nihilo*, this is incorrect thinking and for the same reason. It implies that matter is something distinct and different from God, which God can influence and possibly infiltrate to accomplish his will. Matter is not external to God. It is simply a form of spirit, a result of natural physical evolution guided by a universal physical law that involves the condensation of spirit-energy into basic subatomic particles which then combine under the proper conditions to form atomic matter.

Universal physical law conveys the thoughts and desires of God into manifested physical forms and activity. It is a deliberately fashioned rule designed to guide the transformation of eternal spirit into electromagnetic energy and the condensation of energy into the substance we know as matter. All of the material manifestations possible within the new physical realm would be subject to the constraints of this law (136-37_6). Physical law is obeyed without hesitation by any material object in the physical world. Matter and energy were the raw materials that ultimately brought to fruition God's conceptual idea for a causal environment in which souls would have the opportunity to reestablish communion and union with him. There is a greater and far more encompassing cosmic law of which the universal physical law is a subset. The physical forces we observe and measure are reflected evidence of the reality of the greater Universal Force that rules the spiritual realm or cosmos (538-20_3). Cosmic law embodies the structure and rules of the infinite nonmaterial realms, including the laws of motion and interaction of nonmaterial objects. This higher law is not well explained in the readings, but there are inferences that can be made. The mind creates thoughts that can be fashioned into ideas that suggest a possible course of action. The desire and directive of the will to activate an idea of particular interest causes the mind to take action and activate spirit to manifest the idea. All of this occurs naturally in the cosmic realm, the spiritual realm of soul birth and activity. This creative ability is a fundamental aspect of God that he passed to his soul children.

The physical law that gives shape and form to the universe is crystallized desire, the activation of the creative force of the Mind of God to fulfill a purpose. The Mind of God, under the control of his Will, is able to shape and mold spirit into desired forms of physical manifestation (3508-1_4). This universal physical law contains God's architectural plans for the construction of an entire physical realm dedicated to the welfare and rehabilitation of his soul children, a realm constructed for the purpose of restoring every soul to the awareness of and communion with its creator. The readings describe the creation of the universe with the words "God moved", or "the Mind of God moved." This is an attempt to describe the power and force of the Mind of God as it brought his Spirit into activity to fulfill a purpose. As expressed many times in the readings, the Mind is the Builder, and the physical universe, like all of his creations, is a product of the creative force that is the Mind of God (254-42_6; 262-83_10; 900-227_11). God encapsulated a portion of spirit within a container that would present the concepts of time and space to a conscious mind and fulfill the role of a theater in which souls would manifest activity. The enclosed spirit would be effectively isolated from the cosmic realm. Scientists recognize this physical expression of the Spirit of God as electromagnetic energy, a small portion of which humans experience as visible light. The physical universe would exist within and be a part of the infinitely larger nonphysical realm variously described as the cosmic realm or spiritual realm, terms intended to describe the immense and grand outer realm that man can only imagine and dream about. Cosmologists have established that the nascent universe was incredibly minute, more than sixteen orders of magnitude smaller than the current size of the universe. It would begin life by undergoing an incredibly rapid expansion phase called inflation that would trigger a series of events that would radically change its nature. Universal physical law would guide the motion and interactions of the encased spirit-energy as the expansion took it through a series of phase transitions that eventually caused it to condense into matter. After 13.8 billion years, this law still defines the way in which matter and electromagnetic energy move and interact (1158-14_12). The initial expression of spirit-energy was a state of chaos and disorder, but with infinite patience God was letting the immutable rule of physical law transform disorder and chaos into a magnificent and incredibly beautiful universe.

A Physical Universe for the Application of Spiritual Principles

A single unified universal law of physics governed the interaction of matter and energy at the enormously high temperature and density that existed in the nascent universe, but inflation would soon cause it to divide into four distinct aspects. As the universe of spirit-energy expanded, the temperature and density rapidly decreased, and the active force of the unified law began to resolve into the four forces scientists today have identified and understand quite well (the gravitational force, the strong nuclear force, the weak nuclear force, and the electromagnetic force). Universal physical law has two main aspects that fulfill different purposes. One aspect of the law establishes the container within which, or perhaps more accurately the surface upon which, energy and matter are constrained to move and interact. This aspect of law delineates the limits of the universe and fashions the structural framework of the universe. Physicists call this structure the spacetime continuum or spacetime fabric. Spacetime defines the extent and boundary of the physical universe, the rate of expansion of the universe, and the container that keeps the physical realm separated from the cosmic realm. During the initial brief and rapid expansion phase of the spacetime continuum, spirit-energy existed as waves of highly concentrated and energetic electromagnetic energy moving randomly across spacetime. This incredibly hot and dense environment precluded the existence of anything other than pure energy. Energy could travel across the early universe because electromagnetic waves are self-propagating, even in the vacuum of empty space, meaning space devoid of matter. The structure of spacetime controls the motion of the electromagnetic energy that travels across its fabric because waves of electromagnetic energy follow the curvature of spacetime. The original spacetime fabric was flat, and energy propagated outward without interruption as the fabric expanded. This flow of energy would occur unimpeded until the universe developed charged particles. Much later, when the universe developed huge and massive material objects such as suns and galaxies, the spacetime fabric would become warped and curved by their presence. and the curvature would cause the path traversed by energy waves to bend as the waves passed near massive objects. The curvature would also cause nearby matter objects to experience the effect we know as gravity.

A second aspect of universal physical law defines the manner in which energy interacts with itself in its pure and condensed forms. It guides physical evolution, the transformation of energy into fundamental particles and various basic forms of atomic matter, the recombination of lighter elements into more complex heavier elements, and the rearrangement of heavy elements into massive objects. Matter can be thought of as a collection of minute droplets of highly condensed energy. It was destined from the beginning to become the building blocks of entire worlds. Within one second of the dawn of the universe, the rapid expansion of the spacetime continuum caused the temperature and the energy density of the universe to decline precipitously, allowing massive amounts of the original spirit-energy to condense into oppositely charged pairs of fundamental particles, one a matter particle and one an antimatter particle. In its more energetic state, each unit of spirit-energy could split into a quark and anti-quark pair. In its slightly less energetic state, each unit of spirit-energy could split into an electron and anti-electron pair. Soon thereafter, these particle pairs participated in a massive slightly un-symmetric annihilation event, which, for reasons not yet fully understood by physicists, left the universe with only matter quarks and electrons, the fundamental components of atomic matter. The quarks subsequently condensed into quasi-stable triplets called protons and neutrons (depending upon the type and charge of the combining quarks), and soon thereafter a portion of the protons and neutrons clumped into helium-4 nuclei and trace amounts of a few other light nuclei. The larger portion of excess protons remained unaltered as free hydrogen nuclei, leaving the early universe with a composition of about 75 percent hydrogen nuclei; about 25 percent helium-4 nuclei; and trace amounts of neutrons, deuterium nuclei, helium-3 nuclei, and lithium-7 nuclei. The consciously established quantum laws of physics were bringing order out of the chaotic expansion of vast quantities of spirit-energy by directing the phase transitions and particle reactions that brought forth quarks, electrons, and first basic nuclei. The fundamental particles of the early universe were prepared and ready to create the first atoms, the basic building blocks of all objects in the physical universe.

The binding of quark triplets onto protons and neutrons and the clumping of these particles into atomic nuclei was controlled by a component of physical law that physicists call the strong force. Another force, called the weak force, controlled the natural transmutation of protons into neutrons, and neutrons into protons, a process called radioactive decay that was quite active in the early universe. The force of physical law that controls the interaction of electromagnetic energy and charged particles is described by Maxwell's four equations of electromagnetism. These equations reveal the inherent rule that all electromagnetic energy will travel at a constant speed when propagating through the vacuum of space unhindered by matter. This constant finite propagation speed of spirit-energy limits the speed at which information can be transmitted across the material universe and impresses causality upon the universe. The readings suggest that this limitation on propagation speed does not exist in the cosmic realm and is a contributing factor causing souls to be relatively unaware of the damage caused by their propensity to ignore and "violate" spiritual law. The first light atomic elements did not appear in the universe until about four-hundred thousand years after its creation when the temperature had cooled and the density of energy and matter decreased sufficiently to allow free negatively charged electrons to attach to the positively charged nuclei and form charge-neutral atomic elements. These first elements would become the raw material for heavier elements that would be created later by thermonuclear processes in the interior of the trillions of suns that would eventually form by gravitational collapse of interstellar hydrogen and helium. It would take about 1.6 billion years after the first atomic elements were produced before the first suns would begin igniting and form points of light in the universe, a long period during which the universe was dark and cold. Once the process had begun, it would occur again and again as collapsing matter heated and ignited thermonuclear fusion, burned itself out after several billion years, and explosively threw out the new elements it had formed into interstellar space. New suns would reuse the matter previously ejected and dispersed by dying suns, thereby building up the concentration of heavy elements needed for rocky planets to develop within the solar systems that were created as matter collapsed to form suns. The heaviest element that can be produced by thermonuclear processes in the interior of a star is iron. Atomic elements heavier than iron can only be produced during the explosive death of the most massive suns, an event called a supernova.

This was the fiery beginning of the new universe, the pouring of the foundation on which the estimated two hundred billion galaxies, each of which are composed of about a hundred billion stars and a central black hole, and the several planets that revolve around each star would eventually be built. The creation of the physical universe was a conscious act by God, but was carried out passively. Passive in the sense that God formulated a set of rules embodied in a physical law that directed the transformation of spirit-energy into a condensed form we call matter. Once he set the universe into motion, God let it continue to its own conclusion without micromanaging every one of the uncountable number of energy-matter or matter-matter interactions that would need to occur as the universe evolved to the mature state we now observe 13.8 billion years after the initial event. Universal physical law is inflexible. It unyielding and unerringly leads spirit-energy through a developmental process that yields matter in its various forms and configurations. These forms include all of the richness of the universe that astronomers have identified as spiral galaxies, globular galaxies, black holes, and various classes of stars such as red giants, white dwarfs, and neutron stars (3508-1_4). A condensed form of spirit-energy became the building blocks of trillions of planetary worlds. Most planets that developed in the outer region of a solar system were composed of light elements and gases that were frozen because of their long distance from the warmth of the sun's radiation. Other planets that developed nearer the sun were rocky and extremely hot because they received an intense amount of solar radiation. Some planets developed near a sun that emitted a favorable electromagnetic spectrum at a distance that gave it a moderate average temperature with the ability to retain an appropriate atmosphere and the presence of bodies of water that could support complex carbon-based biological life. One of these planets was chosen to temporarily house souls to give them the opportunity to understand and correct their failure to stay true to the purpose for their creation.

The unique physical conditions and precise physical law that allow energy to condense into matter will not exist forever. Physical law will invariably guide the evolution of the universe and the matter it contains to its final outcome. Much of the matter will be ripped apart and separated from further contact with the rest of the universe as it becomes captured by the massive gravitational wells called black holes that are at the center of galaxies. There it will devolve into the higher vibrational state of pure energy and remain isolated from the rest of the universe, perhaps merging with the source spirit of the cosmic realm. Some matter will be flung into an abyss of eternal darkness by the continuing outward expansion of the spacetime fabric. It will diffuse away from all other units of matter, suffer heat death, and become incapable of reacting with other matter. Eventually, galaxies will no longer be able to communicate by electromagnetic energy with other galaxies because objects in the outward racing universe will move away from each other faster than energy can traverse the distance between them. No one knows how this will end, but as matter becomes more diffuse and cools toward absolute zero, it will be incapable of serving any known physical purpose. The physical universe will effectively die. A much more detailed review of the current findings of cosmological science in relation to the readings was previously published by this author, and the reader is encouraged to review that material to gain a more in-depth understanding of cosmology in relation to the readings (Imes, 2022, see God Moved - The Creation of the Universe chapter, and references therein).

The progress toward soul rehabilitation and restoration of God consciousness was to be deliberate and unhurried to allow the willing soul ample opportunity to rediscover its spiritual roots and regain its honored position as a child of God created in the image of God out of a portion of God. The successful completion of this course of training would require patience and a willingness on the part of the soul to change its pattern of thinking. Souls addicted to selfishness and self-centeredness would be required to learn about and work on their weaknesses and periodically participate in material activity that provided opportunities for them to apply their spiritual lessons in a way that would express and demonstrate their understanding of God (or lack thereof). It is God's desire that every soul take advantage of this redemption opportunity, a form of grace bestowed by God upon his wayward and underserving children. Souls would need to become embedded in this new realm in a way that would facilitate soul-to-soul interaction. Each abusive or selfish activity in relation to other souls would bring consequences in the form of repeated opportunities for spiritual growth including the restoration of God consciousness (1602-3_9). Altruistic soul activity conducted in accordance with the spiritual principles embodied in the behavioral rules to love God and to love and serve fellow souls would be mentally and spiritually beneficial to the soul. Dedicated and sustained activity in the application of spiritual and moral principles would draw souls into a closer companionship with God and eventually give them the right to share in God's creative endeavors for all eternity. These souls would have proven themselves capable of accepting and embracing a restored relationship with God. Along the way they would acquire a new state of consciousness and a more spiritual individuality. They would learn to honor and respect the fact that every soul is a portion of God and accept the responsibility to act accordingly.

Souls would have to use an intermediary to transform their thoughts into manifested physical activity and to communicate with other souls. The combination of the law of causality as incorporated into physical structure and the spiritual law to which souls are bound made it certain that every action initiated by a soul would result in an appropriate physical-spiritual causal response. The inclusion of the spiritual principle of like begets like, which can be thought of as a type of spiritual resonance whereby the mental and spiritual vibrational patterns given off by one soul can resonate with the vibrational patterns of other souls, would allow like-minded souls to be drawn together. A loving attitude could attract souls for whom love was meaningful and important in their lives and was a significant part of their overall outlook and approach to life. Expressions of anger could attract souls that felt the need to use anger as an emotional response in their relationships or as a way to convey their sense of superiority or show their power over others. Physical events in the lives of souls embedded in the material realm would not only be influenced directly by the physical activity initiated by the soul, but would also be influenced indirectly by the overall spiritual attunement of the soul. These factors would influence the unfolding of the individual and collective future to be faced by the souls participating in material experiences. Souls would be required not only to enter the realm and demonstrate their mastery of spiritual principles, but also be obliged to cycle through the causal realm until they were purified and purged of their propensity to rebel against their creator and had embraced the ideal of loving service to fellow souls.

The laws of physics tell us how an object moves through space and time. Newton's first law of motion tells us that when an object is in motion, its velocity remains constant and its trajectory unchanged until it is acted upon by an external force. Newton's second law of motion tells us that if an external force is applied to the object, the force will cause the trajectory and velocity of the object to change in proportion to the inertial mass of the object. Mass is a measure of an object's resistance to change. Consider this imperfect but interesting, analogy. Spiritual law helps souls redirect their attention toward God as they navigate the world as incarnate beings. When a soul has set itself on a trajectory that leads it away from God and God consciousness, that path can only be altered by an application of force. The soul can apply its will to the problem and initiate change that will return it to a better trajectory that leads toward God, or spiritual law can cause material opportunities to arise in the life of the incarnated soul that can awaken the soul to its predicament and encourage it to alter its ungodly decisions and behavior. Spiritual law brings forth the force needed to effect meaningful change in the life path of a rebellious soul. The magnitude of that change is proportional to the mental resistance of the soul. More recalcitrant souls require a greater application of force.

Physical causality is embedded in the physical laws of nature that we humans experience every day and can best be understood in the law of action and reaction. In the domain of macro-scale objects, causality is experienced as the result of one action triggering or initiating another action—cause and effect. For example, a person throws a material object that collides with another object and sets off a chain reaction of collisions until enough energy is dissipated to cause the thrown object and all of the objects being struck to no longer gain enough energy to change their motion. Even after the macro-scale objects have ceased all motion, the original action continues to create future causal events through the vibrational motion of atoms in the objects and radiation of energy from the objects. Likewise, spiritual law, the law of sowing and reaping, is a causal law. It forces souls that are guilty of rebellion or sin against the purposes of God to face consequences for their actions and the thoughts that preceded them. In the cosmic realm, spiritual law enforces a code of ethics on souls, but the environmental conditions in that realm are not conducive to making souls aware of their spiritual failures. Experience in the physical universe encourages souls to rediscover and reevaluate their relationship with God. If the soul manifested thoughts in the physical realm that ignored spiritual principles that encapsulate the essence of its purpose, it would be faced with physical and moral challenges in the form of unpleasant experiences, including physical pain and mental anguish. The soul would be required to repeatedly confront the causal effects of its spiritual error, until it learned that its discomfort was related to the severity and magnitude of its defiance of spiritual law. Physical causality works in conjunction with spiritual law to bring awareness of spiritual disobedience and will ultimately bring the soul mind to remembrance of its true relationship with God, and ideally will awaken a strong desire to embrace that relationship and its spiritual promise. These trials and temptations are designed to bring the soul mind to remembrance of its failure to remain true to God and offer the opportunity for the soul to correct its spiritual shortcomings. Inappropriate soul-to-soul behavior that is disrespectful instead of loving—that is, full of spite, anger, and jealousy instead of respect, kindness, love, and patience—generates real world consequences that souls are required to endure as a matter of spiritual law, not as punishment inflicted by God. The law of the Lord (not man) is perfect, and it converts the soul (Psalm 19:7). It leads souls away from self-centeredness and the desire for self-gratification to the realization that salvation and happiness is to be found in reunion with God and respect for spiritual law.

Mental-Spiritual Training Centers for Soul Education

If the Earth is the plane of application where the soul applies its understanding of God, where does the majority of the actual training occur? It is of no value to toss a soul into a rehabilitation facility without some established process to educate or re-educate the soul mind. To that end, the entire solar system that includes the Earth plays a role in the education and spiritual growth of the soul. There are various mental-spiritual training centers associated with the planets of the solar system that are facilities for realigning the habitual selfish mental and emotional patterns of soul expression into more spiritual avenues of expression. All rebellious souls are required to attend these training centers but not necessarily between every period of activity on the Earth. There is a borderland region between the universe and other spheres of activity where souls may briefly linger then return to the Earth without entering the training centers (538-28_4; 900-10_6). This may be more likely to occur after violent death, which seems to be followed by a more rapid return to the Earth plane (Gershom, 1992). Souls are expected to learn spiritual truths in these nonphysical training centers and align their minds to the mental patterns that represent these truths. They are given the opportunity to apply these truths during experience in the physical realm on the Earth, primarily through interaction with other souls. These training centers, in conjunction with recurring earthly incarnations, guide the soul mind away from a predominately self-centered consciousness toward a predominately God-centered consciousness. They focus on bringing awareness of the soul mind back to the core soul attributes that are part of the soul's inherited spiritual nature. Mastery of these lessons is demonstrated by the consistent expression of godly characteristics such as love, patience, kindness, generosity, grace and mercy.

The readings supply no details about the creation of the nonmaterial training realms but there are some tantalizing bits of information that connect them with the planets of our solar system. These training centers are not located on the surface of the physical planets, but are nonphysical locations that are in some obscure way dimensionally associated with the physical planets (900-289_8). Souls typically enter one of these centers between activity on the Earth to receive training that addresses specific areas of emotional and mental deficiency, or to strengthen mental awareness of a specific spiritual or moral soul attribute. Some of the emotional defects and flaws that are worked on include the propensity to express anger, hatred, jealousy, resentment, bitterness, and other negative emotions that present themselves as forms of animosity toward fellow souls. Others training centers include lessons that help souls to balance mental and emotional forces to avoid extremes, feel and express love for other souls, and even recognize and appreciate the often misunderstood spiritual attributes that occasionally express themselves in the physical realm as psychic abilities. The readings emphasize that "psychic" means "of the soul" and in this sense it means the ability of the conscious mind to be aware of the presence of information that resides in other parts of the soul mind. One center takes especially difficult cases to completely rebuild the soul's mental attitude toward spiritual matters. As the soul cycles through earthly experiences, it is given the opportunity to put into practice these mental and emotional lessons to determine if the training is leading to real and permanent spiritual development. Souls that begin to consciously and consistently express love of God and love of fellow souls will eventually be cleansed of the selfish desires that draw them away from communion with God and will fulfill their destiny to become companions of the Almighty.

The Active Consciousness of Group Mind

The active consciousness we perceive as evolutionary biological law emerges out of Group Mind, an aspect of the Mind of God that expresses as the unification of the biological urges that drive self-preservation, acquisition of food, and reproduction in living creatures.

God used a passive form of mind and consciousness to construct the foundation and structure of the universe. He established a universal physical law that embodied his idea for a causal rehabilitation facility and applied it to a portion of the spiritual realm to construct a dimensional framework that would trap and contain energy, the physical analog of spirit. The law contains an ordering principle that encapsulates the rules that dictate how confined spirit-energy can disassociate into a suite of fundamental charged-particle pairs and how these charges attract and repel to form a vast array of nuclei, atoms, and molecules that can combine to form gases, liquids, and solids. The universe was certainly impressive, but even after billions of Earth years of physical evolution, it was not a suitable facility to house souls and help them to rectify their dire spiritual situation. The ability to communicate and physically manifest thoughts was a necessary precondition for a soul to interact with fellow souls in the physical realm. Souls needed a form of matter that could be animated and controlled by their minds because soul rehabilitation is a mental process whereby souls demonstrate their understanding of God within the context of community. The universe was sterile and lifeless and could not be manipulated in any spiritually meaningful manner. But God wasn't finished. He patiently waited for the formation of a suitable planet and for the physical conditions on the surface of that planet to become capable of supporting life before he took the next step in the preparation of his soul rehabilitation facility. When the universe had matured enough to form a suitable planet, God initiated a second creative event, a conscious intervention in the unfolding physical evolution of the Earth on behalf of his soul children, to initiate the formation of a world of carbon-based organic biological beings on the surface of the planet we call Earth. The rock, soil, and water at the surface of the planet became the substrate upon which these mobile organic life forms, activated and controlled by mind, could move and interact with similar organic beings. This life would be diverse and capable of supporting a higher form of life through which souls could express themselves and interact with other souls expressing themselves through similar bodies. The Earth would become the stage on which a great drama would play out as billions upon billions of souls learned to choose good over evil. As individuals, in groups, and in masses, souls would sow creation and destruction, beauty and ugliness, hope and despair, and elation and depression, as they alternately looked toward God for guidance and support or depended on self and descended more deeply into selfishness and rebellion.

Matter provides the necessary and suitable structural building materials for biological life, but matter alone cannot become self-aware or form itself into a suitable medium in which a higher consciousness can spiritually mature. The readings strongly suggest that even though a planetary system is gravitationally attached to most or all of the estimated twenty trillion stars that exist in the universe, not one of them will self-evolve biological life. For the newly created universe to be useful as a facility for soul rehabilitation, it had to be a place where souls could perceive and experience the consequences of their unbridled use of free will. The facility had to allow them to use their free will and minds to manifest their poor choices and then reap the consequences of those choices. To that end, the Earth would need to support a higher-order biological life with which and through which soul minds could interact. Like all matter, molecules are a manifestation of concentrated spirit-energy, but molecules do not have minds that direct their activity, and clusters of molecules cannot unite and form a collective mind to produce the intentional activity of animated biological life. A group of organic molecules, no matter what the type or how sophisticated and complex, can only be the material components needed for cellular life, not life itself. The readings describe cells as miniature universes in which the positive and negative charges in different regions of biochemical molecules attract and repel in ways that move energy into the cell and distribute it throughout the cell to nourish and repair its various components. An active consciousness had to be brought to bear on the Earth to elevate inanimate molecular matter to cell-based life and guide the evolution of that first life to form an environment in which and through which souls could express and manifest their thoughts.

The Rise of Cellular Life

About 3.8 Bya (billion years ago) something remarkable happened on the planet Earth near one of the mid-oceanic ridges where molten rock flowed onto the ocean floor from active magma vents and kept the surrounding areas at a warm and stable temperature. Clusters of organic molecules began to act in a cooperative fashion to extract energy from the sulfur- and iron-based minerals that spewed from the vents (Margulis and Sagan, 1997). These first primitive biological cells would eventually migrate to the surface of the ocean, where they adapted their metabolism to use the carbon-dioxide-rich atmosphere and photosynthesis to generate energy while releasing oxygen into the atmosphere as a waste product. Millions of years later, this oxygen would become the source of energy for an entirely new class of organisms. The formation of these first cells, their ability to adapt to new environments, and their ability to become mobile cannot be explained by the passive consciousness of physical law. For example, the motion of an object entirely subject to physical law is the result of an external force being applied to the object, but many cells developed the ability to launch themselves into motion using only their own cellular structures. But what are cells and what was and is their greater purpose in God's plan for soul rehabilitation? Whether the organic molecules that made up the first cell came together by chance or by design does not change the fact that cells are the organic basis of life. If they came together by chance as theorized by scientists, such an occurrence would only produce a momentary instance of the mechanical components of cellular structure, but these collections of molecules would lack the organizing principle necessary for the cell to function as a living biological unit.

What precipitated the amalgamation of the specific inert molecular components needed to create a cell having the ability to protect, sustain, and reproduce itself; what gave motility to these first cells; and what transformed them from clumps of molecules into a living organism? Physical law alone, even with the element of chance, cannot predict or explain this phenomenon. Cells, singly and in complex organized masses, became repositories for an entirely different mode of consciousness than that held within their inert components, a higher level of active consciousness that could reason and direct the behavior of matter. When the environmental conditions on the chosen planet were favorable for the activity and survival of these most basic biological organisms, God brought the necessary organic molecules and elements together in an environment conducive to survival to form viable functioning cells. The readings describe this appearance of the first biological life on the Earth as a direct conscious action of God to introduce a higher level of consciousness into the material world, a type of self-consciousness that is localized within a group of molecules directing them to cooperate and act in unison to form a self-organizing cellular unit (694-2_3; 433-1_6). Biological processes at the cellular level obey the laws of physics, but scientists have not identified the overarching law of molecular organization that explains why the activity of certain amino acids and proteins becomes coordinated for the good of the greater cellular whole.

That organizational force lies outside of the realm of the chemistry and physics of biological activity.

Cells are the basic units of life for all living creatures that are part of the biological ecosystem of the Earth (694-2_3; 900-273_7). Molecules on the surface of cells form ion gates that allow a cell to extract energy from its surroundings, energy that gives it the power to support the regenerative processes needed to repair damage and keep the cell functioning properly and gives it the capability of reproducing itself. God does not need to continuously create new cells as old ones break down and expire. Molecules in the interior of cells participate in the exchange of charged particles, electrons, and ions, to provide energy for cell nourishment (433-1_6; 1800-4_2; Larsen, 2019). Each cell is isolated and distinct from its surrounding environment, being separated from it by a membrane that is strong enough to protect the cell and form a localized environment within that allows it to carry on necessary internal chemical reactions without interference from external forces, and yet porous enough that the cell can extract energy from its environment and transfer it across the cell wall to supply fuel for the vital functions that support cellular life. Nucleic acids, proteins, lipids, and carbohydrates are the four important biochemical molecules that support the metabolic functions of a cell. They are necessary to maintain the physiological processes and are essential for the survival of the cell and continuity of life. Lipids are integrated into the overall cell structure, including the protective cell membrane. They also control the movement of molecules and ions through the cell membrane. Carbohydrates are a source of energy for the cell derived from plant photosynthesis and from animal digestion of plant tissue that is rich in starches and sugars.

Cells can replicate. The nucleic acid DNA (deoxyribonucleic acid) carries genetic information that can be passed from one generation of cells to the next to preserve the genetic information about that cell. The architectural plan for each cell of every living biological organism is encoded in the DNA strands within the chromosomes of the cell. Genes are specific segments of the DNA strand that contain the encoded instructions needed to synthesize proteins that express an inherited characteristic or trait, such as eye color. In sexual procreation, one half of the offspring's DNA strand comes from the father and the other half comes from the mother, ensuring that the genetic traits of each parent are passed to the progeny. Barring genetic mutations, the integrity of the genetic code in the DNA of the offspring remains true as each cell divides to create a new pair of cells. As cells divide and multiply to create the material framework, external features, and internal structure of a biological organism, genes are switched on or off to create the various types of cells (leaf cells, cambium cells, blood cells, muscle cells, nerve cells, etc.) necessary to ensure the proper functioning of the future plant or animal life form. The factors that determine which gene will be expressed and when it will be expressed during the life of the organism include the stage of growth of the organism, hormone secretion, environmental setting and stressors, and the current stage of the overall cell life cycle. But DNA, as powerful and as fantastic as it is, only contains information that enables the construction of the physical structural components of a cell and does not contain the information needed to allow those components to work together in a cooperative manner to produce the activity in the cell that we recognize as life.

The nucleic acid RNA (ribonucleic acid) is formed from one of many specific small sequences of DNA base pairs by the process of transcription and is used to construct various replacement parts for the cell. There are also many regions within the human DNA that are gene-like but produce noncoding RNA (Salzberg, 2018). One form of RNA extracts information about a single gene sequence in the DNA and passes the information from the DNA into the surrounding cell cytoplasm, where the data is decoded by other forms of RNA and is used to assemble a specific string of amino acids that, when completed, will fold into a desired protein. Proteins are used in a variety of cell functions. They act as enzymes that catalyze the biochemical reactions needed for cell metabolism and are used in inter-cellular communication. The number of genes that contain the instruction sets for forming new protein molecules to replace those that have finished serving their purpose varies widely from plant to animal and from the simplest to the most complex biological organism. The simple prokaryotic Escherichia coli bacterium, commonly found in the intestines of humans, contains one circular chromosome with about 4,400 genes that can encode 116 RNAs (Serres and others, 2001). Human cells have a more complex eukaryotic structure where the DNA is enclosed within a central nucleus. The estimated number of genes in the human genome has changed over the years depending on the source of information, but seems to be settling in at about twenty-five thousand protein-encoding genes. The more-recent estimates range from about twenty-two thousand to about thirty-one thousand protein-encoding genes. Cells in higher biological organisms like a human body have become extremely specialized to provide the specific functionality needed for complex organisms. The coordinated activity of these specialized cells gives form and function to organs, and the coordinated activity of organs allows the creation of larger and more complex creatures. The bodies of large animals possess specialized organs that support various functions needed for respiration (lungs), digestion of food (stomach), and absorption and assimilation of nutrients (liver and pancreas), elimination of wastes (intestines), and cogitation (brain). Organs cannot stand alone as independent biological units, but in a healthy body are always of one mind and function for the good of the total organism. The organs in higher animals are connected by a vascular network that provides a constant flow of blood to bring nutrients to and remove waste products from each cell (121-1_6). They communicate with the nerve ganglion or brain of the organism through a neural network that sends signals to indicate their physiological needs and receive instructions that allow them to fulfill the greater cooperative obligations to the overall organism (263-13_10-11). What unifies and coordinates the group activity of these cells? The organism can only remain healthy if the trillions of cells that make up a typical large animal body work together with a sense of common purpose.

The passive consciousness of physical law produces the raw materials of biological life, and an active consciousness brings purpose to the cell, but how do these mental forces work together to coordinate activity within a cell? What animates cells? The rule-based generation of proteins according to the script prepared by DNA and RNA explains how nature designed a miniature protein factory with interchangeable dies that can be used on a protein assembly line and the mechanics of cellular construction, but it does not explain unified purposeful cellular activity. Science and the readings tell us that all biological life forms are based upon cellular units, but the readings also tell us that all assemblages of organic molecules that act as an organized cohesive cellular unit are activated and animated by spirit and mind (262-114_29; 294-70_5). Life comes from the union of physical matter with mental and spiritual forces, nonphysical partners that bring consciousness and coordinated activity to a collection of chemical compounds (3976-8_3; 1776-1_19). Life is an active consciousness that forms when mind and spirit animate a functionally viable biological organism (900-17_5). The source of the creative force that imparts purposeful animation of cellular matter comes from outside of the physical universal and is not part of, or constrained by, physical law. Life in all of its various manifestations is creative force in action, a loving expression of God that reveals the truth of his presence and power (262-46_4). The health and harmonious functioning of a cell depends upon how well these material and nonmaterial components cooperate to fulfill their various roles. Life must have function and purpose that transcends the mechanics of biology and gives an organism the ability to consciously react and interact with its environment. All forms of biological life are animated by this active consciousness of God, just as all forms of inert matter are sustained by the passive consciousness of God expressed as physical law.

Every individual cell is brought to life by the Mind and Spirit of God (900-237_4). Each living creature holds within itself the potential to propagate, to release the forces of creation (900-274_13). It is an instinctive innate activity present in cells at conception and in seeds at germination that ensures the propagation of the species. Spirit, the substance of which God is made, is the life force that works with the mind to prompt this cooperative cellular activity that we observe and call biological life. Electrical energy, the physical activity of spirit-energy, is the physical force that most embodies and represents this motivating life force (440-20_7). Spirit provides the creative self-ordering stimulus that brings biological molecules together to work in a coordinated and cooperative manner as individual cellular units and brings order and function out of an otherwise random collection of lifeless molecules. Mind is the force that spans the spiritual and physical realms, brings awareness and consciousness to all living creatures, and brings forth physical manifestations of conscious thoughts and spiritual purpose. DNA can manifest the desire of the mind and spirit at the cellular level and transmit that desire into the physical activity necessary to build the components of a cell. DNA encodes the information for constructing the building blocks of cells, but each cellular unit is bound together by the combined action of mind and spirit to bring community and cooperation to the component molecules and ions and draw them together into a cohesive unit, a self-contained body. This life force is a different application of the same spirit that is the foundational substance of the universe of energy and matter and the same mind that shaped universal physical law. But what is the origin and nature of the activating mental-spiritual force that brings conscious awareness to all sentient living organisms, from the smallest single-celled creature to the largest plants and animals?

Consciousness, Group Mind, and Biological Evolution

The mind brings a rudimentary environmental awareness to cells and the ability to interact with that environment to extract energy to power its various components and to survive in a hostile world. The level of cellular awareness is rudimentary, not simply because cells are inherently dumb, but because they have only the most basic sensory system with which to explore their environment. The readings indicate that the consciousness of the various species that form the biological ecosystem arises from an aspect of cosmic consciousness called Group Mind. This portion of the Mind of God is a mental force that permeates living matter and allows each life form to develop its own consciousness and self-awareness. This form of consciousness allows the living reality of a biological ecosystem to be impressed upon the dead reality of the universe of matter and energy, sort of a one-sided symbiotic relationship between the living and the dead. The mind is the essential animating principle that gives physical motion, perception, and awareness to the organized inanimate matter of a living cell. The mind gives motivation and specialized purpose to cells and cell clusters that form organelles; conduct photosynthesis; and create leaves, bark, flesh, muscles, bones, and organs, which combine in various manners to create living plants and animals. The physiological processes that sustain life in plants and animals, such as respiration and digestion, are not entirely mechanistic, but are partly managed by Group Mind.

There is very little information in the readings about Group Mind, but it appears to have some elements of similarity with portions of various hypotheses that have been proposed whereby a universal or cosmic consciousness guides or directs nature and the ecosystem. For that reason, two of these hypotheses (Panpsychism and Gaia) have been briefly mentioned in a previous chapter. It should be stressed that Group Mind doesn't appear to impart consciousness or project consciousness control into a living organism, and its mention in the readings should not be taken as an endorsement of either Panpsychism or Gaia. Instead, it sets the conditions whereby cells, plants, and animals can generate their own individual physical consciousness through interaction with their environment. The readings associate Group Mind with the mineral kingdom, the plant kingdom, and the animal kingdom (262-80_5). The facet of Group Mind that the readings associate with the mineral kingdom is perhaps a transitional phase of consciousness between the passive consciousness that builds matter and the active consciousness of biological organisms.

Most people probably think of minerals as the beautiful crystal specimens that form many varieties of semi-precious and precious stones, but two-thirds of the 4,300 known minerals are associated with biological activity. As the biological ecosystem matured and flourished, the number and type of minerals greatly increased (Hazen and others, 2008). The form of consciousness attributed by the readings to minerals may be a simple ordering principle.

Biological evolution is the physical expression of the drive, desire, and purpose of Group Mind as it guides plants and animals to successfully adapt to their environment to ensure species survival, including the acquisition of adequate daily sustenance and the propagation of the species. More complex and efficient organisms that out compete and out perform their evolutionary ancestors go on to create new generations of species, while those that cannot effectively compete are eliminated. Evolution has successfully transformed the Earth's ecosystem from a few cells into a seething mass of diverse organisms seeking to find environmental gaps into which they can expand and gain traction. From the perspective of religion, it is tempting to think that evolution proceeds through direct manipulation of DNA by God, whereby he modifies the DNA in existing life forms to occupy an emerging environmental niche and enhance the overall biological diversity of the planet. But does God really mentally touch each new cell that arises from the act of conception and cell division or activate the life force in each seed to cause it to grow a certain way? God is consciously aware of the Earth's biosphere and its ongoing biological processes, but evolutionary law does not need to be constantly monitored and directed by God. The readings suggest that an impelling force derived from Group Mind helps sustain the evolutionary process, but that cellular life evolved into an integrated biosphere without the need for God to micromanage the ecosystem. The projection of instinctual desires by Group Mind into living creatures and the mutation and dispersal of genetic material cooperate to form the evolutionary process that gives the developing ecosystem the means to explore the adaptability and survivability of new variant organisms. It forces species to constantly probe for new and better methods of extracting nutrients from the environment. The appearance and progression of new creatures during the evolutionary process is not foreordained, and is not the result of God periodically introducing new, fully formed creatures into the ecosystem but is a result of the overall design parameters of biological evolution.

Scientists understand evolution as a purely biological process whereby random DNA mutations cause organisms to survive or die depending upon how well the new biological structures they form allow the organism to compete with other life forms in their immediate surroundings. Successful creatures are the ones able to fill a biological niche and extract energy from the plethora of less complicated and less aware organisms that fill their environment. The entire ecosystem is constantly shifting as DNA mutations alter the characteristics of each species. The readings suggest that the procreative cells of biological organisms exist in a latent state of potential future activity until they are brought together, at which point their union causes the infinite forces of spirit, under the direction of the creative universal thought of God, to manifest and activate the cellular division that ultimately forms the new organism (262-78_14; 136-37_8). So, it appears that God does not micromanage evolution, but in some way Group Mind patiently monitors the progress of evolution and supplies the impetus for life as biological conditions align to make the nascent organisms susceptible to the life force. Evolution effectively guided the biological ecosystem to provide a support system for the life form that God planned for souls to use to experience life in a causal environment, the means by which souls would be brought to their senses and restored to God consciousness.

What can we infer about the relation between Group Mind and the many ways in which it expresses itself in the biological world? From the perspective of the physical realm, the conscious mind associated with each species and each member of those species appears to have a wide range of awareness, intelligence, and reasoning capacity. Plant consciousness forms as Group Mind infuses a plant seed as it emerges from dormancy and grows to maturity. Animal consciousness forms as Group Mind makes contact with the immature brain and endocrine system of a newborn chimpanzee. These vastly different forms of intelligence and consciousness arise out of a single universal Group Mind consciousness. The level of awareness in the members of each species is mainly a product of the enormously different range of physical sensory stimuli that can be detected by the organisms. More complex animals having several sensitive sensory organs can sample a diverse range of electromagnetic waves and physical vibration, which gives them a greater ability to interact with the physical environment. A plant may only be able to detect the particular frequency of light it needs for photosynthesis and aim its leaves toward maximum light intensity.

Newly forming conscious minds in sentient species develop and mature as Group Mind catalogs, organizes, and analyzes sensory information collected by the physical body of the organism. The greater the variety and complexity of the sensory data and types of physical interactions, and the more sophisticated the neural network of the organism, the higher the level of cognitive awareness and intelligence that can be formed. More advanced animals with larger concentrations of brain and ganglia neurons spend longer periods of their life to bring their minds to maturity. These animals can develop recognizable and unique personalities that are backed up by a larger mental capacity and greater reasoning ability than less advanced animals or plant organisms. As the mental force that brings conscious into the life of every advanced biological creature on the Earth, Group Mind drives evolution in the plant and animal kingdom. Each unique set of physical phenomena that is fed to an individualized portion of Group Mind and the reactions of the mind to those phenomena cause an individual conscious mind and consciousness to form. The organism uses this developing mind to better understand its environment and increase its ability to fulfill the mental directive to survive in a hostile world, gain sustenance for the proper maintenance of the body, and procreate to ensure species continuity. The conscious minds of plants and animals do not have a free will component that allows them to act in ways that violate their evolutionary mandate or defy their maker. Cells can break down physically and can lose the ability to function as they were meant to, for reasons involving disease, physical injury, and old age so that the consciousness of the organism can be disrupted, damaged, or made to disconnect from the physical activity that it is attempting to guide. It may lose the ability to restore or maintain the proper function of the cell, but normally plants and animals always strive to express the will of their creator and to fulfill their appointed purpose in life.

From the perspective of the spiritual realm, Group Mind would seem to be a uniform field of mental force. It doesn't seem possible that the Group Mind, as part of the Mind of God, is divided into trillions upon trillions of sparks of plant and animal consciousness that appear and disappear as each unit of life lives and dies. If it is a universal consciousness, then how does it manifest in so many different ways among the various plant and animal species and the vast number of creatures that live today and have ever lived? Let us use some of the information the readings give about "human" consciousness, which we visit in later chapters, to try to understand Group Mind. Imagine the junction between a uniform field of Group Mind and a single plant or animal physiological system as a nucleation site where physical consciousness emerges, expands, and grows in awareness and cognitive ability. The point at which Group Mind makes contact with the physical organism may stimulate that instance of the Group Mind to develop a localized physical conscious mind with both nonphysical and physical aspects. The initial state of that conscious mind will be an unrealized potential that will blossom according to the neural system and physiology with which the Group Mind interacts and the quantity and character of the sensory data it is able to access. When the creature is able to transmit sensory data to a central nerve ganglion or brain, the portion of Group Mind that is associated with and animates the creature uses the sensory information to form an awareness of its physical environment, assess the types of interactions it can have with other creatures, decide how to react or proceed in a given situation, and learn how to behave in its social group.

The readings do not make it clear if the spirit-mind activation of single cells is the same force behind the development of consciousness in multi-cellular organisms formed by the presence and influence of Group Mind. Group Mind, as described in the readings, is definitely the mental force behind the individual development of physical consciousness in higher plants and animals. It seems that the conscious knowledge required for the survival of animals primarily is passed to the offspring by the activities of the parents and members of their social group rather than through Group Mind, but perhaps some knowledge or mental acuity is transferred to the animal through a form of evolutionary intuition, a more basic transitional or muted form of spirit-mind activity that brings life and awareness to individual cells and perhaps to lowest-order creations. It is not clear how or if the collective mental experiences from a species is passed to the mind of an organism, but if it is, it may be through an aspect of mind called Group Soul or Group Consciousness (262-80_5, 1641-1_76), perhaps meaning a nonphysical relation or connection among species that directs, enforces, or provides the impetus for evolution. It may be acquired as part of the activating force that impels propagation of the species (262-78_14). There is also the question of instinctual behavior. For example, what makes a bird belt out its first song, and what makes the seventeen-year and thirteen-year cicada emerge from their long sleep at the appropriate intervals of time? Is the instinctual and inbred behavior of so many different species solely a function of the Group Mind, or does it have its roots in some other aspect of physical reality or cosmic conscious-ness? Is it partly inherited through cellular DNA? Reading 2464-2_13 associates instinct with a group soul impregnation, by which is meant the predominate nature of the class of animal that is seeking physical expression. This entire concept of the transfer of collective mental infor-mation in animals is speculative because there is too little information in the readings to determine for certain the existence or nature of the concept. We will assume that the coordinated internal activity of cells, the spirit-mind activation of cellular awareness, the infusion of instinct from group soul influence, and the power of Group Mind to initiate the formation of consciousness in plants and animals are all aspects of the cosmic consciousness of God.

The conscious minds of plants and animals are created at the interface of Group Mind and the sensory system of the organism. The sophistication of the mind, its reasoning capacity and its level of awareness are mainly the product of the quantity and variety of sensory information the organism can transmit to the physical-spiritual interface, and the complexity of the organism's neural system. The activity of DNA and RNA does not explain purposeful cellular activity. Every biologically evolved organism, from the lowly single-celled amoeba to extinct human-animals, was and is animated by a conscious mind that is a temporary localized aspect of cosmic consciousness. This mind animates biological organisms and gives them what we call life, the ability to move, acquire sustenance, coordinate vascular and neural networks, metabolize food and excrete waste, grow and reproduce, and respond to environmental stimuli (262-114; 294-70). All of God's creatures function at the mental and spiritual level for which they were designed. They don't need to be reminded of their spiritual nature, but do need to have a daily period of rest when their physical structure can be replenished and restored in preparation for the activities of the next daylight period (900-31_5). When an animal sleeps, its conscious mind is put aside so that its physical body can rest and repair.

Single cells such as bacteria can exist as independent units of life but depend upon air currents or moving water to gain mobility. Some single-celled organisms are capable of self-directed motion and have the ability to make decisions and learn from mistakes and successes as they seek sources of energy and protection from danger. The single-celled amoeba is capable of movement, but it does more than distort its cell wall to induce random motion through its environment. An amoeba can interact with its environment through touch, thereby identifying the location of nearby objects and perhaps gaining a tactile overtone such as the roughness or smoothness of the object's surface. This interaction with its environment gives it enough information to purposely navigate, remember specific routes to food, and even work its way through mazes (Jabr, 2012; Latty and Beekman, 2011; Reid and Latty, 2016). The construction of a suite of protein molecules and their assembly into an amoeba pseudopodia does not explain the amoeba consciousness that uses them to direct the amoeba's body left or right to reach and encircle a diatom or other morsel of food that it has detected and wishes to consume for energy. The varieties of species in the ecosystem and the level of intelligence possessed by these creatures is truly amazing; unfortunately, we rarely take the time out of our self-important lives to learn that nature is far smarter that we realize. The sea snail Aplysia has become the object of neurological research because it has large neurons arranged in a relatively simple neural system containing between about ten to twenty thousand neurons organized into nine different ganglia. The snail has been shown to store learned behavior in both short-term and long-term memory, depending on the duration and number of training sessions. Sensitization studies using a mild electrical shock show that long-term memory can be extended and involves protein synthesis that encourages the growth of new synaptic contacts and enhances the release of neurotransmitters from sensory neuron axons to the motor neurons causing an increased contraction of muscles. Even snails have a complex neurological system (Agranoff and others, 1999; Kandel, 2006).

Consider the case of Alex the Grey Parrot, a research subject, thirty-year companion, and close friend of his trainer Dr. Irene Pepperberg. Alex learned to name about fifty different objects, distinguish among seven colors and identify five shapes. He could recognize numbers and understand and add quantities up to eight. He could use labels, colors, and shapes to describe more than a hundred different objects in his environment; had the ability to request specific objects and specific foods; and would refuse to engage with Irene or students during training sessions when he felt slighted or sometimes when he didn't get his own way. He routinely used the phrase "want to go back" when he was tired and didn't feel like engaging in a training session to indicate his wish to return to his cage. Once he learned to identify and label a new type of object, he could easily distinguish between different colors of the same object. He was not taught to say complete sentences, but only to say the necessary words needed to communicate during his training sessions. Nevertheless, he learned several expressions that allowed him to give vent to his emotions, such as "I love you" and "I'm sorry." Whether he understood those concepts in the same sense that a human would understand them is not certain, but his use of those terms was generally appropriate for the time and situation. He needed security and stability in his life, and at the end of the day, or when he had to be left in a strange place, such as at the veterinarian overnight, would often ask Irene if she was coming back tomorrow and would be consoled when Irene responded with "I'll be back tomorrow." His speech was quite clear for a parrot despite the fact that his lack of lips gave him a decided disadvantage when attempting to say words that used strong consonants such as B, P, or V.

Despite the difficulty of pronouncing those sounds, he was able after practice to adequately construct those sounds in other areas within his larynx. When he produced words with sounds that more easily fell into the natural range of his larynx, the sounds of the words that he produced were quite similar to the corresponding human sounds, not only to the human ear, but also to the electronic equipment that analyzed the frequency spectrums and compared the words he spoke with human speech. Alex figured out the concept of none, as related to the concept of zero, without being taught that concept. This is an amazing leap of mental ability. Not only did Alex deduce this concept himself, but it was he who also introduced his understanding of the concept to Irene by getting her to ask the appropriate question so that he could express the concept of none. Alex was highly intelligent and capable of learning much more than most humans would give him credit for, but he probably was not highly unusual among his species. In nature, birds communicate by using their voices and body motion, but because we have no special insight into these forms of communication, and because few birds or animals are capable of producing human speech or using sign language, we generally refuse to admit that they are capable of higher thoughts and understanding or conclude that they would never be able to communicate with humans. In reality, it seems that it is not so much a lack of ability as it is a lack of the appropriate environmental situation that would encourage the bird or animal to try to communicate with a species such as humans (Pepperberg, 2009).

It is quite difficult for humans to relate to a mineral, cell, or plant, but there are many members of the animal kingdom toward which humans can display affection and concern because they obviously use their minds to interact with the physical world and appear to show and reciprocate emotions. These are characteristics that they acquire from a loving God. The consciousness of an animal is mainly a sensory-trained physical consciousness, and its associated personality is derived from an analysis of its environment, including interaction with other animals of the same and different species. But, except for the underlying influence of intuition that participates in the evolutionary processes, their minds are no deeper than or more complex than their physical consciousness. Apparently, they do not form an identity or individuality in the spiritual realm. Animals may receive some form of evolutionary instruction or guidance from the universal consciousness during the sleep period but they do not commune with an associated subconscious mind in the spiritual realm. There is no subconscious mind that allows them to retain their conscious memories after death. Their destiny, their fate when they complete their earthly life cycle, lies in the Mind of God who granted them life, and if there is retention of memories after death, they reside within the Group Mind through which God animates his earthly biological creatures (900-24_4; 900-31_5). In one cryptic answer to a woman who asked if she had previously been associated with her dog, the response was, to paraphrase,

Yes, in a Roman experience, but then it was a lion (268-3_33-35). It only adds to the confusion about animal consciousness.

The Rise of Human-Animals

There have been many varieties of plants and animals that have evolved, had their moment of glory, and then became extinct since the first cells appeared about 3.8 Bya. Undoubtedly, the most well-known extinct animals are the dinosaurs, a class of reptiles that achieved massive proportions relative to other evolved animals and ruled the Earth from about 230 Mya (million years ago) to about 65 Mya. Their reign was terminated by a devastating asteroid strike in the Gulf of Mexico that altered the Earth's climate for many years (Larsen, 2019). They would be replaced as the rulers of Earth by mammals that first appeared about 130 Mya. Our earliest human-animal ancestors, pre-Australopithecine and Australopithecine species with new physical and behavioral characteristics that distinguished them from chimpanzees, appeared about only 6.0 to 7.0 Mya. These animallike humans or humanlike animals retained the physical features of apes, including the tilted face and the prominent brow ridges of their close relatives, the chimpanzees, but, like modern humans, they walked upright on two legs and did not have the inner blade ridge that sharpens the canine teeth of apes during chewing. They couldn't speak because their throats had not yet evolved the hyoid bone necessary for speech. Four million years ago, in a burst of rapid evolutionary advances, human-animals started changing physically and getting smarter at a much faster rate than they had during the previous two to three millennia. *Homo habilis*, which exhibited true bipedal locomotion on short legs, lived from about 3.0 Mya to 1.8 Mya and was the first truly humanlike species to biologically evolve from Australopithecus. It was succeeded by *Homo erectus* (about 1.8 Mya to 0.3 Mya), the species that exploded out of east Africa and in a short time could be found in Europe and central Asia. These human-animals had a modern arm-leg ratio and large brow ridges, and used tools, including a new tool, the hand axe. *Homo erectus* is also credited with learning to control fire.

What do we know about these human-animals that evolved along with many of the plants and animals that we observe in today's environment? Scientists who study early man have made substantial progress over the past few decades as better methods of DNA extraction from ancient bone fragments and more advanced and precise analytical tools and methodologies have been developed and applied to investigations of ancient DNA. Partial human skeletons and bone fragments found at ancient archaeological sites are being used to infer the physical characteristics and lineage of early human-animals. Improved age-dating techniques applied to artifacts excavated from newly discovered habitation sites across Europe, Asia, and the Americas have extended the known range of ancient human-animal species. Archaeological investigations at these sites and on these artifacts have shed new light on the relationships among early human-animal species and the cultures of these peoples, especially the Late Archaic *Homo sapiens* called the Neanderthals, named after the Neander Thal valley in Germany where their fossil remains were first found, and the Early Modern *Homo sapiens* who were our predecessors. The *Homo sapiens* looked even more human than their ancestors when compared with the physical appearance of humans today, but their appearance belied the fact that they had animal minds.

Age-dating methods applied to recovered artifacts and analysis of skeletal remains yield an estimate for the time frame of Neanderthal activity of about 350 Kya (thousand years ago) to about 30 Kya. The presence of fossil hyoid bones in Neanderthal remains suggests that the Neanderthals could speak, and the readings, as we will see, can be used to infer that this was indeed true. The Early Modern *Homo sapiens*, who appeared about 200 Kya, would be extinct by about 10 Kya, and would coexist with the Neanderthals for nearly 170 thousand years. They were the human-animals that began the physical transition toward the flatter faces, higher and more vertical foreheads, rounded and taller skulls,

projecting chins and much smaller brow ridges that are physical characteristics of modern man. The Earth had evolved advanced life forms and a
biological ecosystem that could support them. It is important at this point
to inquire about the development of intellect in these human-animals.
By comparing anthropological evidence and the readings, we can arrive
at the conclusion that the conscious minds and intelligence of naturally
evolved human-animals developed at the interface of Group Mind and
human-animal bodies, and that their activities were controlled by intu-
ition-driven biological evolution. We will explore the complexities and
caveat that come with this reasonable conclusion in the next chapter. The
species *Homo sapiens* was a prime candidate and had significant potential
as a suitable life form to host souls, but God still had not completed his
preparation of the rehabilitation facility. God's patience was paying off,
but the impatience and selfishness of many souls would cause chaos on the
Earth and draw them even farther away from God consciousness. They
would interfere with the earthly paradise and maturing rehabilitation
facility God was building for them.

Scientists have concluded that the transition of human-animals
from *Homo habilis* to modern man occurred through purely biological evolutionary processes and the readings seem to agree in principle
with this assessment—with a notable exception. The readings generally
support the Darwinian theory of evolution and are consistent with the
scientific reasoning that points toward an evolutionary progression of
ancient human-animals (3744-5_46). Scientists believe that the mind
of man arises out of the neural network of the brain, and that a large
brain means a greater intelligence (Kandel, 2006). They do not consider
the possibility of a nonphysical source for the minds of animals because
they cannot measure, quantify, or verify the presence of a nonphysical
mental influence in the life of a living creature. Anthropologists infer the
mental capacity of early man on the basis of brain size as determined by
measurements of the interior volume of skull remains. The transition from
the pure animal mind to the higher intelligence and analytical reasoning

mind of a human-animal or modern man is explained as being the result of the larger number of neurons packed inside the human brain. This is one instance where science and the readings part ways when describing the animal kingdom. Although the readings support the idea of biological evolution, the basis of that biological force and the physical consciousness of all animals, including evolved human-animals, is identified in the readings as Group Mind. The ultimate source of animal and human-animal intelligence is the cosmic consciousness of God that activates, animates, and gives life to biological organisms, not a consciousness that emanates from the neural network of an animal brain. Perhaps in the future, as neuroscience research pushes closer toward the physical-spiritual interface within biological organisms, scientists will identify neurological phenomena that have no purely physical cause and will be forced to undergo a paradigm shift that will allow science to push into uncharted territory in the search for the mind.

Scientists conclude that the Early Modern *Homo sapiens* evolved into the people we see around us every day, and that we are the culmination of the evolutionary progress of human-animals and the pinnacle of biological evolution on the Earth. The readings are consistent with the concept that modern man is a genetic mixture of the evolved Late Archaic Neanderthal and Early Modern *Homo sapiens* but, in contradiction to science and in partial agreement with religion, the readings also state that a non-evolutionary human form whose design was based upon the evolved Modern *Homo sapiens* is the key to understanding modern man. At this point in the narrative, the perceptive reader may be wondering about the persistent use of the term "human-animal" in the text as opposed to the simpler word "human." This is done intentionally to stay true to the readings which categorically state that events that occurred about 106 Kya altered the natural evolution of human-animals, and to stress the point that human-animals and humans refer to similar, but not identical, life forms having different origins, sources of consciousness, and intellectual capacity. We will learn in the following two chapters what caused the transition from human-animal to human. We will see how anthropological science and the readings can be combined to explain the rapid mental development in early human-animals, understand why a new human form based on the Modern *Homo sapiens* was created, and learn why the relationship between modern humans and Neanderthal and Early Modern human-animals is far more complex than a simple evolutionary progression of human-animals. We will begin by investigating the amazingly rapid rise in human-animal intelligence from a nonphysical and spiritual angle involving the unsanctioned activity of rebellious souls.

The Conscious Interference of Soul Minds in Biological Life

From before its creation, it was always God's intention for souls to use the physical universe and the Earth's environment as a spiritual reha- bilitation facility to bring them back to awareness of their loss of God consciousness (262-114). Many errant souls in the spiritual realm had been acting on selfish mental desires that caused them to lose awareness of God as their creator and source of life force. They were intoxicated with their creative power and abused their free will to indulge in selfish activity that mentally separated them from their Father. They no longer remembered that they were portions of God and needed to remain one with God in spirit and mind. Souls were spectators to the unfolding universe, the flowering of the Earth, and the evolution of biological life. At some point in the evolu- tion of Earth's biological ecosystem, souls came up with the idea of vicari- ously experiencing the earthly environment through biological organisms. Energy and matter are constrained by the nature of the spacetime fabric to move and interact within the confines of the physical universe, but the soul mind can pierce the fabric and interact directly with matter under some circumstances. Souls began interacting with biological organisms as a way to explore the fascinating ongoing creative processes in violation of God's plans for the evolving species. In their rebellious state and desire to explore the limits of their mental powers, souls injected themselves into the lives of evolving biological creatures without regard to the consequences of their actions. Souls that had strayed the farthest from God saw selfish opportunity in the evolving biological system to indulge in a bit of role-playing, imagining themselves participating in the Earth's teeming biological world, feeling the intensity of physical activity through the sensory network of various animals, and even manipulating physical bodies into various concoctions of distorted biological life (364-10_11). This would eventually include manipulation of the most advanced human-animals.

Before considering how souls might have interacted with our biological ancestors, we need to clear our minds of preconceived ideas and understand the fact that, within the context of the readings, the naturally evolved *Homo sapiens* were animals. They were linked to Group Mind and not controlled by souls. *Homo habilis* was the human-animal that biologically evolved from or branched from the animal predecessor called Australopithecine. It had human physical characteristics, and its successors, *Homo erectus* and *Homo sapiens*, looked even more human in comparison with the physical appearance of humans today, but although all of them looked like modern humans in appearance to one degree or another, they all had animal minds. Their similar physical characteristics compared to modern humans lull us into the false conclusion that they were mentally similar to us. In fact, their intelligence and social activities were a result of the physical-spiritual interface of the animal's sensory network and the portion of Group Mind that imparts consciousness and the instincts needed for them to survive and evolve. This is the same type of conscious mind that all animals today use to interact with the material world. They were not people like us; they were not animated by souls. The first humanlike animals were not human in the sense of the soul-directed humans that we encounter today. But we will see how soul interference with natural evolution completely altered the nature of human-animals.

Souls may have at first been passive observers of the unfolding physical evolution of the universe, perhaps with a sense of wonder and excitement and maybe the anticipation of seeing the next supernova disintegrate in a massive fireball. But then something changed, and souls began to get other ideas about this new world. The first cells appeared, developed photosynthesis, began working in cooperative clusters, and evolved into a wide variety of complex plant and animal forms. Souls were watching this exciting process of biological evolution that transformed the most basic DNA-manufactured organic matter into a vast number of fascinating new mind-animated body forms (228-2_15). In their fantasies about what it would feel like to mentally immerse themselves in such a world and in their wanton yearning for sensual experience in the tantalizing biological diversity of the Earth, souls began to interfere with various life forms. Soul interference in Earth life was an extension of their irresponsible behavior in the spiritual realm and once again displayed their willingness to push the limits of their freedom without regard for the consequences to their mental and spiritual health. Once again, soul rebellion upset the good order of creation, but this time in an entirely new way. The readings state that these first meddling souls were driven by the desire for material selfish expression and self-gratification (264-50), the same mental drives that are dominant in far too many souls even today.

Souls are spirit-mind beings and are more like energy than matter. As mind-directed beings with mental roots in cosmic consciousness, they have something in common with the Group Mind that animated plants and animals. The main difference is that they have an independent existence as a soul body in the nonphysical realm, and they have free will that they too often use to get into spiritual trouble. They have the ability to inject themselves into the physical world and observe ongoing biological processes at the cellular level, as well as the higher level where plant and animal organisms interact as individuals and form societies (364-10_4). Much of this early activity was in the form of thought-form projection of immaterial soul bodies into the Earth environment, more akin to an amorphous form than a solid form, resulting in mental entanglement in the physical bodies of existing organisms (364-3_5; 257-201_8; 364-7_5). These souls at first retained certain mental abilities that are called psychic today (364-10_4) and their material manifestations on the Earth were largely driven by their desire for sensual gratification. The biological effect of these activities would carry through descendant generations long after souls were forbidden to enter the Earth plane as thought forms (5756-11_8; 2072-8_18).

Souls watched the interplay and competition and dependency of one species upon another. They watched cell division, asexual and sexual methods of reproduction, the evolution of plant and animal species, the battles for survival, and the competition for resources, and they imagined what it might be like to be directly involved in such activities. These souls were engaging in selfish activity that would eventually create a mental barrier between their subconscious minds and the Mind of God, and they were not above clouding that line of communication even farther by embedding themselves into materiality in inappropriate manners. We should probably think of soul interference with animal life forms as part of a progression of activity starting with passive observation and moderate interference. When these pastimes became blasé they advanced to outright manipulation of animal behavior through biological modifications that would permit a closer union of soul mind and animal body, culminating in outright mental control of human-animal bodies with suppression or forceful replacement of the animal mind. What exactly is it within the nature of a soul mind that allows souls to infiltrate and interfere with the Group Mind that activated early human-animals? Remember, souls were looking at the biological world from the reverse side, from the spiritual realm toward the physical realm. Could they "see" or sense the mental-neural connections that allowed Group Mind to integrate with an animal brain to produce physical consciousness? Did they use brute force to maneuver Group Mind to the side and insinuate themselves into a position of authority over a body, or did they slip in around the fringes with subtle mental tentacles, testing and trying different connections, slowly gaining more control, until they assumed full command of a body?

Soul Interference with Biological Life

The readings state that souls interfered with a variety of plants and animals in ways that caused mixtures of plant and animal traits in some life forms

(2072-8_18; 1066-1_37). These creatures were called monstrosities in some readings and referred to the effects of misuse of creative power to manipulate plant and animal forms in ways that would never be produced by normal evolutionary processes, including the appearance of appendages, feathers, and scales on otherwise human bodies (364-10_11; 2072-8_18). These biological mixtures of different species are said to be the source of many of the tales of mythological creatures in ancient folklore and legends. Although the readings don't specify how such creatures were formed, it seems that direct soul manipulation or mutation of gene sequences within DNA could have been a major factor in the creation of such creatures, especially considering that humans share many genes with animals and plants. For example, humans share about 60 percent of their DNA with chickens, bananas, and fruit flies. The method by which these intriguing and fantastic biological creatures were produced will not be explored in this book because it would be pure speculation. We will concentrate on soul interference in human-animal creatures because that mental interference had significant long-term ramifications for soul rehabilitation and implementation of God's desire to lead souls back to awareness of the source of their life.

The desires that can be expressed in the animal mind when the animal is in its natural environment are limited to instinctual desires that are inherent in the rules of evolution (349-17_3). The earliest human-animals were guided by animal instincts to seek food (sustenance), protect their physical body (survival), and ensure continuity of the species (procreation), just like the other members of the animal kingdom. Their actions would not have been driven by higher-order reasoning and thoughts channeled from and controlled by the will of a soul. They had sufficient mental capacity for survival and basic community organization, but did not have independent wills that could generate the desire or manifest the ability to make higher-order rational analyses or engage in deductive or inductive reasoning. Like all animals, they did not have free will (an attribute of soul minds, not an attribute of animal minds derived from Group Mind), and could not defy their creator (900-31_5; 262-63_10).

These early human-animals were intelligent, but their tribal activity may still have had more similarities to modern ape tribes than to even the most primitive modern human tribe or societal group. Even apes can learn to communicate with modern humans through sign language, but that doesn't make them human. The Late Archaic *Homo sapiens* species called Neanderthal and the contemporary Early Modern *Homo sapiens* were the pinnacle of biological evolution in the animal kingdom and were highly intelligent human-animals—in fact, the most advanced human-animal to populate the Earth.

An animal personality is formed when Group Mind makes a link with a new biological organism and subsequently matures as the animal explores the physical realm through sense perception. This temporary personality dissipates when the animal dies and the connection between the Group Mind and the source of sensory information is severed. Reading 262-80_5 describes this dissolution of consciousness as the Group Mind returns to its author and maker, the Creative Force. This statement by itself doesn't absolutely preclude the retention of some or all animal memories in Group Mind, but it strongly suggests that the collective experiences of plant and animals and the personality traits of higher animal are not retained by the cosmic consciousness of God after the death of the biological organism. This would mean there is no continuity of experiences and memory that thread across multiple lifetimes and link individual plants and animals in the biological succession of lives. There is no permanent animal subconscious and individuality active across many lifetimes behind the conscious mind that each animal develops from its steady diet of biological sensory phenomena (900-31_5). The personality that natural human-animals acquire during life on the Earth is transient and does not extend to an associated subconscious mind and individuality within the spiritual realm. Therefore they do not have an independent existence within the spiritual realm after death in the sense that a soul does. Souls that have interfered with plant and animals, including human-animals, do retain memories of those experiences after they become mentally disengaged from the physical forms. When we see pictures of human-animal skulls in an anthropological textbook within the context of the intellectual capacity of ancient man, we correctly think of them as intelligent thinking beings like us, but the consciousness of these beings was strictly a product of a single lifetime of interaction between Group Mind and their physical environment and with other members of their species. Can souls access the material experiences of Group Mind from the spiritual realm while it is guiding and developing a plant or animal consciousness? If they can, those transient memories might have been available to the souls that were interested in investigating the mental-physical activity of Earth life forms. These metaphysical-spiritual considerations generate too many questions, for which there are too few satisfying answers to be found in science, theology, philosophy, or the readings.

We have previously discussed the evolution of human-animals after their ancestors became physically distinguishable from chimpanzees about 6.0 to 7.0 Mya. But here is the most amazing part of the story of the emergence of modern man. It took about four million years of evolution for the brains of the pre-Australopithecine and Australopithecine human-animal ancestors to increase in size from about 350 cc (cubic centimeters) to about 450 cc, an average rate of increase of about a twenty-five cubic centimeters per million years. Then, about 4.0 Mya, the rate of intellectual advancement in human-animals started to increase at a much faster rate than would be expected by normal evolutionary processes and a much faster rate than during the previous two to three millennia. During the progressive appearances of *Homo hablis* (about 3.0 Mya) and *Homo erectus* (about 1.8 Mya) and until the arrival of the first *Homo sapiens* (about 350 Kya) the brain size of these more advanced human-animals nearly tripled, going from 450 cc to 1,250 cc. The average rate of brain-size increase during that time interval had jumped to about 225 cc per million years—about nine times faster than the rate of increase of their predecessors. The Late Archaic Neanderthals and then the Early Modern *Homo sapiens* with a brain size nearly equal to modern man (about 1,500 cc) would become the dominant human-animal species (Imes, 2022, see Soul Incarnation and the Rise of Man chapter, figure 3).

The readings state that souls were actively interfering with biological species in the Earth plane at least during the past three to four million years, which would have begun about the time *Homo habilis* appeared on the Earth. What would have attracted souls to the biological activity of the Earth and to the first human-animals in particular? What are the implications of that soul activity and what were the potential effects of that activity on the development of the earliest human-animals? How would human-animal life have changed if souls were beginning to engage with them in large numbers over an extended period of time? Would the rate of increase in the physical brain size and intelligence of the developing *Homo* species have remained similar to the much slower rate of increase exhibited by their immediate Australopithecine ancestors in the absence of soul interference in the Earth's biosphere? Let's speculate on the possible means and effects of soul activity in relation to the minds and behavioral patterns of these early human-animals using the readings as a guide. What follows is not directly from the readings, but are inferences made by the author using the information available in the readings in relation to the current scientific understanding of the origin of the human species.

The first excursions of souls onto the Earth plane to intrude into human-animal biological life might have been more like a scouting trip where the nonphysical soul entity hovered around a human-animal body. After observation of the behavioral patterns and daily activity of the subject got boring, souls moved on to observe some other members of the tribe or other animals. We might think that these souls saw the panoramas of nature and rich biological life in the same way that the early human-animals saw them, but we don't know how these souls detected light waves. Was their vision limited to the same color spectrum that the human eye can detect? There is no reason to believe this is true and every reason to believe it isn't. The spiritual realm doesn't obey the same foundational law that controls energy (the physical equivalent of spirit) in the physical realm; otherwise, there would be no distinction between the realms. We don't know what images appeared in the minds of souls when they first studied the Earth's evolving ecosystem and observed the activity of early human-animals and their environment.

Before long, souls probably began to imagine what it would be like to form a direct connection with the objects of their fascination. Perhaps they conceived the idea of tapping into the human-animal neural network to directly sample the various sensations that were constantly being activated in the animal's sensory organs. By accessing neural electrical pulses as they entered the human-animal brain, souls could experience the physical world in a way that more closely imitated the perception of the human-animal mind. These first tentative ventures into the intricate neural network of human-animals were probably passive, with the soul along for the ride, perhaps staying just beyond the range of consciousness of the subject human-animal body while sampling neural impulses associated with physical sight and sounds, and observing and listening to the movement of wildlife in the forest and plains. Maybe they were admiring the native plant and animal life, learning how animals identified various sources of food and their unique taste preferences, eventually learning to feel the texture of a plant as it brushed an arm. It was an intentional and transient action, like stepping into a surround-sound theater for a movie and then leaving at the end of the show. Were these first, and perhaps clumsy, soul intrusions detected by the naturally evolved human-animal minds or did each animal mind simply fade into the background as souls made contact with the pineal gland and the neural ganglia of the central nervous system and began sampling and cataloging the electrical signals coursing through the human-animal bodies? Surely the Group Mind consciousness would have had to remain active to some degree, otherwise how would the human-animal retain the ability to function at the level of awareness necessary to keep it alive?

Soul Entanglement with Human-Animal Life

At some point, the souls probably wanted more than they were getting. This, of course, is the problem with a strong desire for self-gratification. It leads to addiction—whether it is addiction to drugs, sex, power, or to other sources of pleasurable sensory phenomena. These souls were no different from us, and for many of us, these souls were us. As the excitement and stimulation of passive sensory detection became more routine and mundane, souls began to consider ways to get a greater high. Let's assume this urge got stronger over time, and by the time the Late Archaic *Homo sapiens* came on the scene about 350 Kya in the form of the Neanderthals with a developed hyoid bone and the ability to speak, souls saw an opportunity to take the next step in biological interference. It may have already started before the Neanderthals, but the abrupt unprecedented increase in brain size in the Neanderthals suggests that something unusual happened at that time. Perhaps it was the sensations of a pounding heart and adrenal rush as a Neanderthal chased and killed large mammals in its quest for food, or the sexual sensations that burst into the brain as the Neanderthals mated that made souls decide to up the ante. These feelings and many others associated with the life and death struggle of the Neanderthals as they worked to survive in a harsh environment would have been completely foreign to the souls that first mentally touched the animal mind of the Neanderthals.

Somewhere along the line, the misdemeanor of neural eavesdropping transitioned into the felony of body snatching. Souls learned to enter a body when they desired to take partial or full control and leave the body when they were finished. When did the passive eavesdropping on the Neanderthal neural system by souls evolve into active control of their bodies—replacing the existing instinctual messages from the Group Mind with purpose-driven signals designed to direct their muscle movements for their own purposes? How long did it take to transition from the initial infrequent sampling of natural neural messages in an adult to the forceful incursion into a newborn Neanderthal child by pushing aside

Group Mind at its birth? When the soul hijacked the pineal gland and neural network of the newborn, could it have also influenced biological changes that included the growth of more neurons in the brain? Scientists believe the Neanderthals were capable of speech, and the readings indicate the possibility (294-11_2), but we can speculate that souls may also have encouraged the greater development of the muscles associated with the hyoid bone through the pineal gland. Souls were now taking full control of human-animal children at birth. The invasion of the body snatchers was underway, and one of the major consequences of this would be the development in the participating soul mind of a full blown physical conscious mind (263-13_8). The incarnated soul would come to believe that this artificial and contrived Earth mind was its only source of consciousness for the duration of the forced injection into a human animal. It would become trapped in a material body until the death of the body. It should be mentioned that soul interference and soul incarnation into human-animals was not limited to the Neanderthals but continued in the evolved Early Modern *Homo sapiens* that separated from the Neanderthals about 200 Kya. For convenience and brevity, we will use the term "Neanderthals" to mean the combined Late Archaic Neanderthal and Early Modern *Homo sapiens* populations in some of the following text.

As the intensity and breadth of the soul incursion and interference escalated, the Neanderthals transitioned from human-animals entirely controlled by animal minds driven by the three basic animal instincts to human forms controlled by will-directed soul minds with a much higher level of intelligence and a deeply buried and well-hidden set of spiritual and moral values. These soul injections created the first overt soul mind interface with biological life and probably caused the number of neural cells and the complexity of the neural network in the early human population to increase more rapidly and beyond that which would normally have occurred during the progress of natural biological evolution. Because they were still animals living in a biological world, the three basic animal instincts continued to be a factor in the life of the possessed Neanderthals, but those instincts of the natural world could be overridden by a completely different set of priorities important to the occupying souls. The interfering souls had the ability to make major changes in the natural environment of the Neanderthals and tamper with their natural rate of biological evolutionary progression. The Neanderthals suddenly got smarter faster, and their daily activity included thoughts and behavior that had not existed when they were in their natural state as part of the animal kingdom. Their ability to fashion and use tools became more sophisticated, and new tools were designed and produced more frequently. Their tribal society became more complex as they developed a civilization with customs that included art and the practice of burying the dead, possibly indicating a latent conscious awareness of the spiritual realm and ideas of an afterlife. The formation of a soul physical conscious mind mirrors the process whereby an animal physical conscious mind emerges out of the interface between Group Mind and newborn human-animals. Soul minds had replaced the mental control once reserved for Group Mind in the human-animal population.

The neural pulses that travel from the brain to the muscles of a human body are not transmitted by the flow of electrons along the neurons in the same way electrons move through a copper wire. The pulses move as a series of action potentials, which are a migration of voltage differences across the cell wall of the neuron produced by a sequence of opening and closing ion gates in the cell wall (Kandel, 2006; Imes, 2022, see Physical Consciousness and Causality chapter). Once a pulse is initiated, it can propagate the length of a neuron and be chemically transferred across a synaptic junction to the next neuron in the chain. The end result is the activation of a specialized muscle cell that can move a portion of the body, such as an arm or leg or eyelid. Souls that took possession of Neanderthal children or adults would have had to learn how to initiate and control these action potentials to do tasks and engage in activities that were already under the direction of Group Mind. This would seem to be a difficult task that would be almost impossible to master by observation alone. It would require on-the-job training that might be highly disruptive to the human-animal body and would perhaps be noticed in the society of individuals in which the body functioned on a daily basis. It might indicate that Neanderthal possession predominately occurred by taking control of a newborn infant and remaining attached to the body for the duration of its life. One serious consequence of this activity is that the soul would begin losing awareness of its true nature as a nonmaterial spiritual being for the duration of the incarnation, during the life of the body, because its subconscious memories would fade as it relied upon the physical consciousness it was building by monitoring the senses of the growing body and by learning to activate the body's muscles.

Soul control of highly evolved animals resulted in the first entanglement of souls and biological organisms in a way that gave souls the ability to manipulate the physical world—the environment of the Neanderthal—in a profound and extreme manner. Without the interfering presence of soul minds, the natural minds of the early human-animals probably would have continued to evolve in a similar manner to the minds of creatures like chimpanzees and apes that made up the rest of the higher-order animal kingdom. The ability to manipulate the muscles of the Neanderthal body allowed souls the opportunity to react to and modify the physical environment around the body within the limits set by the strength of the muscle groups being activated. Their ability to manipulate the physical realm was limited to changing the motion of material objects using human-animal muscles. This was physical interaction on a macro level, the manifestation of thought as applied through the neurons and muscles of a body, not direct mind manipulation of the physical environment. A soul could animate a body to manipulate its environment in ways that the human-animal Group Mind could not fathom. But the primary concern of these self-centered and self-serving souls was to explore yet another means of self-gratification (364-7_6). Souls were likely unaware of the potential of the causal material world to awaken their lost God consciousness and its potential to restore them to a proper spiritual relationship with God. They were entering the Earth plane without waiting for God to complete the preparation of the facility and without his permission. They probably did not understand the implications of physical-spiritual causality or realize that the consequences of spiritual error committed in the material plane must be met in the material plane (2308-4_10; 3023-1_5).

Perhaps this initial monitoring of the evolving Earth and its flourishing biological activity had no causal effect on souls, but the readings make it very clear that souls that repeatedly choose to experience the sensual pleasures of the physical realm usually become mentally attached to that realm. A soul that samples the delights of sensory stimulation is like a first-time drug user. The powerful sensory overload caused by the drug produces a mental response that causes it to want more of the drug. The conscious mind quickly becomes enamored with the sensations it is receiving from the body and is reluctant to give up those sensations. As the soul is drawn by the mental desire to repeat the physical activity that brings intense immediate pleasure and continues to taste the forbidden fruit, the urge to repeat the action is strengthened, and soon the soul is unable to release itself from the lure of sensual materiality. Souls mentally bound themselves to this world and exacerbated their mental separation from God as they focused on the flood of sensory information perceived by the soul mind. We can think of their predicament this way; The uncontrolled earthly physical conscious mind of the soul is the recipient of an unhealthy high-carb diet laden with fats and sweets from the material world. In contrast, the super conscious mind of the soul is the recipient of a healthy diet full of nutritious fruits and vegetables from the cosmic consciousness of God. The health of a soul mind is determined by the nature of the food it consumes, and the interfering souls were on a junk food binge (254-68_7).

Soul excursions onto the Earth may originally have been a form of soul tourism, but it developed a sinister twist. It may have begun with an innocent monitoring of plant and animal life, but it progressed into more direct and invasive experiences that included illicit soul interference with biological life for the purpose of intercepting neural sensory signals, the injection of soul minds into plants and lower animals to experience or control their bodies, and the incarnation of souls into human-animal life forms. All of this illicit activity occurred before God had finished preparing the biological ecosystem as a proper facility for soul restoration. Many of these soul activities could, and often did, result in the inability of the soul to escape from the Earth and its immediate nonphysical surroundings. The spiritual law, to which all souls are subject, works to bring the soul to an awareness of the impact of poor decisions through physical and spiritual causality. The soul is directed to repeatedly meet its spiritual deficiencies and shortcomings until it has learned to reject self-gratification and embrace God consciousness. The soul must learn that its thoughts and actions are separating it from God, a process that requires the soul to be repeatedly and continually faced with physical situations that eventually cause it to realize the error of its ways and decide to change its behavior. This spiritual rehabilitation aspect of the Earth's environment, operating as a law to which the soul is bound until released by good behavior, means that the soul must continue the process of incarnation until it has resolved the issues that are preventing it from experiencing full conscious awareness of its creator.

These interfering souls probably did not realize, or perhaps did not care, that the material world can be a mental snare that traps the unaware. As souls continued their quest for new and exciting material sensory experiences, their minds became more attached to the pleasures they were experiencing. At some point, the indulgent souls became unable to fully control their excursions and could no longer extricate themselves from materiality. They became bound to the Earth, trapped by the combined forces of causality and spiritual law. They would be required to keep returning to the Earth environment where they were defying God until they could sort out the messes they had created (5753-1_23). Souls could no longer come and go as they pleased. When they were not incarnated or projecting onto the Earth, they had to remain in the adjacent local nonphysical environment, where they were required to pass through the associated realms of mental-spiritual training between earthly incursions. Their repeated incarnations would allow them to gradually assess and compare their thoughts and manifested activities in relation to the Will of God written deep within their soul minds. Souls had opened Pandora's Box and could not close it. Incarnation became part of the equation of life for every soul that repeatedly placed the desire for personal and selfish gratification before the desire to bring its will into alignment with the Will of God.

Souls can be strong-willed and obstinate—the same character traits exhibited by many modern humans. Of course, all human words and actions are direct manifestations of the desire and activity of incarnated souls. Humans do not utter one word or take one action that is not first conceived in the soul mind and acted upon at the behest of the will of the soul. All the weakness and imperfections we see in humanity today are projections of the same character flaws that are present in souls. Human speech and actions appear to originate in the neural system of a human organism. In reality, they are the physical expressions of ideas and desires that have their origin in a soul mind. The decision to direct a human body to engage in an activity that runs counter to the higher spiritual principles of the soul testifies to the willingness of the soul to rebel against God. The chaos kindled by the unauthorized soul manipulation of the early animal life forms was not conducive to soul spiritual restoration but simply drew souls farther away from God consciousness as they reveled in previously unimaginable physical pleasures and became embedded in the competitive world of tribalism and resource competition. Souls became so fascinated with the exciting and complex visual, auditory, and kinesthetic images of their surrounding physical environment that they came to believe the imagery was the totality of reality, whereas it only represented a miniscule, limited subset of the greater reality of the cosmic realm.

Animal minds derived from Group Mind do not make decisions about their physical needs in the same manner as incarnated souls; they have entirely different agendas and goals. Souls began altering their environment in ways that seriously distorted the natural evolutionary process on the Earth. This chaotic condition was leading to a downward spiral where souls, in their unquenchable thirst for physical experiences and material gratification, indulged their desires without regard to, or realization of, the great damage it was causing themselves and without care about the harm they were inflicting on the bodies and minds of fellow incarnated souls. Their activities were often atrocious and an affront to God, as they abused the free will of fellow trapped souls. There were no spiritual leaders to teach them the need for a moral life before God, no one to explain the spiritual purpose of morality, and no written guiding principles that could be passed down from generation to generation of incarnating souls to help them come to their senses. There was nothing and nobody to look to as an example, and none or few who could tell them where they had gone wrong and how to extract themselves from their self-imposed predicament. As long as the siren song of sensual pleasures was first and foremost in their minds, they could not even remember God and could never make meaningful progress toward escaping from the Earth and its immediate nonphysical borderland realm. God would again have to intercede in the affairs of souls and would need to alter the rules of engagement for souls in materiality in a way that would facilitate their spiritual growth and lead to their eventual extraction from the physical world. This would be the third major intervention by God on behalf of souls that had lost conscious awareness of his presence and their relationship to him. He would bypass the normal evolutionary process that had been greatly compromised and insert an improved biological form through which souls could incarnate. He set, and enforced, new rules of engagement that required the trapped souls and any other errant souls still in the cosmic realm that were in need of its physical-spiritual properties of causality to reincarnate, but only in the new body type.

The Righteous Consciousness
of the Adamic Race

While many souls engaged in rebellious activity as they explored the limits of their creative freedom in the cosmic realm and interfered with biological life in the physical realm, other souls remained faithful to God and the purpose for which they were created. They did not abandon God and retreat from God consciousness as they developed their independent identity and explored the realms of activity available to them. They matured into loving, caring entities that stayed in communication with God through the open channel of their super conscious mind. They were well aware of the anguish God felt over the behavior of the rebellious souls. These faithful souls shared God's concern about the destiny of the rebellious souls and the discord they were sowing across the spiritual realm and among the biological creatures of the physical realm. God could sense the mental withdrawal of each rebellious soul and tried to encourage all such souls to re-attune their minds to his presence and the purpose for their creation, but the gift of free will and the lure of selfish desires that could be manifested and experienced in the spiritual realm and now in the physical realm, combined with their weakening spiritual attunement and lack of communication with God, proved too much for them to overcome. God knew he had to modify his original plan when souls began interfering in his evolving rehabilitation facility before he had completed its preparation and authorized its use. The Earth and its human-animal species was not yet ready for souls, and their ungodly and unnatural interference in biological evolution was causing havoc in the plant and animal kingdoms and in the minds of the souls that were indulging in inappropriate biological experimentation.

To rectify the situation and complete his plan to rescue souls from self-destruction through selfishness, God created a new body type for soul incarnation—a more appropriate earthly human form for souls to use while they engaged in activity in the Earth environment and interacted with their soul-incarnated neighbors. God knew that the rescue mission would be a certain failure if he allowed souls to continue to enter the Earth plane by commandeering Late Archaic Neanderthal and Early Modern *Homo sapiens* bodies, so he designed and created a new human form that was patterned after the evolved *Homo sapiens* bodies and their soul-influenced variants. This improved human form provided a better temporary residence for souls as they worked through and resolved their spiritual deficiencies and shortcomings in human society. This intentionally designed and refined human body, the Adamic body, was created by a method that bypassed the natural process of evolution. It was close enough in appearance to the existing body forms to be accepted by the existing soul-animated human-animal populations and, because it was biologically within the same species, was capable of engaging in sexual activity with the Neanderthals and Early Modern *Homo sapiens*. This new race of humans could only be animated by soul minds and not the Group Mind that had animated the original human-animal populations.

Amilius and the Adamic Incarnations

Amilius, the first soul to be created (262-52_25) and one of a group of souls that had remained faithful to God and held true to the purpose for which God created them, offered to lead a rescue mission to bring comfort and spiritual enlightenment to the souls that were trapped in the Earth environment (364-8_3). The decision of Amilius to work with God to rescue the trapped souls would eventually gain it the title of Savior, but the path to that exalted position would not be smooth or easy. Amilius began this journey of mercy by entering the society of souls that had incarnated into human-animals. He brought with him many like-minded souls. It was a loving action and a risky venture into a world of temptations and snares that could lead them to soul entrapment in materiality. The initial influx of Amilius and the souls that accompanied him was by thought-projected Adamic bodies. They appeared on the Earth at five separate geographical locations (Atlantis-Caucuses-Sudan-Andean-Gobi), regions roughly corresponding to the present-day areas populated by the five racial groups. From these five locations they dispersed and spread their message to the population centers of the world (364-13_6; 364-9_7; 1580-1_53). The readings focus on the Adamic group that projected into the Atlantean lands because, through successive incarnations, those souls strongly influenced Egypt, the Middle East, Europe, and America, where Cayce was born and the readings were being given. The souls of the four other Adamic projections have their own preferred succession of incarnations, but the readings only give brief mention to these nations and civilizations in reference to their interaction with the Atlantean soul group. The appearance of Amilius and the Adamic group is symbolically described in Scripture as the creation of Adam, the biblical name for the incarnated soul Amilius and an archetypal representation of the Adamic group and its mission.

The reader is reminded here that souls are genderless in their native celestial domain, but we will begin referring to Amilius using both the masculine pronouns "*he/his/him*" and the neutral pronoun "*it*" because of this soul's intimate association with the man Adam, an expression and projection of the masculine-like positive energy of the soul, and to prevent some awkward sentence structures. Amilius would devote its mental and spiritual energy to teaching souls caught in the quagmire of materiality how to extricate their minds from selfish attitudes that drive the desire for physical gratification in its various forms. To accomplish this in a meaningful manner and prove that the task can be accomplished by souls immersed in materiality, Amilius, as Adam, would allow himself to descend into a conscious state of sin and then extricate himself from that sinful state by realigning his soul mind with the Mind of God (364-8_3; 262-59_10). His teaching would have far greater force if he walked the walk as well as talked the talk. This act would be recorded in Scripture as the fall of Adam from grace and his ejection from the garden of Eden. The readings imply that there was a sexual component to the fall. Reading 262-115_31-36 defines the prince of this world as the drive to satisfy arrogant self-interests, including the unbridled desire to procreate, and states that "*in their early days they [Adam and Eve] were tempted by the prince of this world, and partook of same.*" It also discusses the innocence of the Adamic souls that had plunged into a world ruled by the prince of selfishness as expressed in "*darkness, hate, malice, jealousy, backbiting, uncomely things.*" The lamb of God and his companions had entered the lion's den. The process of disengaging himself from mental and physical entanglement in the material world would take Amilius through multiple appearances on the Earth in incarnated form through descendant Adamic bodies. Part of this millennia-long story is recorded in biblical Scripture.

The story of the creation of Adam as given in the book of Genesis suggests that Adam's appearance was instantaneous, or at least occurred over a brief interval of time as a random collection of earthly matter was molded, shaped, and transformed into a human being. The description of the earthly appearance of the Adamic group as indicated in the readings is that soul-created thought forms were projected onto the Earth, which subsequently solidified into physical bodies. These bodies were modeled after the members of the evolved soul-animated human-animal communities they intended to join (257-201_8-9; 364-3_5). There are many unanswered questions left to ponder about the nature of the subsequent transition from spiritual thought form to physical flesh and blood as suggested in the readings—just as there are many unanswered questions about the nature of the transition between a clump of dust or dirt and a flesh-and-blood human body as given in biblical Scripture. In a later chapter we will see how the transition of Adamic soul projections from thought form to flesh and bone may have been similar to the resurrection of Jesus. The sudden appearance of a large number of ephemeral thought-form bodies in existing societies could not have gone unnoticed, but perhaps was not as unusual at that time as it would be now, because this was a time when many self-centered souls were experiencing the Earth through nonphysical means including various forms of projection into materiality. In any case, it was necessary that Adam and his followers be able to communicate the fact that they were missionaries from God and teach rebellious souls the necessity to reform their behavior and the associated thought patterns that had brought them to their degraded position. The new Adamic group was adept at using intuitive subconscious forces in conjunction with their developing conscious minds to help them to make more spiritually oriented decisions and keep their decisions tied back to the spiritual purpose for which they had appeared on the Earth. The more spiritually adept members of the group may have been able to foresee the conclusion of events or at least intuitively predict the outcome of the events in which they participated to a fairly high degree of accuracy (2464-2_4-6; 255-12_9).

The souls that were part of the Adamic influx were not the first, and would not be the last, souls to enter Earth by thought-form projection. However, the age of thought-form projection onto the Earth was coming to a close and souls would eventually be required to shift away from human-animal bodies and projected forms and incarnate only into physical descendants of the Adamic bodies to accomplish their spiritual training. It would take many generations of Adamic descendants before this new procedure was fully adhered to and practical. The original Adamic populations generally were more closely attuned to their subconscious minds than are people today. Despite their material experiences as thought-form projections with a propensity toward ungodly behavior, even the non-Adamic populations retained a strong connection with their subconscious minds and perhaps even their spiritual roots because their minds had not yet become fully weighted down with the material needs of a body and the attractions of materiality. But they were not above using spiritual forces to serve their own selfish purposes, including dangerous manipulation of their environment and abuse of fellow incarnated souls (2594-1_49). This misuse of creative power by rebellious souls was so gross and evil that it eventually led to the total destruction of the island continent of Atlantis. The entire process included a series of three major cataclysmic events (about 52.7 Kya, 24.0 Kya, and 12.7 Kya) over a period of at least forty thousand years (262-39_17; 364-4_9).

The readings state that the last thought forms were removed from the Earth during the time of Noah and the biblical flood (257-201_11; 364-6_6), and associate this event with the second major destruction of Atlantis at about 24 Kya (364-6_6). Other readings suggest that this second destruction occurred earlier and may indicate a series of geologic upheavals instead of one single event (2625-1; 470-22). According to the readings, Adam appeared on the Earth about 106 Kya (364-3_5; Imes, 2022, see Soul Incarnation and the Rise of Man chapter). Therefore, thought form projections would have been active on the Earth for about eighty thousand years after the influx of Adamic bodies. Note that scientists have not proven the existence of the submerged continent of Atlantis. Plato wrote in his dialogues *Timaeus and Critias* that Solon (ca 640 to 560 BC), an Athenian statesman and lawmaker who was instrumental in bringing democracy to Athens by reducing the power of the wealthy and allowing more citizens to participate in the political process, had conversed with Egyptian priests, who told him of an ancient Atlantean people who fled from their homeland about 9.6 Kya because it was being destroyed by the forces of nature (Plato, 2008). The existence, fate, and time frame of Atlantis as described by the Egyptian priests are consistent within the descriptions of Atlantis in the readings. By the time thought-form activity had concluded at about 24 Kya, the Neanderthal population had passed into extinction and the Early Modern *Homo sapiens* were nearing extinction. Only Adamic bodies would survive. The Neanderthal and Early Modern *Homo sapiens* were allowed to become extinct because their bodies had been misused and abused by souls and because of the spiritual directive that future incarnations would only be allowed through Adamic bodies. The descendants of the new Adamic forms, the human species now identified by anthropologists as the Late Modern *Homo sapiens*, would become the only advanced species to survive. The Adamic body form has the general physical features of the evolved human-animals, but contains improvements that make them more appropriate channels through which recovering souls can reconnect with God.

Amilius and his followers intentionally avoided incarnating through available human-animal newborn infants. This avoided the decade or two normally required for an incarnated soul to develop a mature physical conscious mind. It also ensured each soul could more easily retain awareness of its spiritual purpose since it did not have to build an entirely new physical conscious mind based on sensual interactions with the subsequent loss of its subconscious identities. Their early training and developing consciousness would have been in the hands of the non-Adamic populations, and they would have lost awareness of their mission before it began. Many souls would never have been able to recover that awareness. This would have defeated their mission immediately because there would have been no mental continuity of purpose for their entry into the Earth plane. Instead, Amilius and his followers animated the thought-form bodies using their subconscious minds and retained an awareness of purpose as they developed physical conscious minds. The readings describe a higher form of group mind or united consciousness that the souls that participated in the mission could invoke through concentration that enabled them to subconsciously commune among themselves and with those souls that remained in the spiritual plane to receive guidance and knowledge to help the mission (2464-2_4-6). Perhaps this form of extra-physical communication resembled the biblical description of the gathering of Jesus, Elijah, and Moses on the mountain, or perhaps it was more along the lines of a deep group meditation. Over time, these thought forms would devolve into physical bodies as the animating souls used them to engage in material-world activities. The transition from thought-form bodies to physical bodies was necessary so that the Adamic bodies could be used to sexually conceive descendent bodies through which souls could incarnate into the Earth plane as they cycled through the dimensions of mental-spiritual training and earthly lives. The method of soul incarnation into descendant Adamic bodies would be nearly identical to the method that the rebellious souls had been using to force themselves into the human-animal population. The physical consciousness of the children born to the Adamic race and their descendants would need to be continually reeducated about the nature of their souls and the reason for their being incarnated to retain continuity of the purpose of the original mission through the generations of offspring.

As Adamic bodies hardened and became able to produce offspring, they multiplied and became the modern *Homo sapiens* that populate the Earth today, the only surviving human species. Many good and godly souls incarnate in these bodies to cleanse lingering moral and spiritual deficiencies from their conscious personalities and subconscious individualities. Many selfish and evil souls animate these bodies because they are in need of spiritual restoration and have chosen to ignore the inner voice of God that constantly urges them to repent and return home. The readings state that it took many thousands to millions of years for the natural physical environment to evolve until it could support [pre-Adamic] man, and that it will be used by [Adamic] man for hundreds to thousands of years to come (3744-5_46). Patience is truly an attribute of God. Human bodies will be available for a long time so that every soul will have the maximum number of opportunities possible to change ingrained thought and behavioral patterns that stress selfishness into new thought and behavior patterns that stress love for God and fellow souls before the window of opportunity closes.

Reading 364-4 sets a minimum time span of soul activity in Atlantis at about two hundred thousand years, which would indicate activity beginning at or before about 212 Kya and ending about 12.7 Kya, when the last islands of Atlantis sank into the ocean, a time span of at least 180 thousand years. For a hundred thousand years before Amilius arrived on the scene, souls were routinely projecting onto the Earth, manipulating human-animal life and probably incarnating into newborn human-animal bodies. Most of them had already lost awareness of their true origin and their initial close relationship to their creator. The Neanderthal human-animals made their appearance about 350 Kya and survived until about 30 Kya, roughly to the second period of destruction of Atlantis at 24 Kya. The Early Modern *Homo sapiens* human-animals appeared about 200 Kya and survived until about 10 Kya, roughly to the third and last period of destruction of Atlantis, which the readings suggest occurred about 12.7 Kya (364-11_7; Imes, 2022, see Soul Incarnation and the Rise of Man chapter). If we accept the appearance of Amilius as Adam on the continent of Atlantis about 106 Kya, and if we accept the scientific evidence of human evolution and ancient human activity, we must conclude that the Neanderthals, Early *Homo sapiens* and the Adamic race jointly occupied the continent for about seventy-five thousand years.

By the time Amilius entered the Earth plane, the Neanderthals and Early Modern *Homo sapiens* had spread across Atlantis, Europe and Asia; were organizing villages and towns; and were developing socially and culturally. The Neanderthals had already been active on the Earth for about 250 thousand years and the Early Modern *Homo sapiens* had been active for about a hundred thousand years. Soul-dominated human-animals were probably outcompeting and outnumbering their Group Mind animated cousins long before Amilius started the process of bringing God awareness back to these souls. The readings give us a logical physical and spiritual basis to explain the reason why the Late Modern *Homo sapiens*, the only human species that exists today, flourishes while similar and related human-animal species dwindled and perished. They explain why this advanced species deviated from the normal evolutionary pattern of human-animals. It did not find an ecological niche and compete with other species within the limitations imposed by its evolved mental and physical capacities, but suddenly and abruptly in geologic time become the de facto ruler of the entire biological world, while human-animals dwindled into extinction. Archaeologists date the emergence of the intelligent Early Modern *Homo sapiens* with their 1,500 cc brains to about 200 Kya, and ascribe the phenomenal mental advancement of their *Homo* ancestors during the previous three million years to an increase in brain size, which really means number of brain neurons. The readings suggest, but do not confirm, that the increased brain capacity and intelligence of these ancestors was influenced by frequent soul activity among the human-animals and the deeper penetration of soul minds into their physical bodies.

The rise of the Early Modern *Homo sapiens* bodies coincides with the rise of Atlantean culture about 212 Kya and the transition from the Early Modern to Late Modern *Homo sapiens* occurred around the entry of the Adamic group of souls in new body types designed to replace the human-animal evolved body types. Soul incarnation would gradually shift away from descendants of soul-inhabited human-animals and concentrate within the pure and mixed descendants of the Adamic group. The original evolved human-animals would become extinct as the more intelligent soul-animated humans began to dominate the species. The surviving humans we see today would be identified by science as the Late Modern *Homo sapiens*; modern man. Science generally supports this concept that human descendants of the Adamic group interbred with soul-animated human-animals in that Neanderthal DNA is mixed with modern human DNA in European and Asian populations at about 1 to 4 percent (Fu and others, 2015). The projection of so many Adamic bodies at five widely scattered places across the world, their biological and genetic similarity to the existing *Homo sapiens*, and their interbreeding with the existing evolved populations implies that scientific research on ancient DNA will never genetically lead to the single unique pair of original humans that is implied by a literal interpretation of the biblical story of Adam and Eve (Reich, 2018; Imes, 2022, see Soul Incarnation and the Rise of Man chapter).

The Sons and Daughters of God
and the sons and daughters of Belial

Let's contrast the moral and emotional state of the soul-animated human-animals with the soul animated descendants of the Adamic human beings during the time frame we previously discussed. We will speak in generalities and stereotype the two groups. Our characterization will be more accurate just after the influx of Adamic souls and less accurate as time passed and the groups mixed. The general immorality and lack of God consciousness of the souls that animated human-animals earned them the title of the sons and daughters of Belial in the readings (877-26_8). The readings do not mention the name "Neanderthal" or "Early Modern *Homo sapiens*" and, therefore, do not directly connect these human-animal populations with the sons and daughters of Belial. This connection is inferred through a comparison of the current scientific understanding of ancient human-animal populations and the nature of soul activity around the time of the Adamic influx as extracted from the readings. These souls had forgotten or suppressed their spiritual origins as soul children created in the image of God. The title was also applied to genetic mixtures of soul-animated human-animals and Adamic descendants. These interfering souls had already experimented with their creative freedom in the spiritual realm as their minds developed and matured and, like modern teenage humans, discovered that the pleasures of self-indulgence, the power of unbridled egotism and the addiction to sensation could override their common sense and inherent love for their creator. They found much enjoyment in thoughts and activities that were causing them to lose awareness of their creator, rarely thinking about the potential consequences of their behavior. They had chosen to pervert and misapply their spiritual life source to satisfy their self-centered desires. Their activities in the world of human-animals and human beings brought joy to themselves at the expense of the mental and physical well-being of others. They could and did show love and kindness at times, but far too often displayed the emotions of anger, hate, intolerance, and disregard for the welfare and desires of others. Their sense of personal well-being overrode or suppressed their better innate moral qualities. Their greatest joys in life came from activities that gave them power over other souls and that brought them wealth and material goods well beyond their needs, usually at the expense of the mental and physical welfare of those who were forced to serve them. The gross disregard of the sons and daughters of Belial for the welfare of other human beings, other incarnated souls, would become a major point of contention between the two groups.

The readings characterize the sons and daughters of Belial in Atlantis as having little concern for the rights of others and a people who routinely used and abused those they deemed inferior, including subjecting them to forced labor, servitude, and slavery. They had developed the consciousness of rebellion against God, which is the true meaning of sin according to the readings (3976-9_4). Rebellion against God is the only sin, and all of the wide repertoire of sins recognized, identified and cataloged by man are variations on the theme of rebellion against God and his purpose for souls. Sin is enjoyable in the moment, but in a world of causation where souls are bound to the physical and spiritual laws of cause and effect, the pleasure of sinful rebellion against God always leads to pain, suffering, sadness, and sorrow when the moment arrives for the fruit of the sin seed to be harvested. In the absence of proper mental alignment of will and mind to their spiritual purpose, souls were having difficulty mentally linking the suffering they were encountering in the world with their thoughts and activities that were violating the purpose of their creation. God would patiently wait for the force of physical-spiritual law to remind the rebellious souls of their purpose to be loving companions of God, not lovers of self and perpetrators of self-indulgent and self-glorifying actions.

The people of the soul-animated, pure Adamic race are called the Sons and Daughters of God in the readings. These people were animated by souls that remembered their spiritual origins; chose to keep the lines of communication with God open; and did their best to express the inherent soul attributes of love, patience, gentleness, kindness, and mercy when they interacted with other humans who were active on the Earth. They were not emotionless in their piety and respect for God, but were full of joy and the knowledge of their close mental and spiritual association with God. They allowed that joy to radiate through the spiritual realm and express itself in their countenance and actions in the physical realm as they dedicated themselves to giving hope and help to other souls. The Adamic soul group represented a soul consciousness that nurtured and cultivated the loving relationship with God that was always available to them through the super conscious mind. They tended that spiritual-mental link with divinity and listened to the advice, encouragement, and inspiration the Mind of God offered them. They felt the flow of love, kindness, and concern from their Creator. These souls felt a sense of oneness with their creator, remembered that they were actually portions of God, and projected spiritual goodness and loving concern toward their less-godly soul siblings.

The use of the term "Sons and Daughters of God" and "sons and daughters of Belial" in the readings denotes far more than two separate biological, social, or political groups that were active shortly after the arrival of Amilius. The terms have a deep spiritual connotation and indicate the radically different mental dispositions and states of consciousness held by the two groups of incarnated souls. These two states of consciousness are an outgrowth of the mental patterns that souls chose to activate and glorify as they exercised their newly acquired free wills. Souls split into two major camps, and there were probably many who were trying to dabble in the pleasures of self-gratification while attempting or pretending to hold true to their creator. That tight rope act was doomed to failure from the beginning. Souls are either with God in mind and activity or against God by allowing selfishness to enter their minds and become manifest in their activities. Human behavior is soul behavior, and all human activity reflects the nature and mind of the incarnated soul.

The readings and Scripture strongly emphasize that the Lord thy God is One. No person can entertain the thought of Oneness as it pertains to the nature of God and his soul children and have any thought that slavery can be justified, whether in the form of outright ownership of people, segregation, or economic disassociation and inequality (3581-1_24). Slavery doesn't always come in the form of Southern plantations and cotton fields. It can exist by default when greedy individuals and corporations pay workers such low wages that they cannot sustain a reasonable lifestyle, including the inability to purchase shelter or adequate food for themselves and their families (281-60_6). All souls were created equal in the eyes of God. Personal and institutional actions that cause racial and economic inequality and promote the selfish material benefit of one soul or group over another soul or group pervert God's plan for souls. Souls that embraced the tenets of the sons and daughters of Belial when the Adamic group arrived continued to incarnate through the millennia, carrying their morally corrupt and ungodly attitudes of racial superiority and self-righteousness with them and sowing seeds of discord, strife, and divisiveness in their wake. Despite the evil they perpetrate across the world, if those souls were prevented from reincarnating, they would never have had the opportunity to recognize the depth of their spiritual degradation or someday awaken and lay claim to their destiny as companions of God.

There are other similar terms used throughout the readings to indicate these two groups. The terms "Sons of God" and "Sons and Daughters of God" are used more than eighty times to indicate the spiritually pure group that projected onto the Earth with Amilius to rescue the lost souls. The nearly synonymous term "Law of One" (meaning those who hold to the idea of the Oneness of God) is used over three hundred times in various forms (one half are of the form "the children of the Law of One") to indicate the spiritually pure group and to indicate the spiritual principles held by the group. The term "Sons of Adam" is used to describe the descendants of Adam and his co-workers who held to the precepts of the Law of One and who joined with the Sons of God and remained true to the principles promoted by the Sons of God (884-1_31). The terms "sons of Belial" and "sons and daughters of Belial" are used more than 120 times to indicate the human-animals whose minds and bodies were commandeered by rebellious selfish souls and who were the focus of the rescue mission. The terms "sons of men" and "sons and daughters of men" are used over 130 times to indicate the original Belial group, the mixed offspring and their descendants from the sexual union of Adamic group and Belial group members, and are also used as general terms for the present-day human population. The phrase "sons of Belial," "sons of men", and similar phrases are also used in the Bible to refer to persons who are wicked or godless, who are worthless and good for nothing to themselves or society, and who are likely to lead others away from God toward ruin and destruction (Genesis 6:2-4; Deuteronomy 13:13; Judges 19:22; 1 Samuel 2:12).

Because of the entrenched immoral activity of the soul-possessed human-animals, God warned Amilius and the group of altruistic souls that entered the Earth with him to remain spiritually and racially pure and refrain from having intimate physical relations with the existing populations (262-119_14; 294-189_12). It was especially important in the first years after the entry of the Sons and Daughters of God that the incoming souls and their biological descendants refrain from sexual activity with the sons and daughters of Belial so that the Adamic souls could support each other and sustain the mental focus they needed to remain true to their mission while interacting with those whom they came to help (5245-1_10). Intermixing would bring the Adamic souls too close to the material temptations and forms of gratification that led to the downfall of the lost souls and could cause the Adamic souls to lose sight of their mission. They would no longer be effective messengers from God and would become part of the problem instead of part of the solution (364-7_3). This warning was generally ignored as time passed and members of the two groups and their many descendants became better acquainted with each other and began cohabitating or marrying as any two distinct populations that are thrown together are likely to do. Despite the best efforts of the original Adamic group, their failure to remain aligned with the spiritual precepts of God and their willingness to compromise with the forces of Belial would contribute to the political and physical destruction of the continent of Atlantis (364-4_5). The mention in Scripture of inappropriate sexual mixing between the Sons of God and the daughters of men may very well be a reference to the Sons of the Adamic group and the daughters of the soul-possessed human-animal populations (Genesis 6:1-4; 364-11_8). The same verses make an intriguing reference to a mysterious race of unusually large humans called the Nephilim (giants), possibly a group of human-animals whose hormonal secretions were altered by the influence of soul minds (281-38_19). The readings state that these giants were ten to twelve feet in stature and well-proportioned individuals.

The readings refer to a group of individuals called *things* among the mixed group offspring. One reading states that they were the offspring of the Sons of God with the daughters of men and the Daughters of God with the sons of men (281-44_10). This physical mixing was probably accompanied by a dilution of the higher spiritual consciousness of the original Adamic souls. The word *things* was also used in one reading to mean evolutionary individuals (3027-2_38), which strongly suggests that this group may have included soul-inhabited or even Group Mind-controlled human-animals. The *things* may also have even included some soul-inhabited lower animals (364-10_11). *Things* were sometimes intentionally bred to provide a class of laborers and skilled workers and even beasts of burden (5245-1_10). Perhaps the souls that manipulated these *things* were not able to fully and smoothly interface with the bodies they were possessing. These offspring were considered by the sons of Belial to be second class citizens and often had physical and mental defects. It is unclear why they were often defective in mind and body, but it is possible that the spiritual impurity of the sons and daughters of Belial and their intentional desire to produce a subrace of dependent workers to serve them as slave laborers, servants, skilled artists, and craftsmen was part of the reason (1416-1_41). Was this also why God directed Amilius and his followers (the original Sons and Daughters of God) to refrain from sexually intermingling with the soul-animated evolved human-animals? Perhaps there was both a spiritual need to keep the groups in different communities and families so that the mission of the group would not be compromised and also a physical reason because the offspring of sexual activity between the two groups could be physically and mentally compromised.

The use of *things* to do household chores, agriculture work, and to construct buildings was not just practiced by the sons and daughters of Belial, but was also a practice of some of the Sons and Daughters of God. Apparently, over time even the morally and spiritually advanced group was not above the practice of taking advantage of others for their convenience. The influence of evil through the immorality of the Belial group was often overwhelming to the descendants of the Adamic group (and perhaps even some of the original members), and many of them succumbed to the material gratifications that were available to them through ownership of the *things*. Some of the Adamic group accepted the enslavement of *things* for convenience and self-gratification even though the souls of these *things* could have been saved from their degraded condition through education; retraining of the mind; and the application of patience, love, kindness and longsuffering when interacting with them (3463-1_23). Using them as slaves or coerced menial labor was not spiritually consistent with the original purpose of the Adamic group, but the descendants of that original group were different souls with different ideas and experiences. This spiritual shortcoming became a point of contention within the now tainted Adamic group descendants as it raised the question of good and evil in relation to the original purpose of the Adamic group. It was an indication of the moral decay that had set in as the ideals of the Adamic souls were abandoned by new souls that were entering the Earth through their pure and mixed descendants.

The original high spiritual ideals were becoming diluted and weakened by the overall tendency toward more material thoughts and desires (1968-2_5; 3298-1_31). Of course, this was inevitable because the Adamic group descendants were destined to be human bodies for reincarnating rebellious souls. These *things* are part of the genetic group called the sons and daughters of men in the reading, and many of them became remote ancestors of modern man. The manner in which the *things* were bred and ill-treated by the Belial group was a major point of contention between those of the Adamic group who remained spiritually and genetically true to their original purpose and those of the sons and daughters of Belial and the fallen descendants of the Sons and Daughters of God who had become physically entangled with them. One individual who lived before the second destruction of Atlantis (ca 22 Kya) is mentioned as having attempted to better the living conditions and alleviate the suffering of the *things* (3027-2_38). From the very beginnings of humanity, incarnated souls were violating the commandment that Jesus would reiterate a hundred thousand years later; to love our neighbor as we love ourselves. This reluctance or aversion of souls to treat their siblings with decency, compassion, fairness, and a sense of equality would bring turmoil to the society of humans for generations to come, even to this day.

The readings also describe beings called automatons, perhaps indicating creatures of low intelligence and little aptitude for stimulating, intellectual conversation. They may be synonymous with *things*, but Reading 1435-1_10 also uses the term "automaton" in a way that implies a lack of free will, which makes automatons more like the natural biological world instead of a creature with a reasoning, independent mind. Perhaps this condition was caused by the inability of the interfering souls to properly and fully express free will while improperly or only partially bound to a human-animal body. These souls may have brought memories of their previous insertions into animal forms with them when they started choosing human forms in which to incarnate, resulting in biological defects in the mixed-parentage offspring. The main function of automatons appears to be to conduct repetitive and menial tasks, although their mentioned artistic talents and craftsmanship would indicate that at least some were skilled individuals. Reading 281-43_4 characterizes them as entities without purpose, which indicate only partial or imperfect control by a soul, and Reading 2464-2_12 also suggests that many souls were pushing themselves into materiality without considering the possibility that they may not be able to retain their full mental faculties while they animated the physical body they had chosen. Apparently, there was an influx of these creatures into ancient Egypt when the Atlantean immigrants who were fleeing the third and final major devastation of their country brought them as part of their household goods. They were present in sufficient numbers and were of such concern to the ancient Egyptians that special facilities were built to care for them. The physical and mental deficiencies of these abused groups would eventually be purged, largely by the activities of caring individuals dedicated to the service of fellow souls through the Temple of Sacrifice and Temple Beautiful (2570-1_35). These institutions were dedicated to removing nonhuman appendages from the bodies and correcting the mental condition of the souls that were causing them to exhibit the remnant animal features.

The decision of many individuals to help the *things* gain a sense of humanity and advocate for their proper treatment was not acceptable to some others in the community who preferred to see them kept in their subservient position (3027-2_38; 2072-1_39; 2251-1_44). This attitude is reminiscent of that of American and colonial European slave owners, who too often viewed their slaves as subhuman and could not imagine that anyone should or would consider treating them as humans of equal value. Also, a major concern of the native Egyptians was that the Atlanteans were beginning to look upon the Egyptians as inferior people, much like the subservient *things* and automatons that they were used to ordering about and considering as property (281-43_5). This caused added tension between the incoming Atlanteans and the native Egyptians, who increasingly became concerned about the number of immigrants. The readings state that many Atlantean souls were entering into the Americas during the time it was transitioning from a nation of Native American tribes into a European colony (884-1_16). It is highly likely that many of those souls had previously lived as sons and daughters of Belial and brought their ungodly attitudes of racial superiority and disregard for other people along with them. They were quite agreeable to the use of slaves for agricultural production and as personal servants. The stain of the consciousness of racial superiority has been around for at least a hundred thousand years. It is difficult to cleanse this spiritual sickness from a soul.

Initial Excitement Meets Harsh Reality

The consciousness of the original members of the Adamic race was the consciousness of the hope, joy, and satisfaction that comes from living in constant communication with God by actively seeking him through the super conscious mind, even while exploring the mysteries of the spiritual and physical realms. God consciousness is the spiritual enlightenment that illuminates our souls and radiates from our human countenance to brighten our lives and those who we touch. It allows us to explore our coveted intellectual freedom without making God repent that he created us (Genesis 6:6). Our physical lives as incarnated souls will be much more happy, healthy, fulfilling, and soul satisfying when our thoughts and actions include unconditional love for our creator and the souls that came into existence with us. Souls must realize that communion with God is their life blood. There are consequences to mentally blocking and ignoring that flow of life force. It eventually leads to loss of independent identity and soul individuality. A spiritually dead soul, a soul that becomes mentally isolated from the community of souls and its creator, will eventually cease to exist because it will be absorbed back into the cosmic consciousness that is God (826-8_9).

The consciousness of souls that formed the Adamic group was a shared hope for the spiritual enlightenment and salvation of souls trapped in materiality, an exciting opportunity to be the hands and feet of God in a totally new world of sensations and experiences that none of them had ever before encountered. There was probably a strong unified sense of purpose in the coordinated activity of the hundreds or thousands of souls that entered the Earth as thought forms to mentally build the shape and form of the new Adamic body type designed by God and Amilius. This mass soul projection was the beginning of a long series of incarnations by well-meaning souls that taught the words of God and lived godly lives in the societies to which they were assigned. They were eager to spread the message that God was calling for repentance and spiritual renewal among the lost souls. It must have felt quite rewarding and fulfilling to be part of such a grand and noble campaign. Perhaps they thought that the mission would not take long—maybe a few generations for the Earth-bound souls to realize how much they had left behind and recognize the great need for them to show respect for their creator and return to a state of God consciousness. Did they become disillusioned as their mission began to crumble as soul after soul made the decision to intermingle physically with the bodies of the lost souls they had come to rescue, and their once unified force disintegrated into fewer and smaller enclaves that held true to the original mission?

Did the righteous, joyous consciousness of hope and purpose descend into the consciousness of despair and defeat as their initial excitement faded in the face of reality? Did they feel remorse and sadness at their apparent failure to change the course of history? Did the souls and bodies of this original group eventually assimilate with the existing populations? Did many souls simply refrain from reincarnating after it became clear that there would be no quick resolution of the problem of lost souls? Perhaps some of the original group chose to continue to incarnate together at different periods of human history to rekindle and keep alive that initial hope in the hearts and minds of the souls that were trying to hearken to their message. They did not abandon the material-bound souls to their self-fulfilling fate, but continued their efforts to redirect the consciousness of material-minded men and women toward spiritual matters and to reawaken their awareness of their creator. According to the readings, some of the Atlantean Adamic souls entered the Earth in group incarnations in the earliest period of Egyptian history during the reign of Ra-Ta, in Persia at the time of Zoroaster, in Palestine during the appearance and activities of Jesus, in America in the early twentieth century in association with Edgar Cayce, as well as during other periods of history. But the greater hope for the spiritual restoration of incarnated souls still resides with Amilius, who was given the directive to subdue the Earth, mentally conquer the propensity of the soul to become trapped in materiality, and bring knowledge of the Way to restore God consciousness out of the quagmire of materialism and selfishness to the new human race (364-7_7; Genesis 1:28). We will see later why this directive to subdue the Earth was necessary, why it was so important, and how it relates to the mission of Amilius.

It took a long time, as man counts time, and many incarnations before the influence of the relatively small group of souls that came to the Earth to bring spiritual enlightenment would grow and become a serious contending force that could counter the self-centered consciousness and selfish activity of the multitude of trapped souls. That process is still ongoing today and modern history records when the teachings of Amilius gains ground and peace endures for a generation or two, and when those who still mentally embrace the rebellious mental state of the sons and daughters of Belial gain ground and discord and wars rage across the planet. The battle between good and evil is ongoing, not as some cosmic battle between God and some sinister demon called Satan, but within the mind of every soul-animated human. It is a battle between the lure of spiritual rebellion and self-gratification and the promise of peace and contentment that comes from seeking the higher spiritual calling to align the will of the soul with the Will of God. Where do we fit in this grand scheme of things? Will we choose to align our soul with God and thereby do our part in moving the human race toward more a perfect harmony with God, or will we continue to revel in spiritual ignorance and the selfish pleasures that attract a carnal conscious mind and leads to personal animosity, societal disharmony, wars, and continued separation from God?

The mission of the Adamic group of souls was to bring salvation to humanity, to help spiritually lost souls restore their relationship with God. It was not a successful mission if the expectation was a quick worldwide revival with multitudes of trapped souls declaring their allegiance to God, forgoing all selfish activities, and refraining from further entanglement in materiality. The mission might have been more effective if so many of the Adamic group had not succumbed to the temptations of materiality or perhaps the belief that they had a better plan than God. There is no reason to believe that all these souls failed in their mission, but the readings definitely indicate that many of these souls did fail. The lure of material self-indulgence is strong and difficult to resist. Many of the souls in the rescue team became enamored with and sexually entangled with the people they had come to rescue. This failure to hold true to the purpose of the mission is mentioned in the Bible and the readings as the fraternization between the Sons and Daughters of God (the group led by Amilius and their pure descendants) and the sons and daughters of Belial, which has been interpreted herein as soul-animated, biologically evolved Neanderthal and Early Modern *Homo sapiens* bodies. The mission now became more complicated and would take longer because of the inability of many of the souls in the rescue team to ignore and overcome the lure of the material world.

Souls would become symbiotic companions of Adamic biological bodies as they explored personal relationships that would expose their selfish tendencies and bring about suffering and tribulation when those forms of behavior were expressed (262-26_26). Souls jumped the gun and meddled in the evolutionary process before God had finished preparing the biological ecosystem and the specific biological form that would give them the best opportunity for mental-spiritual transformation, but God made a course correction and put things in order so that the process of soul restoration could begin in earnest. But what actually happens when a soul incarnates into a human body? How does the soul accomplish the deed, how does it affect the soul and why don't humans that are animated by souls have recollection of their soul mind, its broader memories, and the true nature of their soul? How can biological bodies help a soul recover God consciousness when the conscious mind that controls the body cannot even remember that it is part of a soul mind? Let's look at these questions and the concept of soul incarnation from the perspective of a human being immersed in modern society.

The Physical Consciousness
of the Incarnated Soul

For man was created a little bit higher than all the rest of the whole universe, and is capable of harnessing, directing, enforcing, the laws of the universe. (Edgar Cayce Reading 5-2_3)

The Department of Economic and Social Affairs of the United Nations published population estimates from 1950 to the present for 237 countries across the world and population projections to the year 2100. The 2023 worldwide births were estimated to be 134 million persons and worldwide deaths were estimated to be 61 million persons (United Nations, 2022). That means, on average, about 4.25 births occurred each second and about 1.93 deaths occurred each second of that year. Of the total worldwide births and deaths, more than a hundred million births and fifty million deaths were estimated to have occurred in Asia and Africa. Every live birth represents the entry of a soul into the world of materiality and human society (3744-5_47) and every death represents the passage of one soul from the world of materiality back into the spiritual realm (610-1_10), the natural environment of the soul. The total world population is about eight billion, which sets a lower limit on the number of souls that God created in his desire to find companionship, and it raises the unanswerable questions, "Why did God feel it necessary to create so many souls" and "How many of these souls will become eternal companions of God."

Souls must incarnate onto the Earth plane to begin or continue the process of atoning for their selfish and self-centered thoughts and behavior and, ideally, to repattern the mind into more spiritual avenues of thought and expression. Today, incarnated souls exclusively animate human bodies and use these bodies for spiritual development. Spirit supports the body by keeping it healthy and properly functioning, while the physical conscious mind of the soul infuses the body with intelligent activity and intentional experiences that can transform the soul mind and reawaken it to its spiritual roots. To be very clear, humans do not have souls, but souls animate human bodies through the process known as incarnation. The soul is central, the soul is fundamental, the soul is the higher-order creation, the soul is the true child of God, and the human body is only a tool, a biological organism used as a temporary vehicle to facilitate soul expression in the material world. Reincarnation is part of an ongoing process of soul restoration that uses interpersonal activity in a material world to correct the souls' penchant for self-indulgent and self-gratifying behavior and rectify their subsequent loss of God consciousness. Every human being represents a soul that has strayed from God consciousness and embraced an unhealthy sense of self, causing it to lose sight of its true destiny as a companion of God. Once a soul enters the Earth for the purpose of spiritual growth and development, it does not leave this sphere and move on to further spiritual activity until it has successfully completed its course of instruction and the intervening periods of practical application of spiritual principles (115-1_13; 441-1_3; 900-25_3). The minds of incarnated souls need to be spiritually rebalanced. Souls that have established mental patterns that intentionally or unintentionally focus on any of the many forms of self-glorification or self-gratification have abandoned God and have lost the awareness of their true spiritual origins as portions of God. These morally and spiritually deficient souls must reincarnate into materiality until those tendencies are purged from the soul mind (262-79_11; 262-81_13; 281-16_25). The movement of these souls is limited to the Earth, the nonmaterial borderland region, and the mental-spiritual training centers used for the education of the soul mind (2753-2; 2405-1). Souls that complete their training and prove that they have internalized the lessons by consistently expressing them as love toward God and their fellow souls in human society can decide to return to the Earth environment to continue aiding the souls that are still trapped in this realm (311-2_6; 900-25_3).

Incarnation from a Human Perspective

So, what happens when a soul incarnates into a human body and embarks upon a lifetime of new physical and mental experiences? First consider incarnation from the perspective of the physical realm and a pregnant mother in whose body the new life is forming. Conception initiates a series of events that starts with cell division. The pineal gland is formed in the early stages of fetal development and is instrumental in directing the development of the brain, neural ganglia, and hormone-producing glands of the fetus and in bringing the inherited genetic traits into the visible physical attributes of the forming body (294-141_6; 281-57_9). The pineal gland acts as a nucleation site around which the brain grows and its effect on the fetus can be influenced by the mental attitude of the mother throughout the period of gestation (281-53_8). Strong emotions such as love and anger, and ingested chemicals such as alcohol and drugs, leave their particular imprint on the mother's body, and their effect can be transmitted to the developing fetus. The attitude and intentions of the parents before conception can influence the character and spiritual disposition of the soul that is attracted to the developing fetus. The readings recommend that the mother consecrate herself and the unborn child to the service of God as part of the preparation for motherhood (5752-2_5). She endures morning sickness as a different mix of hormones flood into her blood stream and changes the chemical balance of her body. She senses the growth of the fetus within her womb over the next few months, feels the first stirring of activity of the developing fetus around five months after conception, and soon joyfully endures the occasional kick as the new body takes on a more human form and develops arms and legs. Parents and family eagerly await the time for birth of the child and dote over the tiny wet form after it is released from the mother's body to begin life independent from the protection and nourishment once provided by the mother.

During the years from infancy to childhood, the parents and family will tend to focus on the physical transformation of the growing human body and its mastery of bodily functions and new skills. The parents proudly watch their child become engaged in the physical world as it manipulates physical objects and learns the concept of three-dimensional space and applies that knowledge to more practical social activities such as taking its first steps and saying its first words. During the years from childhood to young adulthood, they are more likely to focus on the accompanying mental development as the child matures intellectually and makes its own decisions. Over the next decade or two, the family will watch the child grow physically into a young adult and mature mentally as it develops its own ideas about the world from its daily experiences. At some point in time it will decide to leave its parents to find its own place and role in the larger society of men and women that make up community and humanity. In the process of gaining independence, the young adult will make choices that will bring happiness and heartache to its parents. The new independence of the child's developing conscious mind will become increasing obvious during its teenage years when its decisions may begin to clash with the expectations of the parents. It is unlikely that the parents will seriously think of their child's achievements, talents and newly acquired independence as the material expressions of an unfolding physical consciousness that is a portion of a more extensive and complex soul consciousness that is seeking its destiny through material activity.

Incarnation from a Soul Perspective

What does the birth of their child look like from the perspective of the spiritual realm where the soul resides, and how does the infinite soul become part of the finite human child? The soul begins its search for a new temporary home by looking for or sensing a female body in which conception has sparked the process of cell division that initiates the formation of a fetus. It may have a fairly definite idea in mind as to the best home-life situation as part of an inner spiritual urge rather than a visual perusal and logical analysis of the potential candidates. It usually does not scour the world for an appropriate body, but because of past lives and spiritual needs, it may be drawn to a specific region, society, and possibly even family. The mental and spiritual attitude of the parents and the circumstances under which conception occurred can influence which soul is attracted (457-10_15; 457-10_18). The material, mental, and spiritual desires that the parents hold during conception and gestation can draw the soul to a family (281-53_9) and even influence the sex of the infant (780-5_4; 281-55_9). Many souls incarnate in groups because they are dealing with unresolved emotional and relational issues that involve other specific souls, especially the parents and siblings in a family group. The desires and purposes that guided the parents during their own incarnations and their personal spiritual journey will impact the life of the child during its formative years. The life of the child will become entangled with the life of its parents, the primary moral and spiritual influence, for good or bad, in the early years of the maturing child (281-54_11).

The soul may observe the developing fetus, especially with regard to the pineal gland that forms early and directs the ongoing growth of the brain's neural system; the musculature arrangement; the vascular system; the bones that bring structure and form to the body; and the organs that will give the body the ability to ingest, digest, assimilate and eliminate the food that will be needed to nourish the body after birth. The soul mind may monitor these fetal changes and may possibly influence the fetus's development in a limited manner through the pineal gland, but the actual incarnation will not take place until the infant has been born and is physically separated from the mother's body. The soul mind typically takes control of the infant body within minutes or hours of the birth and in some instances a short while before the birth (457-10_16; 2390-2_26; 538-30_13). The incarnation is physically associated with the first breath of the infant and is symbolically associated with the breath of life that made Adam a living soul (Genesis 2:7 KJV). Biological cellular function alone does not impart life to a newborn infant, but it can survive biologically for a brief interval on residual nourishment received from the mother. If the soul delays taking possession of the newborn body, the Spirit of God that activates every biological cell keeps the body alive temporarily until the soul takes full control of the physiological processes of the body (2390-2_27). The soul controls the process of bringing a unified consciousness to the body after it is born. The soul will coordinate the biological functions needed for sustained life as it merges with the sensory and hormonal network of the infant body and takes control of the somatic and autonomic functions of the body (281-53_9). The infant is then able to live an independent life. This union of soul and body is referred to in the readings and Scripture in terms such as "the breath of life" and "becoming a living soul" (3744-5_47; 5749-7_23; Genesis 2:7), to convey the idea that human flesh is not truly alive until it has been quickened by the activity of a soul.

The soul cannot take control of the fetus during the pregnancy because it would compete with, and be in conflict with, the soul of the mother that is carrying the fetus. Two souls cannot control the same unborn fetus. The incoming soul would not be able to control the immature biological organs necessary to produce the blood supply, or grow the assimilation, digestion, and elimination organs needed for proper nourishment at birth. Until the infant is born and capable of surviving on its own, it is a portion of the mother's body, just like any other major organ of the mother's body. The incoming soul may, and often does, hover around the fetus and monitor its progress through tenuous connections until the infant is born and the soul makes a secure and unbroken mental link with the body for the duration of the life of the newborn human. If for some reason the soul decides to reject the body, it will become a stillborn infant, physically viable with all of the biological activity of a normal infant, but unable to survive because it lacks the necessary spark of life given by the presence of a soul mind (281-53_9). The readings mention one soul that entered a newborn infant mainly because of the spiritually oriented hopes and dreams of the mother, but within a few hours changed its mind and left the infant body because the father had been in a drunken rage the evening of the birth. This descent of the father into bouts of inebriation violated a previous agreement between the incoming soul and the soul of the father that it would refrain from drinking alcohol during its incarnation. The incoming soul previously had unpleasant life experiences with the soul of the alcoholic father and refused to become trapped in that type of environment again (2390-2_8; Kirkpatrick, 2001).

The physical structure of the fetus is built from the genetic code contained within a new DNA strand formed from the merger of the DNA of the father and mother. The incoming soul typically does not manipulate the physical characteristics of the new body by influencing or interfering with the bodily functions of the mother or by direct influence from the spiritual realm. However, the physical features of the new body approximate those that the soul needs and can work with during its incarnation for the lifespan of that body. The soul does not choose an available body at random, nor does it meet people entirely at random during its incarnation. It selects a body that has the greatest potential to fulfill its spiritual needs based upon the familial and societal human interactions that it will potentially encounter. A soul does not have a gender but must choose the appropriate body gender that best meets its current spiritual needs. It will also select the cultural and racial environment in which it is born (136-27_13; 294-189_4). Sometimes the soul may be directed to a particular mother to meet a specific need as an urge driven by spiritual law influences the decision of the soul. Other considerations include the physical environment in which it will spend its childhood and the inherited biological traits and physical health of the child. All these factors work together to provide an opportunity for the soul to correct one or more spiritual deficiencies or shortcomings that it has brought upon itself by elevating its sense of self and selfishness and turning away from God.

The process of incarnating, mentally connecting to an infant body, must be exciting but also somewhat scary for the soul. In the moment the soul takes possession of the body, the awareness of the soul mind shifts toward the material world. It shrinks from what was near infinite awareness to a narrow finite awareness concentrating on the stream of incoming sensual data being transmitted from the skin, ears, tongue, nose, and eyes of the infant body. It will begin the process of developing what we call the human mind, but which is really the physical conscious aspect of the soul mind. The soul does not move from the spiritual realm and flood the infant body with its essence. It does not saturate every tissue and organ of the body. The soul remains in the spiritual realm, and a portion of the mind of the soul makes contact with the specific neural and hormonal centers within the body that will allow it to receive the sensory information being transmitted through the neural network and activate various muscles and organs of the body for movement and bodily health. The major contact centers are the cells of Leydig, the gonads, and the adrenal, thymus, thyroid, pineal, and pituitary glands, with the balance of activity between the cells of Leydig and the pineal being of great importance to the spiritual inclination and advancement of the incarnated soul. The idea that these centers of hormonal and neurological activity are used by souls to interface with a human body is also part of the belief system associated with yogic practices, which are mentioned in the readings as a beneficial form of exercise for the body and mind (Avalon, 1974; Iyengar, 1979).

The Physical Conscious Mind

The nature of the soul mind was previously established as a single mental unit that has two basic aspects: the subconscious mind and the super conscious mind. The subconscious mind is that portion that controls the normal functioning of the soul in its natural nonphysical environment where it interacts directly with other souls through the movement of the soul body and through mind-to-mind communication. It is the center of the soul's sense of Self and the individuality that distinguishes and separates the soul from its many siblings. It is that aspect of the soul mind that makes it unique in the world of souls. The subconscious mind stores the memories of the soul and serves as the analytical tool that permits the soul to establish and comprehend its independence from its creator and assess its relationship with its creator and fellow souls. The super conscious mind is the mental bridge that connects the subconscious mind to the Mind of God. It can be an active source of spiritual vitality and mental support to the soul but only when the soul desires to remain aware of its creator and makes the mental effort to keep those lines of spiritual communication open. The strength of the mental union between a soul and God, the quality of the soul's mental awareness of its maker, directly impacts the flow and quality of spiritual sustenance a soul receives through the super conscious link from the Mind of its Creator. The strength of the rapport and comradeship between the soul and God determines the extent to which the subconscious mind can incorporate spiritual principles into the soul and the strength of its inclination to manifest those principles in its activities.

When a soul incarnates, the mental perception of the soul mind narrows as it is compelled to focus its attention on the sensory stimuli experienced by the infant body, the coordination of the body's physical functions, and the training of the body's muscles by electrical stimuli sent from the brain. As the soul organizes and processes sensory data, a physical conscious mind is formed and the seat of awareness of the soul shifts away from the fullness of the subconscious mind with its individuality and knowledge of the cosmic realm and previous life experiences. The physical conscious mind will become the center of awareness of the soul when the human body is in its waking state and makes the incarnated soul unique in the world of human beings. It will be the mental bridge between the subconscious mind of the soul and the physical world of matter and energy, and it will be used to project the desires of the soul into the physical world. This triune conception of the mind of an incarnated soul is not intended to mean that the soul mind is divisible—only that the focal point of the soul attention can be different in different circumstances and surroundings, and when different intentions are expressed by the soul. The physical actions taken by the conscious mind in relation to the soul's veiled inner spiritual awareness is important to the spiritual progression or regression of the soul (262-10_6). The subconscious mind also participates in the process of animating a human body. It monitors and controls some of the basic physiological functions of human life, such as heartbeat, respiration, digestion, and elimination via the autonomic nervous system (3744-1_54; 4208-1_1). The neural system of the human body is influenced by the forces of the physical conscious mind, the forces of the subconscious mind, and the forces of the super conscious mind in accordance with the needs of the body and the spiritual attunement of the soul. We will look at some of these forces in subsequent chapters.

The working hypothesis of most neurobiologists is that consciousness is basically a neural electrical phenomenon arising out of a complex interaction of genetics and biological function, the type of sensory information extracted from the environment, and accumulated physical and social experiences. The rapid expansion of the number of neurons and associated synaptic junctions in an infant's brain are idea conditions for the emergence of a conscious mind, and the analysis of acquired knowledge and accumulation of memories leads to the formation of physical consciousness. The readings disagree with the scientific community with respect to the idea that the mind arises out of the collective neural electrical impulses of a brain, but are generally consistent with the idea that physical consciousness is the interaction of the mind and environment. The readings are adamant that what we call the human mind is an aspect of a soul that preceded the body, and that physical consciousness and life experiences are part of the process of spiritual growth. Consciousness evolves gradually and is unique to each individual because every collection of life experiences and interpersonal interactions is unique, but it is also an outgrowth of the existing consciousness of the soul. The metaphor "drinking from a fire hose" seems appropriate to describe what the soul mind experiences in the first moments after incarnation. The flood of sensory data, while necessary for the long-term well-being of the soul and the body it animates, diminishes awareness of the inner stream of spiritual nourishment that God wants to bestow upon the soul. In the coming years, the soul will learn how to filter the data stream so as to ignore those portions of the data that are not really necessary for the moment to prevent inundation of the mental faculties or saturation of the new conscious mind. The soul must create a new identity for the duration of the incarnation. From the human viewpoint, the consciousness of each individual appears to be completely self-contained and isolated from all other expressions of consciousness with no roots in or connection to any other forms of consciousness. The readings ascribe this apparently independent self-existence to the mental veil that descends between the subconscious mind of the soul and the newly developing physical conscious mind of the infant.

At the moment of incarnation, what we think of as the nascent human mind—which is actually the budding physical conscious mind of the incarnated soul—is truly a tabula rasa, a blank slate to be filled by new experiences. The brains of newborn babies are receptive to the sensory organs of the body. From the first moment of incarnation, the infant will begin collecting and sorting a rich stream of new information and experiences. It will detect environmental changes, discomforts (cold and heat), and bodily needs (hunger and discomfort) but will be unable to put those sensory experiences into the context of immersion in a physical environment of three-dimensional objects and relative motion. Emotions and sensations related to physical discomfort or pleasure are not clearly connected to the environmental sources of those feelings and are not analyzed or examined for meaning or significance. The consciousness and future knowledge base of the incarnated soul will primarily come from its analysis and perception of these sensory experiences. Sensory information is first simply stored and catalogued until the developing brain and mind are capable of comparing the different experiences and feelings and are able to build images and ideas relating to the outer world of phenomenon. Reasoning and experimentation in relation to muscle movement directed toward such basic tasks as reaching, clutching, touching, and tasting provide information that the brain and mind needs to correlate and coordinate various physical activities. The rapid formation of new synapses between neurons and the growth of the prefrontal cortex support and strengthen the storage of memories and the more advanced cognitive functions needed for learning. There may be a feedback mechanism whereby loving, nurturing experiences that promote emotional stability influence the expression of different genes that influence brain development. Infants experience the first stages of physical awareness, but generally, their self-awareness is rudimentary and not continuous in time. Not until about eighteen months are infants able to recognize their own image in a mirror, which is an indication that they are developing awareness of themselves as an independent being separate from their environment. Infants spend the majority of their time exploring their environment through sensory perception, but at some point in their development begin to entertain more abstract thoughts, a basic sense of time, and the first use of words to express desires to others. These more abstract ideas are likely to lead the infant toward the concept of self and perhaps toward the expression of selfishness. Scientists describe infancy as a period of brain plasticity, when it is easier to absorb new ideas and formulate new concepts of life.

As an infant develops toward childhood, the emergence of language is believed to greatly accelerate the development of consciousness and its transition from an immature to a mature human. Language influences the ability to self-reflect and helps build the reasoning ability of the brain. There are indications that bi-lingual children have an advantage in cognitive development, such as problem solving. The outward verbal expression of language is also associated with the ability to talk through life issues and problems silently within the mind, which allows children to better order their thoughts to guide their actions. Thoughts are typically more self-centered in the early stages of consciousness, in that children focus on their immediate needs and desires, but their thought patterns gradually mature to include concern for the feelings and needs of those around them. The awareness and comprehension of external surroundings leads to a better understanding of the passage of time, including the concepts of past and future. The child builds more refined social skills as it interacts with family and community in new and more demanding ways. Childhood is a period of imaginative thinking characterized by role playing, pretending to be someone else, or constructing alternate exciting worlds and taking on the starring role in those worlds. There is a broad range of outcomes that can exhibit during this interval of an increasing sense of self-awareness. It can lead the child into introverted feelings and the desire to withdraw from group activity or into extroverted feelings that can bring about the desire to inject itself more forcefully into group activity. There are intense cultural influences also at work on the child. Different cultures can impress different values on the maturing mind, like cooperation versus independence, which can foster suspicion and intolerance between peoples. As a wider variety of experiences is cataloged and the memory base expands, a more coherent self-identity develops that persists into the future years. Some psychologists have speculated that during the period from age two to age six—with its rapid development of the hippocampus, critical to the formation of long-tern memory—the mind is more receptive to non-sensory information derived from dreams and imagination. They are beginning to study how sleep and dreams might influence memory retention and the formation of identity. Children between ages two to four may be more likely to have vivid dreams and memories that have the appearance of past-life experiences. These inner mental experiences generally fade when the child becomes more deeply immersed in its culture and engages in more intense interpersonal activity, such as that usually associated with entering school. Children are more likely to talk about memories they believe are past-life related when the culture and family are receptive to the concept of reincarnation, but the lack of this receptivity does not always prevent children from speaking out strongly about their belief in a past life.

Dr. Ian Stevenson (1918-2007), founder and former director of the University of Virginia School of Medicine, Division of Perceptual Studies, spent decades scouring the world for children who claimed to remember previous lives and were able to divulge the names of specific places and individuals that could be used to support their claims. Almost all these cases involved children between the ages of two to six years. Dr. Stevenson was able to study about three thousand cases of possible reincarnation, many of which offered the opportunity to investigate the claimed location, names, and personal characteristics of previous relatives, many of which were still living. Some of his most intriguing reincarnation cases involve the apparent transfer of mental trauma suffered during violent death or physical abuse to the physical features of the body that it was seeking to occupy (Stevenson, 1997; Pasricha and others, 2005). Under some circum- stances, soul minds apparently can alter the physical features of a child during the most formative periods of fetal development or upon taking possession of the infant. He investigated 225 instances of reincarnation where birthmarks, physical abnormalities and defects, and even missing limbs in children corresponded to bodily damage received in a previous incarnation just before death or as the cause of death. These childhood memories and visible occurrences of biological defects and deformities support claims of previous lives and provide strong circumstantial evi- dence that confirms the historical events related to the previous death experienced by the subject. They appear to demonstrate the ability of the soul mind to directly influence and transfer previous mental trauma to a new human body and seem to support the idea that a soul mind can directly influence the physical development of a fetus or the newborn infant. The readings suggest that this physical expression of mental trauma may be transferred to the new body through the activity of the pineal gland (263-13_10-11; 294-141_6).

By the time a child is maturing into adolescence, its sense of self identity begins to surface and becomes apparent in its activities. The maturing prefrontal cortex brings about an increasing ability to make decisions and choices, and a better understanding of moral concepts, including how morality relates to fair play and respect for other children. This leads to a better self-understanding of the young person's emotions in relation to interpersonal experiences and ability to analyze those experiences in relation to the personalities of its peers. The intellectual reasoning ability of the conscious mind matures as the soul interacts with its physical environment and navigates the mental and emotional challenges a young human faces in human relationships. The associated personality of the young person develops into the unique temperament that he or she wants to use to project character, beliefs, values, and emotional responses into society. It is a period of exploration and use of imagination, and the building of thought patterns that lead to a clearer distinction between the inner play world and the outer world of society and family. Children begin the process of introspection and questioning of their nature and thoughts. Educational opportunities have a profound impact on childhood development through reading comprehension, expression in writing, and learning to converse and express ideas. Education also bring a notable increase in attention span. In the later adolescent years, the increasing ability to control the body muscles results in more graceful movements. The child also usually becomes more proficient at inhibiting negative impulses that can lead to trouble with friends and family. As the child grows toward adulthood it develops the capacity for more abstract thinking and long-term planning that will be useful when the adolescent leaves the protection of the family and makes its way into the larger society. The ability to plan for the future has by now evolved from a limited ability to understand unfolding events to the consideration of life from several different less self-serving perspectives and even to more abstract thinking about moral concepts and personal identity as it relates to society. Many teenagers spend more time reflecting on the meaning of life and death and more thought about the future and their possible greater role in society as their career and educational choices become important considerations

The succession of personal encounters and sensory experiences a person has experienced as an infant, child, and adolescent greatly increases the complexity and depth of his or her physical consciousness and intelligence. The transition from adolescence to adulthood is characterized by a longer attention span and a more well-developed memory. There is less willingness to leave old habits and beliefs, as they become more ingrained and fixed in the belief system that has evolved during the previous decade. New ideas are more likely to be viewed within the context of previous life experiences and previously accepted ideas. The mature mind usually has better control over emotions and is able to evaluate different opportunities in life as they pertain to talents that have been identified and the urge to express them. There is more introspection associated with the development of long-term goals, and a greater realization and acceptance that people are different, have different ideas and sense of right and wrong, and see life from entirely different perspectives. With a more focused consciousness, young adults are able to accept life as it is and work within its limits rather than wanting to change it according to idealistic principles. They are less distracted by less important external events that are mostly uncontrollable, and usually don't let themselves be easily distracted from the life goals they have set. They may be better able to express sympathy and empathy and share emotional experiences with friends and family. Early adulthood can also be a time of a deep inner search for the meaning of life that involves the concept of an afterlife and the exploration of religion or spirituality to find that meaning in material existence. The later stages of human life bring a variety of mental and physical experiences and multiple opportunities for the soul to manifest the strength and quality of its spiritual attunement with God, which is one facet of the spiritually focused cosmic evolution and expansion of the subconscious mind of the soul.

The readings place considerable importance on the nature of the environment and the type of training received as a child grows from infancy through adulthood. The behavioral changes that accompany the growth of a human child mainly result from the development and expansion as described above, but the readings also emphasize that there is some supervision of the conscious mind by the will of the soul. If the soul lets the mind become enamored with materiality and self-gratification or embraces selfishness instead of service, if it chooses to respond to others by using expressions of anger and greed and foments discord and strife in its relationships, then the soul is driven away from God. It will see the results of its ungodly activity in the lives that unfold before it. It will also see the negative results of previous life decisions playing out through its life, but may have a difficult time realizing that these seemingly external problems are self-created, and not entirely the result of outside societal forces. Selfish souls that refuse to seek their spiritual purpose in life will project the qualities once associated with the sons of Belial. On the other hand, if the incarnated soul seeks and is receptive to the inner voice of spiritual guidance and expresses its human behavior in a godly manner consistent with the inherent soul qualities of love, kindness, patience, and mercy, then it will have chosen to be a Son of God on the earth (3376-2_9; 5753-1_22).

The physical consciousness of the incarnated soul is limited and unique. It is limited, shallow, and narrow in breadth as compared to the awareness of the subconscious mind because it is constructed almost entirely from sensory information channeled from the surface of a human body to the human brain. From the moment of incarnation, the soul is required to control the body it animates, build an image of the physical environment that surrounds the body, and make decisions about how to respond to that environment. From that information, especially as it relates to the souls that constitute human society, it has to construct a new conscious mind and new personality to use for the duration of its incarnation. Much of the information it uses to build this new reality comes from its responses to the behavior of other incarnated souls, the good or bad actions it directs toward other incarnated souls, and the loving or hateful words it uses to communicate with other incarnated souls. The mature conscious mind of every incarnated soul is different because all of the events experienced and compiled by the soul as the body transitions from infancy to old age are unique to that soul. The accumulated mental storehouse of facts, the truths it learns, the fiction and lies perpetrated by others and self, and the emotional response of the soul to this wide variety of information are the bricks used in the self-constructed reality of each conscious mind.

The awareness of the conscious mind constantly shifts as it perceives and interprets the daily flood of sensory information, organizes the data to develop an image of the current environment surrounding the body, and studies the relation between various ongoing events within its immediate surroundings. The flood of incoming sensory data keeps the conscious mind active, growing, and changing, and also keeps the soul mind mentally tethered to the physical world. To make sense of the physical environment, the conscious mind must detect the movement of objects within its immediate surroundings and compare the most recently acquired information with previously received information. It is constantly learning to assess its environment to make decisions and choices about such things as the next movement the body should make as an appropriate response to external stimuli, the speech that the body should utter in response to a question, the action it should take to protect the body or to help another person, and a myriad of other situations that arise every day. This conscious mental activity takes place during the waking state of the body, when the sensory organs are being actively monitored. The rise of the information age with its movies, sitcoms, computers, mobile phones, social-media platforms, and the many almost-real-time news outlets are challenging for the conscious mind to absorb and process. This purely physical data stream can capture the attention of the soul mind to the extent that the flow of spiritual sustenance to the soul through the super conscious mind is ignored or reduced to a trickle.

Through a Glass Darkly

For most people, the conscious mind is largely isolated from the greater body of information, experiences, conclusions, and previous failures and successes held in the subconscious mind. What is the cause and purpose of severing the present conscious mind of the individual from the previous mental knowledge relating to its past history and all that it has learned in previous incarnations and past nonphysical experiences? Why is a veil put up between the subconscious mind of the soul and the newly forming conscious mind, causing the soul mind to basically start over and build another consciousness from scratch with what appears to be little or no benefit from its previous experiences, knowledge, or memories? Is it simply to satisfy the need for the mind to intently focus on the material world and acquire an attachment to the sensory system of the body? We will find that this separation of conscious mind from the subconscious mind is a fundamental and necessary aspect of incarnation that ultimately contributes to soul growth. We will also recognize that there is sufficient continuity of consciousness across the veil so that, at some level of awareness, the conscious mind remembers its purpose for incarnation and understands that this life should be used primarily as a period of physical activity for spiritual development rather than as an opportunity to enjoy sensual physical experiences. The soul probably would not be able to focus on the particular spiritual problems to be addressed during its present incarnation if it knew all of its deeds and misdeeds in every previous incarnation and in the nonmaterial realm. This would likely distract the soul mind and perhaps weigh it down with the guilt of previous actions. Each incarnation allows the soul to focus on a specific weakness or set of weaknesses of the soul mind on which the soul needs to concentrate for maximum spiritual benefit. The soul can best approach its rehabilitation by addressing spiritual issues in manageable bites. The specific spiritual weaknesses faced in this life likely will have been the subject of training in the dimensional planetary realms before incarnation. The current life is an opportunity to demonstrate the level of understanding the soul gained during that training and the degree to which it became integrated into the soul mind. This immersion of a soul in the material world is where the rubber meets the road. It is where God learns if the spiritual training has been effective, whether it has formed deep roots or is superficial. It reveals whether or not the soul has made a conscious decision to restore its relationship with God.

Much of the information the soul receives from the physical world is mundane and pertains to the necessary daily care and feeding of the body to keep it healthy, but some of it is of great value to the mental and spiritual future of the soul. The thoughts that arise in the conscious mind and that gestate into feasible ideas are projected or transmitted into the physical world through muscle movement in the human body. The interaction might take the form of pushing pedals and pulling levers to operate a mechanical device, rearranging the environment around the body for increased comfort or entertainment, or using the human voice to directly communicate with another human being. The exchange of words and actions between or among humans is particularly important to the soul and often bears directly upon the reason that the soul was incarnated. The manner in which the soul responds to material trials and temptations will determine its progress or lack of progress on the long road to spiritual restoration and release of all selfish tendencies. The incarnated soul always has the option to look to God or materiality for mental nourishment and pleasure, and its choices in the matter substantially impact its current circumstances and immediate future.

The activity and words of each human being are a physical manifestation of the thoughts of one individualized portion of God, one soul that represents the smallest viable individual unit of Creative Force guided by an independent will. Human beings can come to the realization that there is more to being human than being a complex biological organism with a conscious mind that has physical drives and desires. An incarnated soul that cannot conceive of itself as a spiritual creature first and a physical creature in passing is doomed to remain focused on and attached to selfishness and materiality, whether that be in the form of power over other humans; desire for material wealth and the temporary tangible goods that can be acquired and accumulated by wealth; or the craving for self-gratification through sexual encounters, mind-altering drugs, fantasy, and escapism. All of these activities can and often do strengthen the sense of self and selfishness in the individual at the expense of activities that strengthen awareness of the need to manifest loving service to other persons. When unspiritual physical activities are excessively pursued, they make it more difficult for the soul to become aware of its true spiritual identity and trap it in cycles of material experiences that further separate the soul mind from God, causing it to lose its ability to perceive and communicate with its creator (816-10_19).

It is natural for the incarnated soul to identify with the human body, but it is spiritually dangerous for the soul to forget its true identity as an independent portion of God made in the image of God for the purpose of companionship with God. We will find that the conscious mind is not really left totally to itself as it learns once again how to manipulate a human body and interact with its environment and fellow souls in its family and community. From the perspective of a human interacting with the biological world and human society, we feel that our actions are totally directed by our conscious mind. We don't recall that our conscious mind is only one facet of the overall soul mind. Our intense focus on the neural information that transmits news of our surrounding environment can cause us to become so mentally attached to the material world that we forget to make an effort to seek out and explore the other aspects of our mind. We form a material-oriented mind, and it takes effort and intentional focus to peek behind the veil and discern the other world that exists beyond the demands and clutter of our conscious mind. We usually ignore or fail to pursue the still small voice within (1 Kings 19:11-13) and the spiritual message it can bring to us in favor of the exciting clamor and cacophony of the much louder voices from without. Let's take a quick look at the mental forces operating behind the veil and the ways in which we sometimes become aware of them.

Consciousness and the Sixth Sense

The sixth sense is not a well-defined and accepted psychological term but is used informally and loosely to refer to the ability of a person to perceive or understand something without the use of the five physical senses (sight, hearing, taste, smell, and touch). Extrasensory perception is generally not considered a valid phenomenon by scientists, and is not considered a proper scientific field of study, partly because of skepticism in the scientific community but primarily because there is a dearth of repeatable scientific evidence to conclusively demonstrate its validity. Attempts to prove the existence of extrasensory perception have invariably been stymied by the inability of those who claim to have experienced or observed the phenomena to provide repeatable and verifiable empirical physical evidence for its existence. The boundaries of science are restricted to the ability to prove or disprove a hypothesis or theory by experimental evidence, and rightfully so, because the scientific method allows the truth of the laws of the physical universe to be separated from conjecture and speculation. Even researchers in the mental medical fields of psychology and psychiatry generally focus on more traditional areas of investigation like cognition (the acquisition of knowledge and understanding through thought, experience, and the five physical senses) and consciousness (the mental awareness and perception of thoughts and feelings, memories, and the environment surrounding the body from sensory information).

A question posed to Cayce about the nature of the sleep state and the sixth sense led to a discourse on the relation between the conscious mind and subconscious mind of an incarnated soul and the interaction between the soul personality and individuality (5754-1; 5754-2; 5754-3). The readings make it a point to emphasize that the sixth sense is not the soul, not the conscious mind, and not the subconscious mind. It is a force associated with and arising out of the accumulated material and nonmaterial experiences in which the soul has been involved as it passed through various realms. The experiences the soul has gained in nonphysical realms are just as important as those it has encountered in the Earth plane. The soul animates a physical body and so develops a conscious mind, but the sixth sense is a separate emanation of forces related to the activities of the soul in relation to its spiritual attunement. It is a force of experience in relation to the soul's fellowship with God (5754-2_12). The most important sixth-sense influences transmitted into the conscious mind and life of an incarnated soul are cumulative emotional urges arising from past-life opportunities to make better moral choices, intellectual urges from mental-spiritual training to repattern the mind to God consciousness, and spiritual urges from a loving God encouraging us to seek communion and companionship with him. The term "sixth sense" may be thought of as including influences that are variously described as conscience, intuition, so-called astrological urges, dreams, and visions. There appears to be no sharp division or distinction between these various forces, but each of them refers to a slightly different method by which the conscious mind can be influenced through the activity of the subconscious mind and the will of the soul.

The availability of the subconscious mind as a hidden mentor to the error-prone conscious mind may be a comforting idea, but the subconscious mind and its associated individuality can be out of sync with the spiritual sustenance that is available through God consciousness. In that case, it may not be a true spiritual advisor and not particularly effective in leading the soul toward greater spiritual development and enlightenment. The subconscious mind receives its spiritual nourishment from the super conscious mind when it uses, acknowledges, and retains the spiritual guidance that is always available and accessible through this portion of the soul mind that links the soul and the Almighty creator. The soul grows spiritually only to the extent that it keeps that channel of communication open, purges all selfish tendencies out of its individuality, and replaces them with selfless modes of thought and activity. In the physical realm, the incarnated soul must guide the physical consciousness to alter its material expressions to better reflect that deeper spiritual insight during its daily physical activities. As the subconscious mind becomes more spiritual and more spiritually attuned and more selfless and more oriented toward glorifying God, the conscious mind is able to better receive guidance as to how it can best approach the life situations with which it contends and the choices that it has to make. The subconscious mind then becomes the spiritual mentor and consultant to the conscious mind and the human personality takes on more of the spiritual characteristics of the soul individuality.

Conscience and Intuition: Knowledge from Within

The conscience typically is active during the waking hours of the conscious mind. The sense of conscience comes from deep within the soul mind and makes itself known as a feeling that nags the conscious mind when the behavior of the body violates the accepted norms established in the subconscious mind. It is a force that makes itself known when the soul mind compares the decisions of the conscious mind as manifested in the present activity of the body with the principles of morality and spirituality that the soul inherently knows it needs to manifest in materiality to fulfill its purpose for incarnation. The mature conscious mind and personality of the incarnated soul are continually urged to set ideals and manifest thoughts that will fulfill the inner spiritual desires of the soul and will bring the conscious mind to the place where it feels most comfortable. If the soul has determined that the physical sensory stimuli that it samples daily or the feeling gained by exerting personal power over others or disrespecting of the rights of others holds the greater attraction, it will pursue those pleasurable moments repeatedly, like a drug addict seeking the next fix. When the actions of the conscious mind and the body repeatedly violate or belittle spiritual principles held in the super conscious mind, there can be a persistent feeling within the conscious mind of something wrong, a sense of guilt, and a sense of knowing innately that the will and mind just participated in an activity or event that violated the innate moral and spiritual goals of the soul. The feelings of disquiet and uneasiness that arise in the conscious mind are a reminder that there is a better way to behave and that its current thoughts and activities do not please God, will not contribute to the redemption of the soul, and do not fulfill the soul's purpose on the Earth.

Probably every person has at some time or another been warned by an inner sense of conviction, their inner conscience, when their daily actions are deviating from the higher sense of morality that would be more appropriate for a child of God. This conscience may be insistent and frequent or weak and infrequent, depending upon the spiritual ideals that are held dear within the soul mind. These warning messages are generated for the benefit of the conscious mind, to help the soul make better life decisions and to let it know when it is going down the wrong path, but these warnings can be drowned out, suppressed, or prevented from reaching the conscious mind because the will has consistently decided to override the conscience, has made too many wrong choices, and has become too attached to the pleasures of the physical world. The problem is that far too many souls are too strongly attached to the sensory input from the conscious mind and cannot hear or choose to ignore the good advice that comes from a subconscious mind attuned to the voice of God (5754-3_7).

Intuition is defined by psychologists as the ability to gain knowledge without the benefit of or interference from logic or rational thinking, without using the reasoning power of the conscious mind. At times it seems to be a form of understanding that transcends the acquisition of knowledge by the physical conscious mind because it comes from a source beyond the physical realm. It is a natural part of human cognition that is especially helpful in solving complex problems and in interpreting the subtleties of human relationships. Although its depth and breadth and limitations are not well understood, it is known that intuition is not a more accurate cognitive process than deductive or inductive reasoning. In general, intuition is not infallible and cannot always be relied upon to arrive at truth. This may be indicative of poor spiritual attunement. Intuition often expresses itself through internal feelings that direct the individual toward certain modes of behavior or influence it to react or act in certain ways when interacting with other individuals. It can make itself known as a hunch, an idea of what to do without the conscious mind having previously compiled information on the topic or attempted to make a decision based upon analysis of the existing data. Sometimes intuition brings closure with respect to a difficult and complex problem that the conscious mind has been mulling over without arriving at a solution. Often the individual will set that information aside, intending to come back to it later without realizing that the subconscious mind may be continuing to analyze the data.

Intuition can make itself known as a momentary insight or flash of unexpected knowledge about a problem without the individual making a conscious effort to solve the problem. The subconscious mind may have arrived at a conclusion or solution without the conscious mind being aware of the intellectual activity that has gone on behind the veil until that conclusion is projected into the conscious mind as an intuitive feeling or a eureka moment (357-2_13). Intuitive advice may take the form of an inner voice during daily activity or make its appearance as the body awakens from sleep in the morning. Several successful inventors, scientists, and businessmen have credited intuition with a role in their ability to come up with new ideas. They may intentionally alternate a comprehensive study of a problem with a period of time in which they set aside the conscious attempt to come to a solution and let their subconscious mind work on it. Intuition can appear as a positive or negative feeling about an individual that the person has just met or a journey on which the person is about to embark. The feeling may be presented to the conscious mind as a reminder that the soul knows an individual from a previous encounter. It may be pleasant and comforting, reflecting the many good experiences that the soul has had with the individual, perhaps indicating a loving familial relationship. It may be a suspicion or a warning, a premonition to the conscious mind about becoming involved with a certain individual. This knowledge, embedded in the depths of the subconscious mind, is usually more readily available to a receptive conscious mind, a mind that accepts the possibility of its existence. These subtle hints and clues about interpersonal relationships become stronger and more readily available to the conscious mind as the mind seeks and listens for these moments of spiritual guidance (792-2-18).

To a question that was asked about how to train intuition, the readings compared the harnessing of intuition to the harnessing of electricity, or more accurately compared the training of intuition to the training of electricity (255-12_10). It is not a matter of training one's intuition but is more a matter of keeping the conscious mind focused on the higher purposes that are set before the soul as part of its incarnation. We are more receptive to intuition when we prevent our soul mind from getting sidetracked by the various attractions and sensual experiences that can be had in the material world. The soul cannot be infatuated with materialism and also be receptive to the presence of the intuitive force. An intuitive mind will be more attuned to the celestial forces that are available through a spiritually oriented consciousness and less attuned to the earthly forces that are commonly experienced and cataloged through the senses of the body by a materially oriented consciousness. The gift of access to the intuitive forces is a gift granted by God as a consequence of a spiritual law that holds true for every incarnated soul. The ability of the conscious mind to protect itself from seemingly overwhelming material temptations and distance itself from the desire for excessive self-gratifying material stimulation earns the mind the reward of access to the natural psychic forces of the soul (255-12_10). It may take years and multiple lifetimes for an incarnated soul to become more intuitive, remain in closer communication with the inner intuitive forces, and better able to rely on intuition to guide the decision-making process of the conscious mind. This communion with the inner mind can be made more dependable as the will intentionally and actively draws the conscious mind closer to the spiritual aspects of personal relationships and teaches it to listen to intuitive guidance to help it through stressful physical circumstances. The constant and repeated effort of the conscious mind to radiate spiritual goodness in the form of love and service to others will cause it to be more receptive to the force of intuition and will allow the force to become more readily recognized and more easily brought to the attention of the conscious mind (412-5_8).

The spiritual force of intuition normally is expressed or manifested in the female more often than it is in the male (262-20_7). This has to do with the emotional forces that are more commonly expressed through the female disposition than through the rational temperament of the male. An individual can try to develop or enhance intuition and other psychic abilities using creative forces that are brought into activity by prayer and meditation, but they should understand that there also is danger in taking that path. If the development of psychic forces is pursued before the soul mind has first grounded itself through a closer spiritual attunement with the creator, there is the possibility that the forces it unleashes may lead the soul to its own destruction. The individual who focuses on spiritual matters and allows the conscious mind to be fed by life forces that arise from within the super conscious mind may become a light unto the world and bring enlightenment to many individuals. Along the way, intuitive forces will naturally become part of the life of the individual. One who feeds the mind primarily upon the material forces of gratification, self-indulgence, and self-glorification will became as a monster that is running amok in the world without any true concept of its spiritual roots and with a complete lack of God consciousness (262-20_7). Such people have ravaged the societies of humans for thousands of years and will continue to do so until they open their minds to the call of their Creator and let him into their hearts.

Mental-Spiritual Training and Astrological Urges

The physical body needs daily periods of rest to remain healthy and retain the ability to construct new cells to replace aged and damaged cells so that it can reliably function for many years. This sleep state varies from person to person but typically averages about eight hours for adults during the period of nighttime darkness. In like manner, the soul needs a period of rest from material incarnation to evaluate its spiritual progress, study the choices it made with respect to the opportunities that it was given, and undergo further mental-spiritual training to correct any tendency toward selfish behavior that will engage a corrective response as dictated by spiritual law. There is a judgment at the end of each life (Hebrews 9:27), but its purpose is not to decide whether to condemn the soul to a specific reward or punishment, but to assess its progress or lack thereof and determine the appropriate next phase of mental-spiritual training. The cycles of incarnations on the Earth give souls the opportunity to apply their mental training in practical situations and demonstrate the extent to which they have mastered the spiritual lessons. In this manner souls are purged of their selfish traits. The soul attends these mental-spiritual training sessions and refresher courses on spiritual principles to encourage itself to focus on higher ideals and to re-pattern the soul mind to better apply spiritual truths during incarnations and eventually return to the greater cosmic realm. The period of training that the soul needs or is given between incarnations, or the absence of a training period, seems to partly depend upon the manner in which the soul left the physical world. Violent death may result in a brief stay in the borderland regions and a quick return to the Earth (Gershom, 1992), whereas a spiritual life and peaceful transition into the spiritual realm may be followed by a longer period of activity in the training centers before reincarnation. In any case, the transition of the soul mind away from the mental focus and stress that comes from animating a human body in the material world doesn't permit the soul to forget about its purpose for incarnation and the spiritual shortcomings that it needs to address. This activity between lifetimes has a direct influence on the subconscious mind and an indirect influence on the next conscious mind constructed by the incarnated soul.

Astrological urges—as defined in the readings—are inclinations, tendencies, and talents that are made available to the soul because of its recent activities in the dimensions of mental-spiritual training associated with the planets of the solar system. Because soul incarnation generally immediately follows the conclusion of a training period, there is a strong connection between the time the soul takes possession of a newborn infant and the relative physical position of the Earth and the planet associated with the mental training dimension just prior to the incarnation. Astrology, as it is generally practiced and understood today, has little to nothing to do with the astrological urges described in the readings. Astrology assumes that every planet in the solar system affects the life of a newborn child only because of the relative physical positions of the planets with respect to the Earth at the birth of the child, whereas the readings indicate that the apparent influence of a planet is really the influence of the mental-spiritual training that the soul received before its incarnation (8-1_4; 526-1_3; 849-11_13). The planet does not control the future actions of the individual, but only indicates the type of mental-spiritual training in which the soul participated before incarnation. Astrological urges often present themselves as fairly weak mental influences because they are easily suppressed by the soul's will and are not activated unless the mind seeks to become receptive to them (189-3_14; 464-32_11; 640-1_2; 649-1_4; 790-1_3). Under no circumstances do these urges supersede the will of the individual to make choices and decisions. Soul activity in a training center does not cause the material activities of an incarnated soul to unfold along a certain path, or influence the decisions to be made in an individual's life. The lessons learned during the training reside as latent deep-seated spiritual urges and mental influences that may or may not be recognized or heeded.

These hidden urges within the subconscious mind can only be brought forth into the conscious mind when the soul determines that the conscious mind needs to become aware of them for its spiritual benefit and acts upon that assessment. Interim training between physical incarnations helps instill spiritual values in the individuality of the soul, strengthening the moral fiber of the soul. The intensity of astrological urges indicates the magnitude of the impact of the training on the soul mind and individuality. It manifests as a desire or yearning of the subconscious mind to influence the physical activity of the body through the conscious mind. These urges can help the soul materially express the particular moral and spiritual precepts it was taught. They are often felt as an intuitive influence in the conscious mind when the conscious mind is receptive to the spiritual forces. But the stronger and usually dominant influence on the personality of the individual is usually more associated with the causal effect of events experienced during previous physical incarnations, especially those that involved interpersonal relationships (812-1_12).

The soul's decisions and choices during an incarnation with respect to its current knowledge of spiritual principles generally controls where the soul goes after the human body dies and the soul mind disengages from the human body and the Earth. The training that a soul mind undertakes between incarnations depends upon the particular needs of that soul, which spiritual deficiency is more serious, and which spiritual quality needs to be enhanced for the well-being of the soul. Spiritual law will determine which training subjects are of a higher priority to the soul and the lessons to which the soul mind will be most receptive at the moment it leaves the human body. Some forms of training might address poor choices that the soul may have made in the previous incarnation and some might focus on a series of behavioral problems that began in a long-past incarnation tens of thousands of years ago. The lessons taught in these various schools are designed to correct specific unspiritual and ungodly thoughts and activities such as anger, hatred, greed, and other self-serving attitudes and to instill positive moral and spiritual traits into the soul mind and individuality, such as unconditional love, patience, or mental strength and stamina in the face of temptation. The application of the knowledge acquired at the training centers is at the behest of the will, and the will can always override any of these urges (2533-1_9), can ignore them and decide to focus on the latest pleasurable sensory feelings, the elation of gratification that the conscious mind can experience in materiality, and ignore the latest training received by the soul mind.

Visions and Dreams

The readings indicate that visions and dreams are a complex interplay of mental experiences that can originate from the conscious mind, the subconscious mind, and the super conscious mind or even as various combinations of these influences (39-3_2). Although visions and dreams are both described in the readings, there is a much larger body of information related to the occurrence and interpretation of dreams. Visions are information provided to the conscious mind in a manner that involves the visual cortex of the brain. When this brain center becomes activated, the conscious mind can receive and construct visual images in a way that is similar to the way it receives information from the retina through the optic nerve. Visions usually occur in the waking state when the body is very relaxed or at rest, or when the mind has entered a state of mental quietness, such as during meditation. They usually are of a more spiritual or mystic nature, arising from a concerted spiritual activity or desire to seek spiritual guidance. Visions can be triggered by the spiritual need of the soul mind to compare the thoughts, manifested activities, and concerns of the conscious mind with the spiritual principles and standard of morality that the soul mind has established and aspires to express in materiality. They may be interpreted as messages from divine or supernatural sources that provide revelatory insight into the nature of the nonmaterial realm.

One reading states that some visions may actually be projections of the subconscious thoughts of other soul minds interacting with the subconscious mind and individuality of the soul (903-5_4).

The dream state is probably the most readily accessible sixth sense. The ability to recall dreams and the value of the information projected into the conscious mind greatly depends upon the willingness of the person to learn to become more receptive to dreams and the messages they contain, and make a conscious and sustained effort to remember them upon awakening in the morning. The messages delivered through dreams often unfold as a series of separate dreams over time, which may require the dreamer to expend the time and effort to record and study dreams. The message is often couched in complex symbolic images that need to be carefully studied to be understood. Dreams can be activated because of the physical health issues that the body is facing or perhaps as a warning mechanism because of the misuse of the physical body for inappropriate gratification of the senses. They can be called forth by the subconscious mind as it assesses the daily activities of the physical body and determines that guidance is necessary to course correct behavior in relation to higher mental and spiritual concepts held in the subconscious mind (136-7_5). The most valuable dreams originate as the transfer of a spiritual message of love and comfort from divine sources through the super conscious mind. As with visions, the Mind of God can speak to the sleeping individual to bring hope and help during times of trouble. The recurrence of a particular category or class of dream imagery and the source of the imagery can vary depending upon the mental and spiritual development of the individual and peace or turmoil currently being experienced in the life of the individual. Most of these excursions into the mental equivalent of Alice's Wonderland aren't simply weird forms of entertainment, but have a purpose relative to the spiritual growth of the soul. Because dreams and visions are expressed in highly symbolic imagery, it is not easy for the conscious mind to understand or interpret their spiritual content. There may be a need for training the conscious mind to the proper manner of interpreting the symbolism used to convey the information so that it can be of spiritual value to the incarnated soul (262-9_7; 294-15_5).

The physical body needs to rest and sleep for about eight hours every day. This gives the conscious mind relief from the steady torrent of sensory stimuli it must constantly monitor when the body is active. The conscious mind recedes into the background during sleep, and the body uses that time to recuperate from the physical demands of its daily activities and repair and rebuild its cellular structure. It also gives the subconscious mind the opportunity to digest the information collected by the conscious mind and the decisions that it made during the day. Every notable, serious, or even commonplace interpersonal incident in the life of an individual is an opportunity prepared by spiritual law that gives the soul a chance and choice to glorify God or glorify self. The sleep state gives the soul mind the opportunity to assess the daily physical activities the conscious mind has set in motion in relation to the previous material experiences of the soul and the spiritual training the soul mind has received. The actions that the conscious mind and its associated developing personality have manifested during the day are compared with the actions that the super conscious mind perceives as the most spiritually promising approach to those life situations. Ideally, the soul will discern spiritual progress. If not, the soul may consider alternative methods of handling the situation. It may review memories from similar situations it faced in a previous life and transmit suggestions, encouragement, or perhaps chastisement for the physical consciousness to access through dreams. In the quiet time of the night, guidance and suggestions on the best path forward, concerns about lack of spiritual progress, and criticism about a tendency to forget spiritual matters in the face of material delights or stressful situations will be reviewed. The soul needs this period of relative calm to collect its thoughts and reassess the decisions of its conscious mind with respect to its greater spiritual purpose.

Many people aren't aware of their dreams because the rush of physical sensory information that floods the conscious mind as it awakens to the material world in the morning sweeps aside the dream information. The ability of the conscious mind to remember dreams and derive spiritual benefit from them is strongly dependent upon the degree to which the conscious mind has made an effort to remember the dreams, the degree to which the conscious mind has willfully and consistently focused upon spiritual matters, and the degree to which it holds to the desire to be receptive to dream information (Thurston, 1989). Dreams are more readily remembered when the conscious mind begins to actively seek guidance from the inner self instead of being mostly focused on the material world. The readings actually hint that the inability to remember dreams is an indication that the dreamer is not making a concerted effort to seek spiritual guidance in their lives and may be related to their lack of spiritual attunement (5754-3_10). The conscious mind that makes an effort to consistently remember and analyze dreams can receive information that will help it to make proper moral and spiritual decisions during its incarnation and be better prepared to face temptations and situations that may be highly stressful or that may lead the conscious mind astray. The conscious mind needs an anchor to keep it focused on the purpose of the incarnation, and dreams are one way of getting spiritual assistance. The conscious mind can be very weak when it comes to making spiritual decisions, and the sixth sense can be used by the soul to strengthen its resolve to make proper choices through the conscious mind and turn every opportunity into a positive experience for soul growth. Dreams can bring much useful information to the conscious mind relating to the need for applying higher spiritual principals in personal relationships or by suggesting how physical activities may be harming the body and the mind. Dreams can inform the conscious mind about the dangers of an inappropriate diet, the need to treat a neighbor differently, or just give encouragement to carry on during periods of hardship and despair.

Latent Talents and Past-Life Memories

Because of the accumulated effect of life experiences, souls enter the Earth plane with latent talents. Talents may be deeply buried and undiscovered or may reside just below the surface of consciousness, where they are easily tapped and more likely to be expressed in a person's life. A few children are born with the ability to easily express a previously developed talent, some people are able to sense an underlying skill or talent and build on it with conscious effort through rigorous training, and many go through life consciously unaware of any innate talents. What determines how deeply our talents are hidden or how accessible they are to our conscious minds? Part of the answer probably lies in the particular needs of the soul, the particular spiritual shortcomings with which the soul is dealing. The application of a specific talent during its current incarnation may lead the soul into a different occupation, physical location, or societal status with a different mix of employees, acquaintances, and friends than would another talent. One talent might be more beneficial and offer more relevant opportunities toward the resolution of a particular spiritual problem that the soul needs to face at an early stage of life, and another talent might be more relevant and surface at a later stage of life. Any talent that a soul has previously developed is, in theory, available to the conscious mind. Every acquired talent will be more easily accessible if the soul has intentionally made the effort to retain some level of God consciousness or connectivity to the influx of information that is available from the subconscious and super conscious aspects of mind while the soul is incarnated. Such a soul is more likely to use its talents to express patterns of thoughts and behavioral traits that are beneficial to its spiritual development. Talents don't necessarily mean artistic abilities or capacity to earn a living, but can mean filling a position in a church one is attending or conducting an open-minded investigation of different concepts of spirituality to find the belief system and practices that strike a resonate note within the deeper mental and emotional regions of the soul mind. The talents that are of most value are those that are used in the service of God and neighbor.

There is a category of latent talents that go against the norm and are more strongly and insistently expressed than the usual talents that are part of a life. These are the demonstrations of genius that occasionally appear in a child or young person. One of the more notable manifestations of genius is in the form of musical talent. Talents in music and fine arts, such as painting, sculpture, and literature, can involve expressions that evoke strong emotions and reactions in the public mind (963-1_5). Talents may also manifest in the form of science and business acumen. The intelligence quotients (IQ) of the famous composer Mozart, the scientist Albert Einstein, and the businessman Bill Gates are estimated to be about 155 to 160, and their particular talents are well-known in their fields of endeavor by the general public. At an age when most children in the mid-1700s in Europe were learning to do basic chores on the farm or around the house, or were playing hopscotch, hide-and-seek, or marbles, Mozart was making musical history. He was one of those rare children who were unconsciously aware of a talent they had developed during previous life-times, and were able to tap into those talents while consciously navigating their current life. It is obvious that Mozart did not gain his musical ability from music lessons he took in the first few years of his life, even though his father was also a gifted musician. He did not inherit his musical talent from the DNA of his father, but from soul memories of past-life experiences where he had developed exceptional musical abilities. This mental transmission of musical ability allowed him to bypass, to some extent, the need to begin anew the process of training his conscious mind to the proper hand-eye coordination required to play complex music and his ears to identify pure tones. He was already playing the clavichord at the tender age of three, was beginning to play musical scores by age four, and composing his own works by age five. He was displaying a musical talent in his first few years of life that many students in prestigious musical conservatories only dream of attaining. The readings indicate that the appearance of the more gifted forms of genius in the population may be related to the coordinated effect of earthly sojourns and astrological urges, perhaps a sort of resonance where memories of previous expressions of the talent combine and cooperate with recent experiences in the mental training centers to strengthen and bring forward a particular talent (963-1_6). The idea of talents being correlated with soul memories and soul training and the operation of spiritual law that directs the soul toward earthly activities that best present needed spiritual opportunities is much more reasonable than perceiving them as random handouts from God to worthy individuals (Romans 12:5-8).

Genius can also appear as an adverse effect in some individuals and must be countered by the intentional application of will to weaken the potential for negative expression and behavior, and to redirect these impulses into socially positive directions. There is no evidence that Adolph Hitler was a genius, but he was known to be a persuasive speaker with the ability to rally people to his cause. There are indications in the readings that Adolph Hitler had the opportunity and the talent to help the German people emerge from the disastrous economic hyperinflation brought about by WWI and post-war reparations in a way that would uplift the people, but that he chose to let his narcissistic tendencies draw him into self-glorification that lead to madness and disaster for the German people and the Jewish population he chose to use as scapegoats (3976-13_6; 3976-15_15). Souls have the freedom to choose to use their talents for the good of mankind or to use them to commit great evil. When talents are used for evil or self-aggrandizement at the expense of others, it is symptomatic of a loss of God consciousness and glorification of the Self.

There is another category of communication from the subconscious to the conscious mind that is probably less well known, especially in Western cultures. Investigated claims of past-life memories in children reveal that the veil between the subconscious mind and the developing conscious mind is weak in young children. The more permeable veil sometimes allows an active exchange of previous life information between the subconscious mind and the newly forming physical conscious mind. This leakage of information through the veil can occur during dreams or even during the day while the young mind is contending with the sensory information coming into the body. It involves the projection of bits and pieces of past life experiences into the mental awareness of a child and the communication of the child's mind with souls in the borderland realm. This transmission of past life memories to the conscious mind was studied extensively by Dr. Ian Stevenson, as mentioned previously in reference to the presence of birth defects and abnormalities in newborn and young children. The memories appear to occur at random within the general population worldwide, but they are more readily noticed, recognized, or acknowledged in populations with philosophical and religious beliefs that include the concept of reincarnation, where family members are more likely to be receptive to the claims of the child. These memories usually come to children from about age two to age six and often fade as the child becomes more involved in society, especially with the onset of more frequent human interaction, such as when they begin to attend school. Dr. Stevenson conducted extensive research and interviews to compare the claims of each child about the manner of death, previous familial relationships, and the names and physical characteristics of neighborhoods that were mentioned as previous places of residence. In many cases he was able to interview individuals who were claimed to have been previous family members and friends during the life of the deceased person the child claimed to have been and to locate historical documents such as medical and police records that mentioned recalled names and described events. He extracted the strongest cases from his initial interviews and preliminary research as candidates for more in-depth and longer-term investigation. Many of these claims have been verified to a greater or lesser degree, and a large body of evidence strongly indicates that many children remember their previous lives while they are establishing new identities and a new life (Leininger and Leininger, 2010; Stevenson, 1983; Stevenson, 2001; Tucker, 2007; Tucker, 2008).

Be Receptive to the Voice of God

The sixth sense is a latent mental force that can help the soul become consciously aware of aspects of the soul mind that generally are not apparent to a conscious mind because it is absorbed in the daily activities of material existence. The sixth sense forces are typically subtle, furtive, and weak unless and until the conscious mind makes a determined effort to strengthen the activity of the spiritual aspects of the mind at the expense of some of the more base material aspects. Our conscious mind and the personality that we acquire through activity in relation to our current material condition and life experiences influences our ability to become receptive to spiritual messages through the sixth sense and inclination to use them to enhance our spiritual growth. All of this available aid from the spiritual realm is for naught unless the conscious mind opens itself to these sources of information and is willing to absorb and utilize the spiritual guidance it receives. With some concerted effort and intentional training, these forces can be brought into physical consciousness and can help reorient the soul toward spiritual matters. The conscious mind can learn to recognize spiritual opportunities, identify and use the sixth-sense spiritual information, and loosen the grip of obsessive materiality and self-centeredness upon the mind. An individual can more easily become aware of the sixth sense as a beneficial force when the mind is relaxed, in a period of quiet reflection, or intentionally directed toward a state of receptive stillness. The nightly rhythm of sleep can become a particularly fruitful period of sixth-sense activity through dreams, and a valuable source of spiritual guidance from our higher consciousness.

The conscious mind must be reconfigured to successfully and consistently avoid falling prey to the temptations of the material world, especially into expressions of selfishness and self-centeredness that gain the body and mind power, material wealth, or position at the expense of other souls. It is not that the spiritually minded individual cannot acquire wealth; aspire to some high office; pursue and accept a position as a community leader, religious leader, or politician, but it is a fact that any soul that goes down one of these leadership paths has a moral imperative to use its wealth, knowledge, or position for the benefit of others. If it does not, the ability of that person's soul to benefit from sixth-sense knowledge will be impaired in lifetimes to come, and soul memory will ensure that the individual will reap in a future life what it has sown in its present life. When our attention is drawn too intently toward material attractions and sensations, we lose the ability to perceive the inner flow of information from the storehouse of the soul's accumulated physical experiences and mental-spiritual training. Individuals who are closely attuned to the spiritual nature of their soul and who exhibit some level of God consciousness will have more frequent visions, intuitive experiences, and dreams. They also are more likely to remember those experiences when they are in the normal awakened state where physical activity is directed by the conscious mind.

There is always the need for the soul to encounter the consequences of past actions, thoughts, and words that do not respect the spiritual law to which souls are bound. There is a force of mental-spiritual training and collective experiences that sets the conditions and circumstances that activate spiritual cause and effect, the process of coming face-to-face with our inner spiritual weaknesses. The residual memories of physical and nonphysical experiences of the soul constitute an active force that can provide positive spiritual feedback to the conscious mind of the incarnated soul. These are the ways in which God speaks to his incarnated soul children. They are all aspects of the still small voice that God uses to remind us that he is present in our lives and is ready and willing to help us on our journey toward redemption, restoration, and salvation. Too often, humans are unreceptive to the spiritual messages that are sent to help us negotiate life's challenges and opportunities in ways that will bring us closer to our creator and restore God consciousness to our soul minds. The failure to make proper use of these material-spiritual opportunities sets up a tension among the current activities of an incarnated soul, residual memories in the subconscious mind associated with past activities, and the spiritual ideal consciously or unconsciously held in the soul mind of the individual. We need to learn to listen to the still small voice that calls us from beyond our earthly domain of human activity, from beyond what we perceive to be the boundaries of our conscious mind.

The Tension between the Conscious and Subconscious Minds

In latent urges, two great influences are apparent. They may be compared to hereditary and environmental influences in the material plane. But these, of the real self, are the spiritual environments, the spiritual heredity. Spiritual heredity, then, is a combination of what the entity or soul has done with its opportunities for creative influence in this and all other experiences. That inherited is what the entity has made of such. The spiritual environment is the sphere of activity in which such influences have found expression, whether in this or in the other environs of this same solar system; much as the manners of activities in the earth have been in the various classes, the various ages, the various periods through which each soul passes. (Edgar Cayce Reading 2581-2_15-17)

The soul mind is a basic unit of self-awareness released from the Mind of God and given the freedom of self-expression. On the one hand we, as souls, have developed a subconscious mind out of a blend of experiences in nonmaterial realms, during previous material incarnations, and from the measure of our more-godly super conscious mind that we have chosen to let guide us in spiritual and material matters. The individuality of the soul embodies the hopes and desires of the soul and is that unique mental-spiritual mannerism that the soul uses to express itself in the nonmaterial realm as it interacts with and communicates with other souls. On the other hand we, as human beings, have developed a physical conscious mind out of the various environmental, relational, and societal experiences we encounter during a single human lifespan. Our associated personality is the unique set of personal characteristics that define the way we choose to express our conscious thoughts and feelings in the community of men and women. Ideally, the individuality and the personality will be one in purpose, even though they may differ in nature (5246-1_17). The arena of activity of the conscious mind is entirely in the physical realm, the proving ground of the soul mind. Each limited conscious mind we have created is active for only one lifetime, yet in their entirety they are vitally important to the mental and spiritual health of the eternal soul. We may at times become aware of the presence of the subconscious mind when it is presented to us as sixth-sense experiences, but for the most part we are not receptive to these messages or discount their validity and value. Is the mental health of the soul compromised by this partitioning of the soul mind, perhaps causing it to lose hope as it loses conscious awareness of the greater spiritual reality beyond the physical world?

The subconscious mind and soul individuality are transformed and spiritually mature as the soul engages in self-centered behavior or respect for spiritual law and honor the purpose of its creation and the expectations of God. The subconscious mind contains the summation of all reasoned and deduced conclusions, expressions of faith, understanding, wisdom, and habitual behavior patterns created by the soul during its accumulated experiences. This includes material experiences as well as the nonphysical experiences it had before it first entered the Earth environment and the periods of mental-spiritual training in planetary dimensions (2581-2_15-17). The likes and dislikes of a soul, its attitudes and emotions, and the way that it expresses itself with respect to other souls are wrapped up in its individuality. This individuality is real, permanent, and eternal (in potential) but is subject to change as the soul grows and acquires new experiences and information; and observes the outcome of its choices and decisions relative to its awareness and understanding of its kinship with God. As the soul becomes more spiritually enlightened, it will become more desirous of seeking its spiritual roots and staying true to the purpose for which God created souls. The mind of a disincarnate soul will ideally partake deeply of the offered spiritual nourishment through the super conscious mind, but still retain a healthy, thriving independent existence guided by the free will that it has been granted. Its thoughts will respect the authority of God as its creator and its will respect the rights of its fellow souls.

The conscious mind and human personality, on the other hand, are primarily formed as the soul mind contends with sensory information, including stimuli from the human activity of other incarnated souls. During the process of organizing and collating the sensory information stream, the personality will also begin to incorporate the soul's core values, morals, residual emotions from the ways in which it previously acted and reacted toward other individuals, and its justification for those forms of interaction. From its earliest phases of development, the physical conscious mind is the interface between the subconscious mind and the physical world. Its earliest reasoning and deductive abilities primarily relate to the physical activity of the body, but it evolves and becomes more complex as the soul gains new information and experiences. The mind's experiences from childhood through adulthood, its interaction with fellow souls during a particular lifetime, the social and material environment in which it was raised, and the veiled soul memories that influence the individual's decisions and desires are factors that influence the development of personality. Our personality encapsulates the manner in which we will manifest the sense of awareness and sense of self that the conscious mind has acquired and projects it into the world. It projects the temperament and disposition of the individual, the outward verbal and physical responses toward friends and acquaintances, and affects the way in which the person reacts to external temptations and events. It is also a protective shield that the soul erects to contend with the vagaries of the material world and the particular experiences in which it is required to participate.

Situations that elicit strong emotions arising out of previous earthly experiences are thrust into the life of the individual by spiritual law, especially when they relate to interpersonal communication and societal interaction with other incarnated souls. When forceful outbursts and disagreeable behaviors turn nasty and hateful, it is a sure sign that the soul has not mastered the challenge that that particular life situation is giving the soul. The type of personality that develops in a mature adult is indicative of the spiritual growth or retardation of the soul during its incarnations. The personality can reflect the spiritual attunement of the soul mind because of the activity of the will (900-22_5). From the perspective of the material world, mental faculties dissipate and are extinguished as death comes to an individual. In reality, the memories collected by the physical conscious mind during the soul's incarnation—all of the willful decisions and choices that the soul made in response to various life situations—are remembered and added to the existing record of soul memories (288-27_4). The essence of the "human" personality is absorbed within the individuality of the soul upon the death of the human body and becomes part of the greater soul identity and individuality that is tied to the subconscious mind (900-306_4).

Balancing the Conscious Mind and the Subconscious Mind

The soul mind will ideally be well-balanced in that while it is active in the material world, it will retain awareness of and receive guidance from the more mature subconscious mind and will perceive the spiritual nourishment available through the super conscious mind. The soul mind becomes unbalanced when the attractions of the material world lure its thoughts and actions into directions that lead to a reduction of awareness of its spiritual component. It loses its spiritual rudder, which causes it to flounder and be tossed to and fro by the storms of life that the soul has merited. The decisions and choices that it makes during the relatively short span of a material incarnation reveal how well the subconscious mind and the will of the soul have absorbed spiritual lessons and the strength of the mental union between the soul mind and its creator. There is a constant mental-spiritual tension in the mind of a soul that has become unbalanced by giving in to an inappropriate and excessive obsession with material attractions. Scripture refers to this inner tension in terms of a conflict between spirit and flesh (Matthew 26:41; Galatians 5:17–18). When lives are turned upside down without apparent reason, it is an indication that there are underlying unresolved spiritual issues that need to be addressed and worked out within the context of the present human environment and activities. This internal conflict is driven by various expressions of selfishness or spiritual rebellion that appear as manifested forms of self-indulgence, self-gratification, and other activities that glorify the soul and its human experience but denigrates the God experience. The soul mind can also exist in a state of mental imbalance if it allows a belief in its superior religious or spiritual convictions to induce a sense of self-righteousness in its dealings with its fellow man. This imbalance can be observed in the forceful and overly assertive personality of a preacher who harangues his congregation with threats of eternity in hell if they do not immediately recognize and accept the spiritual message he is bestowing upon them. This tension is like a stretched or compressed spring that seeks to return to its equilibrium state. Our life experiences are dictated by our previous behavior in relation to spiritual law and physical causality, and are designed to release the mental tension in the minds of souls through appropriate and righteous decisions and choices.

When the human body is awake and active, the soul lives in a world of matter and energy that unfolds before it as the conscious mind samples the ebb and flow of the material world that surrounds the body. It assesses this information, compares it with previously compiled data to evaluate the current situation, and makes the response it deems appropriate. Sometimes this assessment is near instantaneous as habitual reactions to familiar events, and sometimes it is more deliberate as thoughtful reflection or considered analysis of the meaning and possible interpretations of the incoming data. In either case, the response is transmitted into the environment of the material world through the vocal cords or muscles of the human body as words and actions. These responses indicate how well the conscious mind is integrated with the subconscious mind and how well the subconscious mind is integrated with the Mind of God. When the soul's conscious mind is seriously out of balance with respect to its spiritual purpose and in conflict with the spiritual principles innately held in the soul's super conscious mind, the soul's materially manifested activities will not lead to spiritual growth. The constant mental and emotional stress and tension of a serious mental-spiritual imbalance in the soul mind can eventually cause dis-ease and disease in the human body (257-228_10). Why do we generally not perceive this interaction between the material and spiritual realms? One reason is that most of us don't look for it. Our immersion in the material world and the daily demands of family and occupation, the need to spend most of the week doing physical or mental labor that tires the body and mind, and the desire to spend the little remaining time at play or relaxation keeps us so busy that we devote little time to introspection and spiritual matters. But the subconscious mind is present and active whether or not we are consciously aware of it, and the ability to interact with our subconscious mind is within all of us. The potential of the conscious mind to perceive and use subconscious guidance during its incarnation is greatly affected by the type of material activities in which the soul chooses to indulge. If the soul routinely expresses its inherent spiritual attributes as a moral code that glorifies God instead of self when it interacts with other incarnated souls, it will increase the ability of the conscious mind to become aware of so-called psychic information. If the soul mind spends its days focusing on and gratifying material desires while neglecting to respect its spiritual heritage, it will greatly hinder its ability to experience the flow of love and guidance that God wants to pour into our lives (1440-2_20).

The personality that we form during the first couple of decades of our life significantly influences how we will interact as adults with the society of incarnated souls in which we live. It will affect how we respond to abuse from our fellow humans, how sharing and caring we will be, and how loving we will be, especially when faced with unusually stressful circumstances and events that test the limits of our patience and endurance. Consider the case of a child who is playing in the house with a ball. Before long, the inevitable happens, and the ball ricochets off a wall and knocks a coveted vase off the table. The personality (and fatigue) of the parent who hears the crash of ceramic on the floor and discovers the shattered vase will determine his or her response. It can be anger and shouting that ends with a spanking and banishment to the bedroom, or it can be a serious conversation about playing with balls inside the house and perhaps a temporary ban on getting possession of the ball. The choice of anger instead of patience may have its roots in previous life experiences with the soul of the child, experiences that are so deeply buried in the psyche that they cannot be consciously considered or imagined under the circumstances. A childhood filled with abuse can be overcome at the soul level by a willingness to see beyond the physical and mental damage and focus on the future. It undoubtedly is not easy and may require the help of counselors and psychologists, but the aftereffects of abuse can be mitigated to where the incarnated soul can change its life path and prevent the damage from causing the soul to descend into self-loathing or revengeful behavior that can seriously harm it. When rightly used, soul incarnation brings understanding and wisdom out of pain and suffering (439-1_18). All of us may not have to go through severe episodes of hunger, disease, abuse, or debilitation, but we all will have temptations and trauma to face because of our previous willingness to let our minds and bodies descend into materiality so deeply that we cut off the love and spiritual energy that God desires to bestow on us. Until we decide to change and make God consciousness a habitual pattern of life, we will continue to face these hardships. The difference between one personality and the next in a series of incarnations is primarily a result of the reaction and response of the soul to its physical experiences in relation to the particular soul deficiency that is being brought to the conscious mind. A series of personalities will consistently exhibit a more loving and caring attitude if the soul mind keeps a strong and firm mental grasp on spiritual principles, maintains and holds the desire to manifest those principles in its life, and stays true to the purpose for which God created the soul.

The first experience of a soul in the Earth plane may primarily have been to satisfy its curiosity about the physical sensations of a human-animal body, a purely selfish and intentional action that gave physical activity and physical pleasure without regard to the soul's origin as a child of God or to the spiritual cost with respect to its relationship with God. Perhaps its first experience was driven by a sense of altruism that prompted it to offer its services to come as part of the Adamic group projection to help reawaken the minds of trapped souls and encourage them to remain faithful to the purposes of God and attuned to the Mind of God. These faithful and idealistic souls worked to bring rebellious souls back to God consciousness and restore them to their proper relationship with their creator. No matter which approach to life an incarnated soul took initially, the purpose for all soul incarnations today is to realign the will of the soul mind with the Will of God. There are strong mental forces at work in the mind of an incarnated soul, creating a mental tension between right and wrong, good and bad, and carnal and spiritual thought patterns, each constantly vying for our attention. The most powerful force originating from our subconscious mind arises from the accumulated store of past memories from the thought patterns we projected, our experiences and perceptions, the various personalities we created, and the mental-spiritual training we received that are stored in the soul mind and have been absorbed into the soul individuality (294-1_1; 136-7_4-5).

These records are not simply a passive account of history, but are an active force for soul evolution that introduces the incarnated soul to forms of activity that can lead it toward spiritual development with the ultimate purpose of companionship with God (Todeschi, 2007; Todeschi, 2011). These Akashic records facilitate causal continuity between soul incarnations by recording current and past-life experiences, choices, and thoughts while active on the Earth (288-27_4). They are referred to in Revelation as the Book of Life, a book used in the dispensation of divine justice (281-36_11). The Akashic records are accessed and reviewed by the soul along with the topics studied in the dimensions of mental-spiritual training to prepare for its next incarnation. They help to indicate the most suitable future experiences and opportunities for soul development and the most favorable places and situations in which to incarnate. Ignorance of spiritual law does not allow us to circumvent or avoid the law. The law is always in effect. Until we take concrete action to change our selfish mental attitudes, we will continue to create conditions that force us to incarnate to face our spiritual deficiencies and self-inflicted troubles. A pattern of intentional spiritually correct choices will gradually lead the soul mind toward release from incarnation and a pattern of intentional or even unintentional poor choices that disrespect others and violate the dictates of spiritual law will perpetuate the cycles of incarnation and the need to face new opportunities to change spiritually incorrect behavior. Just as the biological heredity of the human body flows from the DNA of its ancestors, the spiritual heredity of the soul flows from the Book of Life and the soul individuality (2581-2_16-17).

Soul memories are the source of mental heredity and can be mani-fested as material experiences that range from poverty and depravation to wealth and prosperity, and in human relationships that range from abuse and intolerance to love and patience. Spiritual law uses these memories to ensure that major events in the current life of a soul unfold in a way that gives the soul a wide range of opportunities to correct previous failures by making decisions that are in accord with the spiritual principles it inherited as a child of God (903-23_9; 288-27_4). This isn't a statement about predes-tination, but is a statement about cause and effect at the subconscious level, about the soul reaping what it has sown in previous incarnations in relation to its awareness and knowledge of God (Luke 6:38). These opportunities are tailored to the specific needs of the soul and offer choices between acting and reacting in ways that emphasize serving the self and selfish interests or in ways that stress loving and selfless service toward God and other souls. One or another of these two possibilities is brought to fruition according to the manifested material activity of the soul during each lifetime. The memories of the soul in relation to its entrance into materiality contain the soul's destiny (903-23_9). The soul mind doesn't suddenly get more spiritual because the body died, no matter how religious the person, how faithfully the person attended church or participated in communion and other rituals, or how fervently the person declared allegiance to a particular doctrine or dogma (254-92_9). The inner awareness of God consciousness is developed slowly over time in space where there are physical and spiritual consequences to our human activities.

The soul is more likely to develop a positive personality trait in its current life if it previously held to spiritual principles that expressed respect through love, kindness, and patience, and created a positive godly personality that became integrated into its soul individuality. The fact that we can love others, have hope in the midst of seemingly hopeless situations, have compassion for our fellow man, and can demonstrate many other noble moral and spiritual attributes is because our souls can physically manifest higher spiritual and moral qualities. Despite what we imagine from our myopic perspective as human beings, the mental and emotional qualities that we see in others and the spiritual precepts they espouse are not human traits. They are soul traits refracted through the conscious mind that are transmitted or projected into the world by the animation of human bodies (3744-1_53). Humans display the moral character of the soul by the manifested thoughts of the conscious mind and force of its personality, but they also express veiled qualities and attributes that radiate from the subconscious mind. These human expressions of soul character traits are similar but not identical to the traits exhibited during the interaction of souls in the incorporeal spiritual realm. It is as important for souls to acquire character traits that respect the scriptural fruits of the spirit and apply them in the society of souls in the nonphysical realm as it is for incarnated souls to apply those traits in human society in the physical realm.

The Supremacy of the Soul's Will

If the cycle of action and reaction by the conscious mind to events in the material world was the only way that souls could become mentally and spiritually educated and regain their lost knowledge and awareness of God, it would be a losing proposition. But there are other factors at work as a soul guides its human body through the world of matter and energy, and interacts with fellow soul-animated humans, that help the soul learn to make spiritually correct choices with its conscious mind even in the face of stressful life situations. The soul that has aligned its mind with the Mind of God and is attuned to the patterns of thought and behavior that God expects from us can influence and override negative thought patterns developed from responses to physical events. Remember, the will of the soul is paramount (1909-1_19) and when the soul acts with the best of spiritual intentions, it can alleviate the deleterious effects of evil intentions or temptations. With proper application of the will, the soul mind can be trained, repatterned, and awakened to its full potential and a greater awareness of God. The grace that God granted souls by allowing them the opportunity to be redeemed through physical activity in a material world also extends to forgiveness for specific actions we take during activity in the world. Grace doesn't mean that the soul no longer has to face the consequences of previous spiritual error, but that God will mitigate those consequences to where they are more manageable for the soul.

The veil between the conscious and subconscious mind isn't a massive impenetrable barrier, but is somewhat permeable, more like a thin membrane that can be penetrated under certain conditions. The conscious mind is not entirely left alone as it attempts to sort out its place in the material world and its approach to the environmental and societal situations it faces as a result of its previous decisions in materiality. The will of the soul is that part of the soul body where desire and even yearning arise and begin their march toward manifestation. The will can direct the attention of the soul mind toward specific avenues of thought and areas of concentrated focus. It affects the entire soul mind, the physical conscious mind that contends with materiality, the subconscious mind with its core individuality of the soul, and the super conscious mind and its connection to the divine life source. Each of the three aspects of the soul mind has the capability and ability to alter a different portion of the soul's environment and the overall mental pattern of the soul mind (262-8_5). The will is that aspect of the soul that makes decisions, that influences the soul mind to act on specific desires that arise in the will, and that moves the soul mind to the fulfillment of its envisioned experience. The will oversees all aspects of the soul mind (1742-4_7). The will, as the overseer of the thoughts and manifested activities of the soul mind, is largely responsible for the spiritual quality of the communication between the conscious mind and the subconscious mind and the frequency with which the conscious mind will receive guidance from the subconscious mind. The will opens and closes the lines of communication between the physical and spiritual worlds and determines whether we will be children of men or children of God.

The will gives the soul freedom of expression, the ability to make decisions and choices that are not dictated or limited by the will of its creator. As the developing conscious mind of the growing child becomes familiar with the functions and abilities of the human body and begins to understand how the body can be made to interact with the environment that surrounds the body, the will of the soul can emerge from the background and gradually guide the mind toward various forms of expression. Because the cognitive development of each child can vary depending on the amount and type of social interaction it receives, the forceful expression of independent will emerges at different ages, but generally by about age three children are asserting their independence and making their personal preferences known. This process changes the conscious mind from a mainly receptive state in which sensory information is processed and sorted to a more proactive state in which the will can direct the mind to entertain one type of experience over another type. As the sense of mental independence expands and the mind learns how to better control the body, the influence of the will on the growing child and within the society of its peers grows stronger and is able to more forcefully express the soul's likes and dislikes. A spiritually advanced soul may choose more altruistic, selfless experiences, and a spiritually retarded soul may seek more selfish, carnal experiences. By the time the child is interacting with other children in meaningful life situations at middle school or high school, it is freely expressing its own opinions and asserting its own preferences within the limits set by adults for that protected society. Children begin to choose their own friends and associates and select the available activities that attract their interest. They become more and more independent as they form their own sense of self-identity and self-worth within society.

Humans can be influenced by both their environment and heredity, but the readings indicate that the influence of both social and biological factors can be mitigated by the intentional application of the will of the soul toward its physical and spiritual development. The will of the soul is paramount and can elevate the life of the human it animates to a saintly level or cause it to descend into a degraded caricature of the soul's true self (900-340_12-13). The application of will to raise a strong mental desire for spiritual improvement can lead the body out of a mental and physical ghetto, change its physical circumstances, and put it on the path that leads to spiritual salvation and soul redemption. The soul's most reverent and loving level of consciousness is in the super conscious mind that bridges the soul mind and the Mind of God. During incarnation it is deeply buried beneath the accumulated thoughts that concern our daily activities. When the will is intently focused on its relationship with God, the carnal aspects of the conscious mind become less important and the super conscious mind becomes more active and brings the presence of God into our daily mental activity. This releases the mental tension between these two competing aspects of the soul mind. Within this more spiritual consciousness is the awareness that our spirit, the essence of the soul, is one with the Spirit of God. Not as one in the sense of similarity, or in the sense of being close to God in a shared sense of ideals, but as one in the sense of unity. Our souls are a portion of God. The spirit component of our soul is a portion of the Spirit of God, and the mental component of our soul is a portion of the Mind of God. The will of the soul can rebalance the soul mind and reclaim the awareness of our oneness with God and lead us back to full and constant communion with God.

We should never forget the importance of the will in soul redemption. The soul maintains a presence throughout the life of the body, and it expresses its physical and spiritual desires through the conscious mind. The will may be strong and impart or impress some of the higher ideals of the soul mind into the developing physical consciousness. It may play a subdued or weak, passive role and let the conscious mind meander through life with little interference or guidance as the mind and body are buffeted by physical events set in motion by itself and others. It may fall in love with the material world and direct the mind and body to seek physical pleasure in its various forms, such as sexual gratification, the feeling of power over others, the sensory overload obtained when drugs and alcohol invade the body, or simply instill a desire to accumulate more and more material goods, well beyond the needs of the body and perhaps at the expense of the welfare of others. The will of the soul has enormous power over the conscious mind. Many people go through the motions of a dissatisfying life without realizing that the will can be used to change lives for the better. The readings state that there is no power on the Earth that exceeds the power of the will (5254-1_4; 262-81_13). Unfortunately, that power can be used for both good and evil to the spiritual benefit of the incarnated soul or to its spiritual detriment. The will must be harnessed to the soul's spiritual purpose. The soul that does not apply the influence of will to awaken the conscious mind to its limitations and focus its attention toward the proper resolution of life's conflicts is being negligent and careless regarding its spiritual purpose. The soul should intentionally direct the conscious mind away from carnal influences and teach it how to get the most spiritual benefit from a life filled with opportunities that, with the right decisions, can return it to a state of God consciousness.

The soul mind may be satisfied with the current status quo, a mental place where the soul may feel comfortable and does not have to exert itself. But God does not intend the wayward soul to be comfortable. It cannot rest on its laurels and memories from one life well lived in the service of God or one set of good, even excellent, deeds within a lifetime. God needs souls to express their innate spiritual qualities of love, kindness, patience, grace, and mercy toward him and toward fellow souls consistently and eternally in all realms of activity. As the soul mind begins to consistently make spiritually correct decisions, the soul is better able to receive sustenance from the more spiritually oriented super conscious mind and reduce its propensity to engage in and exaggerate selfish patterns of behavior. It can use this spiritual nourishment to influence human activities in upcoming incarnations. The soul's relationship with God is strongly affected by the thoughts that the conscious mind most persistently dwells upon and manifests as the soul samples new material experiences. Each soul opportunity evokes a mental and emotional response in the conscious mind, and the moral quality of the response determines the spiritual value of the lesson to the soul (189-3_14; 146-10_8). The conscious mind is transformed by the desires it most frequently and fervently activates. A mind that holds fast to spiritual precepts retains a closer relationship with God, but the mind that revels in self-aggrandizement or self-gratification places the mind in opposition to God (262-78_14). The soul cannot for long be both a force for good and God, and be intensely devoted to carnal pleasures. The mental tension that results will wreak havoc within the soul and separate the conscious mind from the presence of God.

The most important source of mental and spiritual nourishment to a disincarnate or incarnate soul is the love of God, as channeled through an open line of spiritual communication. The super conscious mind understands the unique relationship between the soul and God, but access to that knowledge is corrupted and compromised by inappropriate thought patterns formed from selfish intents and purposes. This spiritual congestion inhibits communication between the subconscious mind and God, and can inhibit expressions of good and righteousness in the individual. There is an ever-present call from God to the subconscious mind, but the rebellious soul becomes deaf to that call. The strength of the mental link and flow of spiritual sustenance depends on the willingness of the soul to keep that channel open by keeping its mind spiritually attuned to its creator and attentive to its spiritual purpose. Once the link is firmly closed, it can take a concerted, sustained effort of the will, perhaps triggered by a major life event, to begin restoring that connection and reestablish a meaningful relationship with God. When a soul decides to concentrate on material pleasures, it becomes more difficult to maintain a healthy mental and spiritual relationship with God. This spiritual blockage can only be removed by the intentional action of the will. The will truly determines the spiritual value of the incarnation. It determines whether the soul mind advances closer to God and godliness or recedes from God and descends further into selfishness, rebellion, and love of materialism as it seeks pleasure, happiness, and fulfillment in the physical realm without respecting spiritual law. The stakes are high, the reward is great, and failure can be devastating to the soul.

Almost every soul that has incarnated on the Earth today is here to restore its relationship with God, to reopen and revitalize communication with the divine through the super conscious mind. What should be an active conduit for the flow of love and blessings from the Whole of God to the free-willed portions of God is too often ignored. Loss of God consciousness accelerates powerful selfish tendencies that lead souls to seek material gratification instead of companionship with God. If the will is not grounded in spiritual truths and a commitment to a higher purpose, the poor choices the soul makes and the desires it activates will manifest in the tendency of the individual to be self-serving and to live life without regard for the welfare or needs of other souls. If the soul becomes too enamored with the sensory world, with its various opportunities for self-indulgence and self-gratification, it will use the conscious mind to explore the seamy back alleys of the sensory world and to further degrade and diminish its awareness of the presence of God. It will cause the soul to fail to fulfill its purpose for incarnation as it urges the conscious mind to act on inappropriate desires that are best left to wither away and die. The materialization of soul imperfections in human lives in relation to spiritual ideals allows the soul to perceive its shortcomings and gives it opportunities to rectify its past failures. When the causal effects of its selfish behavior become too harsh for the soul to ignore or a consequential emotional experience shakes the soul to its core, the soul may begin to realize the error of its ways and begin its journey back to God.

Incarnated souls are mostly working on problems associated with relationships and morality, spiritual deficiencies at the conscious and subconscious level, and various weaknesses in will and mind. These factors cause the soul to drift away from the source of its life force. It is essential that these spiritual flaws and imperfections be addressed or else the soul cannot be fully reunited with its creator and fulfill its destiny as a companion of God. When the soul decides to act on desires that more closely align it with the Will of God and the purpose for its creation, it will more likely use the conscious mind to express godly desires that fulfill its mission to project the love and peace of God into the daily activities of the human body and into human society. When strong moral and spiritual attitudes are projected through the conscious mind into material society, there is a feedback effect that reveals and reinforces the innate spiritual qualities of the soul. The interplay of the conscious mind coupled with the subconscious mind and the force of the spiritual-mental law of cause and effect helps direct the soul mind away from thoughts and actions that are detrimental to the soul. The will of the soul is the catalyst for change. The manner in which a soul applies its will in any given life situation determines if the soul will exist in a state of spiritual lawfulness, mental tranquility, and harmony with respect to God, or in a state of spiritual unlawfulness, mental conflict, and dissonance with respect to God. The soul can tap the infinite source of divine spiritual strength when it willfully chooses to lessen its dependence on the conscious mind for advice and starts listening to the inner voice of God. The central focus of the soul mind will shift back and forth between materiality and spirituality as the soul alternately makes decisions that reinforce its desire for the carnal pleasures of materiality or that reveal the inner presence of God, but with sustained effort the soul can recall its original mental-spiritual relationship with God and reopen communication with God. Souls that fail to do so and remain mentally attached to materiality must undergo more mental-spiritual training and more earthly incarnations to purge the desire to act in rebellion to the Will of God from their will and mind.

There are several methods by which the conscious mind can be made more aware of the higher mental-spiritual aspects of the greater soul mind. They can help the soul break habitual patterns of poor choices, help it be more aware of the greater spiritual realm that is its true home, and help it recover knowledge of its origin as a child of God. These practices are only effective to the extent with which the will of the soul chooses to apply them during life situations. This opening of the mind can lead to consistently better moral and spiritual choices as the conscious mind participates in human social activity and enhances the likelihood that material opportunities will result in spiritual growth of the soul. Fortunately, God has taken the position that he will do his utmost to bring every soul back into the fold so that no soul need remain lost unless it willfully chooses to remain in that state (2 Peter 3:9; 1909-1_19). There are ways to mitigate and reduce the disunity that keeps the conscious mind, subconscious mind, and super conscious mind from working together effectively and in coordination with the Mind of God. We will address some of the methods by which a human being can become more aware of his or her spiritual nature and intentionally shift the focus of the soul mind from the physical conscious mind toward the super conscious mind in the next chapter.

Expanding Consciousness Through Ideals and Meditation

Then the more important, the most important experience of this or any individual entity is to first know what is the ideal - spiritually. (Edgar Cayce Reading 357-13_6)

Many people engage in everyday activity without conscious consideration of the spiritual needs of their soul or fellow souls. They may misuse or abuse other humans for their own pleasure, to gain materially, or to enjoy the intoxicating feeling of power over another person. These souls are flirting with the eventual loss of soul identity and dissolution of self. God won't force souls to change their thought patterns and behavior because that would negate the very purpose for their creation. He still wants souls to be loving companions despite despairing that he created beings that have so much capacity for selfish, uncaring behavior. He knows there is great spiritual goodness at the core of every inconsiderate immoral soul, but he knows that he cannot force the soul to keep true to that goodness and manifest only loving, unselfish activity. When the conscious mind has so degraded itself that it cannot perceive of anything beyond materiality and self-centered actions, the super conscious mind will remain inactive, and the soul will be unable to spiritually advance (357-13_3). If the self-created separation between the conscious mind and the Mind of God becomes large, it may take many lifetimes until the soul can realize its future is decided by the way it uses life's challenges.

There are mental exercises that can help us become more consciously aware of our mental separation from the subconscious mind that will help us learn to recognize this limitation and overcome it in a way that brings spiritual benefits to the soul and human society. Proper moral and spiritual decisions and activities can reveal that life is more than a comfortable material existence and can allow us a glimpse of the glory of a loving God. We will look at the practices of prayer, meditation, and the setting of ideals to induce mental changes that help restore the soul to God consciousness.

There are limits to what a soul can and cannot do and still remain in spiritual attunement, but God does not impose limits on the thoughts or activities of a disincarnate or an incarnate soul. There is an enormous spectrum of thought and activity in which a soul can engage without violating spiritual law, but selfish thoughts and activities that belittle or injure others invariably push the soul away from the law of grace and trigger the law of cause and effect. Any soul can exercise its free will in defiance of its maker and cross the boundary between acceptable and unacceptable behavior, but there are consequences to every inappropriate thought and action. When unacceptable behavior occurs in the physical world, its consequences are met in the physical world. The soul must revisit and reevaluate its previous error and face new opportunities to make a more appropriate response; that is, a response that has its basis in the fruits of the spirit and similar moral and spiritual precepts that define the higher standard of behavior that is appropriate for a child of God. Repeated failure to correct these errors leaves the soul rudderless in a sea of material attractions and selfish desires (696-3_4). The discord and hostility seen in personal relationships and the conflicts and wars between nations are created by souls that have chosen to leave the service of God and fellow souls in favor of thoughts and activity that glorify their own minds and material bodies.

What can a soul do to extract itself from the recurring consequences of previous rebellious activity based on the inappropriate and delusional insistence that it can go it alone without acknowledging or considering its true relationship with God? How can God and souls use physical incarnation in the environment of the Earth plane and mental training in the supporting nonphysical realms to educate the soul of the need for it to re-orient its mental focus away from rebellion and selfishness so that it can rediscover its lost awareness of God and free itself from the seemingly never-ending cycles of rebirth? What role is played by God, and what role is played by the soul in this restoration process? We have seen that God has already taken the first steps in soul restoration by constructing a causal environment with a complex biological ecosystem, and designing a superb physical human body through which incarnated souls can express their current understanding of God, but where do we go from here?

Souls that were and are engaging in spiritual rebellion—and thus sinning against God—are compelled to cycle between the various education classes that are designed to reactivate the part of the soul mind that still retains latent memories of its spiritual roots. Every soul must learn the necessity for respecting the spiritual law that applies to it as a creature created by God. Far too many people on this Earth, perhaps even the vast majority of people, live in a state of unintentional consciousness whereby the pursuit of their daily physical needs and pleasurable activities absorb most of their time and attention. People become so deeply absorbed in sports, fashion, social media, and other forms of escapism that they lose sight of the more important aspects of life. Others are focused on acquiring greater wealth or just making ends meet and surviving for another day. It is vitally important that every individual maintain a proper balance between material attractions, material needs, and spiritual imperatives. The physical consciousness that is too strongly attached to material experiences of the body can become a mental cage in which the soul paces back and forth, and beyond which it is not willing to fully explore. Few people glimpse the true reality of the broader consciousness that lies beyond their material existence unless they have sensed the occasional mental tendril of latent spiritual urges or previous talents. The soul mind must learn to break out of this passive state of awareness and take the initiative to embark on a path of proactive intentional change in its spiritual and mental outlook and physical activities.

The soul's path forward in spiritual development is enhanced by making better choices and decisions during incarnation, decisions that demonstrate practical application of the spiritual lessons it has been taught, and that correct the poor choices it made during previous lives. It must demonstrate mastery of the mental and spiritual lessons it received in the nonphysical training centers while living in a material realm and engaging in social activity with fellow souls. This is where we take the final exam after we complete a training course. Every Earth-bound soul faces the same spiritual struggle. Spiritual law is the impersonal force that keeps souls returning to this rehabilitation facility until they are purified, perfected, and worthy of being in the presence of God. Souls must take the initiative to embark on this voyage of discovery with the faith and perseverance to see it through. God will always make sure that the temptations and trials of material life will not be more severe than the soul can tolerate, if the soul asks for his help in navigating the challenges ahead. This is where faith is essential, because without it the soul is unlikely to take the necessary first steps. It will be less willing to accept the suffering that it may endure and use suffering as a stepping stone on the path of spiritual progress. With concerted effort, secure in the certainty of spiritual success, the incarnated soul is able to use its inherited soul qualities of love, patience, kindness, mercy, and grace as the main operating principles for interpersonal exchanges during social activities involving family, community, and nation. Souls that rise to the challenge and are successful in keeping the conscious mind attuned to God and spiritualizing material activities reap mental and spiritual harmony, better physical health, and communion with the Creative Force that we worship as God (378-14_4). Each soul must do its part to bring the kingdom of God to the Earth by its thoughts, words and activities, and in so doing will realign its will and mind with the purposes of God, redeem itself, and claim its destiny to partake in eternal companionship with a loving Father.

There are several spiritual practices that can help train the soul mind to shift its center of mental awareness away from a purely physical awareness to a proper balance of spiritual and material awareness. This is true even when the incarnated soul is actively pursuing the usual occupations and interests that are necessary to sustain a human body and conscious mind in a complex human society. This shifting or rebalancing of the soul mind toward a more spiritual orientation is easier said than done. What practical steps can a soul take to begin the process of restoration? What can a soul, with its conscious awareness largely constrained and limited to the physical world and with a severely weakened mental connection to the knowledge of its true self, really do to make the best use of each incarnation? How can it best use each incarnation to understand its true nature and reconnect its often ignored mental link with God? How can the individual, the human being active on the Earth, regain consciousness of its real identity and individuality, which usually are only briefly glimpsed through remembered symbolic dreams and rare instances of intuition? There are several powerful tools that can be used to bring mental-spiritual understanding and even spiritual enlightenment to the conscious mind. Consistent application of these tools naturally leads to a redirection of human activity toward a more outward-oriented serving life and away from an inward-oriented self-serving life.

The readings, in common with many religions, recommend spiritual centering practices such as the use of prayer for self and others, the use of affirmations to bring the mind to a spiritually receptive state, and the regular reading of Scripture and other spiritual material. Prayer, meditation, and the setting of ideals are strongly advocated in the readings as practices that are highly effective for intentionally guiding the soul mind from a lower state of material consciousness to a higher state of God consciousness. The individual who dedicates time to these practices will notice a rising sense of peace and greater happiness and will be more prepared to properly respond in a loving manner to any mental and physical crisis that arises in their lives. Prayer and meditation will be briefly mentioned, but the main focus will be on the use of ideals. The mental techniques of meditation and the setting of spiritual ideals are complementary methods of training the soul mind. They help elevate the soul mind to an understanding of the need to suppress selfishness and enhance a sense of community and service. Meditation involves cooperation with God, and ideals involve cooperation with fellow souls. The mental transformation achieved by regular application of these spiritual tools not only leads to a better personal morality through more good and godly behavior in society, but also lessens the attraction of the conscious mind toward the fulfillment of material desires.

During life and at physical death, any new habituated patterns of thinking and modes of behavior that have elevated the spiritual awareness of the conscious mind will be transferred to and absorbed into the subconscious mind. A righteous life will help dilute and replace any poisonous, self-centered mental patterns accumulated by the soul during previous experiences. It will make the soul mind more receptive to and appreciative of the power of love and more open to the spiritual guidance that is always available from God through the sixth sense. When the soul is again ready to incarnate, its previous ability to successfully overcome a spiritual deficiency will allow it to more easily tackle other shortcomings that it needs to address instead of repeating previous lessons. The soul may still have to face some of the same or similar life situations again as a refresher course to make sure that the spiritual knowledge it has received is thoroughly ingrained into the soul mind and has become part of its core pattern of thought and activity. The gradual change of mental attitude will draw the soul closer to God, transform its physical activity from a selfish search for power and wealth into a selfless desire to show love toward others and assist those less fortunate in physical necessities and spiritual understanding.

Humans usually think of the spiritual realm as a place where all is perfect, everything is in a state of harmony, and we can bask in the radiant love of God for all eternity. But death does not radically change our mental outlook and attitude; only our seat of consciousness, our seat of awareness within the soul mind. Reading 254-92_9 puts this in blunt terms; "For do not consider for a moment ... that an individual soul-entity passing from an earth plane as a Catholic, a Methodist, an Episcopalian, is something else because he is dead! He's only a dead Episcopalian, Catholic or Methodist." The physical realm and the Earth, where cause and effect reign, is the plane of application where we are required to prove and demonstrate our understanding of God and become aware of our mental-spiritual relationship with him. We are not granted a peaceful, holy, and harmonious state of mind at death, but carry the remnants of our likes and dislikes; weaknesses and strengths; and propensity for discord, strife, and bickering with us into death. We underestimate the personal effort required to move out of this physical realm in a state of harmony and peace with God. Expecting the soul to suddenly love God and sibling souls because it has been released from the chore of animating a human body is a false belief. Only when we successfully complete and pass our spiritual lessons here on the Earth and learn to project harmony and peace as we instinctively and routinely make correct spiritual choices, will we carry those better traits beyond the Earth plane into other realms. Physical death does not make the soul mind more spiritual. The spiritual realm is not conducive to the restoration of God consciousness and is not an ideal place for redemption of the soul. Remember, the soul needs to be subjected to the causal environment of the Earth precisely because the soul mind has already failed in the noncausal spiritual realm to hold true to the spiritual purpose for its creation.

Communicating with God in Prayer

Individuals can prepare themselves to be of greater service to God and their fellow incarnated souls by a combination of prayer and meditation. The practice of daily prayer can prepare the individual for the more mentally intensive practice of meditation. Prayer is perhaps the most common mental tool used worldwide by persons who sense or know that a higher power exists and who feel the need to bring their hopes, concerns, worries, and fears to God. We pray for many things and for many reasons. We implore God to heal our bodies or our loved ones, especially if the illness is too serious to be cured by basic medical treatment or we consider it a matter of life or death. We ask that others be comforted during illness or stressful life situations. We pray for financial relief or for safety while on a trip. We ask for forgiveness when we have sinned or for the strength to do the right thing toward another person while in a difficult or confrontational situation. Sometimes we don't have any particular request in mind but just want to keep the lines of communication open or offer our thanks for God's many blessings. Why do we have to express our desires in prayer when God is widely understood to be omniscient and knows what we need before we ask (Matthew 6:7–8)? God is not omniscient when it comes to the free will decisions and desires of the soul. He knows what we need, the decisions that we should make for spiritual growth, and he gives us every opportunity to make them correctly, but he doesn't know what we will decide. He doesn't know our thoughts before we formulate them or how we will respond to a given life situation. The act of coming to God in verbal or mental prayer reveals our inner desires to him, indicates whether we are physically or spiritually focused, and indicates our spiritual attunement to him (262-64_11). God answers sincere prayer (Luke 11:9–13; Matthew 7:7–8) but some prayers aren't godly or appropriate. Public prayer can become a self-serving outward projection of pride and personality when an individual uses it to show off his gift of oratory, eloquence, or sense of superiority instead of serving God. Jesus brought this spiritual deficiency, a form of self-exaltation and self-righteousness, to the attention of his followers (Luke 18:10–14).

Why is prayer an effective tool for reestablishing our connection with God? It is not that God wants us to repeatedly or frequently ask him for some favor or request, or that he wants us to show our dependence upon him by constantly reciting a shopping list of things that he already knows we need. Sincere prayer directs our mind toward the one who created us and who always stands ready to help us meet demanding and frustrating life situations that we have created by our selfishness and rebellious behavior. Prayer is perhaps the most basic form of mental training. It can begin the process of moving our center of attention away from ourselves and the world around us toward a source of hope greater than ourselves, toward our creator and the source of all life. It temporarily breaks our preoccupation with life's difficulties by allowing us to share the burdens we carry, bringing peace and quelling anger. In prayer we admit that we cannot pull ourselves up by our own bootstraps, and learn to seek spiritual help from our creator. When we convey our private thoughts, feelings, fears, and hopes to God, we open ourselves to guidance from him and cooperation with him. Prayer brings the impersonal intelligent mind of an infinite God into an intimate personal relationship with the mind of the soul as we communicate with our creator (1158-14_12). It is effective when practiced individually, but becomes even more effective as a cooperative practice with like-minded individuals. The focused thought of group prayer can enhance the spiritual power of the prayer (900-23_7).

You have probably heard the expression that all prayers are answered, but sometimes the answer is no. We usually assume our prayer has been answered with a resounding "no" when we perceive apparent inaction or silence from God on the subject of our prayer. On what basis does God answer prayer? Does he assess each request on the degree of sincerity he hears when we pray? Does he ignore requests for material goods if there appears to be a selfish element involved? Are some prayers answered in ways that are not readily apparent to us because we are not properly attuned to the Mind of God? Are there any overall criteria that can help us assess whether or not our prayer was answered? Yes, there are, but first we must realize that the answer to any prayer is, at the end of the day, for the glory of God and serves his purpose. It is not a boon to satisfy a personal request in the manner expected by the supplicant. If we really want to know if and how our prayers might be answered, we need to ask ourselves if God will be glorified if he were to answer the prayer in the manner and with the outcome we expect. We need to be aware that requests for material help and even physical and mental healing may not align with the needs of the soul, and the soul is far more important to God than the corporeal body or our acquisition of material goods.

A request to God for healing always has a conditional, but usually unappreciated and unrealized, aspect that is rarely recognized. What would you (or the subject of the prayer) do with your life if you were healed? This question is always in the Mind of God when we pray to him for healing. The answer to this question may affect the way in which God responds to healing prayer. Why would God want to heal a physically sick individual if he knows that there little likelihood of an accompanying inner spiritual healing of the soul? What is the spiritual purpose of granting physical healing to an individual suffering from a serious illness but who intends to resume a life of decadence and debauchery and will continue to squander his or her spiritual inheritance? God is far more concerned with the eternal soul than the transient and temporary body. There are times when the answer to our prayer is no, because God knows that, with the right attitude, the suffering we are enduring will make us a better person, a better soul. He is giving us the opportunity to use the situation for positive spiritual change. People who seek healing of the body while recognizing the parallel need for inner spiritual healing receive the most benefit from their restored health (2482-1_20). The physical condition of the body reflects the spiritual condition of the soul. Perhaps the tenth leper recognized his need for spiritual healing as well as physical healing and his expression of thanks was indicative of that insight (Luke 17:11–19). Sometimes a prayer is finished with the words "not my will but thy will be done." This is an acknowledgement that we don't have the answers, and our desires may not coincide with God's purpose for us or for the individual for whom we are praying. It allows us to place the final outcome with God and removes any thought that we can use prayer to tell God what to do. Prayer does not absolve us from the responsibility of doing all that we can physically do to aid ourselves or another person, but it helps us to remember that there is a higher power that cares about us and wants us to lean on him for moral and spiritual guidance and support.

Not long ago, there was a flurry of messages, phone calls, and social media activity to inform family and friends about an individual who had been diagnosed with a serious disease the previous day. There was a lot of discussion over how the disease would likely disrupt the person's career and affect his immediate family, how the spouse would have to get a job to help support the family, and how much of the looming medical bills would be paid by insurance. There were even discussions about helping the spouse get out of the pending purchase of another residence that was part of a planned career move. Of course everyone volunteered to pray for the sick person. These discussions and prayers were no sooner underway when new information surfaced that the affected person had a rare type of the disease that was treatable and would likely be challenging, but probably would not be the calamity that was being predicted in the discussions. Upon hearing the news, one of the individuals involved in the discussions stated that the new information was the result of prayer, that it was God's answer to the prayers that were offered during the past twenty-four hours. As much as it might feel good to believe that prayer works this way, there seem to be serious questions as to the accuracy of that statement. The patient's disease had likely progressed for months or years before symptoms developed that led the patient to seek medical advice. The blood samples that were used to diagnose the disease had been collected and delivered to the laboratory before the patient or the patient's family and friends were notified of the initial findings. So, did the collective prayers retroactively change the laboratory test results or alter the disease from a more virulent form to a rare but manageable form? Prayer works and prayer should be offered for sick individuals, but one should be careful about blindly interpreting a favorable outcome of events as proof of an answered prayer or evidence of the prayer's ability to influence God.

Listening to God in Meditation

Meditation is a spiritual training technique that applies the commandment to love God with all our heart, mind, and soul in a way that brings spiritual growth and enlightenment to the soul. It attunes the soul mind to the Mind of God and helps the soul to focus on its relationship to God and its true spiritual nature even when the soul is incarnated and attentive to the demands of human society. Meditation enhances the mental-spiritual union of soul and God and brings the soul mind into alignment with the Mind of God. It is a powerful and direct application of will that encourages the soul to remember the fact that at its core, it is one with God and can reclaim God consciousness (Puryear, 1992; Cayce and Van Auken, 2007). It is a form of mental training that involves intentionally setting aside or bypassing the conscious mind and allowing the seat of awareness to migrate into the celestial realm of the soul toward the subconscious mind and the deeper level of super conscious mind. It is a powerful technique for reorienting our desires such that the soul mind is brought to a higher level of consciousness. The most difficult part of meditation comes from the need to be mentally quiet. The key to overcoming this obstacle is patience—an inherent soul trait that is too often atrophied from disuse. During meditation the will is used to tightly control the thoughts of the conscious mind to keep the soul mind from being distracted by the constant flow of sensory information from the body and the mind's desire to review current events, problems, and experiences. With persistent practice the conscious mind is awakened to the inner presence of the subconscious mind, and the higher spiritual values and moral principles of the soul are brought into activity in the material world.

Meditation also works directly at the interface of the soul and body to spiritualize the body by bringing its activities under the shared control of the subconscious mind and the physical conscious mind. It alters the connectivity between the soul mind and the human body that it is animating. As the regions of higher consciousness in the soul mind are activated in the incarnated soul, the spiritual principles that are held in mental pattern can be more easily accessed by the conscious mind. As the conscious mind becomes more receptive to the influence of the subconscious mind and assimilates its spiritual advice, it will begin to reevaluate its choices in life. It will seek to rediscover and reactivate the original mental pattern of the soul mind that holds the key to God awareness and that allows the mind to rediscover its connection with God. Over time, these higher spiritual principles will be more likely to be expressed through the normal daily activities of the body (Thurston, 1996). Meditation can teach the soul to recognize and distinguish between God's Will and the will of the soul. Initially, there may be some difficulty in determining whether the individual is simply listening to his own mind expressing its thoughts and desires or is truly communing with God and properly interpreting God's words. The individual can learn to attune his or her mind to the inner "voice" of God, listening for God's response to questions posed in earnest prayer or simply listening to hear what message God might wish to impart to the conscious mind. The meditation experience may include a vision, an inner voice, an intuitive feeling, or only silence. As the individual becomes more attuned to the presence of God, it becomes easier to be aware of the voice of God and the influence of God in daily activities.

Meditation can cleanse the thoughts and manifested activity of the practitioner as the conscious mind is guided to a closer union with the subconscious mind and elevates the spiritual attunement of the cells of the body. It influences the activity of the hormonal centers of the human body and the distribution and amount of blood flow through the brain (Newberg, 2012). It brings the activities of the body into better alignment with the soul's spiritual purpose and diminishes the urge of the conscious mind to derive its sense of self-worth from the material world. It can reduce the desire to seek satisfaction from material power and wealth. Meditation affects the soul mind at the subconscious level to bring the subconscious mind into action as a partner with the conscious mind. The conscious mind becomes aware that it is only a portion of the larger soul mind. Long-term application of meditation techniques can transform the conscious awareness of the practitioner and allow the conscious mind to more clearly recognize its spiritual origins through the thick fog of materialism.

The Application of Ideals to Raise Spiritual Awareness

The incarnated soul can use the conflicts that arise during interpersonal interactions to realign its patterns of thinking to include more purposeful and intentional expressions of spiritual truths. One technique highly recommended by the reading is the use of ideals, specific intentionally directed life activities or practices based on a standard of perfection. Ideals can be used to alter or remove habitual patterns of thinking and acting that cause the soul to lose awareness of its spiritual purpose for incarnation. This involves setting physical, mental, moral, and spiritual rules of behavior that, over time, will lead the soul mind to a closer union with the Mind of God, toward a stronger sense of God consciousness and a better ability to perceive the presence of God. Everyone sets ideals, whether or not they are aware of the fact. An unconsciously set ideal is a pattern of behavior that a person establishes as he or she encounters various people and engages in daily interpersonal activity in the absence of a conscious effort to set and live by a higher standard of morality and spiritual values. It is the spiritually lazy approach to life. An individual who has not set a spiritual-based ideal or that has allowed the formation of an ideal to have occurred haphazardly or arise out of the attractions of physical consciousness to materiality disrupts their ability to contact spiritual forces. They lose contact with that aspect of the soul mind that contains stored experiences and knowledge of spiritual principles.

The use of ideals actuates the physical consciousness to the meaning and value of the commandment of Jesus to love thy neighbor as thyself (Matthew 22:36–40) and makes practical application of the spiritual force awakened during prayer and meditation (270-33_11). Ideals are used to modify and transform conscious thought patterns and physical activities that are counter to the higher spiritual purpose of the soul. They are deemed by the readings to be especially powerful and effective in bringing major spiritual transformation to the seeking soul. The setting of ideals incorporates the idea of communal or corporate salvation and the concept that souls are a portion of God and are not entirely independent from the cosmic intelligence that is God. Souls are not completely isolated from or separate from their soul siblings because at some level of consciousness and spiritual development, soul minds that are mentally and spiritually attuned to God are also attuned to one another. Souls are the children of God and the true images of God. Human beings are physical expressions of those soul children. As soul children of God, we must learn to show love, honor, and respect toward our sibling souls, both in the cosmic realm and the material realm. The idea that no man is an island unto himself is true not only because humans need fellow humans to live, grow, and survive in the physical world but also because humans, as incarnated souls united in the Wholeness of God, are mentally interconnected at the subconscious level. It is essential to soul survival that we do not use our different individualities or human personalities to keep us divided. Souls have a much greater mental and spiritual bond than is apparent or obvious from our daily human interactions.

How are ideals set, and how are they put into practice to effect change in the mind of the soul? Humans intentionally acquire ideals when they make a concerted effort to establish a spiritual ideal, but they also unintentionally acquire ideals when they inadvertently let the mind attach to material desires that are selfish and elevate those desires into an ideal. The readings stress that a spiritual ideal should cause the soul mind to stretch beyond its current material-minded state in an attitude of faith and trust in God. It should mold the mind into a true image of God by intentionally realigning its will and mind to the purpose and plan of God for the soul. The readings place great emphasis on the value of ideals and their role in reshaping the soul mind to a more spiritual state of awareness. Meditation can be used to activate an ideal and enhance the individual's ability to consciously apply the ideal in life situations. Several of the 262-series readings are devoted to the beneficial effects of higher ideals and the necessity of holding fast to those ideals to affect mental advancement and spiritual growth. These readings were compiled into two books of twelve lessons devoted to the application and explanation of their core teachings (Study Group #1, 2019; Study Group #1, 2016). The third lesson in the first book describes the power of ideals and the means or manner in which ideals can be used to help the soul prosper spiritually and evolve to a greater God consciousness. As the soul grows spiritually, its innate godly attributes will begin to be habitually expressed as higher modes of moral behavior within human society. The application of higher ideals to everyday living is an effective tool that can permanently instill a high state of spiritual consciousness and God awareness in the soul that decides to value and respect the biblical injunction "If you will be my people, I will be your God" (Exodus 6:7; 2 Corinthians 6:18; 520-3_19; 5752-5_14). The setting of ideals and their application involves changing the way we interact with our fellow humans to better express and put into practice the commandment given by Jesus to love our neighbor as we love ourselves.

The proper intentional application of ideals changes the way the conscious mind perceives other incarnated souls and the way the conscious mind directs the body to interact with them. It sets the mind at peace with God and with neighbors; helps eliminate responses to life situations that end in anger, fear, accusations, and fault-finding; and restores peace and harmony in personal relationships (357-13_15). The use of ideals makes practical application of the biblical injunction to treat others as you would like them to treat you (Luke 6:31). It not only involves better modes of interaction with other people in human society but involves the concept of service whereby we redirect our energies and efforts toward helping other people who are less fortunate than us. This help may not only alleviate the material needs of those around us, but the act of extending a hand in loving service can cause another soul to become aware of its need to embrace a more spiritual frame of mind. It might influence the person to seek guidance and help from God as it struggles to face the material impact of its spiritual errors and deficiencies. Service to others can help them become aware of what they lost as they focused too strongly upon materiality and too little on spiritual growth. As the conscious mind is guided into making choices and decisions that more fully implement patterns of human behavior that express love, kindness, and patience toward other human beings, the conscious mind itself is modified and becomes more spiritually oriented in its thought patterns and priorities. This process not only brings spiritual growth to the soul and brings it closer to salvation, that is, to reunion with God, it also uplifts the larger society of incarnated souls.

If we seek God only through prayer and meditation, we miss the transformative power of the fruits of the spirit—a power that allows our minds and attitudes to be changed through a genuine desire to serve others. When we let God express his love through us, we become more virtuous, more righteous, more moral, and more incorruptible in the face of evil and temptation. The application of ideals through service not only benefits the individuals who experience our better side, who receive help or comfort from us, but also strengthens the will of the soul. As the will of the soul becomes more aligned with God's Will, the soul naturally activates God's purpose for the soul. The application of ideals can repattern the mind into a channel of blessing toward others by exchanging negative and harmful thought patterns with positive and beneficial ones. The will and mind of the soul construct new patterns of thought that, in time, become ingrained in the mind and routinely manifested in human behavior, bringing the soul into attunement with God. As we express love through the exercise of ideals, we begin to better understand the truth of God, not as an intellectual exercise of the mind but as an inner awareness from the heart, a form of mental-emotional awareness where the presence of God is revealed to us. Reading 262-81_13 tells us the nature of the spiritual truth we should all seek in our quest for understanding and wisdom in the following words, "What is Truth? That which makes aware to the inmost self or the soul the Divine and its purposes with that soul." As we become more aware of the truth of his presence and understand his immense love for us and desire for our companionship, our inner being will be warmed like the sun's rays striking our bodies on a warm summer day.

Establishing ideals encourages the physical conscious mind to aspire to specific moral codes of conduct during interpersonal activities and sets manageable spiritual objectives that, through time, patience, and multiple experiences, redirect the mind away from self-centeredness and self-gratification. The dedicated long-term practice of this technique develops habitual patterns of thinking and acting that emphasize manifestation of the fruits of the spirit while constantly reminding the mind of its spiritual roots. Remember that the mind is the impulsive force that acts on spirit to fulfill the process of creativity in the spiritual and material realms. It takes intent and determination to break detrimental activity that has become persistent and habitual. It takes a sustained mental effort to substitute ungodly habits with spiritually sound practices and actions. It involves retraining the conscious mind to release old habitual patterns of thought and their manifestations in everyday life to bring the mind and the directed actions of the physical body more in line with the spiritual roots of the soul (357-13_15). It truly makes the body the hands and feet of God (Matthew 25:35-40; 1 Peter 4:10-11) in a seamless manner by integrating the higher spiritual purpose and inherited godly qualities of the soul into the thoughts of the physical conscious mind and the actions of the body.

Undesirable habitual mental patterns with little or no spiritual value may not be readily recognized or identified by the conscious mind. Many of these activities have severe physical and emotional consequences, which become part of the physical and mental suffering that are key elements in the re-education of the lost soul. It isn't that God wants us to suffer and wants to inflict pain as a form of punishment, but that the thoughts and behavior of selfish rebellious souls naturally and consequentially through spiritual law lead to physical and mental pain and suffering. Ideals work directly on the conscious mind and personality by encouraging individuals to make willful changes to material-oriented and selfish habitual thought patterns and modes of behavior so that they gradually become more spiritually oriented and aligned toward a higher sense of morality and even righteous behavior. Ideals work indirectly on the subconscious mind and individuality as the new thought patterns based on spiritual principles are incorporated into the overall character of the soul. These new patterns are advantageous for the spiritual growth of the soul mind, and their effect goes far beyond a simple alteration of lifestyle within a single lifetime. Drug addicts let their insatiable desire for drugs become the guiding light of their conscious minds and therefore their mental ideal by default. It is the only course of action that their mind can comprehend, and their will is along for the ride instead of directing the mind toward higher spiritual ideals. Their life revolves around satisfying that unintentional ideal. Unless the person can suppress or replace the thought patterns that keep urging them to take another fix or another drink, their efforts are likely to end in failure. The will of the soul is instrumental in making the initial decision to allow the body to ingest the drug but soon is unable to exert itself to tamp down or stop the rising flood of desire for the next fix and the rush of pleasure it will bring. The independence and integrity of the will has been compromised, and it is quite difficult for it to restore moral principles as the basis for physical activity. The soul must be willing to establish a valid spiritual ideal to override and replace the physical desire, but it is not easy for a soul to make major life changes that rip it out of long established indulgent modes of activity that are pleasing in the short term but damaging in the long term.

Unless harnessed with a spiritual ideal, the soul mind can become engulfed in the myriad of environmental and social problems of the physical world, letting the world control the soul's destiny instead of letting God lead the soul to a higher calling that brings love and peace into the world. The application of ideals is one of the most important ways to guide human life for the spiritual benefit of the soul (357-13_6). When used in conjunction with our conscious knowledge of the life and teachings of Jesus, they help us to understand and fulfill our spiritual purpose in life and elevate our self-consciousness to include awareness of the presence of God. The highest ideals encourage an individual to take specific actions that will achieve change in his or her mental attitude and bring spiritual awareness of the immense benefit of applying the teachings of Jesus to everyday life situations. The desire to live according to the teachings and life example of Jesus is often mentioned as the highest ideal that any person can desire to attain (2533-7_7; 436-2_29), but be aware that the profession of belief in a church tenet or dogma does not meet the standard of an ideal (5392-1_6). A soul that retains consciousness of its close relationship with God even when immersed in a physical world that constantly demands its attention, and often places distractions and temptations before it, will be a conduit that allows God's love to flow through the soul into the society of humans. As this channeled flow of love alters the propensity of the soul to live life selfishly and brings to it the desire to live life selflessly, human society will be transformed.

The effort required to successfully change old habits and to stop falling prey to the lure of material and sensual attractions would be too great if undertaken all at once. It takes tremendous mental effort and will power to alter the destiny of the soul. It requires disrupting and sidelining the accumulated negative influences of a long string of selfish decisions and actions, many of which have occurred during previous incarnations. That is why it is more effective for the soul to work on one or a few deficiencies during a lifetime, and the reason that apparently good people are not immune to tragedy and suffering. The consequences of poor choices may be postponed until another lifetime, but the soul will ultimately face and need to correct its propensity to make spiritual errors. Progress in a given lifetime is made by using a step-by-step progression of smaller changes and accomplishments that will lead the dedicated person to manifest and embrace higher spiritual morals and truths in daily life

(303-14_16; 922-1_6). In the words of the readings, the spiritual growth of the soul is best accomplished when the mental challenge of overcoming its spiritual faults and failures is met a little here, a little there, line upon line, and precept upon precept (39-3_5). One graphic analogy given by the readings is of a lily unfolding itself from the muck of the Earth to raise its face to its Master, the difficulty of pushing itself out of the muck being comparable to the difficulty the soul meets in trying to lift itself out of the mire of doubt, fear, and anxiety it faces in materiality. But the reward is tremendous, and the soul mind is ecstatic in success as its new-found conscious awareness of God radiates as a glow from the face of the human body it animates to bring hope into the hearts of its fellow incarnated souls (827-1_11).

The incarnated soul must climb out of its decadent material comfort zone, make choices that may initially make it uncomfortable, and learn to make decisions that allow consideration for the rights and needs of others. It may well require multiple lifetimes before the deliberate behavioral changes that are needed to activate new thought patterns become a permanent mindset, but progress will be made and will eventually allow the individual to break spiritually damaging habits. Souls will learn to recognize the causal effects of inappropriate thoughts and actions and learn to consciously make course corrections that lead to the cessation of inappropriate activity. The process of breaking a negative spiritual habit is usually a long-term process because souls are not released from the consequences of previous poor choices just because they make a commitment to change and are demonstrating some signs of success. Only as the will of the soul holds true to a long-term course of spiritual renewal can it strengthen and reinforce the desire to reverse sinful soul habits and reinforce the likelihood of long-term success. As the soul mind and will cooperate and consistently and forcefully stop inappropriate and unwanted manifested activity, the new patterns of thought become stronger, and the individual is better able to navigate away from the old harmful pattern. To become a valuable tool for spiritual growth, new intentional ideals must be of a higher spiritual value than the old patterns of thought and activity and must lead to a more spiritual way of thinking.

Individuals can easily define, set, and work toward an ideal, but most individuals probably will find it difficult to carry forth with their honorable intentions with the same intensity, focus, and strength day in and day out. The initial excitement and good intentions bring out a strong enthusiasm for a dedicated and valiant effort to achieve the greatest possible effect in the shortest amount of time, but this effort will likely wax and wane according to the current life situation the individual faces and the emotional stress that comes from hardship and fear. The soul mind must undergo a transformation from self-centeredness to God-centeredness that transcends merely living a mostly good life. Every good life is beneficial to soul growth, but soul restoration and perfection like that manifested in the life of Jesus is a long-term process that is impossible to achieve in one lifetime, but with perseverance, prayer, and a willingness to let God help, it can be accomplished. The setting of proper ideals helps the conscious mind to course correct itself during the soul's incarnation to effect spiritual growth. Memories of each well-lived life will elevate the subconscious mind of the soul to a higher spiritual state and lead it closer to the companionship that God envisioned when he created souls. Ultimately, the soul mind is brought closer to the mind of its creator and the antagonism between the material-oriented conscious mind and the spiritual-oriented super conscious mind is resolved in favor of a higher state of consciousness that reveals the abiding presence of God.

It is the responsibility of each person to develop and activate ideals that will meet the spiritual needs of their soul within the context of its previous experiences and interpersonal relationships. Nobody else can truly know and understand the circumstances that led to our current life situation or the character traits that are in most need of repair, although some character flaws may seem obvious to an unbiased observer. The readings suggest that individuals draw up a list of spiritual ideals and any inappropriate thoughts and behavior that have been hindering the progress of their spiritual development toward those ideals. Spiritual ideals might include the exercise of patience, the desire to be more generous, the perceived need to be kinder, or other patterns of behavior that might be appropriate to correct perceived spiritual weaknesses or deficiencies. For each particular spiritual ideal a person identifies as worthy of pursuit, they are to write down specific mental and physical actions that could be taken to alter inappropriate thoughts and behaviors. The readings encourage each person to work on one spiritual ideal until they are satisfied that they have achieved a measurable and observable change in their life before moving to a new ideal (5091-3; 3051-6_6). This mimics the broader pattern of recurring lives, each of which have a primary purpose to cleanse the soul of one or more specific spiritual problems. This approach to producing a workable set of ideals and applying them in everyday life has been compiled and published to encourage use of the technique and to aid in its practical application (Shambaugh and Puryear, 1981). Although it is impossible to develop personalized ideals herein, a general approach to the concept of ideals is given in the hope that it may provide motivation and guide the reader into the process of setting specific ideals that will be of personal spiritual benefit. Readers are encouraged to study the referenced book and prepare a set of spiritual, mental, and material ideals that will be of the most benefit in their lives.

Spiritual ideal: I resolve to realign my will to better represent and imitate the Will of God, to draw on my soul's inherent godly spiritual attributes of love, kindness, and patience for inspiration and strength. I resolve to seek pleasure and satisfaction from the higher pursuit of spiritual perfection instead of the lower pursuit of self-gratification and self-glorification so that I will be better able to fulfill my soul's purpose as a child of God and future companion of God.

Our ideals should be chosen to correct our perceived personal spiritual shortcomings. We may draw inspiration for our ideals from the lives of spiritually adept individuals who have proven that they were willing to sacrifice their self-interests, self-centeredness, and sense of entitlement for the greater benefit of mankind. The living examples and highest moral teachings of well-respected philosophers and leaders (The Buddha, Mahatma Gandhi, Mother Theresa, John Wesley, St. Augustine, etc.) can be sources of inspiration that lead to spiritual growth when a sustained effort is made to mentally and physically follow the example of such leaders and their most spiritual teachings. The best spiritual ideals that can be used to improve and enhance the life of a human being and so give spiritual meaning and value to the life expressions and experiences of an incarnated soul are embodied in the fruits of the spirit and other moral and spiritual principles that meet those high standards. No one should be satisfied when a particular goal has been achieved or when one bad habit has been conquered and no longer takes holds on the conscious mind.

The soul should ever aim higher than the example provided by any contemporary or historical religious or spiritual leader. However, the readings identify Jesus as the unique and only human representation of the highest spiritual ideals and declare that no ideal that we may imagine or formulate will be better than those that seek to emulate the moral teachings and actions of Jesus (2116-2_5; 2533-7_7). The purpose of soul incarnation is not fulfilled by belief in a particular philosophy or adherence to the prescribed doctrine or teachings of any particular religious organization, but only by finding the truth that is revealed as the soul embraces its creator. No soul should consider that it has achieved its highest possible spiritual aspiration until its activity in human incarnation equals in all respects the high standards set by Jesus the Christ in spirit, mind, and manifested activity. This is not a call to accept the Christian religion, Christian theology, or even the writings of his apostles, but is a statement that every seeking soul will eventually come to know of Jesus and his sacrifice for all of mankind. Because souls reincarnate and because spiritual growth is an evolution, many souls that have not had the privilege of learning about the historical Jesus in their previous lives will have that privilege in future lives when it is necessary for their further spiritual development. The principles that he espoused reside in memory within every soul mind, and any person can open themselves to the presence of God, follow the Way of Jesus, and commune with their creator.

As a part of daily prayer to keep this spiritual ideal alive and active in our conscious mind, we might ask God to help us to become fully aware that we are his children, created from his essence, his Spirit, and are endowed with the same creative abilities that he possesses. We might pray that we be made consciously aware of our relationship with him and understand that our very existence is solely at his pleasure. We can ask that he help us understand the relationship between our conscious mind and sense of humanity and our true nature that is contained within our subconscious mind and soul individuality. We can ask that he give us the wisdom to apply our free will to further his plan and purpose for our soul. We can pray that God will help us remember that we are a portion of him and understand our need to rededicate ourselves to his holy purpose that we rejected and abandoned so long ago. We can ask his help to understand the concept of Spirit as the life force of all that exists and Mind as the Creative Force by which his Will is made known and manifested throughout his creations.

Mental ideal: I resolve to consistently make choices and decisions that are compatible with my highest spiritual ideals and that reflect a strong desire to reunite my soul mind with the Mind of God. I will seek guidance and strength from my higher consciousness while turning away from the more base desires that arise in my physical conscious mind. I resolve to rebalance my mind by moving my center of awareness away from self-centered avenues of expression toward thoughts that are more consistent with being a child of God.

Our state of mind as we participate in the various societal activities that are part of our life experiences is of critical importance to the spiritual success of our life on the Earth. This includes our mental approach to relationships within our families and our attitude as we participate in the company or business that we own or where we are employed, whether that be in a position of authority, a junior clerk, an accountant, an assembly-line worker, a laborer, or a janitor (5392-1_7). All of these life situations and life experiences require us to daily make choices with respect to the type of interaction we will have with other individuals. We should seek to let those interpersonal interactions be guided by the highest ideals to which we have professed allegiance. We should rely on God to give us strength and encouragement as we seek to spiritually improve our thoughts as we navigate life in the physical realm. We should be aware that every decision and choice we make has physical and spiritual consequences. We need to learn to make choices that not only fulfill our material dreams but that also honor a sense of respect, equality, and fellowship toward the people with whom we interact each day. Our choices must include the concept of stewardship of the Earth's resources and ecosystem that God prepared for our spiritual benefit. We must let our desire to express broader spiritual ideals help us to better understand God and emulate his Son. We will know how successful we have been at expressing our higher purpose through mental ideals by the effect our choices have in the lives of other incarnated souls.

As a part of daily prayer to keep this mental ideal alive and active in our conscious mind, we might ask God to help us activate more godlike patterns of thought that will keep us oriented toward our spiritual desires. We can ask for the strength, understanding and wisdom to refocus and transform our inner awareness so that we change old selfish patterns of thinking to a pattern of mind that mimics as closely as possible the one held by Jesus the Christ. In our hour of weakness, we can beseech him to give us the strength to overcome the old comfortable thought patterns that spawn sinful habits, to give us the power to let them go and cast them by the wayside of life as we embrace the mental awareness of his abiding presence. Only with his help can we purge thoughts that build barriers to better relationships with family members, friends, and acquaintances, and embrace thoughts that bring peace, contentment, and joy to our lives.

We cannot go it alone, but need his help to replace the strong ego-driven desires and selfish ambitions that pull us away from the consciousness of our creator.

Material Ideal: I resolve to apply my renewed and revitalized spiritual awareness and my enhanced consciousness of God's purpose for me during my daily activities in human society. I resolve to manifest my highest spiritual ideals by altering my habitual patterns of selfish behavior and ungodly actions within the society of men and women, and so fulfill my part in bringing the kingdom of God to the Earth.

Material ideals can alter our propensity to excessively collect material wealth and to conduct ourselves poorly and disrespectfully in the presence of other incarnated souls. We should identify specific instances in which our choices and behavior have caused other people to be treated unfairly or where we have taken advantage of others. We should learn to specifically and intentionally make behavioral choices that make our actions morally better and more loving. Perhaps we have been rude to an acquaintance at work, too quick to snap at our spouse, or in too big of a hurry to give time to our child who needs our attention. As part of the practical application of the material ideal, we need to recognize and identify where we are deficient in the application of spiritual principles. It is helpful to prepare a list of habitual actions we wish to correct and refer to it as a reminder of the changes we are trying to make and to monitor our progress. As we correct these spiritual errors and remove the poor patterns of behavior that keep us separated from God, we will learn to recognize that each of these life situations is one moment in a plethora of life opportunities provided by God to help us make step-by-step progress in spiritual growth. As we successfully navigate these challenges, our lives will become more pleasant, and we will face fewer and fewer situations that bring physical pain, suffering, and mental turmoil in our lives. As we bring higher spiritual ideals into the battle for soul restoration, as we realign our mental attitude toward fellow souls, and as we correct our poor behavior in human society, we begin to purify and restore our soul and make progress toward the state of perfection that Jesus asked each of us to attain (Matthew 5:48). As we make progress, we should aim higher and seek strength from God to become a spiritual light unto the people we meet.

As a part of daily prayer to keep material ideals alive and active in our conscious mind, we might ask God to help us grow spiritually as we apply the ideal. We need to ask for his help and strength so that we manifest the love of God throughout the day as we are faced with and contend with different crises and trials that require us to express ourselves in words and deeds. Among the things we might ask for is the strength to consistently express love to everyone we meet, no matter how stressful or negative the situation, and for help to outwardly express the fruits of the spirit such as patience, kindness, long suffering, grace, and mercy as they are appropriate in given situations. As we continue praying, meditating and applying ideals, we will acquire the ability to discern God's purpose for us, feel the loving presence of God within us, and be given the honor of being an open channel for the outpouring of his spiritual blessings into a troubled world.

Prayer, meditation, and the application of ideals are spiritual practices that conquer our failure to seek his will in all things and help us come face-to-face with and correct our spiritual deficiencies. Selfishness causes us to turn away from God and think that we do not need him. As we face our failure to live up to his expectations by intentionally altering our thought patterns and human behavior to better conform to his will, our conscious mind is bathed in the light of his presence, and we experience the awareness of his closeness and the Almighty power that he radiates. When we turn from God, we create spiritual shadows thrown by our desire for self-gratification and our propensity to act on self-centered desires. When we seek and face the light of God, we walk without stumbling because there are no shadows cast by our selfishness (262-28_7; 262-30_6). Our selfish desires interfere with our communion with God's and prevent us from manifesting God's gracious loving spirit in the material world. We must turn away from this absorption with ourselves and our own self-interest and perceived needs that blind us to spiritual opportunities and cause us to increase the suffering in this world. Through the application of ideals to correct and prevent spiritual error, we can dampen and eliminate the carnal desires that draw us away from the knowledge of his presence. Spiritual restoration will follow as we remove from our lives the desire for unbridled wealth, power, and dominance over our fellow souls, and the willingness to trample on others as we seek to selfishly fulfill our desires. The use of meditation and ideals can lessen or eliminate the greed for possessions and lust for self-gratification that clogs our conscious minds and keeps us from truly knowing God. It is imperative that we learn to use that which God has provided us to further his plans and purposes on this Earth instead of dwelling on the selfishness that drives us to find pleasure and solace in material satisfaction and the sense of entitlement.

If we are willing to step out in faith, to let God and Jesus walk with us on this long and difficult path, our efforts will be enhanced and magnified, and we will succeed. We will fulfill our Father's faith in us as expressed by Jesus in the statement that we are gods, by which he meant that we are gods in the making (John 10:34–36; Psalms 82:6–7). If we stay true to the spiritual purpose for which our soul was created, we can fulfill our purpose as companions of God and share in his creative endeavors (165-26_25; 877-21_30; 452-3_13). We will never be the Whole of God, but we can become as close to God as we desire if we let love be the governing personal quality in our lives. We need to integrate our growing awareness of God's purpose for us into our daily lives—a difficult task for many of us who are so used to making habitual responses to certain life situations we face. But the reason we face them again and again is to learn to make better choices that lead to more loving and spiritually rewarding outcomes and to make sure that this better approach to life becomes part of who we are at the deeper level of our soul individuality. Each better choice that a soul makes is a step closer to the reunion of the soul and God and the restoration of harmony and mutual respect among the incarnated souls that manifest their thoughts in human society. With perseverance and patience, we can use these and other methods of mental-spiritual training to reorder our life priorities and redirect our mental attitude to achieve the spiritual mindset that the readings call Christ Consciousness.

Christ Consciousness and the Redemption of Fallen Souls

Then, just being kind, just being patient, just showing love for thy fellow man; THAT is the manner in which an individual works AT becoming aware of the consciousness of the Christ Spirit (Edgar Cayce Reading 272-9_8)

Our conscious minds are only a small aspect of the near-boundless soul mind that is active in the borderland realm, mental-spiritual training centers and greater cosmic realm. It mainly derives nourishment from the use and abuse of physical desires and constantly feeds information about our daily activities to our subconscious mind. Upon the death of the body, it will cease activity because there is no physical sensory data to process. However, the mental residue from the activity of the conscious mind in relation to the physical universe will remain within and influence the subconscious mind after the death of the body. When the soul disengages from the body, it will once again use the subconscious mind to activate thoughts and manifest action, process environmental data from the borderland realm, and conduct soul-to-soul interaction through direct influence on other soul minds. Our recent physical memories will remain intact until they fade in the normal course of activity as we interact with other souls in the borderland realm and training centers. Our mind will not magically transform from a condition of selfish thought patterns to a spiritual state of unselfish thought patterns just because we die repentant of a life of sin and spiritual error. Our souls will not be restored to a higher state of spiritual perfection or even to a more godly state of mind by the death of our physical body. Salvation is not bestowed upon us at death; we merely revert to our nonmaterial natural state. However, the process of soul salvation is greatly influenced by the nature of our most recent activity in human society. If our minds and our manifested actions are not already acceptable to God before we die, we will again have to face similar life circumstances that bring use face-to-face with the mental attitudes that are keeping us from reintegrating with God. We precipitated the mess we are in, and the onus is on us to make the mental and physical effort in the material realm to effect positive spiritual change and to take steps in faith that will remove the need to repeat cycles of incarnation and mental-spiritual training. God will strengthen us for the long journey and ensure that the spiritual lessons we learn become a core part of our psyche. This loving spiritual force from God comes to us as the Christ Spirit.

The word "Christ" comes from the Greek word *christos* meaning anointed and is used in the New Testament to identify Jesus as the anointed one of God. It is used in an inconsistent manner that can easily confuse the reader and is often used incorrectly to refer to the man Jesus. According to the readings, the term "Christ" should be considered from three different perspectives that have more to do with the conscious state of the soul mind and the relationship of the soul to God than with the conferring of a title of authority. There is more to the word "Christ" than is apparent from its use in biblical passages and traditional Christian theology. The readings use the word in reference to Christ Consciousness, the mind of Christ, and the Christ Spirit, What is meant by these terms? First, "Christ Consciousness" is the inner mental awareness of our soul's oneness with God. It gives us the sure knowledge of the presence and activity of God within our inner being. Although, as souls, we are portions of God, we have used our free will, our freedom to make independent choices, in ways that have mentally separated us from God. The sustained spiritual growth of our soul restores our relationship with God and culminates in the mental state of Christ

Consciousness. Second, to have "the mind of Christ" means that the will and desires of the individual are aligned with the will and purpose of God, a frame of mind that all souls should strive to acquire. The readings repeatedly stress the fact that the mind is the builder that manifests and shapes spirit to satisfy desire (364-10_6). The mind of Christ is the mental state that precedes and guides all manifestations of God's Spirit in the world. The acquisition of material needs and comforts should be a natural outcome of a Christ-like mind, not the greater center of attention and desire of the incarnated soul. Having the mind of Christ embodies the concept of being in the world but not being of the world, the ideal state of mind of the incarnated soul immersed in the daily activities of the material world. It allows the conscious mind to perform the necessary functions of life needed to maintain the physical body while also realizing and understanding that life has a greater spiritual purpose. Third, the "Christ Spirit" is that power of God that can be manifested in the material world. The most important spiritual connection between man and God derives from the activity of the Christ Spirit, the part of God that resides within the deepest recesses of the mind of every soul and can be accessed by conscious effort. The Christ Spirit is manifested on the Earth through acts of love and similar expressions of God-given soul qualities that are imbedded in the super conscious mind of the soul. Its earthly manifestations are seen in human relationships by the attitude and actions described in Scripture as the fruits of the spirit (Galatians 5:22–23 NIV; love, joy, peace, patience, kindness, goodness, faithfulness, gentleness, and self-control) and all other words and actions that project love for our neighbor.

The soul mind partakes of the material world through the physical conscious mind during incarnations and the spiritual world through the super conscious mind that interfaces with and communes with God as the Christ Spirit. The Christ Spirit is called the "motivative force" in Reading 2420-1_18 because it continually but subtly urges the soul to seek union and communion with God. It is the activity of the Will of God expressing the desires of God for our well-being. Mind is the creative force or activity that builds that which the will of the soul desires (262-64_11; 262-64_14). Just as the mind can be a force for good, it can also be a force for evil. When the soul mind opens itself to the presence and activity of the Christ Spirit, it becomes the preserver of soul unity with God, but when the soul mind primarily dwells upon and becomes attached to selfishness and materiality, it becomes the destroyer of unity between soul and God. We hinder our awareness and reception of the Christ Spirit and prevent its manifestation in our lives when we dwell on and indulge in selfish desires (262-29_9). The soul that tethers its unruly mind and reforms it into the mind of Christ can manifest the Christ Spirit in the world as a form of cooperation between the Spirit of God and the soul of man. The Christ Spirit stands ready to work with our soul to bring the knowledge of God's presence to our soul mind. The Christ Spirit is ever-ready to manifest on the Earth, and its potential activity in our lives constitutes the greatest spiritual opportunity given to man. The Christ Spirit is a force, a force that is of God, an active force for good that can strengthen and comfort man in his trials and temptations on the Earth and allow him to have a peek at God himself. The unselfish soul can sense the presence of God as the Christ Spirit and become receptive to the flow of love and goodness that gives man the fortitude to overcome his trials and temptations on the Earth.

Christ Consciousness is the willful remembrance of the state or condition of the soul soon after its creation, when the soul mind first became aware of the presence of God, understood the bond that existed between itself and the Mind of God, and had not yet been polluted with the strong desires for self-indulgence and self-gratification that could separate it from God awareness. It brings the remembrance of all things before the foundation of the world that God promises (John 17:24; 1 Peter 1:20). Not remembrance as a history refresher course or sentimental journey through the memories of times long past, but as a deep, ecstatic comprehension of the original kinship we had with God when we were created, and a deep regret for the poor decisions and choices that we made as our minds grew attached to egotism and the sensory experiences that ultimately drew us away from a state of unconditional love to a state of selfish mental separation. Scripture says to love your enemy (Matthew 5:44), and the readings say to love the sinner but hate the sin, an expression that tells us not to let the magnitude and awfulness of the sins that are committed daily in this world to crush our faith in God and our faith that he has prepared a way for every soul to be released from this merry-go-round of self-created messes. All humans—even those we view as evil and who blatantly display socially unacceptable and outright ungodly traits that harm and destroy those around them—are animated by souls that still, even if only faintly, retain knowledge of their original intimate relationship with God. We may once have expressed ourselves in ways that were just as selfish and evil, and in a weak future moment we may also backslide into decadence as we are brought face-to-face with some serious soul deficiency that we have yet to master.

Christ Consciousness is defined in Reading 5749-14_20 as "The awareness within each soul, imprinted in pattern on the mind, waiting to be awakened by will, of the soul's oneness with God." This definition of Christ Consciousness was coined by Thomas Sugrue, the author of the original biography of Edgar Cayce (Sugrue, 1997), as part of his literary research and was presented to the sleeping Cayce for approval. It was enthusiastically accepted by the source of the readings as an accurate definition of Christ Consciousness. This definition, along with the many discussions of Christ Consciousness, the Christ Spirit, and the Holy Spirit in the readings, gives us insight into and a broad perspective of the nature of Christ Consciousness and tells how it can be attained and its effect on the soul mind. As the name implies, it is a mental awareness, a higher state of consciousness that brings the soul to a more complete understanding of its relationship with God as the Christ Spirit. Christ Consciousness fulfills the promise of conscious awareness of the Christ Spirit and represents the mental unification of spiritual awareness and spiritual activity. This perceptive and enlightened state of consciousness exists as a latent pattern of thought and mental activity in the inner recesses of the soul mind associated with the super conscious mind, which forms the mental bridge between the soul and God. This part of the soul mind still retains the pattern and knowledge of the soul's oneness with God, but that understanding is now buried under layers of thought patterns that have been formed from selfish intents and purposes as the soul sought self-gratification, abandoned its spiritual heritage, and lost the knowledge of its true relationship with God. We have ignored these memories of the presence and activity of God for so long that we do not have the capacity to easily bring them back into our working consciousness. In a sense, this region of our soul mind has atrophied from lack of use as we used our subconscious mind to access and probe the wonders of the spiritual realm and used our conscious mind to sample material pleasure in the physical world. The memory of the presence of the Christ Spirit and the flow of love and spiritual strength that God makes available to the soul that remains receptive to its presence lies unused and unappreciated in the cluttered mind of souls that have developed an inflated sense of self-worth and unquenchable desire for material pleasures. But all is not lost. Spiritual awareness can be awakened by an intentional effort of the will of the soul, can reunite the soul mind with the Mind of God, and can restore the mental and emotional link necessary for the soul to rediscover its spiritual roots (440-16_10). As the soul perseveres in its effort to turn away from self-serving, ego-centric interests toward the service of God and fellow souls, the embers of the old memories are stirred and flare to life in the soul mind. The soul once again realizes that it is not an isolated entity or an island of consciousness unto itself. It becomes aware that it is a portion of God with all of the spiritual attributes of God and understands that it has a responsibility to live in a manner that respects the spiritual law to which it is beholden and bound.

Christ Consciousness is the ideal mental state of soul and man. Christ Consciousness allows the soul to be eternally aware of its oneness with its creator while maintaining its unique soul individuality and identity. It causes all thoughts and actions to be grounded in truth, the truth of the existence of God as the intelligence that creates and animates all realms and all forms of life. It opens our minds to the ultimate source of spiritual and material truth; the knowledge and certainty of God's intimate relationship with his soul children; and the knowledge of the purpose behind the creation of the physical universe, a realm of opportunity designed to reestablish our proper relationship with him. As we mature spiritually and come to the state of Christ Consciousness, we are able to use that knowledge responsibly and with wisdom to the benefit of all souls. Christ Consciousness exists in potential in the mind of every soul God has created but can only be realized and activated by a conscious decision of the soul mind to suppress its rebellious and selfish tendencies and embrace companionship with God. Souls that have made the decision to seek advice and counsel only from the storehouse of memories and the habitual thought patterns they have developed by selfishly exploring the spiritual and physical realms cannot easily perceive the need to seek spiritual sustenance from a higher authority. Christ Consciousness brings awareness of the source of our conscience and the origin of our moral sense and higher standards of behavior that are ever ready to guide us safely through the trials of life and bring us closer to God. It erases all doubt from the mind and exposes all decisions to the guiding influence of Spirit. It fulfills our faith in him and his promise to be our source of strength. It is the inner light that illuminates the darkness of our desire to sin and exposes it for the deception and delusion that it is.

The Christ Spirit is the abiding presence of God and stream of divine love that flows into us as our soul minds acquire Christ Consciousness. It is that part of God within us that continually communes with us, comforts us, and gives us hope (137-125_13). It is the sure knowledge that God will support and protect us as we meet the crosses we must bear. It gives us the strength to stand firm in the face of disappointment and heartache, to persevere and overcome the suffering we must endure to cleanse our souls from the error of glorifying our own minds and bodies instead of glorifying our creator. We receive the Christ Spirit into our soul by letting our super conscious mind become the source of our inspiration and guidance instead of relying on the conscious mind and its unhealthy desire for the attractions of the world. Our super conscious mind connects our souls to the Mind of God and receives and transmits to us the knowledge of God's plan and purpose for our soul. Our fascination with petty self-interests and selfish desires blinds us to the presence of this wonderful counselor and source of enlightenment that is so close to us yet so far away. The Christ Spirit of the readings is the same spiritual force called the Holy Spirit in Scripture. The term "Christ Spirit" is primarily used herein instead of "Holy Spirit" to remain true to the formal terminology and definitions of the readings. Traditional religious education and church doctrine have instilled in Christians concepts associated with the term "Holy Spirit" that are not consistent with its use in the readings. The Holy Spirit of the readings is not an ethereal spirit being with a human-like form or a nonmaterial being with a personality as described by many Christian writings on the Trinity—and certainly not a person—but is the mental-spiritual aspect of God that communes with and illuminates spiritual awareness within the soul mind.

The soul is fully capable of being aware of its true nature as a child of God, but it can only begin to understand the true spiritual purpose for its creation when it decides to cooperate with spiritual law, the code of conduct it inherited from God, and be led by the Will of God. Christ Consciousness, which gives access to the Christ Spirit and cooperation with spiritual law, brings salvation to the soul. The application of moral and spiritual practices, the process of making the Christ Spirit active in personal relationships in human society, guides the soul toward a greater awareness of its spiritual heritage (705-2_8). It allows the soul to rediscover the forgotten mental pattern that holds the key to its recognition of its oneness with the Creator and its original intimate relationship with God. It brings fellowship with God, access to spiritual sustenance and guidance from our creator, knowledge of our spiritual purpose, and imparts a sense of fulfillment to the soul. It is experienced as the harmonious attunement and resonance of the soul mind with the Mind of God. Christ Consciousness is achieved in materiality by a conscious effort to direct the mind and body into activity that conforms to the highest standard of human interaction, to desire no less than to sanctify and purify interpersonal relationships in the society of humans. As we use prayer, meditation, and ideals to resurrect the desire to apply love, kindness, and patience in our daily activities, we awaken our soul mind to the long suppressed inner knowledge of the higher purpose for our lives. Through sincere and persistent effort, the soul can reveal the inner knowledge of truth and perceive the spiritual wisdom that accompanies that knowledge. This is the truth and wisdom that is revealed in the liberal application of love, patience, kindness, humility, generosity, and tolerance in human relationships.

As Christ Consciousness blooms in the union of soul mind and God, it brings the Christ Spirit into material activity. As the Christ Spirit becomes active and the love of God flows through the soul into the world, there is a feedback effect that excites the soul and encourages it to further manifest the fruits of the spirit. It becomes the moral compass of the incarnated soul. The purpose for the creation of souls as companions of God is fulfilled as the incarnated soul recognizes, applies, and magnifies the Christ Spirit in the world and perceives the life-changing effect of applying the fruits of the spirit. We learn to not simply endure the suffering that is part of our life on the Earth but also to embrace the suffering as an opportunity to change our future. We understand and can face the fact that our soul will require multiple lifetimes and life experiences to extricate itself from the quagmire that it created as a consequence of its ungodly thoughts and actions (5749-5_5). With the knowledge that God does not give us more to contend with than the soul can bear, with the inner awareness of God's presence and the flow of his love into us, and with the certainty that the reward will be enormous, we can walk the path to soul restoration and redemption. If the soul refuses to make the Christ

Spirit the center of attention of the soul mind and an active force in its human expressions, it will deny itself its spiritual destiny to be a companion of God. It will wallow in the mental misery that self-centeredness brings until it eventually ceases to exist as its essence is absorbed into the Whole of God and it loses its independent identity.

The voice of the Spirit in Revelation 3:20–21 (NIV) says, "Here I am! I stand at the door and knock. If anyone hears my voice and opens the door, I will come in and eat with him, and he with me. To him who overcomes, I will give the right to sit with me on my throne, just as I overcame and sat down with my Father on his throne." Where is this door? What are the consequences of a closed door, and how can the door be opened? This door is not the entrance to our physical house. The door is the barrier that we have erected by selfishness, the sinful action of rebellion against our creator. When we think and act in ways that keep this door shut, we block access to spiritual truth, our awareness of God's presence dwindles to a trickle, and our soul "days" are numbered. The eternal soul begins its descent into hell, a self-created state of mind, in which the soul has entirely lost awareness that it is a child of God, and that it is sustained only by the spirit and love of God. Spirit is life, and the life force in spirit is love, and the soul that deprives itself of love degenerates into a caricature of its true self. To open the door means to open our hearts and minds to allow the Christ Spirit, the spirit that Jesus so well exemplified and manifested in the world during his lifetime, to have access to our consciousness and a place in our life. The mind is the godlike force of the soul that is constantly urged by an inner spiritual impulse to build a consciousness of at-oneness with the creator (262-123_5). In physics, an impulse is a short duration high amplitude force like a knock on a door. God is knocking on the door that we have erected that blocks communication between the inner recess of our soul mind and his abiding presence. The door is our mental creation, and only we can open it. As the soul becomes more aware that it is a portion of God and seeks reunion with God, this barrier begins to open, dissipates, and becomes null and void. We literally open our mind to accept the presence of the Christ

Spirit and thereby make the spirit the active and guiding principle in our lives. When we open the door and let God become the controlling factor and the standard by which we live our life, we become a channel through which God can work his purpose in the world.

We don't accomplish this spiritual awakening with a well-meant prayer asking Jesus to enter our lives and walk with us as we face temptation and turmoil, although he will do exactly that when we give ourselves to him. We open the door of our consciousness to the presence of the Christ Spirit as we eliminate selfishness from our thoughts, cease the activities that originate from self-centered mental patterns, and replace selfish desires with the desire to be a channel of blessing for God. When we willingly allow God to use our hands and feet to accomplish his will in the material world, we advance his kingdom on the Earth. When we open the door, God's love will pour through us and become apparent to those we know and meet and interact with every day. We open the door by a deliberate willful decision to set aside our own selfish interests so that we can become coworkers with God and spread his message of love and hope to a needy world. God won't open the door because that would be tantamount to him pushing himself upon us, which would violate his original intent to grant us the freedom to make our own decisions in matters of conscience. He waits patiently until we accept the opportunities he provides us every day to change the direction of our life. He waits for us to hunger for him and seek spiritual well-being in cooperation with him instead of spending our days fulfilling our own personal selfish ambitions. This is the work we must do while having faith in the outcome. We must become aware of the spiritual potential and possibilities that are conferred upon a soul in conscious union with God, open our minds to the Christ Spirit, and manifest the Christ Spirit in our daily lives on the Earth.

A Search for God

The sole spiritual purpose of human life is to open the soul mind to the presence of the Christ Spirit through the development of Christ

Consciousness. The eighth lesson in *A Search for God; Book I* is The Open Door. It summarizes the meaning of the open door and how the door is opened as the soul mind abandons its pursuit of self-centered thoughts and activities for the higher God awareness of Christ Consciousness. The selfish rebellious mind degrades and diminishes its ability to receive nourishment from its creator as it figuratively turns its back on the one source of life. The enlightened mind bathes in the flood of life-giving love that washes through it as it faces toward its creator and beholds a joy that was never imaginable or possible when it was enamored with self and materiality. As the mental barrier formed by the soul's self-created ignorance of spiritual law and repudiation of the spiritual principles it inherited as a child of God fades away, the healing power of God's love is able to flow freely into the soul. The soul feels at peace with itself and God because it is fulfilling the destiny for which it was created. When the enlightened soul is at peace with God, it retains awareness of the presence of God and revels in the newly discovered ability to direct nondogmatic love and healing toward those in human society who are in need of physical and spiritual assistance.

The first seven lessons in *A Search for God; Book I* present a way in which the incarnated soul can use everyday life experiences to reorient the manifested activities of the soul mind during interpersonal interactions to bring about spiritual growth and Christ Consciousness. The lessons do not include esoteric practices such as becoming a mendicant or taking a vow of poverty. They don't require seclusion, isolation, or time spent in a monastery for years on end, although some individuals may find those environments conducive to spiritual growth. They don't require knowledge of any particular religious doctrine or the practice of specific rituals. Spiritual advancement is gained through the expenditure of time, energy, and resources in ways that support, encourage, and help other people who are part of our personal and social lives, other souls that are struggling to express their understanding of spiritual principles in a material world. It requires consistent application of moral precepts that have been known to mankind for thousands of years with a liberal dose of love, an attitude of faith, hope, and trust in God, and a consistent dedication to prayer and meditation, or at least introspection, to reinforce and strengthen the good intentions. The first seven lessons are these: (1) cooperation, (2) know thyself, (3) ideals, (4) faith, (5) virtue and understanding, (6) fellowship, and (7) patience. They represent a progression of activity and mental attitude that proceeds from the more practical physical-mental activity of cooperation with fellow incarnated souls to the more mental-spiritual attitude of forbearance and tolerance of perceived faults when dealing with others (Todeschi, 2010; Thurston, 1976). They include the liberal application of the biblical fruits of the spirit. The purpose and value of these lessons are well defined and explained in the *Search for God* books and other publications, so will not be described in detail here but will be briefly summarized to put them into the context of Christ Consciousness. The first three lessons address the material level of consciousness, the fourth lesson serves as a bridge between material and spiritual thinking, and the final three lessons focus on the spiritual level of consciousness. The application of this sequence of practical lessons bears some resemblance to Eastern religious traditions, particularly in relation to spiritual awakening and the raising of the kundalini energy through the chakras—energy centers located along the spine and in the brain (1861-4_25; 2329-3_34). The remainder of the twenty-four lessons of the *Search for God* books contains a description of the physical and spiritual outcome of those practices, including descriptions of the ultimate destiny of the body, mind, and soul of the dedicated practitioner. There are many books that promote various techniques to direct and enhance the spiritual growth of Christians. They usually outline a system of spiritual practices that include prayer, Scripture reading and study, church attendance, and adherence to doctrines and rituals. These spiritual practices are beneficial and can be spiritually uplifting, but do not emphasize the importance of the soul and may not give the individual the intellectual latitude to thoroughly assess his or her spiritual deficiencies and prepare a plan of action to begin intentionally addressing them for the purpose of training the will and mind to achieve a mental-spiritual equivalent of Christ Consciousness (294-141_6).

Why would cooperation be the first lesson? It doesn't seem to be a spiritual practice, so why is it important for soul growth and enlightenment? The cooperation of incarnated souls within the structure and context of human society is an essential element in the spiritual quest to transition from a self-centered state of consciousness to a selfless state of consciousness that embodies service to our fellow man and by extension to our fellow souls. Cooperation allows us to maintain a proper balance between our personal desires and the desires of others in society—a key ingredient for societal harmony. It is essential to the concept of stewardship, which is necessary for the successful long-term acquisition of shelter and food by all of humanity, as opposed to the overexploitation of natural resources which threatens the long-term physical survivability of the human race. Cooperation, as understood from the readings, does not mean to go along with the group so as not to cause disruption, but means to contribute to the group for the fulfillment of a worthy physical goal. It is most effective when the group has a spiritual purpose, a spiritual aspect that is manifested through service to fellow man. At its best, it is the outward expression of a group of individuals who have chosen to be channels of blessing. In this way, we cooperate with our fellow man and with our creator. Lack of cooperation among the members of human society endangers the soul because it sets soul against soul and weakens our respect for the commandment that says we should love our neighbor as we love ourselves. Cooperation is the foundational element that brings harmony and peace to families, communities, and societies, and to our relationship with God. Cooperation is more than a tool used to ensure the smooth operation of a business or corporation. It should partake of body, mind, and spirit in a manner that engenders respect for all members of a shared enterprise. Physical cooperation builds harmony of activity among souls within a family or an enterprise. Mental cooperation builds unity of purpose. Spiritual cooperation brings coordinated activity between souls and God. The act of cooperation helps restore the soul to awareness of its Creator, brings peace and goodwill to men of all nations, and brings souls together in a unified family of God (254-42_6).

We are tasked to truly know ourselves because most of us continue to think of ourselves as human beings when in reality we are incarnated souls animating human bodies. Our minds and thoughts are not rooted in our human bodies, but are aspects of a soul that can perceive life much more fully and abundantly than our limited conscious minds can imagine. Until we realize and accept that we are more than glorified human-animals and that our destiny involves much more than the acquisition of material wealth at the expense of our fellow man or the exercise of political, ecclesiastical, or personal power over others, we will not advance spiritually. We will remain the proverbial swine on which the pearls of wisdom are wasted. Our greatest ambitions may be to become a famous artist, author, scientist, or powerful politician whose words and ideas can move a nation to action. As worthy as these ambitions are in the human world, they can divert our attention from the fact that we are soul children of God, not simply sons and daughters of men and women. The inordinate attention we pay to fame, power, and wealth means little when compared to a future in a realm where souls can aspire to be companions and co-creators with God, share in the excitement of his latest creations, and bask in a love so intense that it is indescribable in any human language. Until we are certain that we are more than human and that our consciousness is the activity of a soul mind instead of a human brain, we will not be able to raise our expectations to include the idea of Christ Consciousness. We must also be wary that we do not become complacent and satisfied as we seek to know ourselves and the truth of our earthly existence and spiritual destiny, for then we will stumble and falter in our spiritual quest.

The setting of ideals is a spiritual practice rooted in physical behavior. It has been discussed previously as a method of raising consciousness, but cannot be emphasized enough. With practice and dedication, ideals can teach us to break old mental habits that keep us entangled in materiality and at odds with our fellow man. Jesus told us that unless we free ourselves from the habit of thinking that we are better than others, treating others as if they are inferior to us, or reacting to others out of anger instead of from a position of love, we cannot follow him. We cannot make progress on the path to Christ Consciousness. By redefining who we are and who we want to be and using that new mind set to restructure our thoughts and behavior, we can take positive steps to recover awareness of our relationship with God and our spiritual heritage. As we take charge of our lives to effect spiritual change and growth, we prepare our minds and bodies for a closer relationship with God. As we begin living our lives so that our intentions, efforts, and actions will be acceptable to God, God will support us when the self-imposed trials and tribulations we face begin to overwhelm us. Only when we take intentional willful action to unselfishly express the fruits of the spirit in personal relationships and selflessly engage in service to fellow souls in the material world can the soul mind be reunited with its creator and fulfill its original purpose as a companion of God. It is necessary for the will of each individual to make the conscious choices needed to bring the mind of the soul back into accord with the Mind of God. With each choice that is grounded in spiritual truth and righteousness, the seeker will be given the strength needed to successfully tackle the next opportunity and to demonstrate its evolving spiritual maturity. Only then does the soul have any hope to rediscover its oneness with its creator and experience the expanded state of awareness it can now barely comprehend. The reader is encouraged to review the concepts of physical, mental, and spiritual ideals presented in the previous chapter on expanding consciousness.

The lesson on faith admonishes us to keep faith in the face of our trials, knowing that God will give us the strength to endure if we will continue to make choices that respect our promise to remain true to him. Faith, defined as the sure knowledge of things unseen, is stressed as a necessary and virtuous quality of new Christians or any person seeking spiritual enlightenment. It takes faith to venture forth on a spiritual quest when the God we seek is not visible or accessible through the senses on which we have come to rely and that serve us well as we navigate the material world. Faith allows us to transition from physical thinking to spiritual thinking. But neither weak faith nor blind faith is good. If we need supporting material evidence to strengthen and solidify our faith and make it more acceptable to us, faith enters the realm of belief and limits our spiritual growth. Faith will be strengthened as we begin to see that a Christ-like life yields tangible physical evidence that God is walking with us, but faith should carry us beyond the physical. Faith should not become a reason to believe everything that we are told. If we rely on blind faith as the driving force of our spiritual journey, it opens us to the possibility of being disciples of the next Jim Jones, willing to take a poisonous drink to prove our commitment and faith and to secure our place in paradise. Or we may become like the followers of William Miller and be left standing in a field staring at the sky, feeling foolish as the clock ticks past the prophesized time of the end of the world. Faith is necessary to take those first steps of a lifelong commitment to God, but we also need to discern the spirit, to compare knowledge acquired consciously with the still small voice of God that becomes audible through prayer, meditation, and frequent communion with God.

To have faith doesn't mean to go blindly where no man has gone before, to paraphrase the *Star Trek* theme. Nor does it imply the ability to read Scripture and suddenly acquire an understanding of the age of the universe or the way creatures of the Earth were created or interact with and adapt to their environment. Faith is not a license to conclude that every line of the Bible contains special infallible truths about the process of creation even when such literal interpretations are outlandish and refute common sense and the accumulated scientific knowledge gained over hundreds of years of painstaking research. To have faith doesn't mean to check your intellect at the door of your church along with your hat and coat. Faith does mean accepting that there is more to our existence than a single life in a frail body in a large and often dangerous world. Faith is something we choose to take hold of when we begin to feel that there is more to life than we are able to see, hear, touch, taste, or smell, but at the same time, faith can lead us to understand and interpret what we can see, hear, touch, taste, and smell in a different way. It can allow us to observe material experiences from an entirely different perspective. Faith opens our conscious minds to a new set of possibilities, the prospect of a new reality of existence and purpose. It lets us explore ourselves and the meaning of our lives in directions not apparent when we are immersed in the daily activities that go into making a living, putting food on the table, and finding shelter for our family. Christ Consciousness is the confirmation and culmination of faith held steadfastly as the soul struggles to find spiritual truth and redemption.

All incarnated souls that embark upon a spiritual path do so in faith that the longed for but ephemeral future will unfold in a way that brings salvation, restoration, and the abiding presence of God. But when faced with the continuing onslaught of life's temptations and problems, the issue of perseverance comes to the forefront. Souls have a tendency toward selfishness, a propensity to sin when faced with the temptation to put self before God or neighbor. The lure of self-gratification and self-indulgence can overwhelm the soul mind. It is easy, especially at first, to slip back into old habits of self-centered behavior even after sincerely dedicating oneself to a new life path and promising to let God guide our thoughts and actions. The soul can cultivate the spiritual quality of virtue to combat this weakness and keep it dedicated to the path of spiritual growth. To be virtuous is to remain true to the spiritual principles to which the will of the soul has decided to dedicate itself. Virtue is a soul quality that allows the individual to remain righteous in his or her activity in family and society, and serves as a safeguard to the possible relapse of the individual back into the ungodly habits that it previously pursued. This inner spiritual force can be tapped to keep our daily activities and interpersonal interactions aligned with the spiritual precepts that we have professed. Virtue allows us to stay true to the spiritual ideal that we have set as a standard of behavior. It is activated as we seek guidance from God and feel his spirit bear witness to our spirit as we make life choices. Virtue keeps our choices and decisions consistent with the spiritual attributes we inherited from God at the creation of our soul. As we learn to be virtuous and hold true to our spiritual principles in the workplace, at the grocery store, and in the family, we will begin to better understand how spiritual law works, how it applies to every aspect of our life, and what it means to be children of God.

When our actions are virtuous, we will begin to better understand our true relationship with God and our ideal relationship with fellow humans. We will gain an understanding of who we really are as the Christ Spirit reveals to us our inner purpose as a soul child of God. The understanding that we will gain is not an understanding formed from sensory information we receive from our five senses, but a deeper spiritual understanding that comes as we open the lines of communication with our creator and begin to work with him for the benefit of our fellow souls. Spiritual understanding is not simply the ability to think abstractly or intellectually grasp or comprehend matters presented to the conscious mind. It is the ability to rightly perceive the truth or judge the merits of a situation. It is the forerunner of wisdom. The consistent practice of virtue in our interaction with our fellow incarnated souls leads us to an understanding of the rightness, righteousness, and value of remaining true to spiritual principles. The quality of virtue leads to a deeper understanding of spiritual principles and the wisdom to apply them when making life choices. It helps the soul mind transition from a material focus to Christ Consciousness.

Every individual who seeks God must first rectify their relationship with their fellow man. All healthy interpersonal relationships among family members, with neighbors, or with members of the larger community must be based on respect, compassion, and a healthy component of brotherly love. The readings emphasize that every person must answer the question "Am I my brother's keeper?" in a way that is acceptable to God before he or she can have a right relationship with God. Many people today are asking this question and coming up with answers that fall far short of the expectations that God has for us. A type of fellowship that embraces the concept of love of neighbor and service to neighbor is required for every soul that seeks its creator. Each soul is a portion of God, with its own unique individuality and idiosyncrasies formed from its particular thoughts and experiences. We cannot love one portion of God while hating another portion. The ability to experience fellowship and friendship with people of shared interests, and even with people with whom we do not always agree, helps us to see God in others. When we open our hearts and minds to express fellowship and love for our neighbor, we strengthen our fellowship with the Whole of God and become more aware of the presence of God within our deepest inner consciousness. As we learn to commune with God, we will develop a stronger sense of our spiritual connection with him until we are able to be constantly aware of his guiding presence. We will be able to receive his advice and counsel at each critical juncture in our lives when we are given the opportunity to choose between selfishness and godliness so that we can choose rightly and remain true to our spiritual purpose. We will learn that there is hope. Although we squandered our original opportunity for divine companionship when we chose to descend into mental and spiritual rebellion, God eagerly awaits our return to fellowship with him.

The dictionary definition of "patience" includes terms such as "tolerance," "endurance," and "stoicism," even going so far as to include "resignation" and "fatalism." All imply that the individual can only passively accept circumstances that are beyond his or her control. The person who practices patience is almost a bystander to the events that are occurring. The readings describe patience from a spiritual perspective as an innate attribute of the soul, a quality that the soul possesses that it may frequently or rarely exhibit depending on its spiritual attunement. From a spiritual perspective, patience is more than stoically putting up with the current life situation. Patience is not passive acceptance of events but active engagement with the goal of affecting positive change while realizing and accepting that the outcome will occur in God's, not man's, time frame. The exercise of patience increases the possibility that opportunities essential to soul growth, that often come in the form of trying circumstances, are correctly navigated within the context of spiritual law (262-26_4). Patience helps us assess the success of our application of cooperation and ideals, of our projection of virtue and understanding, and the depth of our faith in the face of adversity and challenge. Jesus recognized the need for patience, saying, "In your patience possess ye your souls" (Luke 21:19). He knew that the early Christian community would face intense persecution that could turn many new Christians away from their newfound faith, and he encouraged them to stand strong and endure because the reward for steadfast loyalty to God and the Son of God is nothing less than soul restoration before God. Patience allows us to move forward through life without being quick-tempered and intolerant when faced with life situations that need to be managed in ways that honor our status as children of God. It allows us to free ourselves from inappropriate choices that cause us to be caught up in a series of future life events designed to bring us face-to-face with our spiritual shortcomings.

We must have patience with others who intentionally or unintentionally cause us physical and emotional pain by their antagonistic or uncaring attitude toward us. When a person patiently responds to an angry outburst by mentally or verbally forgiving the offending person, he is doing more than just defusing an ugly situation; he is providing a possible path to a more positive outcome. First, he is making a response that will begin the process of removing the need for him or her to be in these kinds of situations in the future. As the soul continues to respond in a loving manner in similar situations, it draws closer to God, and the soul mind becomes more aware of the presence of God. It eventually becomes unnecessary for the body to face these situations because the soul has learned that spiritual lesson. Second, the person initiating the angry encounter will see a different response to his action than was expected.

Perhaps a memory or feeling is triggered that reminds the individual that the angry words are not acceptable to God. It may be enough to change his or her heart or stir something deep inside the soul mind that will eventually lead to a change in behavior. This is where active patience is important. The proper response is not simply to tolerate the anger while holding back the urge to respond in kind, but to also engage the person with a positive, loving reply. The response is immediate but the desired effect upon the instigator may take minutes, days, or lifetimes. It is in God's hands to be fulfilled at the time and place of his choosing, depending on the willingness of the offending soul to let God transform its mind toward a state of Christ Consciousness.

It is essential for the soul that wants to restore its relationship with God to cultivate peace within its mind and patience in its dealings with fellow souls. We serve God by glorifying him in the world through loving interaction with others, by showing mercy toward those who are spiteful to us, and by showing patience toward others as they stumble in their personal search for God. We are required to respect and serve others in our quest to find God and restore our soul minds to God Consciousness because souls are not separate entities but are united within the collective wholeness of God. As we seek him within ourselves, we must also learn to recognize him in others and realize that their shortcomings are no different than ours. We must have patience with ourselves, especially as we begin our journey, and be willing to forgive ourselves for our failures so that we can step out of the way and let God work in us for the transformation of our souls. The fact that we ask God to forgive the many transgressions that led to our current condition does not instantly and automatically transform us into a more righteous individual. It does allow God to begin working with us to effect change in the will and desires of our mind as we cooperate with God within the framework of his purpose and plan for us. As we use our will to activate desires to serve God and our fellow travelers in this world, instead of focusing on ourselves, we grow spiritually and are more able to practice patience.

When the spiritual seeker uses prayer, meditation, ideals, and common Christian practices such as community service, Scripture reading, fasting, ministry, and witnessing, he or she unleashes a powerful force for soul restoration and redemption, and releases the force of the Christ Spirit into the world. As we begin to remove the ungodly thoughts and conduct that separate us from God's active presence and spiritual guidance, through the consistent application of spiritual and moral principles, we can open the door to an active and perpetual communion with God. Only then can God truly work with as we use our presence in the world for personal spiritual growth, showing us how to become individual points of spiritual illumination in society and using us to bring spiritual renewal to humanity. We can come to know mentally and emotionally that we have the privilege to be extensions of God, sparks of consciousness with the greater purpose of co-existing in a spirit of harmony with our fellow souls and co-creating with the preeminent cosmic consciousness of God. Through the development of Christ Consciousness we come to understand this intimate relationship and oneness, and experience it as an inner certainty rather than an intellectual exercise in possibilities. Be aware that the use of Christian terminology and reference to biblical Scripture in this book is not meant to imply that the application of these mental-spiritual principles is limited to adherents to the Christian faith or members of any specific Christian denomination. These are universal principles that can be applied by any person anywhere in the world that desires to lead a more moral and spiritual life (991-1_59). Christ Consciousness is a natural mental-spiritual state of the soul that can be sought by any person of any religious persuasion that desires reunion with God, and that is willing to apply the spiritual teachings of love for God and neighbor in their lives.

The primary factor that prevents God from fulfilling his purposes through us and the society of souls in which we live is the stubborn will of the soul. Until we let a Christ-like mind be among our highest ideals and highest aspirations, we will be unable to fully participate in God's plan for soul restoration and redemption. We have spent eons willfully honing our selfish nature at the expense of our natural generous godlike nature. We frequently use our will to direct our minds into selfish activities designed to accumulate and perpetrate power over others. We generate wealth through the application of our talents while using moral and immoral methods and revel in the material objects that we can acquire through that wealth. We seek sensual gratification and enjoyment as we use our wills to direct our mind and body to explore sexual pleasure outside of the context of a loving relationship. But too rarely do we use our will to seek God's purpose for our life or try to understand where and how we lost our way and how to rectify the messes in which we find ourselves. Changes in the soul mind are achieved as the will of the soul makes choices that alter the intentional and habitual selfish thoughts that we give expression to and project into the spiritual and physical realms. When selfish desires are allowed to dominate our minds and thoughts and when we willingly act on those desires to the detriment of others or for any of the various forms of self-gratification, we interrupt and interfere with the ability of the soul mind to retain its conscious awareness of God and we lose sight of the fact that we are spiritual beings. As we become more and more mentally associated with physical phenomena and sensations, the drug of materiality lures us away from God, the only source of sustenance and life for the soul.

Each incarnated soul, and by extension each human on the Earth, must through training of the soul mind learn to live within the material world, but not be of the world (John 8:23; John 17:11). Spiritual law and the physical universe that we inhabit imparts a perceived causality of space and time to the physical conscious mind and creates a physical framework that ensures every incarnated soul will reap what it sows. As it sows the seeds of love, kindness, patience, and unity of purpose in Christ, it better understands its relationship with God and becomes more aware that it is a child of God. The soul moves closer to God in consciousness and reaps the ultimate reward of Christ Consciousness, the absolute certainty that it is a portion of God, and that it exists in a state of eternal Oneness with its Creator. If it sows the seeds of hatred, anger, divisiveness, and disunity through selfishness and the desire for self-gratification, self-indulgence, or power over others, it reaps the dubious reward of separation from God and loss of conscious awareness of God. It obstructs the efforts of God in the form of the Christ Spirit to work with and through the soul and body for his purposes. The soul shapes its destiny one choice at a time and one life at a time. There are allusions in the readings to other realms of activity connected with celestial bodies in the physical universe where the soul may go for additional experiences and training after it successfully completes the cycles of earthly incarnations and has subdued the temptation and tendency to let self-centered attitudes or desires come between it and God. Access to these other realms requires a higher state of God consciousness than most souls currently residing on the Earth or active in the borderland region have attained. These realms of higher consciousness remain closed to the soul until it is redeemed before God through the enlightened state of Christ Consciousness. This perfected state of mind almost seems unattainable from the perspective of men and women absorbed in the frantic activities to acquire nourishing food, adequate shelter, perhaps a higher education, and meaningful employment. Can the soul mind really achieve Christ Consciousness in this environment, or is it just an arcane and esoteric spiritual concept to be discussed in the abstract? Has any soul actually achieved a state of Christ Consciousness?

The Consciousness of Jesus
Who Became the Christ

*In the beginning, celestial beings. We have first the Son, then
the other sons or celestial beings that are given their force and
power. (Edgar Cayce Reading 262-52_25)*

What does Jesus have to do with the evolving consciousness of souls
and the human condition? How does his life impact humanity,
and why was his state of consciousness relevant to the future of mankind?
To fully understand Jesus and his role in the redemption of souls, we need
to establish some basic facts from the perspective of the readings.

1. *Like every Adamic human that ever lived or now lives on the Earth,
   Jesus was a human body animated by a celestial soul.*

   Many Christians will jump up and down, wave their arms, and scream
   heresy at the idea that Jesus had a soul. Despite the best efforts of
   Catholic and Protestant church authorities to deny or downplay the
   belief that Jesus had a soul that preexisted his birth, it is true. The
   Catholic Church attempted to crush this idea at the Fifth Ecumenical
   Council (Second Council of Constantinople) in 553 AD in Anathema
   1 of the Emperor Justinian against Origen: If anyone says or thinks
   that the soul of the Lord preexisted and was united with God the Word
   before the Incarnation and Conception of the Virgin, let him be anathema (Schaff and Wace, 1900). To be anathema means to be cursed or
   condemned and possibly excommunicated. Despite the declaration

of the council, if we miss the essential fact that Jesus is a soul sibling to the rest of the created souls, we miss the whole point of his mission, the hope of his message, and the potential of all souls to be like him and have a close relationship with their creator. Because, like us, he was a soul-guided human being, his life and his death have a real personal meaning for us. Another false idea, the concept that Jesus was a human manifestation of the totality of the Almighty God, gained traction as a result of the publication of the book "*Why Did God Become Man*" by St. Anselm in about 1100 AD (Davies, 2008). Jesus was not the totality of God, was not the infinite God squeezed into a finite human body. The New Testament speaks of the soul but only in general as to its existence and rarely in meaningful or useful words that accurately describe its nature, relationship to God, or connection to man. Paul alludes to Jesus having a soul (not a preexisting soul) by saying in Acts 2:31 (KJV) that God did not leave the soul of Christ (meaning Jesus the Christ) in hell but raised him up. Later Bible translators would alter the words in Acts 2:31 (NIV) to only say that the Christ (meaning the Anointed One) was not abandoned to the grave, thereby ignoring the Greek word *psuche* (breath of life) and bypassing the idea of Jesus having a soul. It is very difficult to get any kind of meaningful understanding of the soul from the Bible, which probably means that the writers had little real knowledge of the nature of the soul.

2. *Like all souls, the soul of Jesus was created by God out of a portion of himself as a quasi-independent composite unit of mind and spirit given the free will to develop and express its own individuality, including the ability to defy its maker. Like all souls, the soul of Jesus was created in the image of God.*

All souls were created by God to be his companions, but many of them went their separate ways as they learned to use their free will to satisfy longings that built self-created patterns of behavior that were destructive to a harmonious fellowship with God (5749-14_5). Free will is the mental quality that separates souls from the remainder of creation. It is a great honor bestowed by God upon all of his soul children but it is also the aspect of a soul that gives it the ability to make spiritually poor choices. It was God's hope that all of his soul children would manifest their inherited spiritual attributes, remain loyal to him, and become companions and co-creators with him (1549-1_6; 3654-1_8), but the seemingly infinite creative ability of will and mind was too seductive for many souls to resist. The highest achievement of any soul is to harness this free will to keep the soul mind from drawing the soul into patterns of thought and behavior that separate the soul from conscious awareness and knowledge of its Creator. The soul of Jesus was not immune to the tendency of souls to use their free will to dwell on inappropriate thoughts and manifest unseemly actions that contradict the spiritual law to which all souls must conform, but it remained true to and devoted to its creator as it grew into a mature soul active in the spiritual realm. The soul of Jesus aligned its will and mind toward the fulfillment of the purpose for its creation, and remained devoted to and steadfastly loyal to its Creator. It projected all that is good, all that is loving, and all that expresses respect and consideration of fellow souls. Many other souls valued their honored position as companions of God and embraced the spiritual precepts that honor the divine nature of God and the birthright of souls. The soul of Jesus knew God intimately because it was in a state of perfect communication with God and glorified God during its activities among his soul children.

3. *The soul of Jesus was the first of the created souls, which the readings call Amilius, and the same soul that entered the world as Adam. The mission of Amilius was voluntary and its purpose was to bring God consciousness back into the minds of souls that had degraded themselves before God, who were now committing spiritual atrocities on the Earth, and who had become trapped in the Earth plane.*

Amilius is our elder soul brother in the spiritual realm because of its status as the first of the created souls. The theology of the apostle

Paul definitely has its flaws, but he gets it mostly right in Colossians 1:15 (NIV) where he states that, "He is the image of the invisible God, the firstborn over all creation." The readings clarify this statement, especially when we interpret it more broadly to mean Amilius, the soul of Jesus, was created in the image of God and expressed itself through the body of Jesus. Amilius was the firstborn of all creation, meaning the firstborn of all souls in the beginning, before our present human form or the universe existed. This is consistent with a reading that states that there was an order in the creation of souls and that Amilius was the first created soul (262-52_25). The words of Paul echo the even more insightful words that the apostle John used to describe the relationship between Jesus and God, which is discussed below. As was mentioned previously, souls are gender neutral, but we will refer to Amilius using both the masculine pronouns "*he/his/ him*" and the neutral pronoun "*it*" because of the intimate association of Amilius with both Adam and Jesus and to prevent awkward sentence structures.

Because of his great love for other souls, Amilius would volunteer to lead a mass projection of souls onto the Earth to rescue the many souls enamored with and trapped in materiality. This Adamic group would enter as thought forms that would transform into physical human bodies patterned after the physical characteristics of evolved human-animals. Amilius would risk its own spiritual welfare in the process. Amilius planned this universe with God and was the co-creator of this universe with God (Colossians 1:16). It was the first soul to project the Adamic thought form onto the Earth, the new form that became the prototype and archetype of the human race, the first man and the first of the Sons of God to appear on the Earth (1158-5_36; 5749-3_8). Amilius entered the Earth plane about 106 Kya as Adam. The scriptural story of Adam describes a person and the archetype of the many projected forms that would become the forerunners of the physical human bodies we recognize today as modern *Homo sapiens*.

The mission of Amilius was and is to save souls from their tendency to rebel against God through selfish activity by teaching incarnated souls to love and trust God unconditionally and to love their neighbors, their fellow souls, as themselves. To fulfill his mission, he had to demonstrate that it is possible for a material-bound soul to escape the Earth sphere, to mentally extricate itself from the lure and temptations of materiality. He would teach them that by acquiring the mental state of Christ Consciousness, they could reunite their will and mind with their original innate purpose to be companions of God and turn away from the corrupting ideals of self-centeredness, material self-gratification, and self-indulgence. Amilius would descend fully into materiality. The readings equate material manifestation with being in sin (262-59_10). He would willingly move through this state of sin while being repeatedly tempted and enticed to misuse his will for self-serving benefit and power, and would walk the path of incarnation until he was fully released from that sinful condition by living lives that served God and his fellow incarnated souls, spiritualizing his physical activities and restoring of his God consciousness while immersed in materiality (364-8_3; 364-7_7). Adam faced physical death as a material being, but Amilius would face spiritual death when he let sin enter into his consciousness (900-227_11). This full descent of the Adamic souls into materiality and the subsequent transformation of the original members into sexually active male and female human beings were essential for the procreation of future Adamic bodies to be used as an alternative to the evolved human-animal bodies for soul restoration.

Scripture would record the beginning of this altruistic act as the fall of Adam, and Paul would unfairly malign Adam as the cause of sin in all men. Whether some or all of the many souls that entered the Earth environment with Adam also intentionally allowed themselves to succumb to the temptations of selfishness and sensual materiality or simply lost sight of the spiritual purpose for their incarnation is not known. Once Adam allowed himself to succumb to temptation, Amilius had to reincarnate on the Earth to correct this and any other subsequent spiritual errors. Any spiritual error committed by a soul in the physical realm must be met and corrected in the physical realm. Amilius would undergo spiritual and mental training in the spheres of consciousness about the Earth and would incarnate on the Earth until he was able to subdue all forms of inappropriate material desires, such as those that led to his downfall as Adam, until he was able to remain faithful to the Will of God while incarnated in the material world (1158-5_36). Only then could Amilius complete his spiritual mission as the savior of the souls trapped in materiality. He was confident of his success from the moment he took that fateful action that clouded his awareness of and attunement to God (2067-7_21). There is good reason from the readings to believe that many of the souls that were part of the original mission with Amilius continue to incarnate on the Earth while retaining residual memory of their spiritual purpose and still work today toward the spiritual enlightenment of mankind (294-8_24).

4. *The readings indicate that Amilius was the first soul to successfully complete a series of incarnations on the Earth that fully purged any tendency to glorify itself or yield to unwarranted material temptations and desires. It achieved the mental state of Christ Consciousness while immersed in the physical realm.*

God created the stage and the props on which the play of life is performed. He orchestrated the major acts of the plan of salvation from the beginning to the end (Isaiah 46:10; 262-55_15) and Amilius played the lead role as the soul that brought the alpha and the omega full circle, the beginning of the play as Adam to the finale of the play as Jesus (792-1_12; Revelation 22:13). Amilius came in the perfection as Adam, but as the as result of his self-inflicted fall had to relearn how to maintain his mental and spiritual alignment with God during physical incarnation (Hebrews 5:8). Amilius didn't just dip his toe into materiality but became completely immersed in human affairs in ways that stressed his ability to restore God consciousness. He attended the mental-spiritual training sessions in other dimensions and confronted the same physical trials and tribulations that all humans face, even experiencing the terrors of wars and certainty of death (3976-27_8). He lived through the same pattern of reincarnation that we must follow to perfect our souls and be restored to God consciousness (Hebrews 9:26). The Old Testament is not only a record of the history of the Israelites as a chosen people through which the Messiah would appear, but is also a partial record of the activity of Amilius upon the Earth as it learned to subdue the mental enticements of the material realm (Sanderfur, 1988).

Amilius was a perfect soul child of God in the nonmaterial realm. Amilius was the first soul that completed the process of perfection in earthly lives, including the mental-spiritual training in dimensions associated with the planets (5749-14_18). The perfection of the soul in materiality is achieved by mental and spiritual training that leads to Christ Consciousness and applying that mental attunement to successfully and correctly face life situations during physical incarnations. Through a series of incarnations that included mental and physical suffering, he learned to remain obedient to God while in the physical realm. He was able to shift his center of awareness away from any form of material and self-serving consciousness back toward full awareness of the ever-present God as the Christ Spirit and full awareness of his oneness with God. Because Amilius had attained the mental state of perfection called Christ Consciousness while immersed in the physical realm, he earned the right and honor of returning to the Earth as the savior of all humanity. His return as the savior was a voluntary, selfless act (5749-14_19).

5. *The readings accredit Jesus as the first man born in the perfection, meaning that the soul of Jesus had already attained spiritual perfection before it came to Earth to occupy the body of Jesus.*

The perfection of Jesus was a restored perfection acquired as his soul incarnated as various historical figures that worked to bring spiritual enlightenment to other incarnated souls. Only by overcoming all vestiges of selfishness was Amilius able to return to the Earth in the perfection as Jesus (5749-14_18). Because of his souls perfection in Christ Consciousness, Jesus was the savior of mankind from the moment of his birth, not as a result of his life as Jesus and his death on the cross (262-125_18; Hebrews 5:9). The will of Jesus was indistinguishable from the Will of God in its desire and resolve to put the plans and purposes of God before its personal interests. This fact accounts for the confusion that reveals itself in doctrinal statements such as Jesus is "God come down to earth." The life of Jesus was not only dedicated to the salvation of all lost souls, but was proof of his mastery of the physical realm and perfection in Christ Consciousness. Jesus was the first human representative of God that retained full consciousness of his oneness with God during an entire incarnation. Because of this mental union with God, Jesus was the perfect human Son of God and was able to complete and fulfill his mission to be an example to all humanity of the perfect union of God and man. He is our mentor and guide as we struggle to reach the same perfection. His mission is not complete and will not be completed until the last soul that decides it wants companionship with God returns to the metaphorical loving arms of its maker.

Jesus lived a life of perfection from birth to death. His life was the culmination of his training in the ways to subdue the Earth and hold fast against the temptation to become entangled in inappropriate material activities that could ensnare his soul in the Earth plane. He was at-one with his Father, had passed through all of the required training, perfectly expressed love, and demonstrated mastery over the physical laws. He allowed himself to become an open channel for the Christ Spirit to pour forth into the world. He lived the life of a perfect man, and in so doing became the example of intertwined physical-mental-spiritual perfection for all to follow (900-10_8; 900-100_8). He became the Way of human behavior that leads to spiritual liberation, the Truth of the real relationship between man and God, the Light of Christ Consciousness that exposes the darkness and false hope of the material world, and the perfect example of a Life guided by the Christ Spirit (John 11:25; John 14:6; John 8:12). The most intense and agonizing mental test that Jesus faced to demonstrate his complete alignment and atonement with the Will of his Father came at the Garden of Gethsemane, when Jesus would learn that despite living a perfect life in the service of God and his fellow man, he would still be required to face a tortuous death on the cross. What an emotional kick in the gut it must have been to know that he had passed every test without one mark against him and still must face this horrific death. He spent an entire night praying and agonizing over the decision to accept or reject this crucially important task, the strength of spirit contending with the weakness of flesh, chiding his disciples when they could not stay awake long enough to pray for and support him in his hour of need (5277-1_41; Matthew 26:36–46). He stayed true to his spiritual purpose despite the fact that it would cost him his earthly life. Because of that fateful decision on the mount, he reigns with God over the Earth and its inhabitants and left us an example of a perfect life lived in service to God and fellow man. He opened the way for the restoration and salvation of our souls.

Jesus is referred to as our elder human brother in the readings (262-69_8; 1992-1_11) by virtue of his status as the final incarnation of the first soul to successfully complete a series of earthly incarnations and fully conquer the tendency of the will to let selfish desires interfere with God consciousness (452-3_13; 2879-1_18-19). He lived his life in service to others so that they might see his life as an example to be followed, and he laid down his life for us so that his death and resurrection would open the way for our approach to God. He has become an inspiration for all who believe in him and who desire to walk the path that leads to spiritual enlightenment. Jesus was the perfect example of a soul-animated human being and represents the ideal mental and spiritual state that every incarnated soul should strive to attain. Every incarnated soul has the potential and the ability to become like Jesus, and every soul mind has the potential and the ability to become like the Mind of God through Christ Consciousness. Every soul that continues in faith to seek God will reenact the accomplishment of Jesus, will learn about his historical past and his perfect attunement to God, and will naturally desire to emulate his activity and share in his success in subduing the Earth.

6. *Amilius knew that he was destined to be the savior of mankind when he first entered the Earth as Adam and fulfilled that destiny when he successfully restored his mind to a perfect state of Christ Consciousness while immersed in a series of material incarnations. As Jesus, he demonstrated this perfection by living a life that was an ideal example of the mental attitude and material activity that every incarnated soul must emulate if it desires to restore its relationship with God.*

When Amilius became ensnared in materiality as Adam, he lost his initial human immortality and embarked on a spiritual path through materiality that allowed him to become the savior of all souls (815-7_4; 2067-7_21). As Amilius corrected any spiritual errors he perpetrated in the material realm and suppressed the natural tendency to live for self instead of others, he was able to overcome materiality and complete the original purpose of his entry onto the Earth. He walked the entire path of physical incarnation, from sin to perfection. He demonstrated, by example, that the soul of man can extricate itself from the morass of materiality and provide an example of the way of salvation for the souls enmeshed in the physical world. All souls that sin—commit spiritual error—while active in the physical realm are required to be spiritually cleansed by incarnation in physical form. Amilius showed us how to accomplish this spiritual requirement for reunion with God. Before he entered the Earth as the Christ child, he resolved to retain that state of perfection by remaining unsoiled by selfishness, self-gratification, or egotism and to faithfully execute the next step in God's plan for soul salvation. His physical conscious mind was devoted to the fulfillment of God's plan for soul redemption and restoration. To accomplish his mission, Jesus had to keep his mind in a state of Christ Consciousness throughout his incarnation. The free will of his soul mind, including his physical conscious mind, was fully aligned with the Will of God. There was no room for expressions of selfishness in the life of Jesus because he rejected any material desires and temptations that could interfere with his mission. He maintained awareness of his oneness with God throughout his life by keeping his will, his desires, and his mind fully attuned to and submissive to the mind of his creator,

Jesus would complete and fulfill the mission that Adam had begun. The words of Jesus were the words that God wanted us to hear. The actions of Jesus were the physical manifestations of a soul that embraced its divinity and remained in a state of oneness with God. Any soul willing to embrace and activate ideals that conform to the pattern of mind held by Jesus will grow into a more spiritually mature soul and draw closer to God. This is an application of the concept that the mind is the builder. Every soul that seeks reunion with God must come to a state of Christ Consciousness, whereby it is in constant communion and communication with God. The spiritually enlightened mind of Jesus is the ideal mental pattern for every soul mind, and his approach toward interpersonal relationships and life experiences define the ideal way in which thought should be manifested into action. Because Jesus fulfilled his role in God's plan for the salvation of souls, he earned the right to be the savior of all who choose to follow his example (Hebrews 5:9). Jesus lived his life not for self, but for the rest of humanity. He lived a lifestyle that God expects us to emulate in our daily activities. He is the perfect example of a life devoted to serving God and neighbor, and expects us to live similar lives. Each intentional act of service, each selfless application of the fruits of the spirit, helps the soul regain its true spiritual heritage as a companion of God. There is no other better example of a life well-lived in service of God than that of the Master. He is the Son of God in body, mind, and soul and the savior of mankind.

7. *By successfully fulfilling the directive given to Adam by God to subdue the Earth in the spiritual meaning of the phrase, Amilius submitted himself to spiritual law and became the law. As Jesus, he was able to perform what we call miracles because he lived in the realm controlled by universal physical law while using a perfected mind that was open to the realm of a greater cosmic law.*

What does it mean when the readings say he (Amilius / Jesus) became the law? To what law does this perplexing statement refer? The readings tell us how Jesus became the law and give us some clues that may help us understand what that implies. As Amilius, the soul of Jesus, attained Christ Consciousness, he became mentally and spiritually reunited with the cosmic Creative Force of which he (and every soul) is a portion. Amilius achieved perfection in the Earth plane by properly applying the spiritual and mental aspects of the law during physical incarnations, not by birth as the Messiah (2390-7_12). He held fast to that perfection during his life as Jesus (Hebrews 5:8–9). There are two laws to consider; spiritual law and physical law. We can understand the implication of Jesus becoming the law in the sense of the spiritual law that governs the soul by reference to the readings. Because Amelius learned to keep his will attuned to the Will of God, his mind and physically manifested thoughts were fully compliant with spiritual law and were in perfect attunement with the Mind of

God. This conformity with spiritual law released him from the need for further incarnations. His thoughts and actions would not cause him to become mentally and spiritually separated from God. He was able to let the Christ Spirit flow freely into and through his soul and project its loving force into his earthly environment. To see Jesus was to see the perfect cooperation between man and God and a life perfectly lived with respect for spiritual law. He became the law in Christ Consciousness as he subdued the Earth. Because he became spiritual law he could identify the sin source of physical illness and had the authority to forgive those sins when it would be conducive to the spiritual progress of a soul.

We can understand the effect of becoming the law in the sense of the physical law that governs the behavior of energy and matter by studying the actions of Jesus during his life on the Earth. According to scriptural records and the readings, Jesus could directly influence physical law to affect physiological changes in another human body by enhancing the body's ability to heal itself (blindness, fever, paralysis, a withered hand, a severed ear, leprosy). He could indirectly influence the subconscious mind of a soul that had severed or nearly severed its connection with a body to reestablish contact, restore the connection, and reanimate the body. This required that the soul and Jesus work together to first restore the body to good health (Jairus's daughter, the widow's son at Nain, Lazarus). In the case of the resurrection of Lazarus this process would require major reconstruction and rejuvenation of the organs of the body. His perfectly healthy body literally radiated health into his surroundings. His garments radiated healing properties even as a youngster (1010-17_25). The faith of a woman who had a bleeding disorder allowed her to be healed by touching the hem of his cloak (1353-1_41). As part of his perfection, Jesus also attained local mastery over universal physical law, He was able to walk on water, bring calm to a storm, turn water into wine, multiply loaves and fishes, and wither a fig tree. But how did Jesus manipulate or alter physical law to accomplish these miracles? Perhaps the answer lies in the basic tenet of the readings, which is that the mind is the builder. The readings clarify that the mind is a creative force that manifests the desires of the will by acting upon or molding spirit to fulfill those desires. Energy and matter in the physical universe is a form of primordial spirit-energy, a portion of the Spirit of God constrained and bound by universal physical forces established by the Mind of God. We can speculate that the mind of Jesus was able to locally influence, affect, and even control this spirit-energy. Jesus applied his mind, which was unified with the Creative Force of the greater cosmic realm, to momentarily change the natural interaction of physical matter. The Mind of God established the universal physical law that controls the energy-matter reactions of the universe, and the Creator, working with and through the perfect Son, could modify those laws locally to alter normal physical processes. The mental state of Christ Consciousness brings with it a level of mastery over the physical world that engineers can only dream about.

Because Amilius spiritually subdued the Earth and unified the material, mental, and spiritual aspects of individuality and personality, he was no longer subject to the physical-spiritual law of cause and effect (262-36_17; 1662-1_26). He gained the right, the ability, and the authority to reenter Earth as Jesus the Savior of mankind with the power to supersede or override physical law by using his command of cosmic law and spiritual law to intervene directly into materiality and material forces. Jesus didn't violate physical law but used aspects of the higher-order cosmic law, of which the universal law of physics is a subset applicable only to the physical realm, to alter conditions in the physical world (900-17_7). He was able to exert local control over the forces of nature and perform actions that others would call miracles because his mind and actions fully conformed to spiritual law. It is imperative that we also seek this perfect mental union of man and God, of soul and God, and open wide the door to our super conscious mind and the fellowship with God that permits us to receive his guidance and encouragement as we navigate the nonmaterial and material realms. It will allow us to fulfill the directive given to Adam, and through him to all men and women, to subdue the Earth; that is, to overcome our propensity to indulge in selfish behavior, to crave sensual pleasure, and to gather material wealth and power at the expense of others.

8. *The readings indicate that no person can find a better ideal, a better pattern to guide the conscious mind, interpersonal behavior in society, and approach to spirituality than the life and teachings of Jesus. The mental act of naming the Name is associated with the setting of ideals that are based on the words and actions of Jesus, the Christ.*

Jesus called the practical application of spiritual principles and the moral code of conduct exemplified by his life "the Way." The setting of ideals based on spiritual principles is tantamount to following the Way. The life of Jesus was dedicated to applying the fruits of the spirit to real world situations, and the most powerful spiritual ideals are rooted in the fruits of the spirit. Amilius was the first soul to accomplish perfection in the flesh and by doing so paved the way for the reunion of all of souls with their Maker. Because Jesus fully submitted himself to the Will of God, he earned the right to be called the Way that all must follow to restore their relationship with God. As an earthly expression of God's Will and purpose, the Christ Spirit could work through him to bless those who were receptive to his teachings. When Jesus said, "I am the Way," he meant that his life was the perfect expression of a life given to God. He was both the ideal pattern for mankind and the living example of that pattern (622-6_20; 954-5_18-19; 1608-1_58; 2533-7_7). During his incarnations, Jesus was confronted with the same temptations that we face during our lives but steadfastly and resolutely found the inner courage and stamina to use those circumstances to strengthen his mental and spiritual bond with God and hold fast to Christ Consciousness (262-82_10). He could ask his followers to "be perfect, therefore, as your heavenly Father is perfect" (Matthew 5:48 NIV) because he had proven that it was possible to do and had prepared the way so that others could follow him. He demonstrated that incarnated souls can overcome the temptations of the material world by applying spiritual princi- ples in their lives and allowing the awareness of God and the action of the Christ Spirit to direct and guide the activities of the soul as it navigates life in the physical realm. The decision to follow the Way of Jesus opens the soul mind to help and encouragement from God and makes it receptive to God's forgiveness, grace, and mercy; otherwise the soul cannot overcome the heavy burden of sin it has created. By following his example we will understand that our soul and the Father are one and will be able to restore our soul to companionship with God. I am the Way, the Truth, and the Life (John 14:6). Living according to the Way leads to Christ Consciousness, which leads to the Truth of the soul's oneness with God, which leads to eternal Life as a soul companion of God.

Jesus showed us how to use our humanity to uncover and activate our underlying innate spiritual origin. Every act of goodness involves a conscious effort, a redirecting of our conscious mind into modes of activity and expression that manifest the spiritual attributes of the soul. Perhaps it is like relearning to use muscles that have atrophied from lack of exercise. As we exercise the conscious mind, teaching it to think more lovingly and caringly toward our fellow souls, we build more godly patterns of thought and behavior that bring to our minds remembrance of previous satisfying and joyful feelings that came from expressing love and kindness toward fellow souls and receiving love and kindness from them. The difficult part is learning to set aside, suppress, and eventually eradicate our tendency to be selfish and to use our lives as an opportunity to gain at the expense of others, whether that occurs in a family, social, business, or political setting. When we base spiritual, mental, and material ideals on the life and teachings of Jesus and the two Old Testament commandments he stressed, and steadfastly work toward the implementation of those ideals in our daily life, we will grow to be more like Jesus. Actions done for the spiritual and material benefit of our neighbors in the name of Jesus are like the application of ideals that are grounded in the teachings and life example of Jesus. They have the power to bring positive change in the life of others and teach them how to become Sons and Daughters of God (262-37_4). Souls that turn away from evil thoughts and actions, that decide to emulate the spiritualized pattern of mind and the selfless activity of Jesus, are released from the law of cause and effect and abide in the grace and mercy of God (262-36_17).

The Spiritual Insight of the Apostle John

Perhaps no writer of Scripture knew the true nature of Jesus more than the apostle John. His incredible insight into the origin and nature of Jesus was surely enhanced by his ability to enter a deep meditative state that carried him into the world of the subconscious and a wealth of spiritual knowledge. One of these incredible meditative journeys was chronicled as the *Book of Revelation*. John's insight into the nature of the man Jesus and the origin of the soul of Jesus as given in John 1:1–14 is striking in its depth of perception. It begins with a description of the spiritual history of Jesus and the spiritual relationship of the soul of Jesus with God. In describing this relationship, he calls Jesus "the Word". This simple expression represents the authority of Jesus to speak for God and to be God's messenger and emissary on the Earth. The soul of Jesus was attuned with God and desired to bring all souls into perfect communion with God. Using the readings, we have identified Amilius as the soul of Jesus and understand that this soul remained devoted to and in perfect communion with God when in the spiritual realm and thereby had the authority to speak for God before other souls (364-7_7). We can now identify "the Word" as an expression for Amilius, the soul of Jesus. With this knowledge we can better understand some of the wording in John 1:1–14 and gain further insight into the nature of the man Jesus. Let's look at the relevant portions of these verses.

In the beginning was the Word (NIV v1) and *He was with God in the beginning (NIV v2)*: The phrase *in the beginning* used in the first part of verse 1 and in verse 2 can be interpreted several ways. It might refer to the beginning of the eternal God or the moment of soul creation when Amilius and his sibling souls were given life to satisfy God's desire for loving companions. We can rule out the beginning of God, because eternal beings have no beginning. It may refer to the creation of souls, but we need to remember that at the moment of their creation, souls were not entirely cognizant of their identity and independence. Souls are beings created from a portion of God that were given intellectual freedom and the ability to mature into responsible beings that can co-create with God in all realms in which the soul chooses to be active. Souls were given the ability to become like God in consciousness, but not all souls remained in a state of mental and spiritual harmony with God as they matured intellectually. However, Amilius was unique as the first of the created souls and as a soul that, along with other souls, continued to honor the Creator as it matured and began expressing its individual free will. Because the phrase *the beginning* is used within the context of the activity of *the Word*, we can infer from the readings and Scripture that the reference is to the mature Amilius. As the elder soul that chose to remain in perfect mental harmony with God, devoted to God, and dedicated to fulfilling its role as a companion of God in all mental and spiritual activity, Amilius could speak with authority about God and was truly the Word of God. The phrase *in the beginning* can mean any moment before the creation of the soul rehabilitation facility we call the physical universe, when the mature Amilius was cognizant of his close spiritual relationship with God and was working with God to help restore God consciousness to the lost souls. Amilius never wavered in his love for and dedication to God. He was unified in purpose with God, became the living spiritual expression of the voice of God among souls, and worked for soul restoration in the spiritual realm and in the physical realm. It can also mean the beginning of the physical universe because Amilius worked with God to create the physical universe. It could refer to the entry of Amilius as Adam because he was the soul behind the person recognized as Adam, the first man and the beginning of the human race according to Scripture. Amilius was also the soul behind the physical and mental activity of the man Jesus and, as Jesus, could rightfully claim to speak for God in matters of spirit to other incarnated souls (364-7_7).

And the Word was with God, and the Word was God (NIV v1): This phrase expresses and clarifies the fact that Amilius was a soul in the spiritual realm that existed in the presence of God, that the soul Amilius was a portion of God, and that he was a true likeness of God. Amilius was mentally and spiritually attuned to the Mind of God in purpose, desire, and manifested activity, and was a true companion of God, in constant spiritual communion with God. To some readers, this biblical statement may seem strange, but it accurately portrays the fact that Amilius was granted an independent existence through the gift of free will, but still was also a full image of God, with inherited godly spiritual attributes. These attributes give souls the ability to express the godly traits of love, kindness, patience, mercy, and grace in all forms of interaction with fellow souls and with God himself. Amilius was not God in the sense of being the Whole or Entirety of the Infinite God, but was God in the sense of being created as a portion of God with an independent identity that matured into an unselfish disciplined soul that knew its spiritual and mental relationship with God and chose to honor that relationship and become a true companion of God. His expressions of independence in the spiritual realm did not extend to the type of rebellious and selfish behavior that violated spiritual law or would have damaged his relationship with God.

Through him all things were made; without him nothing was made that has been made (NIV v3): Here John refers not only to the fact that Amilius was a co-creator with God in the sense that all souls were created to be companions of and co-creators with God, but that he was a co-creator with God in the specific creation of the physical universe. The power to command creative forces was (and is) an aspect of the nature of souls that many chose to abuse by using their creative powers to indulge in their own self-centeredness and selfishness in rebellion against God. Amilius used his creative powers in unselfish ways within the context of full cooperation and union with the desires of God. Amilius was truly a companion, coworker, and co-creator with God. The statement that all things were created through Amilius the Word is correct, but by all things, John is referring to all physical things, all of the physical universe of matter and energy (see Chapter 5), the creation of biological life that flourishes on the Earth (see Chapter 6), and the creation of the perfect human form through which all rebellious and selfish souls would eventually be required to incarnate to cleanse them of the propensity to sin (see Chapter 8). Amilius could be a co-creator in the effort to build a facility for soul restoration because from the beginning of soul rebellion in the spiritual realm, he remained devoted to his creator. He volunteered to become the leader of a rescue effort and primary instrument through which God would bring the promise of soul restoration and redemption to all spiritually lost souls and would become the living example of the Way to accomplish that restoration (257-201_8; 254-2_4).

In him was life; and the life was the light of men (NIV v4) through *The true light that gives light to every man was coming into the world (NIV v9)*: Verses 4 and 9 refer to the spiritually enlightened soul mind of Jesus. Light is used here to mean a state of consciousness, and in particular, a state of higher consciousness that can enlighten the souls of men that have lost the knowledge of God during the pursuit of sensual pleasure and materiality. The light that shone through the man Jesus into the world was the light that comes from Christ Consciousness, the higher consciousness of the creator that allows the Christ Spirit, the source of life that sustains both souls and men, to flow into and through the soul. Christ Consciousness allowed Jesus to remain fully attuned with the Will of God and committed to the plan of God for soul redemption. The Christ Spirit guided and counseled Jesus during his journey on the Earth as the Messiah and spiritual savior of humanity. The word "light" is also used in Scripture to indicate visible radiation shining forth upon the Earth from the sun or emanating from manmade sources. Verse 5 uses the dual meaning of light to make the point that just as visual darkness (absence of visible radiation) cannot overcome visible light, so spiritual darkness (evil and sin) could not overcome the light of the Christ Spirit that radiated from the soul and body of Jesus. No force of evil can overcome the individual who has fully opened himself or herself to the force of the Christ Spirit.

In these verses, the apostle John also tells us about the role of John the Baptist as the forerunner who anticipated and announced the eminent coming of the Messiah. According to the readings and Scripture, the Baptist was an incarnation of the soul of Elijah (Malachi 4:5; Matthew 11:7–15; 1010-17_25; 257-61_16). John wishes to make sure that the reader of his words does not confuse the Baptist with the Messiah. We are assured that the Baptist came as a witness that would testify to the fact that Amilius in the incarnated form of Jesus would come into the world as the true light of spiritual consciousness and that the true light would speak through the man Jesus to the salvation of all mankind. The teachings and life example of the man Jesus had and still has the power to awaken human beings to the realization that they are incarnated souls and to help them to discover a renewed awareness of the spiritual life they had as nonmaterial souls in the cosmic realm in the presence of God. The spiritual light that radiated from Amilius, the Word of God by right of true soul communion with God, through the man Jesus was the powerful light of the manifested Christ Spirit that cannot be overcome by darkness and evil.

Yet to all who received him, to those who believed in his name, he gave the right to become children of God (NIV v12): Verses 10 through 14 explain how Amilius entered the world as the Christ child, a world that he had helped create with God for the purpose of providing a facility for soul rehabilitation and redemption. The mental union of Amilius with God was so complete that Amilius could radiate life, love, and kindness through the words and actions of Jesus into the society of men. He was able to retain the state of Christ Consciousness even while engaged in the material world and with other incarnated souls. Jesus was able to radiate spiritual life and light so brightly and so intensely that those who looked upon him and heard his words with an open heart and unfettered mind understood that God was behind that higher consciousness. Those who received Jesus and recognized that he was the Son of God and that his authority was derived from God were given the opportunity to learn from him the way to repair and restore their relationship with God. John states that those who believed in his name were given the right to become children of God. It should be noted that all incarnated souls, the souls of all human beings, are already children of God, but many have lost awareness of that relationship. What Jesus did was give those who believed in him the Way, the proper way to live in human society, a way that would reveal the truth of their existence as souls, their oneness with the Creator, and that would restore their lost intimate knowledge of God and allow them to once again commune with God as companions and co-creators.

But many of the incarnated souls that inhabited the Earth had become so bound in materiality and so enamored with its sensual pleasures that they could not recognize the presence of Amilius and the Christ Spirit in Jesus and would not accept him or his message. Many were so caught up in their own personal selfish activities that they failed to recognize the spiritual perfection and authority of Jesus. They could not recognize that God was speaking to them through the person of Jesus, and could not open their hearts to accept the message that Jesus was bringing to them. They had descended too far into the quagmire of selfishness and materiality to recognize the presence of God. Some of them were immersed in the religion of their upbringing and were averse to accepting new teachings and doctrine advanced by an outsider about whom they were ignorant. Jesus knew his own people. He knew of the previous unspiritual activities of the many souls that were incarnating in human form and were now manifesting ungodly actions on the Earth, and possibly was acquainted with some of them personally as soul siblings. But each of these people had the free will to remain tied to materiality and remain ignorant of the presence of God's representative in their midst. Those people lost the opportunity to receive spiritual guidance from the Master himself but would still be given new opportunities to learn about Jesus and learn about the need to redirect their minds toward spiritual matters in future incarnations.

The words "children of God" in verse 12 brings us to words that Jesus spoke to the Pharisees, in which he reminded them that their own scriptures said they were gods. Jesus was telling them to rise above their sensory-saturated and religion-indoctrinated minds and open their hearts to the idea that their souls are godlike, created as a perfect image of God. He wanted them to understand the nature of his divinity and to be aware that they had the potential to be restored to that same godlike spiritual condition. No created soul can ever become the Whole of God, but every loving soul that embraces goodness and godliness and recognizes its oneness with God through the state of Christ Consciousness can exist in a perpetual state of companionship and communion with God. The message of Jesus emphasized the truth that we can and should become like him and thereby like God (1 John 3:2; Matthew 5:48). He was the perfect pattern of human behavior, which means the perfect example of the way humans should interact with God and their neighbors, the model of the loving manner of behavior that brings out all of the godly spiritual attributes that are part of the soul by right of inheritance from its creator. When our will is redirected to spiritual matters and we attune our will to the Will of God, we have the potential to rediscover the lost knowledge of his inner presence. We can begin to remember and recognize that pattern imprinted in the deepest recesses of our minds that assures us that we are one with God. As Christ Consciousness awakens that knowledge within us, God is able to communicate with us and we are able to understand God's purpose and plan for us. We can fulfill our true purpose to return to him and live in a state of atonement with him in consciousness. We will be able to better utilize our bodies and minds to serve others and help them achieve this higher God consciousness. When we do this individually and as a society, the towns, cities, and nations of the Earth will be at peace and the kingdom of God will have arrived on the Earth.

Jesus was born as the fleshly incarnation of Amilius, the perfected soul behind the perfect man, the soul child of God that entered the Earth on a mission to fulfill God's desire to provide a path of escape for souls trapped in materiality. Amilius descended into selfishness to fully immerse in worldly human activity but restored its full relationship with God by dedicating its earthly incarnations to the service of God and other souls. Amilius entered the Earth as Jesus to complete its mission to bring knowledge of the plan and method of salvation that God has prepared for every incarnated soul. Truly, the only begotten Son of God, the physical representation of a spiritually perfected soul, that remained fully attuned to the Mind of God in Christ Consciousness while animating a flesh-and-blood human body. Jesus had the authority to communicate God's grace toward other souls through the forgiveness of sins, and to teach the plan for soul salvation through proper use of material opportunity during fleshly incarnation. Salvation involves far more than accepting Jesus as our personal savior and confessing our sins. It involves bringing the will into harmony with the Will of God and a complete transformation of the conscious and subconscious mind of the soul away from systemic selfishness. Jesus wanted us to open our minds to the possibility and probability that the same physical-spiritual connection that existed between him and God also exists between us and God. Salvation is a process, a long process of retraining the mind, of turning the mind away from selfishness and rebellion and embracing a mental and spiritual reunion and union with God. Belief in Jesus as our Savior is the first step of a journey in faith that erases selfish tendencies and nurtures loving service toward others. Jesus doesn't give us salvation when we decide to believe in him, but shows us how to gain salvation, the inner awareness of oneness with God through Christ Consciousness, by manifesting the Way in our lives. We are redeemed, restored, and saved as we open ourselves to the awareness of the Christ Spirit within and begin to project the Christ Spirit into the world.

Events Recorded in Scripture that Reveal the Nature of Jesus

There are three significant events near the end of the ministry of Jesus that we will study in more detail. His response to each of these situations tells us something about his nature and mission on the Earth, the application of ideals, and his attunement with God. Two of his life choices reinforce who he was not, and one event in his life defines who he was. The conclusions from the choices he made and the outcome of the events are as follows: He was not a religious person; he was not a political person; but he was an intensely spiritual person fully attuned to God.

The religious and political rulers of Israel thought Jesus was a blasphemer, a false prophet, and potentially an instigator of an uprising (5252-1_9). Jesus was arrested on the charge of blasphemy by the leaders of the Great Sanhedrin, the supreme Jewish religious, legislative, and judicial court in Jerusalem that ruled over the Jewish population at the behest of the Roman occupation authorities. His forced appearance before the Sanhedrin was an opportunity for Jesus to use miracles and his powers of persuasion to educate the leaders of the Sanhedrin about his true nature and purpose and to exert his spiritual authority to influence the Jewish religious authorities to accept him as the Messiah. But Jesus didn't exert any overt influence on them. He didn't use his intimate personal knowledge of the purpose and plan of God for humanity to correct the theology of the Jewish religion or any other religious group. Jesus was not a religious person in the sense that he did not put doctrine and rituals and ecclesiastical power before the two commandments he espoused. Religions are systems of worship formed around a set of ideas, often promoted by a forceful or charismatic figure whose claims are accepted by other men and women. At times they are spiritual organizations that uplift the lives of their members, and at other times they are full of self-important and self-righteous individuals who intentionally or unintentionally deceive their members and draw them away from communion with God. For example, in 1845 the Rev. Basil Manly, Sr., a wealthy slave owner and a strong supporter of the Confederacy, was the driving force that split the existing Baptist church so that he could lead a pro-slavery faction, the Southern Baptist Convention, in the Southern states of America. Just because religious leaders use many of the right words in sermons and study guides does not mean that they have the right moral and spiritual attitudes in their hearts. When Jesus was brought before the Sanhedrin in the middle of the night to face the accusation of blasphemy, he made no serious move to defend himself or try to change the hearts and minds of these religious leaders. He let their knowledge of him based upon their own observations, their own mental state and religious conditioning, and their own inability to discern the spirit define and form their understanding of him.

Although these individuals were members of the highest Jewish religious authority, their conscious awareness of God, the creator and Father of each soul, was obscured by the self-righteous certainty that they were the most knowledgeable Jewish religious scholars and the purest expressions of Judaism in all of Judea. The self-righteousness that grew in their hearts along with their book knowledge and mastery of tradition interfered with their ability to commune with God and recognize God in Jesus, not because they had learned too much, but because they allowed themselves to become prideful in their knowledge and let that pride express itself through a sense of moral and intellectual superiority over others. Their theological expertise may have brought them knowledge, but it didn't bring them wisdom or a closer awareness of the inner presence of God. They were no longer receptive to the voice of God who is always waiting and ready for the soul to turn its attention away from self-assuredness and self-centeredness and back toward the unrestrained love of God. Only when religious education is used to fully understand and appreciate our limitations and inadequacy before God will we seek God's help and develop a better understanding of Jesus and his role as God's representative on Earth. They could not recognize the true spiritual depth of Jesus. In their embrace of the 613 moral and ritual laws (*mitzvot*) of the Old Testament, they lost sight of the two commandments that really matter, the two Old Testament teachings to love God (Deuteronomy 6:5) and love neighbor (Leviticus 19:18) that were the foundation stones of the body of teachings attributed to Jesus. They failed to express a love of God from the depths of their hearts, minds, bodies, and souls, and in their self-righteousness, could not find the wherewithal to treat all of their neighbors with a loving attitude. Perhaps, in their intellectual pride and ecclesiastical power, they considered themselves better than others, and felt it demeaning to actually engage with and serve the lower classes and the poor and downtrodden.

By taking up the mantle of religious authority, Jesus may have been able to influence the Jewish religious leadership to focus on the welfare of society instead of paying lip service to that idea while reveling in the finer things in life that could be bought with the tithes that poured in from well-meaning and generous believers anxious to secure their place in the afterlife. Think of the societal changes that could have been wrought as the Jewish population adhered to the theology and rituals promoted by a Sanhedrin headed by the Son of God. Surely there would have been an enormous spiritual awakening and great material benefits to society. But would the residents of Judea who came under the protection of the One Jewish Church led by Jesus willingly stop taking advantage of others and expend a portion of their time and resources trying to advance and better the lives of their neighbors? Unfortunately no, and Jesus was well aware of this fact. Salvation is not enforced from the top down, but is acquired as individuals change their goals and aspirations, and that better mindset propagates through families, communities, and nations. Jesus did not want ecclesiastical power. He knew that religion can and will be abused. He knew that any human organization that tries to define, dictate, and enforce the manner in which men should worship was susceptible to corruption and that the leaders of those organizations too often descended into patterns of self-serving behavior to protect the power and the wealth they acquired as a result of their elevated positions. He was also well-aware that his mission extended far beyond the boundaries of Judea. He came for the salvation of the world, not just for the salvation of the Jewish people. Aligning himself with the Sanhedrin would have made it impossible for his message to spread to Samaria, Rome, Greece, Britain, and throughout the Gentile world scattered across every inhabitable continent and island.

The words and actions of Jesus also demonstrated that he was not a political person and had no desire to politicize his mission by taking political power to achieve his spiritual objectives. He didn't use his position as Son of God and his deep knowledge of human nature to establish a political movement to boost his following or get himself appointed to a political position so that he could have his teachings codified into laws of morality and force the population under his jurisdiction to hold closer to the laws of God in their daily behavior. He didn't try to reform the Jewish or Roman legal systems so that justice would be based entirely on moral and spiritual principles, and could be properly and equally served upon the public. He could have reformed the legal system so that those who attempted to violate or deviate from the righteous laws he formulated would get the proper punishment, no more and no less. When Jesus was taken before Pontius Pilate, the Roman proconsul in authority over the Judean Providence, he made no attempt to convince Pilate of his God-granted authority over Jews and even Romans. He simply stated the fact that his authority was derived from God and that it was the desire of God that Jesus stand before Pilate. He did not urge Pilate to accept his claims, nor did he attempt to influence Pilate and work through Pilate's power structure and position of political authority to make policy decisions that would advance his goals and further strengthen his influence among the

Jewish and Roman people. Jesus could have worked with Pilate to become more influential in the power structure of Roman and Jewish society. Jesus could have exerted his influence while in conversation with Pilate, and he could have swayed Pilate, not only to save his life but also to change Roman policy in Judea. He could have caused the Roman occupation forces to be less severe in their policing of Judean society and alleviate the tax burden placed on the urban and rural Jewish populations. He could have caused Pilate to introduce policies that would have resulted in more humane treatment of the Jewish population and perhaps even elevated them to a favored position within the Roman Empire. But he did none of these things because this was not his mission and would not have served his purpose for being on the Earth.

Jesus could have convinced Pilate to set him up in a position of religious authority equivalent to or in place of the Jewish Sanhedrin so that he might have a stronger influence in the religious life of the Jewish people. He could have urged Pilate to give him the leadership position of the Sanhedrin and removed those members who held to incorrect theological ideas or who were simply more interested in the power and comfort that came with their position instead of the spiritual welfare of the greater society. He could have set up a combined political system and state-sanctioned religion with the single directive to actively encourage its members to love God with all of their heart and soul and love their neighbors as themselves. Jesus entered the Earth in a state of spiritual perfection, but to use that perfect life to run a large political organization probably would have caused him to sink into materiality again. It definitely would have interfered with the true purpose of his life, which was to demonstrate the Way of spiritual growth for the restoration and salvation of incarnated souls. His mission was to treat the cause, not the symptoms, of human suffering. He did not come to save the bodies of men and women from tyranny and persecution, but came to save the souls of men and women from the selfish motives and activities that were causing them to lose God consciousness. Spiritual liberation would, in the long run, more effectively and permanently release humans from the physical suffering they encountered during their lives as incarnated souls. He presented his ideas to his disciples and the relatively few people who gathered around him on different occasions as he taught in public, knowing that these core followers would spread the good news of his message across the Earth.

Perhaps the most spiritually significant event in the ministry of Jesus occurred when he posed the question to Peter, "But whom say ye that I am?" (Matthew 16:15–17 KJV; Mark 8:29 KJV). This was the moment Peter began to understand the meaning of Christ, not just in the sense of the anointed one and not in the sense of a title of respect, but in the spiritual sense of the essential component in the spiritual connection between Jesus and God. Christ Consciousness enabled the mind of Jesus to retain awareness of God, receive spiritual support and strength from God, and bask in the unfathomable love of God. The Christ Spirit is the aspect of God that merged with the soul of Jesus to give him his spiritual righteousness and power. It gave Jesus the authority to be God's representative on the Earth and to speak in the name of God. We have no written evidence that any other apostle had yet made this leap of faith or exhibited this power of observation and deduction, although we might infer from his writings that the apostle John had gained an understanding of the spiritual depth of the intimate connection that Jesus had with God. Although this connection exists in principle in all souls incarnated on the Earth in human form, it is largely ignored and invisible to the material-oriented minds of most members of the human race. Of course, Peter previously knew that all men can have a close relationship with God, but perhaps but did not fully understand the depth, intensity, and intimacy of that relationship when it is sealed in Christ Consciousness. Jesus stated that the depth and intensity of the mental relationship he had with God was available to all men and women who were willing to set aside their own selfishness and their own habituated appetites and personal desires. He taught that if human beings wanted to experience soul growth that leads to Christ Consciousness, they had to stop glorifying themselves and start devoting their lives to glorifying God and using their talents for the good of their fellow incarnated souls.

This was a great opportunity for the followers of Jesus to establish a spiritual education program, a practical set of spiritual lessons designed to activate Christ Consciousness in the minds of the faithful and bring humanity to the receptive state needed for the Christ Spirit to become the primary active force within every person (261-15_14; 262-30_18; and many others). Unfortunately, the great insight of Peter and the ensuing conversation was used instead to justify a lineage of ecclesiastical authority. The opportunity would be largely lost as the early Catholic church gained dominance by the projection of power and crushed different approaches to spirituality with their demand that church members show obedience and obeisance to the perceived earthly successors of Peter (Martin, 1981). The widespread use of anathemas concocted during church councils to limit the independent thoughts and beliefs of clergy and lay persons suppressed the flow of spiritual thought and ideas circulating after the death of Jesus. The idea and ideal of Christ Consciousness as the perfect union of God and man took second place to the idea of a universal church organization with a spiritual descendant of Peter at its head. The true meaning of the word "Christ" is revealed to the mind of every individual that seeks mental union with God through the meeting of spiritual weaknesses and the desire to let the Christ Spirit manifest in his or her life. The Christ Spirit is the true strength of every church. The true church left behind by Jesus the Christ is the community of individuals who in faith choose to acknowledge the Christ Spirit within and follow the teachings of Jesus in their worldly activities (262-87_7). Jesus emphasized the Old Testament commandments to love God and neighbor as the foundational tenets for all interpersonal and societal relationships, and the means whereby the Christ Spirit might be raised within the minds and hearts of all mankind.

Many Christians strongly identify with the personhood and life of Jesus but give little thought to the meaning of the word "Christ." When Christians use the word, it is often in the context of a synonym for the word "Jesus" or a title bestowed upon Jesus. Even though it is properly associated with Jesus, it may be too closely associated or improperly associated with his physical being, while its deeper spiritual meaning is often not well understood or appreciated. It is improperly used in the form "Jesus Christ" if it is intended to mean a surname of Jesus. It is partially correct but fails to convey the full meaning of Christhood if it is used simply as an honorific title for Jesus as the anointed one of God. In the language of the readings, the word "Christ" is more properly used when the intended meaning is "Jesus who became the Christ," a phrase that celebrates the restoration of Christ Consciousness to the soul of Jesus, and the action of the Christ Spirit through the man Jesus in the physical world. Too many Christians fail to recognize that Jesus did not want us to worship him but wanted us to identify with him and use his teachings to strive toward mental union and communion with God. Reading 5749-4_9 clearly implies this in the statements "The Christ Consciousness is a universal consciousness of the Father Spirit. The Jesus consciousness is that [which] man builds as body worship." Reading 2533-7_29 also tells us the "The POWER, then, is in the Christ. The PATTERN is in Jesus." Jesus taught the Way and opened the way for us to access God in the holy of holies within our soul. He provided the example of a life that will lead the questing soul mind to the attainment of Christ Consciousness. Because of his perfect attunement to God, his life was a living manifestation of the Christ Spirit. Jesus was not immune to physical weakness and uncertainty, but the mental strength he gained as he overcame the world and resolutely held to the ideal mental pattern of Christ Consciousness allowed him to walk to the cross knowing it was the Will of God and that his actions would open the way for souls to return to God. He was the ultimate fulfillment of the injunctions to be in the world but not part of the world and to love thy neighbor as thyself. The spiritual purpose of human engagement in societal units—whether at the family, community, or national level—is to use the pattern of Jesus to receive the power of the Christ Spirit.

In the broadest sense of the word and in the sense used in the readings, the Christ Spirit refers to the flow of goodness, godliness, and love through the mental-spiritual connection between man and God. This spiritual and moral force resides within the super conscious mind of every soul and can be activated and made available to every human being by conscious effort made during prayer, meditation, the intentional use of ideals, and other spiritual practices that bring the mind closer to divine awareness. We truly can become Sons and Daughters of God. The practical application of the Christ Spirit in the material world is embodied in the deliberate and purposeful implementation of the biblical fruits of the spirit (262-58_3; 262-98_8; 281-16_24), which represent the moral principles of human behavior that are appropriate for any incarnated soul that decides to live life to a higher standard of spirituality and morality and who desires to attain a high state of inner God awareness. The greatest and all-inclusive fruit of the spirit is love, a soul attribute inherited from God that embodies the essence of all other biblical fruits of the spirit to one degree or another. Love is the foundational spiritual quality of God. The commandments of Jesus to love God with all of our being and to love our neighbor as ourselves activate the process of redemption and are the cure for many of the spiritual deficiencies that plague our lives. They are not commandments given to Christians but are given to all humanity. They are not suggestions that the soul can follow occasionally when it wishes to feel better about itself as it continues to pursue material dreams in the physical world at the expense of fellow souls. The mental and emotional surge of pleasure we get from showing love to others reinforces the importance and value of love as a godly expression of our soul mind, and the reaction of others as they respond to love lets us see how love can alter human society.

The Forgivable Sins and the Unforgivable Sin

Jesus told the Pharisees who were intent on destroying him that all sins can be forgiven, even the sin of not recognizing him as the Son of man, but that sins against the Holy Spirit are not forgiven (Mark 3:28–29; Matthew 12:31–32). What did he mean by this statement and what are its implications? Sins are forgiven by God when we recognize that we have sinned, ask God to forgive us of the sin, and willfully change our thoughts and actions so that we make a strong commitment to stop expressing that sin. It is not enough to request forgiveness in a moment of sorrow and dive back into the sin the next day. Forgiveness is not a reprieve from the causal consequences of sin unless God softens the causal impact by an act of grace. There must be a change in consciousness, a redirection or removal of the desire that is behind the mental or physical sin or else forgiveness is futile and will not benefit the soul. The category of sins that Jesus is including under the heading *All sins* includes any of the sinful thoughts and physical actions that we have ever expressed since our souls rebelled against God. He probably also meant sins that were expressed in the spiritual realm but that may not be apparent or directly manifested in the material world. His audience was probably thinking of actions in the physical world that violate the Ten Commandments and the 613 Jewish moral and ritual laws (*mitzvot*).

Jesus singles out the sin of not believing in him as the Son of man for special consideration. Jesus is referred to in Scripture as both the Son of God and the Son of man. He is Son of God by the fact that his soul was created out of the substance of God in the image of God, by right of his full mental attunement with God (Christ Consciousness), and by the application of the Mind and Spirit of God to the body of Mary to spiritually conceive his physical body. He is the Son of man by right of his several incarnations in physical bodies conceived by physical means through the sexual union of two human parents, and his various activities in the society of men to return his soul to a state of spiritual perfection by bringing hope and enlightenment to souls in need of God consciousness.

Man is not to be rewarded only according to his faith in God or his Son, but according to how he puts his faith into action (Matthew 16:27), that is, by how well he emulates the life of Jesus in outward display of love and service. Works as mentioned in this verse are ways in which the faithful individual fully manifests the Christ Spirit in human society in the face of the temptation to consolidate and express personal power that seeks to domineer or crush the will of others and the desire for material goods to the extent that they are worshipped and become idols to the conscious mind. Faith is a prerequisite for the desire to act in ways that glorify God. It only signifies the first step in the spiritual journey, not the end of the trip and certainly not the time to sit back in self-satisfaction. Jesus is implying that a person can be forgiven for not believing in his altruistic works for the good of mankind or the fact that he is united in spirit with God. There is no time or locality constraint on the statement, so it can be equally applied to the millions of persons who lived and died since he walked the Earth, non-Christians who have heard about him or read about him in a Christian religious tract and were unconvinced or who saw the Jesus movie but didn't find in it a compelling reason to turn their backs on the religion into which they were born and the family that might ostracize them. There seems to be something in these verses that goes against the arrogant belief by some Christians that all non-Christians will be consigned to hell because they do not believe in Jesus.

Why are sins against the Holy Spirit so special? How does one sin against the Holy Spirit? To understand the meaning of this statement, we need to remember that the Christ Spirit and Holy Spirit are synonymous in the readings, and that sin is rebellion against God. The term "Christ Spirit" in the readings has a specific meaning that helps clarify the statement. The Christ Spirit is that portion of God that communes with the soul through a mental-spiritual connection that constantly fills the soul mind with the love of God, beckons the soul to recognize its oneness with God, and encourages the soul to return to companionship with God. It is the source of life for the soul that allows the soul to fulfill its destiny when it is willing to be led by God. When a soul mind is in the state of Christ Consciousness, it becomes aware of this oneness with God and aware of the fact that the soul is also a spirit portion of God. This is the concept and the meaning of Jesus as the Christ. Jesus became the Christ as he attained this state of higher conscious awareness. Only when this mental awareness of God is present within the consciousness of an individual soul can it recognize God's presence and let the Christ Spirit be an active force in its life. If a rebellious soul continually refuses to acknowledge the presence and activity of the Christ Spirit and manifests evil instead of goodness, it will permanently damage its ability to commune with God. The soul can do irreparable harm to its relationship with God and block the source of life to the soul. The denial of the Christ Spirit, sin against the Holy Spirit, eventually leads to the death of the soul through its absorption into the Whole of God with loss of its identity. The portion of spirit that God released to become a unique individual identity will lose its birthright and existence.

We cheapen the life and teachings of Jesus and his message when we lay claim to being saved simply because we have expressed our belief that Jesus is the Son of God, or that Jesus is our Lord, or that Jesus has for-given our sins. There is much more to the message of Jesus than a shortcut that allows us to bypass the way of the cross with its trials, tribulations, temptations, and life and death struggles in a material world. We must face our spiritual shortcomings until they no longer govern our thoughts and actions. It takes repeated effort to fully conquer the temptation to put material goods, self-gratification, and selfishness before unconditional love of God and unconditional love of fellow souls even when they do hideous things in the world of humans. Souls cannot perpetually exist in a condition of disharmony and discord with their creator. It is not a natural state of the soul or the cosmic realm in which souls normally abide. Jesus expects us to seek a perfection (Matthew 5:48) that leads to wholeness and oneness with God by making daily effort to free our soul minds from the desire to let spiritually unhealthy and ungodly attitudes control our thoughts and actions in interpersonal relationships. He knows we will not be magically transformed from selfish humans into selfless souls in the infinitesimal instant between life and death. None of us should harbor the arrogance of assuming that because we were good for part of our lives we will be transformed into a state of spiritual perfection just because our soul left our body.

The newly developing conscious mind of the young Jesus was strengthened and guided by the full communion of the subconscious mind of his soul with God and by his early training in the Essene community in which he was born (Furst, 1976). The certainty and awareness of his spiritual mission grew stronger as the conscious mind of Jesus developed through childhood and he approached the years of accountability. Amilius interacted with the material realm through the conscious mind of Jesus while also existing in a state of Christ Consciousness and communion with God. This inner strength and spiritual maturity in relation to his purpose allowed Jesus to fully comprehend and remain aware of his mission to restore the spiritual integrity of lost souls. The distractions of physical life and the attractions of the material world did not cause Jesus to waver from the certain knowledge that he had entered the Earth to do the Will of God. He completed the mission to bring the knowledge of salvation and method of soul restoration to humanity and opened the way for incarnated souls to lay claim to their godliness. To complete his mission, he would have to make the ultimate sacrifice and give his physical life so that we might have spiritual life. (John 15:13).

The Consciousness of the Death
and Resurrection of Jesus

*Nevertheless I tell you the truth; It is expedient for you that I
go away: for if I go not away, the Comforter will not come unto
you; but if I depart, I will send him unto you.* (John 16:7 KJV)

What do the last days of Jesus teach us about him, about us, and
about our relationship with the universe and God? The message
of his early years, with their emphasis on morality, right living (as the
Buddhists would say), service to others, honoring God, and obeying the
spiritual law embodied in the two commandments is relatively straight
forward, but the implications of his death and resurrection are more of a
mystery. Let's look at the last days of his life, starting with the transfiguration of Jesus before his disciples Peter, John, and James. Transfiguration
means that Jesus took on a brilliant otherworldly countenance as he
engaged in conversation with Moses and Elijah. The souls of Moses,
Elijah, and Jesus were joined in spiritual communication and the bright-
ness of the light that radiated from them was caused by the high-energy
vibrational state in which they existed at that moment (remember that
electromagnetic energy is the physical analogue of spiritual energy). These
nonphysical manifestations, which may have been akin to the thought
forms previously created by Amilius and the Adamic group, were clearly
visible to the apostles, but they apparently were unable to hear the conversation between them. Souls communicate by the exchange of thoughts

(5753-1_22; 254-2_2), not by a modulation of air waves or a spiritually equivalent process. Why they wanted or needed to take on this spiritualized form instead of directly communicating with the conscious mind of the man Jesus is not clear but may have to do with the desire of Jesus to show his disciples that he had spiritual support in his decision to submit to the cross.

The three accounts of the transfiguration in Scripture are sparse and devoid of real substance (Matthew 17:1; Mark 9:2; Luke 9:28), but the symbolic meaning of the scene is described in Reading 262-37_5. The three figures were meant to represent three aspects in the journey of every soul back to God and the pattern of thought and behavior that souls must pass through on that journey. Moses represents the law, the moral code, that guides the behavior of incarnated souls in the physical world and that is naturally followed by those who respect their fellow men and seek to obey the commandment to love thy neighbor. The prophet Elijah represents the higher mental ideals that should be held in the soul mind and that all incarnated souls should aspire to emulate in thought and manifested activity. He also represents the need for the spiritual seeker to reorient the will and mental attitude of the soul in preparation for the spiritual journey. Jesus is the completed and perfected soul and man, the Son of God who attained Christ Consciousness in materiality during his service to mankind, and regained eternal companionship with God. He represents the highest spiritual achievement that any soul can attain, the culmination of the spiritual journey. He represents the perfection we must all seek, the ultimate spiritual evolution we can hope to emulate, and the awareness that we too can once again be known as Sons and Daughters of God. These individuals represent a progression of spiritual growth from mortal moral humans animated by souls to immortal enlightened souls that have joined their will with the Will of God and have offered themselves in the service and companionship to God. They represent the progression of steps that incarnated souls take as they move from bearing the crosses that they have created during earthly lives to the crown of glorious eternal companionship with God, escape from the imprisonment of mental and material selfishness and self-centeredness to the spiritual freedom of service to God and fellow souls. When the physical, mental, and spiritual are in perfect harmony and the will is obedient to spiritual law, the soul will be spiritually perfected and restored to its proper relationship with God.

Rome claimed the authority to decide who would live and die in the occupied Jewish territories and throughout their empire. The cross was one method of projecting that authority. It was an instrument of torture designed to inflict maximum pain and suffering on the body of a criminal or rebel that might challenge the might of the Roman Empire. It was the ultimate form of punishment conducted in public in a highly visible location to instill fear and a consciousness of submission in the populace. It was an implement of harsh justice for the Romans and a symbol of subjugation and injustice for the Jews, a brutal method used by a secular authority to reduce crime and maintain peace and political control within the occupied Jewish provinces. Death was a longed for and welcomed event for those who were hanging on the cross.

The most agonizing decision Jesus made was to accept death on the cross. It was the most severe earthly test that he would encounter and the most profound event in his life. He agonized over the decision to accept the cross, a decision that would confirm his total and complete acceptance of God as his guide and mentor. It was a critical and necessary action that would verify and validate his soul's obedience to the Will of God and set the stage for the completion of his experiences as an incarnated soul and his mission as savior. The cross of Jesus would come to represent to his followers the trials and suffering that we sometimes have to endure as we come face-to-face with our personal failure to live life in righteousness fulfillment of our spiritual destiny. We occasionally face extreme situations during our life that cannot be bypassed or avoided. These life events must be accepted and met with the intent to complete the task at hand in the faith that God will give us the strength to persevere and conquer our fears. They must be approached with the intent that our responses and our actions in the face of those trials will conform to the highest spiritual values that we hold within our mind. There is no question that we will have to face a personal cross at some time in our life. We usually don't know beforehand what kind of experiences we may be expected to face. Our crosses might include the unexpected death of a close family member; a divorce; a car accident; a mugging that leaves us disabled; or the loss of our home in a flood, fire, or tornado. We should mainly be concerned that we will approach our crosses in the best possible way so that we come out of the experience spiritually stronger and better able to face any other mentally and emotionally stressful situations that may come our way.

The Jewish religious leaders thought Jesus died for the religious crime of blasphemy, but for Jesus, the cross was not just the instrument of his death, but represented a choice that would determine his personal spiritual fate and that of mankind. It was a highly visible and emotionally charged end to a 104-thousand-year mission that began with the projection of Amilius onto the Earth to restore God consciousness to souls enamored with the sensory experiences of materiality. His death on the cross and subsequent resurrection would open the way for our return to God by bringing to our conscious minds the awareness that we are far more than flesh-and-blood human beings. If he had balked in the face of his knowledge of the pain and suffering he would have to endure in his final hours on Earth, then future generations would not have recognized or accepted him as a savior sent by God. His death on the cross and his resurrection would instill a strong visceral and emotional impact on the minds of those who witnessed the events. Many of those who heard about the circumstances of his death and resurrection would be deeply stirred, and his claims of being the Son of God would ring true in their hearts and minds. His death and resurrection would trigger long-forgotten memories of our real nature as spiritual beings and our prior closer relationship with God that we discarded in our rush to become immersed in the physical world and experience physical sensations. It would awaken the innate spiritual mental pattern that allows the soul mind to understand its one-ness with the Father. Generations of humanity would be emboldened by the dedication, devotion, and submission of Jesus to the authority of God and would believe with absolute certainty that there is life after death. They would come to believe that the purpose of every individual is to prepare for that immaterial life by altering their propensity for selfish behavior and self-serving thoughts and intentionally seeking the light of the Christ Spirit within.

Hebrews 5:8-9 and Reading 281-16_25 state that Jesus learned obe-dience and was made perfect through the suffering that he endured, and that because he was made perfect, he was able to complete his mission and become the author of salvation for all who would obey his teachings and emulate his life. It should be clearly understood that the man Jesus had no need to learn obedience. The crucifixion of Jesus had nothing to do with the disobedience of Amilius when he incarnated as Adam. The crucifixion did not inflict suffering on Jesus for the purpose of bringing his soul to a state of spiritual perfection or instilling obedience to God, as is suggested by a common misinterpretation of Hebrews 5:8. The soul of Jesus was already perfected in the material plane, and he had no personal need to suffer on the cross for the restoration and redemption of his soul. The life of Jesus was a demonstration of his perfection, the proof to humanity of the perfection he had achieved during previous lives and mental-spiritual training, and was not part of the series of incarnations that were necessary for him to attain perfection (262-57_11). Amilius had already acquired spiritual perfection in the physical realm when he regained the state of Christ Consciousness during his previous incarnations. There are no biblical verses that record youthful indiscretions of Jesus in pursuit of selfishness and self-gratifying actions or any other forms of disobedience to God because Jesus never deviated from his mission to bring salvation to souls. One might think that, like many human children, there were periods of mild disobedience toward God during his teenage years that are not mentioned in the Bible. However, the readings clearly state that this was a period of secular and spiritual education for Jesus, just as a modern-day teenager might graduate from high school and move off to college. The actions of Jesus throughout his life continued to speak to his allegiance to God and verify that he was already a fully obedient Son from the moment of his birth. His adult life was totally dedicated to the completion of God's plan to educate incarnated souls about their spiritual origins and establish himself as a living example and savior for the lost souls. There was no time during the life of Jesus when he disobeyed God and needed to endure punishment or suffering to remind him of his relationship with God or to rededicate him to his mission. At age twelve he was already demonstrating his knowledge of Scripture to rabbis. He had slipped away from his parents unbeknownst to them. Three days later, during which time his parents led a frantic search for him, he was found in a synagogue teaching and astounding rabbis with the depth of his spiritual knowledge acquired during his upbringing in the Essene community. He was well aware of his spiritual Father and the nature of his mission at this time and even told his worried parents that he needed to be about his Father's business, by which he meant the business of God, not the business of Joseph (1010-17_19; Luke 2:42-49; Furst, 1976).

The mind of Jesus was fully attuned to God through Christ Consciousness before he died on the cross. That mental state would have caused every cell of his body to be highly attuned to the source of life itself, able to sense and commune with the permeating presence of the Christ Spirit. His body could resuscitate itself, heal itself of any physical injury no matter how severe, and rid itself of any disease that might attempt to invade and breach its defenses (1158-12_48). The body of Jesus was able to heal itself under normal circumstances, but when he was nailed to the cross, he let nature take its course. When the damage inflicted on the body became too severe for it to continue to be animated by the soul, he released it and allowed it to die. It is important to remember that even though the soul of Jesus, had already agreed before it entered the Earth as Jesus to follow God's plan to awaken the minds of his soul siblings, Jesus still could have decided to forego death on the cross (John 6:38; John 12:27). It would have represented a rebellion against the plan God had prepared for the salvation of souls, a plan to which his soul had agreed before entering the Earth as Jesus. Failure to accept the way of the cross would have been detrimental to his soul, causing Amilius to reenter the Earth and endure another series of incarnations to correct a lingering propensity to make self-oriented and self-centered decisions instead of God-oriented decisions. Jesus did beseech God that he not have to take the path that led to the cross (Matthew 26:38) because he was well aware of the physical suffering he would have to endure, but when God made it clear that it was necessary for the salvation of all future incarnated souls, Jesus made the tough but spiritually correct decision to reaffirm his vow, accept the Will of God, and follow the plan to its completion.

By this act of submission to the Will of God in the material world and his subsequent death on the cross, Jesus would become the omega to the alpha that was the entry of his soul onto the Earth as Adam (Revelation 1:8; Revelation 22:13). The statement "it is finished" made by Jesus just before his death not only signaled his imminent physical death, it signaled that the soul of Jesus had successfully fulfilled the purpose for which it had originally entered the Earth. Amilius successfully completed the most difficult physical task he would face as Jesus and ignited a spark of spiritual awareness in the conscious minds of men. That spark will eventually flare into full blown Christ Consciousness in the minds of those souls that choose to follow his example. The cross would represent the pain and suffering Jesus endured and the love Jesus held for us, but is also the symbol of the pain and suffering that we will face in our quest for soul restoration as we struggle to restructure our selfish pattern of thoughts to bring them into a state of atonement and at-one-ment with God. Jesus did not die on the cross so we can claim with adoration, self-satisfaction, or smugness that we are saved because we believe he died for our sins. By his death and resurrection, Jesus showed us the certainty of life after physical death and allowed us to comprehend that we too can be united with God. His life showed us how we can overcome our tendency to put ourselves first as we seek material comfort through goods, wealth, and personal power, and can instead seek and find a restored relationship with God through service toward others. Like Jesus, we can say yes to God; yes we will follow his Will and plan for us and keep our self-directed activities within the limitations defined by spiritual law. The physical and mental strength of Jesus and the single-minded devotion to his mission that he showed during his life, while praying in the Garden of Gethsemane, during the trial before Pilate, and to his death on the cross inspires Christians to persevere when faced with their own trials and tribulation. We know he will be faithful in his promise to help us if we call on him as we make our way through life and traverse the path that he blazed for us. He gives us hope that we can follow in his footsteps and reside with him in a shared state of Christ Consciousness and full awareness of our soul's oneness with God.

When the body of Jesus was removed from the cross, it was prepared for burial and then taken to a tomb donated by Joseph of Arimathea, where it lay for three days. When Mary Magdalene came to visit the tomb, she found the stone that blocked the entrance of the tomb had been rolled aside. Mary looked inside and saw that the body of Jesus was no longer in the tomb (2533-8_5; John 20:1–16). The Bible and the readings relate that in her extreme anguish Mary's first thought was that someone had stolen the body of Jesus. The readings indicate that the body of Jesus disintegrated and was dimensionally translated out of the material world, out of the three-dimensional physical universe (2533-8_5; 900-227_11). It should be noted that the word disintegration is used in the readings to indicate not only the physical breakdown of a body, but also the separation of the spirit and soul forces from a body at physical death. There is no indication as to how this was done, and obviously this event was well beyond the known limit of physical law as applied to matter and energy. Was the disappearance of his body a form of dissolution or the transference in its entirety to another dimension? Was it a last physical miracle performed by the soul of Jesus as it departed to the spiritual realm? Whatever the method, the real question is why was this done?

We can only speculate as to why the body of Jesus was removed from the Earth. It is possible that the reason was to prevent its bones from being used as relics or objects of veneration. Perhaps Jesus did not want his bones to become a rallying point for future generations, yet another set of holy relics to be prayed over or to build monuments and rituals around, and which could detract well-intentioned believers from the true spiritual meaning of his death. The readings are clear that this body was not needed by Jesus to complete his resurrection. Jesus did not want his material remains to become focal points of veneration or worship by material-minded seekers, an action that could cause those seekers to lose sight of the fact they needed to focus on more important mental-spiritual matters. Instead of tying the thoughts of future generations of faithful Christians to a physical relic from the body of Jesus, God wanted them to focus on Jesus as a teacher, an example of a life well lived for God, as the savior who blazed the trail he expects us to follow, and as a soul restored to its rightful place at the right hand of God. Soul restoration is not well served by the reverence of bone fragments or skulls of deceased individuals, no matter who those individuals were or what they accomplished and did for humanity. Soul restoration is a mental process whereby the subconscious mind of the soul tries to balance the conscious mind and the super conscious mind. The spiritualization of the soul mind is not well served by tethering the consciousness to physical objects on the Earth. Those people who look to the life and death of Jesus for strength in their own personal quest for soul restoration and return to God consciousness need a spiritual ideal, not a material object of veneration. They need to look beyond the material, beyond what they can see and feel, and not have their minds tethered to physical relics.

But the death of Jesus would not be the end of his mission on the Earth. As the weeping Mary gazed upon the stone bed inside the tomb and feared that his body had been stolen, angels appeared to her to reassure her that all was well. Soon thereafter, she would see a man nearby who, in her distraught state, she thought was the gardener. She questioned him as to who might have stolen the body of Jesus, but when he spoke, she immediately recognized him as Jesus. It might be easier for the conscious mind to imagine that this resurrected Jesus who stood before Mary was in some way a reconstitution of the physical body of Jesus, the body having been taken away to be repaired by God or some spiritual doctors until it was again functioning properly, and then dropped back on the Earth as the resurrected Jesus, but this would be wrong and would totally miss the point. We need to understand that the soul Amilius did not require and did not use the physical body of Jesus as part of the resurrection process that followed his death. Because of the way the story of the resurrection is written in Scripture, it is easy to assume that the body of Jesus that went missing from the tomb was the same as the newly resurrected body that stood before Mary outside of the tomb, but this would be an incorrect assumption. Amilius did not cause the body of Jesus to disintegrate or translate dimensionally out of the physical world, repair it, and then push it back into the physical realm to reanimate it. The readings clearly state that the resurrection was not transmutation, a changing of one flesh body into another, but new creation using the pattern of the old body (2533-8_5).

The readings state that when we die, the soul retains an ethereal form of the physical body that it most recently animated well after the death of the body. The resurrected Jesus should be more accurately imagined as a thought-form body, a mental creation of the soul Amilius that was the likeness of the physical body of Jesus. This is similar to the processes whereby Amilius projected the thought-form body of Adam on the Earth, the precursor of the physical body that would become the man Adam. Remember, spirit is the substance that is acted on by the mind to manifest reality in the physical world. The mind of Amilius, using spirit and memories, manifested a resurrected body as a thought form of the physical body it had previously animated as Jesus. It was not recycled flesh and blood. At first, this thought form was not yet integrated with the physical world, and Jesus would warn Mary not to touch him. The readings indicate that in this highly energetic state, Mary could have been be harmed if she touched him just as if she had touched a high power electric current (262-87_10). The thought-form projection would soon begin to take on the nature of physical matter just as the Adamic race thought-form bodies had transitioned into more physical forms with the desire and need for physical sustenance.

The resurrected body of Jesus made several appearances as a thought form before its cells were regenerated and the body took on a more hardened physical aspect. On one occasion, the apostles had locked themselves into the upper room (presumably where the last supper had been observed) for protection from the Jews. They were perhaps fearful and uncertain about what was going to happen next in their upside down world and were trying to take stock of the situation. The thoughts and ideas that they were discussing probably included an attempt to clarify in their minds the next step on this path that they had all begun only a few years before. The hopes and dreams that they had placed in the man Jesus may have been shaken by their recent experiences, but they still had strong memories of his life and teachings, and an enduring element of faith. They remembered the admonition to stay in the upper room until he returned. Amilius again reconstituted the bodily image of Jesus "out of the ether" inside the closed and locked wooden door of the upper room and appeared before the apostles (2533-8_5). At first the apostles were warned not to touch the body because "it could not be handled until there had been the conscious union with the sources of all power, of all force." But after several appearances the transition from thought form to physical form was sufficient to enable the resurrected Jesus to eat and digest food, fish and honey in the comb, and he would allow Thomas to touch the hole in his side where the spearhead had pierced his body and drawn blood (John 20:27). The biblical account of the resurrection of Jesus is consistent with the account in the readings and with the entry of Amilius onto the

Earth. Both actions involved the manipulation of spirit by a soul mind highly attuned to God working with aspects of cosmic law that are more comprehensive than the universal physical law that guides the creation and interaction of physical matter and energy.

The resurrection was not another miracle performed by Jesus to prove that he was the Son of God. It was a realized consequence of the perfect union and attunement between the soul mind of Jesus and the Mind of God (5749-10_24). It is an intrinsic expression of a soul body in materiality, a natural product of a spiritually attuned soul. It harkened back to the Adamic race projections and to the interference of souls in the biological ecosystem. The interfering souls were projecting themselves into and corrupting the biological world hundreds of millennia before Jesus was born, but did not create new enduring life forms. The resurrection was a consequence of the ability of Jesus to retain Christ Consciousness during the ordeal of his torture on the cross as he relinquished his body to death. As the new body congealed, each cell of his resurrected body embraced spiritual union with the source of all life, with the spirit and mind of cosmic consciousness that infuses every living cell, and with the unifying consciousness of the soul mind of Jesus. Jesus needed to close his mission with a bold statement to humanity that would instill in the minds of all people the certainty that there is something to look forward to after the death of the body, and to give hope, assurance, and confirmation to his disciples that his words to them were true. Jesus needed to reappear on the Earth to provide physical evidence and proof of the truth of the spiritual message he had been giving to the conscious minds of his followers. His resurrection awakened the minds of those who saw his resurrected body and many of those who had only heard about his resurrection to the fact that there is a nonphysical component associated with the human body that retains conscious awareness of life and body form after the disintegration of the human body. He wanted to stress that this nonphysical component that survives physical death is the animating agent of the human body during life. He wanted us to know that the welfare of the nonmaterial soul is far more important than that of the human body and vitally important to eternal salvation.

The resurrection was not intended to show mankind that a glorified body awaits those who follow in the footsteps of Jesus. It was to demonstrate that there is a continuity of consciousness after death and that if the human consciousness, the physical consciousness of a soul, is brought into alignment with the greater consciousness of God the soul can physically and spiritually subdue the earth. The resurrection of Jesus should not be used to instill hope in the faithful of the possibility of gaining their own personal resurrected body. It isn't a future gift bestowed by God to the righteous human who suffers death in materiality. The ability of a soul to project onto the Earth is not something unique or special to be granted to certain souls because of the goodness they displayed during one physical lifetime. The purpose of companionship with God is not best served by souls wandering around on the Earth in resurrected bodies. Soul activity on the Earth is only a temporary measure meant to bring souls to a higher state of conscious awareness. Earthly activity in a resurrected body would not serve the same purpose. The idea of having a resurrected body like Jesus only detracts us from the purpose for which Jesus lived and the true purpose of his resurrection. The idea that we will be given a fantastic glorified body that is a vast improvement over our current frail and disease-prone body puts too much emphasis on possessing another body that can survive on the Earth and too little emphasis on following the path of Jesus to spiritualize the soul. It causes us to set our sights and hopes on the acquisition of yet another Earth-bound object, even if it is a spiritual substance that can acquire material properties. It is yet another thing that we can desire and seek to acquire, and that draws our attention away from the need to mentally elevate the celestial consciousness of the soul mind toward the divine consciousness of God. The hope of a future personal resurrection on the Earth is a false hope and an incorrect understanding of the meaning and purpose of the resurrection of Jesus.

The purpose of the resurrection of Jesus is that we learn and understand that there is more to life than human existence and more to death than nonexistence. It reinforced and confirmed the validity of his teachings. The resurrected body of Jesus was a visible demonstration of the fact that there is continuity of existence and consciousness after death, and that the perfected soul has mastery over the physical elements (1158-5_18). God will not grant us a new, glorified, resurrected body in the form and likeness of our deceased body simply because we have led a good life on the Earth. We will have no reason to reappear on the Earth as an incarnated soul or as a thought form that solidifies into a human body after we have fulfilled our spiritual purpose and realigned our soul minds to full Christ Consciousness. The future acquisition of a resurrected body is not relevant to the salvation of the soul. The purpose of reincarnation and earthly existence will have been fulfilled when we learn to always and consistently choose God over self-centeredness and materiality. After we have conquered the tendency to let materiality and human sensuality control our thoughts and emotions, we will not need to continue experiencing earthly life in a semi-physical thought-form body that expresses the spirit-energy pattern of the body we last animated or that expresses a composite memory of the bodies that we animated during various previous incarnations. To do so for our own pleasure or pride would only risk bringing back the previous dark days when souls using similar methods interfered with natural evolution. There is no spiritual purpose to be served by a saved soul, meaning one that has achieved a state of Christ Consciousness, to continue inhabiting the Earth. Our future will unfold in other realms of experience when we have successfully completed our spiritual training and testing on the Earth. Jesus wants us to emulate his life, not try to emulate his resurrection.

Amilius became immersed in the material world of selfishness and self-centeredness to prove that incarnated souls can conquer the tendency to express selfishness and disobey God. In his role as Jesus the Messiah, he remained loyal and faithful to God and demonstrated that man can live for a higher purpose and look beyond the attractions of materiality and the urge to exercise power and control over others. He remained faithful to God even unto death. He was not simply a good man who had the misfortune to be condemned to death on the cross. He was not saved from death on the cross by the intervention of God (Surah 4:157). He was not the Whole of God come down to Earth in the sense promoted by fundamental Christianity. Jesus was the physical expression of the perfected soul Amilius and the first human to fully and faithfully represent God and to do the Will of God during his entire life on the Earth. He aligned his will with God's Will and lived so that every undertaking he pursued found favor with God because there was no selfishness in his thoughts or self-indulgent actions during his life. The magnitude of the mission didn't depress him or become an undue burden on his mental health because his mind was united with the Mind of God through Christ Consciousness. His life revolved around a mission of mercy that would change the course of history and the future of mankind, but it wasn't a glum or sad life devoid of pleasure. He laughed and joked with friends and family even in the face of his looming crucifixion (262-33_7; 1158-14_14).

Because of his love for us, Jesus made the choice to endure the agony of death on the cross and the very public disgrace of crucifixion. He knew that by this last physical act, he would demonstrate to all present and future humanity that death holds no power over those who live according to spiritual law, putting others before self and selfishness, and putting God before the Self. He would also demonstrate that his return to Christ Consciousness was complete, secure, and unshakable in the face of the physical conscious urge to express his own will instead of seeking the Will of God. He had already fulfilled in previous incarnations the spiritual law that demanded he subdue the cause of his spiritual error as Adam. Now he demonstrated the strength of that commitment, his attunement to and oneness with God, and was ready to take his place for eternity at the right hand of God. The ordeal on the cross and his acceptance of that agonizing end of his life was the final act that verified, confirmed, and proved his spiritual perfection and closed the chapter on his earthly incarnations on behalf of mankind in biologically conceived human bodies. Jesus demonstrated and opened the way for all of mankind to access the throne of grace and mercy and realign their conscious minds with God. By right of his status as the Son of God and his successful restoration to Christ Consciousness, Jesus (as Amilius) has earned the position of advocate before God for all souls. Because he completed soul perfection in the physical realm and knows our weaknesses and strengths as we try to emulate his success, he can represent us before God. Jesus didn't die for our sins as much as he lived that we might recognize our sinful nature, learn how to release our minds and bodies from the desire to sin, and free ourselves from the spiritual and physical effects of sin. His death was an extension of a life lived according to the Will of God. He was truly Christ Consciousness in action, the living expression of the Christ Spirit, and the physical representative of God on the Earth, and he asks that we also live our lives guided by a Christ-like mind so that we can fulfill our true purpose in life through the perfect manifestation of the Christ Spirit.

Amilius will return to the Earth at least once again to continue his mission. This will be a refresher course or special teaching seminar for those incarnated souls that are seriously interested in his spiritual message. As part of his ongoing mission to save humans from their descent into self-indulgent sinfulness, Amilius will return to the Earth as a thought form in the likeness of Jesus, just as he appeared during the resurrection (364-7_8; Acts 1:11). That thought form will also solidify into a physical or quasi-physical form and Jesus will preach and teach to the many incarnated souls that are earnestly pursuing spiritual perfection and mental attunement with God. This reign of righteousness, called the second coming of Jesus in Scripture (Matthew 24:30; Luke 21:27) and the readings, will last for a thousand years (364-8_3; 5749-4_15), approximately the lifetime of Adam, and will be a time of peace and great spiritual growth for many souls whether or not they were Christians in previous lifetimes. The readings provide a few details about this event that take some of the mystery out of its purpose and the manner in which it will be accomplished. This second coming of Jesus will not automatically enforce a lasting peace but will be a temporary respite from the intentional manifestation of evil thoughts on the Earth. The conscious minds of the souls incarnated on the Earth during this period will not suddenly become purified and spiritualized because of the presence of the Master on the Earth any more than they were when Jesus came two thousand years ago. The difference will be that souls that have not yet made a strong effort to grow spiritually, and whose presence would seriously disrupt the peace and tranquility of an orderly society, will be prevented from incarnating during the second coming.

This period of peace will not violate the free will of the remaining recalcitrant souls, but will only temporarily prevent them from being active in the Earth environment. It will be a special opportunity and period of study for the spiritually gifted souls that are making a good-faith effort to realign their minds with the Mind of God. These souls will be allowed to pursue the ideal of Christ Consciousness under the influence and guidance of the perfect soul that walked among men as Jesus and experienced death on the cross so that other souls might have the opportunity to know God through Christ Consciousness. Perhaps Amilius will be accompanied by many of the enlightened souls that entered the Earth with him 106 Kya who also held to the ideal that souls can remain faithful to God even while engaging with an often sinful human society in a material world. The influx of a larger company of souls with Amilius would bring the effort to restore God consciousness full circle, with the success of the second mission much more likely than the first. The time of this reappearance of Amilius in the form of Jesus is not known by mankind but is dependent upon the concerted effort by incarnated souls to make themselves channels through which the Christ Spirit can flow into society (364-8_3; 5749-2_17; 5277-1_37; and others). The collective prayers and actions of a sufficient number of righteous and godly incarnated souls that have determined to remain faithful to God and who are earnestly striving to live their lives in obedience to spiritual law will usher in the thousand-year period of peace (262-49_7). No one knows when this second coming will occur or what portion of the population will have to be striving to live a moral and spiritual life before it can occur, but the readings assure us that the primary factor will be the desire and dedication of incarnated souls to restore their relationship with God (281-37_10). Scripture also confirms that no one knows when this event will occur, with some manuscripts saying that even the Son does not know (Matthew 24:36). It is the responsibility of each soul, each human being, to set aside selfishness and devote each incarnation to the manifestation of the Will of God in loving service to others and so complete his or her part in making the way passable for the return of the Master.

The Material Implications of Christ Consciousness

... for we must meet ourselves in our dealings with our associates, or friends, or neighbors, or enemies even - for, as has been said as of old, which is the universal law, "If ye will be my people, I will be your God!" (Edgar Cayce Reading 257-85_11)

The path to Christ Consciousness begins when the soul becomes aware that the physical world has a spiritual purpose. We progress along that path when we understand that life is only lived successfully to the extent we honor that purpose and decide to live our lives in a manner that brings fulfillment of that purpose. Success breeds success, and small steps along the spiritual path ultimately lead to great dividends. The universe and the society of humans exist for the spiritual benefit of souls, and not for the physical pleasure of men and women. Spiritual growth can best occur when the individual is intent on approaching the vagaries, temptations, and trials he or she encounters with the attitude that each situation is an opportunity to make spiritually oriented choices that draw the soul closer to communion with God. As the soul mind becomes more attuned to God, the soul is better able to retain awareness of its true individuality and maintain a secure spiritual link with God during its physical incarnations. The conscious mind awakens to the greater knowledge of the subconscious mind and the soul's spiritual core deep within the super conscious mind. This blossoming awareness of our inner being, the feeling that we are part of something far greater than anything imaginable to the conscious mind, gives us the strength to push through difficult times. It opens the door through which God as the Christ Spirit can express his Will on the Earth as we willingly become his hands and feet. It reveals the sure knowledge that the Spirit of God is active on the Earth, working to illuminate the minds of mortals to his power, presence, and infinite love. The life changes that attend the pilgrim's progress toward Christ Consciousness don't just unfold in the abstract and shadowy regions of the mind and spirit, but also manifest as concrete material benefits. Christ Consciousness elevates mere understanding to the soundness of wisdom, the ability to bring good judgment to an experience and rightly apply knowledge and understanding when making decisions. An enlightened view of the material world and its spiritual purpose allows the conscious mind to process the trials and tribulations of life and everyday societal interactions in ways that make practical application of the teachings of Jesus.

We don't know how many souls chose the path of selfishness and are now confined to the Earth plane. We do know that more than eight billion souls are currently engaged in active rehabilitation on the Earth. We don't know if this represents a significant portion of the total soul population. We only know that far too many souls chose a life path based on selfishness and rebellion against the spiritual principles that were established to guide the developing consciousness of souls. There are an unknown number of souls now residing in the inter-between borderland realm and occupying the mental-spiritual training centers designed to reeducate soul minds. We don't know how many souls currently in rehabilitation made their first poor choices in the cosmic realm or how many were part of the Adamic influx of souls that came with good intentions but succumbed to the attractions of materiality. Because so many souls chose rebellion, and each soul has a unique training requirement that best fits its particular set of circumstances, there is a need for millions of combinations of mental-spiritual training and human life situations that incorporate a wide spectrum of opportunities to correct the spiritual deficiencies of every soul and bring them all back to God consciousness (5755-2_10-11). These needs shift and change as souls respond to new opportunities and become more or less inclined to forgo selfish activity in favor of selfless activity in the offered life situations. Jesus would allude to this chaotic state of soul consciousness with his often misunderstood statement about many mansions (John 14:1-3). How we navigate interpersonal soul activities and experiences in relation to spiritual law determines the type and condition of the "mansion" we inherit, the state of consciousness we carry into the borderland after death (555-1_6; 3578-1_8).

God communicates with his children as the Christ Spirit. Faith is a necessary prerequisite that lets the Christ Spirit make expression through the individual. Service, the outward projection of the loving force of the Christ Spirit into human society, works for the material and spiritual benefit of mankind and fulfills the commandment to love our neighbor. The Christ Spirit is only active within men and women who have opened their minds and hearts to the presence of God in the seat of the higher consciousness of the soul mind, the innermost holy of holies where man and God commune. The soul has the responsibility to open the door through which God and soul communicate and to keep it open. The soul has the responsibility to manifest the Christ Spirit in the society of humans. The soul decides whether to take its signals and prompting from the material and carnal pleasures of the sensory world or from the illumination and revelation of the Christ Spirit. It alone decides if it wants to bask in the love and kindness that comes from direct communion with God. As the mind of a more enlightened soul becomes attuned to the Mind of God, the soul draws nearer to the state of perfection that Jesus encouraged his disciples to achieve (Matthew 5:48). This is quite a high bar, and it is easy to water it down by concluding that Jesus really meant we should just try to be as good as we can be, but that would not be correct. Jesus wants us to achieve the same state of perfection that he achieved, the same state of mind that allowed him to focus on the successful navigation of his mission of soul salvation from the day of his birth through his death on the cross. He wants us to learn to forgive even as he forgave his disciples who could not hold vigil with him during the most important night of his life when he agonized about a decision that would affect the destiny of every soul but bring terrible suffering to him, even after he had lead a perfect life (281-27_16). He wants us to open our hearts and minds to the presence of the Christ Spirit, the loving force of God that illuminates the minds of his soul children and that has been available to every person in every society that has existed from the beginning of the incursion of souls onto the Earth.

The readings state unequivocally that all healing comes from God (4757-1_4; 3512-1_5). The ability to self-heal, to fight off a disease or repair an injury, is affected by the degree of attunement of the soul to God. Jesus made clear the connection between sin and physical illness when he used the words "Your sins are forgiven" and "Get up and walk" to announce the healing of a paralytic man (Matthew 9:5 NIV). Healing is a mental process as much or more than a physical and biological process. Remember that the basis of cellular activity is that spirit and mind impress organizing and cooperative principles upon a collection of organic molecules, causing them to self-organize for the purpose of survival, sustenance, and procreation. The active consciousness of God animates cellular life and the higher functions of plants and animals, but the overall biological activity of a soul-animated human body is primarily sustained by the soul mind. Healing in the human body is managed by the influence of the soul mind on the body through the cerebrospinal system, the endocrine system, and the sympathetic nervous system (600-1_21; 281-46 through 281-58 excluding 281-50 and 281-56). The soul mind facilitates healing by enabling the proper flow of blood and the appropriate transportation and distribution of biochemical nutrients to and from various parts of the body to repair tissue and destroy invading organisms such as bacteria and viruses. There are times when the healing system of the body needs the attention of a doctor to administer drugs or perhaps minor surgery, but this chemical and physical assistance only better aligns the body with the spiritual forces that are the source of all healing (262-83_10; 1152-2_2; 1158-3_12). This external assistance is especially beneficial when the damage to the body is extensive, or the activity of the invading organism is overwhelming in relation to the spiritual advancement of the soul. The mind usually can keep a body physically well under normal circumstances, but unless the mind is open to and attuned to the Christ Spirit, it may not be able to bring the body back from a serious injury or virulent invasive organism. Massive physical trauma such as shattered bones and major destruction of tissue may need to be physically repaired by a surgeon to make the body more amenable to the natural healing process because the damage exceeds the ability of the unenlightened mind to coordinate the changes needed to heal the body.

Our human bodies are important, but souls are far more important. Human bodies may be required to endure illness, physical pain, and suffering for the spiritual benefit of the incarnated soul. Chronic mental and physical illness may be the manifested response to a specific spiritual error perpetrated during one or more previous lives. The conscious mind may need to experience emotional trauma, fear, and other forms of mental stress to awaken the soul to its spiritually degraded state. These physical conditions can correct the propensity of the incarnated soul to make choices that serve the Self without consideration of spiritual law or to engage in activities that impinge on the well-being of other souls. The intensity and longevity of these forms of suffering depends on the extent to which the soul has embraced selfishness and the desire for self-gratification, self-indulgence, self-exaltation, self-aggrandizement, and other forms of behavior that serve and glorify the soul instead of the creator of the soul. Without the proper mental-spiritual attunement, the ability of the soul to heal the human body is compromised. The long-term progression of age-related disabilities is linked to the general deviation of the soul from its spiritual roots, the lack of perfect attunement with God as the Christ Spirit, the source of life. Christ Consciousness draws the spiritual elements of the soul into closer contact and communion with the human body and makes it easier for the Christ Spirit and the soul to work in harmony to maintain the health of the body (1152-5_5-6). It allows the soul mind to work in cooperation and coordination with the cosmic consciousness that infuses biological cells and imparts life and purpose to each appropriate union of biochemical molecules. The Christ Spirit will naturally spiritualize the cells of the body and sanctify and consecrate the body as the soul mind unites with and glorifies God.

The biblical accounts of the life of Jesus do not mention any periods of illness. The readings suggest that there were no instances of illness in the life of Jesus (479-1_7). Jesus apparently lived his childhood and adult-hood free of the diseases prevalent in his day, such as mumps, typhoid fever, polio, cancer, leprosy, pneumonia, and perhaps even the common cold. The cells of his body worked in perfect harmony and unison with the Christ Spirit to bring health and fulfill the purpose for his incarna-tion. This physiological condition of perfect health is a natural biological byproduct of a soul mind perfectly aligned with the Mind and Will of God. Under this state of mind, the flow of life force from the Christ Spirit permeates the body. Adam was told not eat fruit from the tree that is in the middle of the garden because it would cause his death (Genesis 3:3 NIV). By this was meant spiritual death and physical death. It would lead to spiritual death because the act of immersing and indulging himself in materiality would weaken the communion of Adam's soul mind with God by interfering with the free flow of life force as the Christ Spirit (900-227_11). It would lead to physical death because his thought-form body would take on solid physical form, and the weaker spiritual life force would eventually lead to bodily death. The mortality of Adam was a direct consequence of his decision to let himself descend into self-indulgence and disobedience of spiritual law (Genesis 2:17). That decision caused Amilius to come under the law of cause and effect, sow and reap, and led to the need for Amilius to reincarnate. It meant that Amilius could not fulfill his spiritual purpose on the Earth in a single lifetime, but that through multiple lifetimes, he could prepare himself to be the example of the Way for all of mankind to return to God. Over time, spiritual disobedience brings about deterioration of human physiological processes and ultimately leads to physical death. The souls that arrived with Amilius were subject to the same spiritual and physical effects.

Jesus was not only healthy, but he also healed others. He knew that the faith of the patient was an important factor that awakened the patient's mind to the possibility and probability of a successful conclusion to the healing process. Jesus attacked the problem of human illness at the spiritual level. The mind of Jesus interacted with and influenced the subconscious mind of the patient. Jesus could connect with the individual's subconscious mind to diagnose the physical-spiritual cause of the physical ailment and directed the activated soul mind of the patient to apply the cure. The medical diagnoses that Cayce gave to those seeking help from him were accomplished by his subconscious mind communicating with the subconscious mind of the person who requested medical advice (294-1_1; 900-22_3). Cayce could not accomplish this feat without first relaxing and setting aside his conscious mind, but Jesus, being fully in the state of Christ Consciousness, could make the subconscious connection while remaining consciously aware of his physical surroundings. Cayce could not direct the subconscious mind of the person seeking help to cure the body, but could provide an accurate physical-spiritual diagnosis. Jesus could give the appropriate suggestions that allowed the regenerative healing energy of the Christ Spirit to move into the patient's body and give the necessary electro-chemical healing impetus by activating the hormonal, neural, and vascular system to make the needed alterations in the physiology of the body. For healing to succeed, it was also necessary that the people who were mentally and emotionally close to the ill person and those that physically surrounded the ill person keep a proper mental attitude (Mark 5:21–43). Jesus sent away individuals whose mental attitude would hinder his healing efforts.

There are other types of healing mentioned in the readings and Scripture that are also difficult to assess and understand within the context of modern medicine and science. Scripture tells the story of a woman who approached Jesus from behind, believing that if she could just touch the hem of his garment, she would be healed of the disease that had afflicted her for many years (Mark 5:25–34; 1353-1_41). Her faith in the healing power that surrounded Jesus was so strong that she was made whole. The question here is whether the robe that Jesus wore transmitted a healing energy to the woman or whether the touch of robe physically activated her faith in his healing power and allowed the life-giving Christ Spirit to flow into her body and heal the disease. The answer seems to be both. Reading 1010-17_25 clearly states that the body of Jesus was perfect from birth, radiating life and heath as a vibration that was destructive to dis-ease (a word used in the readings to indicate any kind of disorder in the physio-logical functions of the body). This bodily perfection was a result of the fact that the soul of Jesus had attained the spiritual perfection of Christ Consciousness before it incarnated with the body of Jesus. As a child, this radiated force of health apparently was in some manner absorbed by the fabric of his clothing and imparted healing benefits to other children who touched his clothing. One reading suggests that, as a child, Jesus was not consciously aware of the spiritual energy that radiated from him, but that he began to be aware that he projected a life force at about age twelve when he started conversing with the rabbis in the temple and was becoming more aware of his spiritual mission (2067-7_9). Many readings associate the healing process with atomic vibrations (the electrical forces of matter) that act to counter-balance the destructive forces of disease (281-3_14), and Reading 443-4_3 indicates that an individual who has sufficiently raised the spiritual and physical vibrations of the body may project those healing forces outward through touch or mental influence. This transmission of beneficial healing properties to other individuals is only possible after the individual begins the process of healing themselves so their body is able to give forth that which it possesses. Other readings seem give a different definition of vibrations as they relate to healing—a more spiritually oriented definition than physically oriented definition. When asked to define vibration in relation to healing, the source of the readings stated that it is the raising of the Christ Consciousness to such an extent that it is able to flow outward and be directed toward another individual. The ability to project the Christ Spirit is a natural result of the union of the body, mind, and soul with the Creative Force that gives life. The spiritual and physical are unified in that the Christ Spirit becomes a physical manifestation of the force of God, attuning the atomic vibrations of the body so that the destructive vibratory force of disease can be counter-balanced to bring harmony to the various functions of the body. Christ Consciousness and the Creative Force of God are the key to healing whether or not material assistance is provided to the diseased or injured individual (281-7_16; 281-3_14-15).

Not every major life event that results in serious injury or death has its roots in previous spiritual error. There are first-cause events happening every day in the world—those initiated by a soul that makes a fateful decision that causes the injury or death of another person, but which are not causally related to a previous spiritual error. People have the capability to make stupid decisions, and sometimes the consequences are catastrophic. When a novice hunter mistakes movement in the brush for a deer and kills his hunting companion, we usually classify the event as an unfortunate accident. When a robbery goes awry and leaves a homeowner dead on the floor of his house or a mentally ill or angry individual goes on a mass-shooting rampage and kills and injures a dozen innocent shoppers in a mall, we are often at a loss to understand the purpose of the action. We are unlikely to comprehend the true magnitude of the personal trauma and mental-emotional fallout of the deaths unless we or a close friend has lost a loved one in the tragedy. Mechanical devices can fail or be improperly operated, leading to the injury or death of the operator, passengers, and innocent bystanders. Natural disasters claim many lives every year. We consider the death and destruction inflicted by earthquakes, hurricanes, tornadoes, floods, wildfires, and volcanoes the result of natural meteorological or geological processes, so-called acts of God. The readings agree that there are accidents in creation (5252-1_29). Accidents are simply part of the human life experience, but man-made tragedies and natural disasters can also have a causal spiritual component that eludes the affected individuals or observers. Without conscious knowledge of the soul memories or spiritual urges that are influencing the activities of human beings, it is difficult to correctly identify the root cause of destructive events that bring injury and death.

What are the implications of soul enlightenment, of embarking on the path that leads to the higher state of Christ Consciousness, for family and community? Members of families and communities often incarnate together because they have unresolved interpersonal issues that offer opportunity for spiritual growth. These are the places where individuals interact frequently, where life situations require a constant awareness of how to behave, interact, and react as personal desires, child rearing, and career dynamics cause unsettling mental and emotional stresses. This is the arena where opportunities to demonstrate our true understanding of God abound. These opportunities are present in abundance in the close quarters of a family unit, where the give and take necessary to keep a marriage healthy can break down as different personalities, opinions, and ideals place strain on relationships and create the potential for conflict. It isn't easy to remain at ones best at all times under every circumstance, especially when many marriages bring two people together who may well have serious unresolved issues left over from previous relationships during prior incarnations. When one or more family members allow God as the Christ Spirit to become a part of their lives and decide to adjust their ideals to incorporate spiritual principles, they are better able to weather crises and are more supportive of each other. A higher spiritual consciousness changes our outlook on life and our particular life situation. Families live in communities where their members go to school and church, attend after-school and weekend sports functions, are employed, shop for groceries, and go to the park for relaxation. These activities involve various levels of interaction with other individuals outside of the family unit, and many people approach them differently. We usually are superficially polite when interacting with the cashier in the checkout line at the neighborhood grocery store but are more focused and attentive when sitting in our boss's office, but both interactions can be used for spiritual growth or decline. More intense and stressful situations usually arise from being a business owner or manager, or an employee, where a typical day might mean many encounters with various people who are working on mental-spiritual problems requiring different approaches and solutions. These stressful family and community environments are the place where the sincere application of ideals can really bear fruit. This is where we can learn cooperation, sharing, and mutual respect or revel in our selfishness at the expense of our family and community relationships. This is where we can show God that we are serious about living up to the commandment to love our neighbor and truly deserve to be called one of his children.

Every life situation we face, every attempt to navigate a marital or business crisis, every serious illness that brings us to the breaking point offers multiple opportunities to make choices that affect the physical outcome of the situation and influence the direction of our future mental and spiritual development. The range of choices may be quite large and challenging for a life situation that plays out over many decades. Life choices made incorrectly will cloud the incarnated soul's spiritual understanding and impede its ability to hear the inner voice that calls every soul to its true destiny. Consistently poor choices will lead the soul down a twisted and tortuous path of ceaseless conflict with family and friends and toward spiritual degradation and alienation from its creator. Some of these paths can lead the soul so far from God consciousness that the soul can lose the ability to understand right from wrong and good from evil. A positive approach to an interpersonal problem that shows respect and concern for others is a step toward inner peace for the soul and greater harmony in the family and community as its effect ripples outward and begins to influence other incarnated souls. God-centered choices keep the soul on the path toward spiritual enlightenment, strengthen the lines of communication between soul and God, and ultimately lead the soul to a better relationship with God. Even imperfect choices made with good intentions can help the soul to grow spiritually. A single godly action based on one good choice can improve the current stressful or distasteful life situation and advance the process of spiritual transformation. A series of good choices may come with the recognition that there is more to life than the pursuit of happiness without concern for our fellow human beings. A consistent pattern of spiritually correct choices will eventually lead to peace within the soul and the inner conviction, mental comfort, and sure knowledge that the action taken is appropriate and arises from a higher source than the Self. A mind that has been reined in by a will intentionally habituated to making choices that honor the soul's purpose and the expectations of God will consistently manifest cooperation, harmony, and peace in the family, business, and community.

What are the implications of a higher state of spiritual consciousness, or Christ Consciousness, for society and nations? The mental and spiritual forces at work within and behind the society of humans, the society of incarnated souls, are extremely complex. The greater cause of human tragedy comes not from natural events but from man's inhumanity to man, mainly in wars that take the lives of humans by the thousands and millions. We might know the historical political reasons for the conflicts and wars that bring so much suffering to humanity, but we usually do not understand the deeper underlying spiritual reasons behind the many conflicts. We may be generally aware that self-serving economic greed, the coveting of others' territory, and the desire for power or ideological dominance are critical factors or the root causes of most wars, but it is impossible to identify and separate which atrocities, injuries, and deaths are influenced by the deeply buried soul memories of individuals and groups, and which are truly first-cause events. The truth may be found only in the soul minds of the affected individuals. Each individual's approach to societal opportunities alters the mental pattern from which the person is operating, and brings spiritual healing, stagnation, or degradation to the individual and nation. The way in which individuals collectively interact with respect to physical reality and spiritual law directly affects the quality and integrity of the government of a nation, the way that nation is seen by the rest of the world, and the future of that nation and its role in the world. Romans 13:1 is a controversial and often misused biblical verse that tells individuals to submit to governmental authority, and declares that there is no authority except that which God has established. The equivalent statement in the readings is that no man and no group is in authority save as allowed by God, even admitting that some governing agencies may appear to have achieved power in conjunction with the forces of evil (1933-1_31). The key word in the readings is *allowed*. God allows governments to be established. He doesn't manipulate citizens to elect his chosen candidate in a democracy, and he takes the same hands-off approach toward the rise of authoritarian and dictatorial governments. When brotherly love in the form of economic and political equality and inclusive policies are used to liberate the potential of all citizens, societies and nations thrive (877-9_22). When sectarian hate and exclusion are used to divide, control, and manipulate citizens, societies wither and break down. When souls that represent the forces of selfless service and good fail to intercept and nullify the activities of those who represent selfishness and evil, a peaceful, prosperous nation can transform into a dysfunctional or tyrannical nation. The destructive effect of selfishness and disrespect for opposing opinions can cause the collapse of democratic institutions by neutralizing the checks and balances that ensure respect for the opposition and prevent the rise of an authoritarian figure.

God allows citizens of democratic nations to elect politicians who will turn their selfishness, racism, and prejudice into civil law, but spiritual law will make the citizens of those nations pay dearly for their failure to love their neighbor and give all citizens a voice and fair representation in their government and equal opportunity in the economy (2509-2_5). Reading 3976-8_8 lays the blame for the terrible wars and conflicts of the twentieth century on the strained relationship between God and man and between man and neighbor as expressed and made visible in racial and social inequalities. The readings declare that societies must be purged as by fire until each incarnated soul learns to be his or her brother's keeper (3976-8_8; 254-55_5; 262-79_11). Reading 3976-15_14, given in 1934, specifically warns that if Americans do not learn to uphold and abide by the principles of brotherly love, then America will lose its status as a beacon of hope for the world, and that the center of Christian thought and practice will be allowed to move Westward (3976-15_14). Like every nation, America's economic greatness, military greatness, and leadership role among the nations of the world is derived from the collective spiritual maturity of its citizens, the extent to which its citizens allow the Christ Spirit into their lives. Reading 3976-29_17 builds on this theme, identifying China as the probable future cradle of Christianity, but also adding that that day is far off as man counts time. The thrust of these readings is that when the people of a nation become prideful in their perceived greatness or one segment of society uses its perceived superiority to oppress another, the nation will stagnate and possibly even disintegrate. America is great only to the extent that its citizens are willing to open their hearts in loving service toward their neighbors, accept and promote the equality of all men and women under God, and align the laws of the country with those beliefs. The barely submerged sense of white superiority and rise of Christian Nationalism in a large segment of American society, with the attendant demonization of immigrants and the inclination to look down upon "others" is the greatest threat to American society today.

Every nation has a spirit, a vibrational energy created by the combined spiritual attunement and personal desires of its inhabitants. The readings indicate that the occurrence and severity of economic and political crises, and even destructive natural events, are influenced by the existence, extent, and intensity of the collective depraved thoughts and misbehavior of its less spiritually oriented citizens. The economic well-being of a nation suffers when economic policy concentrates wealth in the hands of a few who ignore the suffering and hardship of the deprived masses. The readings state that the Great Depression in America that followed a period of extreme economic disparity was caused by too many people turning away from the spiritual principle of love thy neighbor (3976-8_13). Christians might be more inclined to think about the biblical stories of Noah and the Flood, Sodom and Gomorrah, or Jonah and Nineveh as examples of spiritual crises. The Old Testament is the story of God's covenant with the people of Israel and their repeated failure to live according to that covenant. The traditional interpretation is that when the Israelites honor and respect the covenant, they flourish as a people and as a nation; when they dishonor and disobey the covenant, they face judgment and an appropriate punishment. This imposition of spiritual justice may take the form of regional famine, invasion by a foreign power, or exile of the people to a foreign land, perhaps after a series of warnings by a renowned prophet. From the perspective of the readings, God is not monitoring the collective behavior of the citizens of Israel or any nation, reaching the limit of his patience when too many of its inhabitants turn away from him, and venting his wrath through punishment when he can no longer tolerate their immoral behavior. Instead, a nation begins to decline and diminish when a critical mass of its people turns inward and begins acting in ways that glorify self-centeredness, self-gratification, and self-indulgence. Disrespect of the principle of brotherly love and the innate moral and spiritual purpose of the soul, eventually leads to national collapse. It is not mass punishment; it is spiritual law on a national level (877-9_22). All nations go through purifying cycles of death and rebirth as their inhabitants respect or reject the spiritual law to which all souls, and therefore all humans, are subject. There are material consequences for individual sin, but there can also be collective repercussion for widespread sin, especially when the sins contravene the spiritual precepts of love, brotherhood, and service. Christianity denies that the cyclical process of spiritual accountability, suffering, and national rebirth experienced by Israel in the Old Testament also applies to individuals. In fact, members of every nation, soul citizens that animate and express themselves through human beings, also are subject to the cyclical process of spiritual regeneration through suffering, death, and rebirth.

A nation's political system and the quality of the leaders it produces reflect the spiritual maturity of its citizens. Democracy is the political system that, in theory, best honors the second commandment to love thy neighbor as thyself. It is a form of government in which the poor and downtrodden can, at least in principle, share political power with the powerful and the wealthy. The readings specifically state that the concept of being our brother's keeper does not mean we have a right to force ourselves upon others or control others. It means freedom before the law and before God (3976-19_32). Free speech is the political equivalent of free will. It can be abused through the spreading of hate and lies and is a particularly insidious form of abuse when magnified through social media. When citizens of a democracy respect the brotherhood of men and use their freedom of speech to express an opinion without descending into hate, lies, and fear mongering, democratic institutions remain strong and prevail in the face of outside forces. When the force of love from the indwelling Christ Spirit becomes stronger than the divisive dogma of religion and politics, nations thrive. A country whose people collectively try to serve God by adhering to the commandments to love God and neighbor in their personal and social activity will elect caring politicians who serve the people and enact legislation that generally reflects the concepts of love and service. The electorate will be considerate of other people in its society who live different lifestyles, who have different religious beliefs, or who simply have a different skin color or speak with a different accent. They will be willing to share their wealth to see that the marginalized and poor have access to decent nutrition, healthcare, and education so that these segments of society, especially their children, have the opportunity to lift themselves out of generational poverty. A country whose people collectively are selfish, inconsiderate, and intolerant of the beliefs of their neighbors will vote into power politicians with similar selfish traits and the nation will reap the results in the form of internal division, discontent, and chaos. They will elect politicians who will force aspects of their particular religious or moral beliefs upon others. They will stereotype other segments of society, point out their perceived racial inferiority or moral deficiencies, and use them as scapegoats to whip the base into a frenzy of self-righteous indignation. They will blame them for the economic ills of society and disenfranchise and attack them in the name of preventing imagined physical or economic harm. Once a minority inner enemy has been identified or manufactured, the self-styled saviors of the nation can strengthen and consolidate their political position and enact laws that discriminate against the minority, even when those laws are contrary to the previously accepted norms and rule of law. The collective moral consciousness of the people of a nation, their attunement to the indwelling Christ Spirit, determines the quality of their government and how easy or difficult it is for evil leaders to manipulate their minds to gain power.

An enthusiastic or idealistic young person with concern for the plight of others will often get into politics to correct perceived inequalities, to remove or reduce governmental corruption, or simply to serve their fellow man as, for example, a congressional representative in a democracy. Far too often, as those young idealists grow older, their minds become more jaded from the effort required to push against the inertial mass of governmental bureaucracy. Their increasing cynicism and fatigue can make them more susceptible to the temptations that are present in the backrooms of political power, more prone to falter and fail in their original altruistic purpose, and more likely to succumb to the impulse to serve themselves at the expense of their constituents. This is the fatal flaw of politicians all over the world. When they fail to integrate their higher moral and spiritual qualities in a nondogmatic way into their political duties and become corrupted by the system they wished to change, their soul suffers greatly. When leaders abandon the commandment to love their neighbors as themselves, and fail to use position and power to serve others instead of themselves, they severely degrade their ability to access or express the inherent godly traits held within their soul (262-65_4-5; Matthew 18:7). It is an established fact that constitutional democracies can and do die when citizens stop respecting the rights of others and elect officials who manipulate the system to gain undue influence for themselves and the group that elected them (Levitsky and Ziblatt, 2019; Levitsky and Ziblatt, 2023). A major factor that enhances the potential for a democratic nation to slide into political anocracy (a weakened democracy with strong elements of autocracy or dictatorship), and even possibly to descend into civil war, is the existence of a disillusioned and dissatisfied majority that is fearful of losing its long-held political power as population dynamics create change in the country (Walter, 2023). In this case, a segment of the population that cannot let the concepts of equality and brotherly love stand between them and their inflated perception of self-worth and perceived need to retain control corrupts the system. If the self-created barrier that separates a soul from its source of spiritual guidance is strong, it may take many cycles of incarnation and mental-spiritual training to remove the barrier, give the soul a glimpse of the glory of God, and teach the soul to strive for more than a comfortable existence at the expense of other incarnated souls. Self-centeredness, moral corruption, and other human flaws have their roots in spiritual weakness. It presents a problem in government, but certainly is not limited to politicians. Any person who has attained a position of power or leadership over the lives of other people, whether they control a small business or major corporation, whether they are a pastor or priest of a church, are susceptible to corruption when their moral compass gets broken.

History repeats itself because many of the players have not made substantial improvements to their mental-spiritual mindset from one incarnation to another. They harbor the same old selfish attitudes and are prone to make the same mistakes. The sick demagogues and dictators of the past who stoked social discord that descended into civil war or embarked on regional wars of conquest periodically bring their penchant for chaos and division into the world for a repeat performance. The fallout from their intense quest for power is magnified by the sycophants who are willing to blindly follow them without assessing the immorality in which they are called to participate or the spiritual consequences to their soul. The acquiescence of followers and the inaction of those who disagree give free reign to power hungry politicians and allow the destructive power of evil wielded by a few dedicated individuals to blossom and spread across the nation. It is imperative that humans learn to break the cycles of mayhem and violence that ripple through history by refusing to condone or participate in such activities. Real change in the world will only come when enough individuals make a substantial improvement in their mental-spiritual mindset from one incarnation to the next and use their sense of goodness to counter the spread of evil. The magnitude of the task at hand is difficult to fathom. Every day souls create mayhem, division, destruction, and other trademarks of a self-centered mindset severed from God consciousness. It is almost overwhelming to turn on the news on any given day and listen to the many examples of disrespect, racism, hatred, anger, brutality, and other unloving traits that incarnated souls express in the society of mankind. The devastation and damage that unenlightened conscious minds can and do inflict on society is enormous and is symptomatic of the failure of souls to recognize their spiritual origins and live up to the purpose of their creation. Until these modern-day sons and daughters of Belial are brought to the knowledge of the Christ Spirit and allow the fruits of the spirit to manifest through them, humanity will be doomed to repeat the cycles of economic turmoil, conflict, and war.

How are we to cope with this barrage of negative information? We first need to realize that there is much good done in the communities of the world every day; it just doesn't make national headline news. Scripture and the readings tell us to fear not and to hold firm in the sure knowledge that God will walk with us, and will save our body and soul if we will seek his counsel and advice (Matthew 10:28; 3976-26_17). We are to keep faith in the certainty of God's promises, know that there is hope for the future of mankind, and do our share within our sphere of activity to make the influence of the Christ Spirit alive and active in the world. As we seek to attune our will with God's purposes and open our minds in Christ Consciousness, it will become easier for us to understand why we as individuals and members of human society face certain life situations and recognize the best way to approach them for the maximum personal and societal spiritual benefit. We may have to suffer, even unto illness, injury, or death in some situations, but our souls will greatly benefit if we patiently face our circumstances while in communion with the Christ Spirit. We are not required to show the passive patience of submission and acquiescence, but the active patience that speaks the truth of righteousness and brings cooperation that uplifts humanity. To be agents of positive change in the world, we must learn to be a channel of blessings to others even under the most trying conditions. The more attuned to God we become through the application of ideals and the mental pattern of Christ Consciousness, the closer we walk with him, and the easier it becomes to keep strong in faith in the face of unsettling events. We can alter the future for the better instead of repeating the mistakes of the past. We cannot single out any individual or group as being inferior or less worthy than us, for the members of our family, community, and nation are also fellow souls trying to fulfill their destiny to be companions of God. We can help ease our fears and mitigate the plight of mankind by praying daily that God's Will be done in the affairs of man and by doing our part in making that come true by being the hands and feet of God. He never intended that we should wait around for him to solve the world's problems for us through some grand event at some distant point in time, but wants all who know him to do their small share to change the world for the better by being Christ-like in our family and community affairs, and demanding that our local and national politicians be of the same mind.

The False Consciousness of Inherited Sin and Demonic Beings

The concepts of inherited sin and nonmaterial evil forces can too readily be used by the faithful as convenient reasons to abrogate their moral responsibility, excuse their immoral behavior, or explain away their own latest sin. Christians generally believe that Adam's sinful action of eating the fruit of a tree that opened his eyes to the knowledge of good and evil (Genesis 3:5) brought death to Adam and his descendants and caused a genetic cascade of sin that is still sweeping through humanity and causing irreparable harm to individuals and societies. This genetic force of sin supposedly acts on and overwhelms many humans despite their best efforts at being good, but with concerted effort, many good people are able to counter this inherited propensity to sin. The Christian concepts of Adam as the original sinner and the source of sin in humanity come from writings of the apostle Paul that were incorporated into the New Testament. Paul didn't have any special or superior insight into the nature and character of the man called Adam in the creation story of Judaic scriptures. Like many before and after him, he tried to understand and explain the reason that man seems to so easily succumb to the temptation to sin. The concept of original sin that he proposed in his writings and that was incorporated into the New Testament was not a new idea. It reflected ideas already developed and presented in contemporary Jewish texts written over several centuries from about 300 BC. These writers were trying to understand the current circumstances of the Jewish nation in light of Jewish history and were elaborating on the Jewish traditions presented in the Old Testament. Like Paul, they struggled to understand the biblical story of Adam. One category of these written texts is called Pseudepigrapha because they were falsely attributed to a historical figure (a literary technique of the day). These writings are not accepted as canonical Christian Scripture. Another category of written texts is called Apocrypha. These writings were not included in the original Hebrew scriptures, but were included in the Greek translation of the Old Testament. The Roman Catholic Church considered some Apocryphal books to be worthy of study, and they are included in the Roman Catholic Bible, but none of them are included in the Protestant Bible. As a highly educated Jewish scholar, Paul was almost certainly familiar with these texts.

In his writings, Paul portrays Adam as the corrupted progenitor of humanity who brought physical death upon himself and all of his descendants by committing the sin of disobedience and breaking the rules of the game established by God. According to the narrow biblical viewpoint, all humans are biological descendants of Adam. Paul uses this idea to conclude that all human descendants must therefore be tainted with the propensity to sin. Paul desperately wanted to use the sinfulness of Adam and his perceived role as the first human to justify his understanding that Jesus was born on the Earth to be the savior of both Jews and Gentiles. In Paul's view, Adam is not only kicked out of the garden of Eden, but the stain of his disobedience and selfishness is transmitted to generation after generation of his many descendants. Nothing in the Old Testament supports this radical idea of genetic transmission of sin, but, because of Paul's influence, the idea of sin as a genetic disease was advanced by St. Augustine and some other prominent early church figures.

In Paul's theology, the perfect life of Jesus makes restitution for the imperfect life of Adam and all of his tainted descendants. The disobedience of Adam brought death to mankind, and the obedience of Jesus brought life to mankind. Therefore, Jesus became the Messiah for all of humankind, not just the Messiah for the Jews. This perception of Adam as the original sinner and source of death and sin in all humanity is flawed and, as we have seen, is not supported in the readings. Why did the disobedience of Adam bring him physical death and the obedience of Jesus bring him physical death? Why did sinful Adam die peacefully (presumably) at the ripe old age of 930 years, and sinless Jesus die an agonizing and brutal death (certainly) at the young age of thirty-three years? The physical consequences of virtue and sin and the reality of life and death are far more complex than envisioned by Paul and traditional Christian theology. In 2 Corinthians 5:21 (NIV), Paul writes that "God made him who had no sin to be sin for us, so that in him we might become the righteousness of God." Christian theologians generally interpret this verse to mean that Jesus was made to be a sin-offering, a sacrifice for our sins, and not to mean that Jesus was sinful. This thinking fits well with the Jewish idea of blood sacrifice for sin. The readings interpret this scriptural verse somewhat differently, strongly implying that Amilius, the soul of Jesus, came into a state of sin as Adam so "that through Him [Jesus] the Earth, or the spirit of man [souls], might have the advocate with the Father and through Him [Jesus] once for all be made free from sin through that activity of the Christ-Spirit in the Earth" (262-59_10). Jesus didn't just figuratively take on our sins; his soul literally experienced sin and the temptation to sin, and showed that it is possible for a sinful soul to become disentangled from the grip of self-centeredness and materiality. Amilius, as Adam, took on sin to show us it is possible to be restored to God consciousness while immersed in materiality. As Jesus, he demonstrated that we too can restore the conscious awareness of God within our soul minds if we are willing to follow in his footsteps and live our lives according to the Way he lived his life (262-19_5; 262-36_4; 307-3_10).

Several apocryphal books written after the destruction of Jerusalem in 70 AD (after Paul wrote Romans and Corinthians) agree with Paul that Adam is the source of human death but do not name Adam as the source of human sin. The nature of Adam as described in Second Esdras is more closely aligned with Genesis 2:16–17 than Paul's understanding of Adam in Romans 5:12. It blames the transgression of Adam as the cause of his death and the reason why all humans now suffer death. But unlike Paul, Second Esdras only states that Adam brought death upon mankind, not that Adam's sinful nature was transmitted to his descendants. Many of Adam's descendants will repeat his pattern of conduct, but that pattern is not biologically inherited. The book *Second Baruch* blames Adam as the cause of every person's corruption, but not every person's sin. Corruption in this context means an inner weakness in humans that makes them inclined to sin as opposed to the actual sinful act that occurs when we choose to disobey, or rebel against, God. Humans have personal moral responsibility for their actions and can decide whether or not to follow the example of Adam. Adam's disobedience led to universal death, but we are responsible for our own sin (Enns, 2012).

Other much earlier writings, some of which are part of the Dead Sea scrolls, give different perspectives on the nature of Adam. In *Ecclesiasticus* (Apocrypha second century BC), Adam is formed from dust, but there is no mention of a fall or a sinful nature being inherited by his offspring. Adam is portrayed as the most exalted figure in all creation, but one who lacks wisdom. It blames Eve for the introduction of death into the human world, which is a theme taken up later in 1 Timothy 2:14. *Ecclesiasticus* assigns the responsibility for choosing good or evil and life or death to each individual without the complication of an inherited propensity to sin because of Adam. *The book of Jubilees* (Pseudepigrapha second century BC) characterizes Adam as a priestly figure who leaves the garden at some point to fulfill the mandate to be fruitful and multiply without reference to original sin. *The Wisdom of Solomon* (Apocrypha late first century BC to early first century AD) states that Adam was created to be the master over all things but that he fell to the temptation to sin. However, he was delivered from his transgressions. The book equates the serpent in the garden of Eden with the devil, and states that death entered the world through the devil, not through Adam's disobedience. This happens because the devil is incensed because God has ordered the angels to worship Adam, causing the enraged devil and like-minded angels to rebel against God. The rebellion is put down and the devil and his angel followers are cast down to Earth. The famous and well-respected Jewish philosopher Philo of Alexandria (ca 20 BC to ca 50 AD) understood Adam to have been made perfect and immortal, a true image of God. Instead of a fall, there was a gradual weakening of his spiritual connection with God that was instigated by Eve. The true image was gradually and increasingly lost from each generation to the next generation of descendants. This decline derived from the desire of Adam for pleasure with Eve, which precipitated an exchange of immortality for mortality. Philo believed that an individual is responsible for his own sin, and that no sin was transmitted from Adam to descendant generations.

All of these writers were trying to present their best, but always somewhat biased, understanding of Adam based on little information. All of these people, including Paul, were relying on older texts, oral traditions, and outright suppositions that were affected by the quality of their personal spiritual attunement or lack of attunement. There is no reason to believe that any one of these ancient writers really understood or correctly described the nature of Adam. All of these portrayals of Adam are incompatible to some degree with the history of the origin of man and the Adamic race as presented in the readings and explored herein. The idea presented by Philo of a gradual loss of spiritual connection with God is compatible with the concept presented in the readings of a gradual loss of God consciousness by souls that repeatedly indulge in self-glorification and the pursuit of material gratification. These indulgences can become idols that replace God. The traditional Jewish and Christian interpretations of the Genesis story of Adam are based on scant scriptural information, are a misunderstanding or misrepresentation of the voluntary mission of Amilius to bring spiritual relief to souls immersed in materiality, and give a wrong impression of the state of consciousness held by Amilius and the group of altruistic souls that accompanied him onto the Earth to restore God consciousness to spiritually lost souls.

The scriptural idea that physical death is a punishment inflicted on Adam and his descendants doesn't square with the readings, the concept of reincarnation as an opportunity for soul restoration, or common sense. God told Adam that he would surely die if he disobeyed a directive to refrain from acquiring knowledge, meaning violating spiritual law by immersing himself in materiality. God did not tell Adam that he would be condemned to death as a punishment if he violated the directive to, basically, remain ignorant. The distinction may seem subtle, but it is an important one. On one hand, we can imagine a loving, caring God who provides opportunities in a causal world for souls to learn to respect spiritual principles and live within the rules defined by spiritual law. On the other hand, we can imagine a brutal, vindictive God who exacts maximum suffering, pain, and grief for what seems to have been a minimal crime, exercising the human desire for education. Adam's natural curiosity and desire for learning earns him the loss of eternal physical life, banishment from a well-stocked garden of plenty, and hundreds of years of hard labor trying to make a subsistence living before his physical death. When his son Cain commits murder, God just banishes him from the family. Where is the justice in that punishment as compared to the punishment of Adam? We have learned from the readings that the sin of Adam was a result of his intentional descent into materiality and a conscious state of sinfulness so that he could subdue the Earth and then teach humanity how to extricate itself from materialism and restore God consciousness. Physical illness and death are natural causal aspects of sin committed by an incarnated soul in the physical realm because sin prevents the Christ Spirit from being fully active in the soul and throughout the body. The sin of Adam was his own personal sin, and the death of Adam was a natural consequence of his immersion in materiality. He overcame both through incarnation and loving service. As Jesus, he showed us how we can overcome our personal sins, and through his apostles left a book of basic instructions for us to follow. The readings see spiritual and physical death as a natural and straightforward consequence faced by every soul that has turned away from God and ignored spiritual law. Spiritual error committed in the physical must be corrected in the physical. God extends grace and mercy to errant souls by giving then repeated opportunities through successive incarnations to recognize the source of their error, repent, and repair their relationship with him through unselfish loving thoughts and actions. These repeated physical life experiences take the form of various situational interactions in the society of incarnated souls and present multiple opportunities to correct selfish attitudes that lead toward self-righteousness, self-indulgence, and immoral behavior.

Satan

Christians generally believe that one or more powerful sinister evil beings stalk the Earth and prey on the unwary. The perceived underlying purpose of these demonic forces that work against the Christ Spirit is to constantly assail the conscious minds of humans to pull them away from God. This activity is a source of great satisfaction and glee to the other worldly perpetrators of evil as they display their ability to outwit God and deceive mankind. One of the favorite beings we can blame for our failure to act responsibly in spiritual or moral matters is Satan, aka the Devil or the Evil One. He is considered by many Christians to be an otherworldly demonic being that gleefully works to thwart the purposes of God and wreak havoc in the lives of good people. Satan tirelessly trolls human society to find weak people who can be manipulated into turning against God, terrorizing fellow humans, or pitting one group of individuals against another group. Christians believe it is imperative to be vigilant so as to prevent Satan from getting a foothold in our life and leading us astray or delivering us to hell, and are quick to blame personal tragedy and misfortune on his latest schemes and intrigues. Like the concept of inherited sin, these traditional Christian ideas and theologies shift the blame for sin that should fall on individual members of society to powerful external factors.

The meaning of the Hebrew word that is translated in English Scripture as Satan is *adversary*, a force that works in competition with, or in opposition to, any desire of the soul to reestablish a state of communion and oneness with God. The word does not mean *The Adversary*. It is not a proper noun used to identify a cosmic being, but a common noun used to describe people, places, or things. New Testament Interpreters generally have shifted the meaning of Satan from the impersonal to the personal. The new Satan became a real spiritual being with a personality, intelligence, and the will to do harm to humans, the prince of this world that leads the forces of evil into battle against the angels of God. Other interpretations retain the true Hebrew meaning of the word, seeing these verses as symbolic and taking Satan to be a personification of the mental state of man intent on pursuing his willful rebellion against God. The power of Satan, as understood by many Christians today, can be seen in the unexplained personal and collective misfortunes and suffering of mankind, which actually have their true origin in material causal experiences that are designed to lead the soul toward Christ Consciousness. The readings define Satan, the devil, evil, and the serpent as references to the spirit of rebellion that arises in souls that have the capacity to exercise their free will in defiance of the Will of God (262-52_25; 5755-2_9). This rebellion began in the cosmic realm long before souls entered the Earth to fulfill selfish desires and before they learned to indulge in self-gratifying sensory pleasures through the medium of a human body. The solution to immoral, unethical, and irrational human behavior and the cure for mentally deranged individuals is not the exorcism of an imagined devil, but the loving healing power of God and a cleansing of the soul mind that has embraced evil thoughts. The evil that we see manifested in this world, and that is associated in Scripture with the prince of this world, has its origin in the realm of the soul and has made it necessary for soul incarnation in materiality (262-89_6). Rebellion works in opposition to the mental attitude of godliness and goodness embraced by Jesus, the Son of God, the revealer of the Way and source of spiritual light that leads to eternal life and the truth of our existence as souls. When the soul realigns itself to the Will and Mind of God and is mentally at peace with and in communion with God, the decisions and activities of the soul will harmonize with the purposes of God for the soul. The spirit of rebellion keeps the subconscious mind partially isolated from the super conscious mind, which chokes off the closer communion with God that is available through Christ Consciousness. When the conscious mind directs the human body to engage in sinful behavior, it keeps the conscious mind in a state of tension with respect to the spiritual aspirations of the sub-conscious and super conscious minds (262-89_7). It is essential for the inner peace of the soul that all three aspects of the soul mind are kept in a state of balance and harmony through cooperation with the Christ Spirit.

The word "Satan" occurs in eleven verses in the book of Job (KJV) in the course of two conversations between God and Satan (and only in three verses in the remainder of the Old Testament). God is praising and boasting about Job to Satan, and Satan responds that Job would not be so faithful if he lost all of his worldly goods and his health. The idea that God would conspire with an evil being of great power to bring mis-fortune, disaster, and death upon men, women, and children merely to prove a point is the antithesis of a loving God. The idea that God would allow affliction, calamity, and destruction into the lives we have built on Earth—including the death of our loved ones—simply to test our con-viction and resolve to remain faithful to Him runs counter to any sense of fairness or love we believe to be part of God's nature. The readings make it clear that the book of Job doesn't describe an actual person or a true life event. It doesn't document a tragedy fomented by an evil being that gleefully goes about the world doing mischief to deceive and seduce mankind into turning away from God. The allegorical story presents an archetypal answer to the question why bad things happen to [apparently] good people. It explores the notion that it is dangerous for the incarnated soul to assume that material comfort and accumulated wealth are signs of great spiritual worth or spiritual superiority. Satan in the allegory does not refer to an evil spiritual being who cons God into giving him the authority to test a good man by destroying his family and stripping him of all his worldly possessions. The Spirit of God is the essential essence of all that exits, and God is the creator of everything in the material and nonmaterial realms not created by souls. He does not create evil beings, but the souls he created can use their free will to create evil. He does not make us face trials and temptations on a whim or a wager to test our resolve to hold true to him. The common superficial interpretation of the book of Job as the story of an impulsive God giving in to the persuasions of a devious Satan to destroy a good man's life to prove a point is false. The description of God's collusion with Satan is the author's way of introducing calamities into the life of the fictional character Job rather than an actual conspiracy between God and Satan. The soul of Job is in a spiritual state of rebellion against God even though that rebellion is not readily apparent in the material life of Job. The story underscores the idea that man tends to forget his relationship with God and his dependency on God when man is blessed with material goods. Satan, as the adversary or opponent of God, is a personification of the soul's rebellion against God—a rebellion not only on the physical plane but also in the spiritual realm of which the physical is but a reflection.

The interplay between Job and his friends allows the author to present Job's reaction to his material and personal disasters and to explore Job's attempt to understand the meaning of the disasters with respect to his perceived relationship with God. Job uses much of his speech to his compatriots to profess that he is innocent before God, that he has never sinned, and that he doesn't deserve the disasters that God has visited upon him. His three friends, Eliphaz, Bildad, and Zophar were unable to support Job's belief in his innocence and often suggest that he is guilty of sin, otherwise he would not be in this situation, and they tell him that God has a right to do what he wants with man. Elihu is a young man filled with the Spirit of God. He holds his tongue while Job's friends expound at length but finally can hold back no more. He starts by telling the three friends that they have not proved Job wrong, but also have not answered his questions (Job 32:12). He restates Job's claim to be without sin (Job 33:8–9), then tells Job that this is not right thinking (Job 33:12). He states that God speaks to man in various ways to preserve his soul, but does not mention anything about preserving his family or wealth (Job 33:14–18). The apostle John agrees with the conclusion of Elihu by declaring that if we claim to be without sin, we deceive ourselves, and the truth is not in us (1 John 1:8). God does not do evil or wrong to man simply because he has the power to do so, which his friends insinuate, but allows spiritual law to deliver to man those things that his conduct has earned him (Job 34:10–11). To do otherwise would be a perversion of justice. God does not pervert justice (Job 34:12), and to think that he would do so is to condemn God of injustice (Job 34:17). God does not punish the wicked (NIV) but does openly chastise (KJV) the wicked through the impersonal action of spiritual law when they turn from him (Job 34:26).

The readings make it clear that what man may perceive as punishment from God or the nefarious activity of a satanic being is actually spiritual law in action. God does not consciously monitor our every thought, observe our every action, and decide on a future punishment for each error we make. Each spiritual error has a consequence under the law that he established to govern the spiritual framework within which souls live and have their being. Spiritual law serves the purpose of soul restoration because souls earn what they mete out to others; they reap that which they sow and are thereby purified until they sow only goodness and godliness (262-51_14). Justice is not arbitrary, but is governed by an established law that leads souls back to their Creator. The story of Job alludes to these ideas. When Job again declares himself free of sin in response to the words of Elihu, he adds the sin of rebellion against the truth of God to his previous offenses (Job 34:35–37). God makes sinners recognize their sin as part of the process of mental correction that will lead them to repentance and reconciliation with him (Job 36:8–10). Elihu continues by extolling the majesty and power of God (Job 35–37) as a prelude to God's own exposition of his might and the smallness of Job in the greater scheme of creation (Job 38–41). Job finally admits the error of his ways and repents that he thought God's actions were unjust and that he dared to claim before God that he was sinless (Job 42:5–6). God chastises Eliphaz, Bildad, and Zophar for giving bad advice to Job and misleading him even though they disagreed with Job's claim of innocence before God, probably because their explanation included the possibility of injustice, the arbitrary abuse of man by God. Elihu is not criticized by God (Job 42:7–9) which supports his analysis of the cause of Job's misfortunes. Job's problems are a result of his soul's failure to remain faithful to God despite the fact that within the context of his current life and limited conscious memories, he considers himself righteous, ethical, and worthy of the abundance of material goods he has accumulated. None of his friends blame his misfortune on the actions of Satan. All of the conversation is about God, his ability to cleanse a sinful soul, and the inability of souls to perceive their sinful state in the midst of plenty.

The interpretation of the allegory is that good people, and by extension, the souls that animate them, undergo tribulations and hardships because they have sinned against God, even though these sins may not be readily apparent in their present life or remembered in their conscious minds. It expresses the truth that human nature and activity has a visible material component and a submerged spiritual component. The broad range of human activity in which the soul partakes during life is mostly activated by past memories that reside within the soul's subconscious mind. Job was unable to access those memories in his conscious mind because his material awareness, desire to acquire material wealth, and/or his absorption in daily human activity was not balanced by a persistent spiritual awareness of the Christ Spirit. He was a good and respected person in the eyes of those who knew him and in his own mind, but he lacked the strong reliable mental attunement of Christ Consciousness. The current material reality of an incarnated soul does not necessarily reflect the overall spiritual condition of the soul, and an obsession with material comforts and wealth may blind the individual to underlying spiritual defects within their soul. Many men are accepted as good when viewed from the perspective of limited and shallow conscious minds immersed in human activity, but God knows the full depth of the soul (Matthew 7:21–23). The book of Job doesn't say there is no cause for the sometimes intense suffering we may endure during our lifetime, only that we may not be consciously aware of the true cause of our suffering. Not being consciously aware does not mean that there is no specific reason for the suffering or that the suffering is purposeless or of no value. The sub-conscious mind of the soul remembers the choices we made in response to the opportunities that previously came before us to demonstrate our current understanding of God. We continually face material situations that reflect our previous actions and thoughts that expressed selfishness, greed, self-gratification, or actions that harmed others, but not every life will bring forth all or even most of those situations.

The readings ascribe the authorship of the book of Job to Melchizedek, who Abraham identified as the High Priest of Salem with the authority to speak for God (262-55_14). Melchizedek instituted the symbolic use of bread and wine centuries before Jesus used the same objects to impress upon the minds of his followers the significance of his looming death on the cross and the blood he would spill for all who would renounce evil and follow him (Genesis 14:17–18; Luke 22:14–20). Commentary notes in the scholarly Jerusalem Bible describe him as a Christ-like figure (Hebrews 7:1–3). Some early church Fathers (for example, St. Augustine and St. Jerome) believed that Melchizedek was a manifestation of the Son of God. Melchizedek is said to have appeared on the Earth without the benefit of a father or mother and to have left the Earth without experiencing biological death. This description of Melchizedek is supported by the readings, which state that he came as a thought form, the same method used by Amilius to create the body of Adam and the resurrected body of Jesus (2072-4_55). But the readings describe an even more important facet of Melchizedek. He is mentioned as one of the incarnations of Amilius into the world as part of his training to realign his soul consciousness with God while in the material world and to revitalize his mission to bring spiritual awareness to mankind (364-7_8; 3054-4_28; 5749-14_21; 5023-2_5; Sanderfur, 1988). Melchizedek is part of the personal path to perfection in the physical world that Amilius was destined to follow after his fall in the garden as Adam. According to the readings, Amilius accomplished his soul realignment much quicker than any other soul has been able to do, and as Jesus, he completed his mission to bring knowledge of the way to spiritual enlightenment to souls incarnated in physical form.

The Antichrist

The Antichrist is often perceived as a demon-inspired force that reveals itself through a powerful leader who will use his commanding presence, strong anti-Christian bias, and ability to influence and control the minds of his many followers to weaken the influence of Jesus the Christ. He will beguile, urge, and intimidate the people he rules and reject the qualities of righteousness and goodness that are patterns of behavior adopted by followers of the Christ. He will make these godly traits to appear as signs of weakness and will mark those individuals as targets and scapegoats for the excesses and purposes of the regime. Some see the Antichrist as a political figure that will rise to dominate national and international politics in some future end time. Some think this time will be associated with and immediately precede the second coming of Jesus the Christ. Others understand the Antichrist as a series of particularly evil political or religious figures that periodically bring about repressive regimes that oppose Christianity or Christian principles that are an impediment to their consolidation of power or desire for empire and glory. Reading 281-16_24 equates the spirit of antichrist with the spirit of any activity that is opposed to the spirit of truth, spirit being the motivating force or animating principle of that activity. The spirit of antichrist is the adversary of the Christ Spirit, the force of God that revealed itself through the life of

Jesus. The spirit of truth is manifested in human society through actions that project love, joy, peace, patience, kindness, goodness, faithfulness, gentleness, and other forms of human interaction that arise out of brotherly love and obedience to God. The spirit of antichrist is manifested in anger, hate, contention, strife, gossiping, division, egotism, narcissism, and conceit, and other forms of human interaction that disrespect God and other souls (281-16_24). Righteous anger in defense of a moral principle or injustice is a positive trait as long as it is controlled, is not destructive, and is not self-serving or ego driven. The readings categorize righteous anger as a virtue (3416-1_9).

The word "antichrist" as used in Scripture has a much broader meaning than the common concept of the Antichrist as an evil human who works against the Christ. The antichrist mentioned by the apostle John (1 John 2:18; 1 John 2:22-23; 1 John 4:3; 2 John 1:7) is not a powerful demon who roams the world seeking to weaken the influence of Jesus the Christ, or a strong-willed political leader who controls a vast army of supporters who have no regard for Christian principles. John assigned the appellation "antichrist" to anyone who refused to believe that Jesus was the Christ, that Jesus was the Son of God, or who denied that Jesus was sent by God. He concluded that those who disbelieve in the spiritual authority of Jesus and his special kinship with God have no personal relationship with God as Father and cannot know God. John believed that the presence of so many antichrists in his day was evidence that the world was in its last days and coming to an end. This belief is echoed in 1 Peter 1:20 and Jude 1:18. This is a harsh condemnation of the Jewish populace to whom Jesus taught his message of love and hope. Religious Jews were waiting for a Messiah, and John was at a loss to understand why they didn't rush to embrace Jesus as the Messiah who was to come. John had thoroughly tied his belief system to the idea that Jesus was the Son of God, and he could not comprehend how anyone could fail to come to the same conclusion. He may have been especially frustrated to see many of the people who heard Jesus speak as he traveled and taught throughout Judea, or who heard about him from those that had heard him speak, still reject Jesus. Perhaps Jesus did not measure up to their perceived qualifications for and expectations of a Messiah. Perhaps their minds were so imbedded in the material world that they couldn't perceive the spirit.

The vast majority of humanity in the Near East at the time of Jesus adhered to pagan traditions. Other peoples of the Far East held to Hinduism and Buddhism. These people had no tradition of a coming Messiah and no insight as to the spiritual meaning of his life and death. Their religious upbringing may have hindered them from accepting Jesus as a Messiah. Most of them would never hear about Jesus or would only hear about him by word of mouth years after his death. Whether John also labeled these foreign Gentiles as "antichrist" is not clear. John's words do not allow for the longer-term view that must be taken when reincarnation is part of the salvation equation. Jesus understood this broader view, even saying that disbelief in him was a forgivable sin (Matthew 12:32). Jesus would have recognized that the ideals, moral principles, and spiritual yearning of his fellow Jews and the Gentiles were more far important to their spiritual development at that moment than any stated belief in him as the Messiah. There were surely many people throughout the world who tried to follow moral teachings and a lifestyle similar to that taught by Jesus without knowledge of his specific teachings and role in soul salvation. The readings state that the desire to emulate the life of Jesus is the highest ideal to which an individual can aspire (2533-7_7). He would have realized that all souls would eventually have opportunities to learn more about his life and teachings and would be able to make a considered decision to accept his claim to be the Son of God during future life situations.

Too often in human history, the force of evil in one charismatic leader metastasizes, and then spreads like cancer throughout the entire society. The term "antichrist" is often associated with powerful national leaders because of the attention they get and the damage that they can do with their power. The almost unimaginable capacity for destruction wielded by an authoritarian figure who has gained control over a nation with a large and powerful military may lead people to the concept of the Antichrist. In the twentieth century, men such as Adolf Hitler, Mao Zedong, Pol Pot, Kim Il-Sung, and Joseph Stalin, to name a few, stand out as examples of especially powerful and evil men who committed unspeakable atrocities upon humanity. Adolf Hitler is probably the poster boy for the Antichrist or the activities of an antichrist to people of the Western hemisphere. He unleashed the Nazi Party and the power of hate and intimidation on the Jewish minority. He divided the German nation and gained control over those who stood by and let his power of evil magnify and spread though society. He used divisive language, suspicion, and terror tactics to scare and intimidate the German people into bowing to his ever more strident political demands and militarism, even despite the mounting evidence of his growing insanity. He didn't single out Christians unless they spoke out against him, but whipped up hatred of the Jews to unify and energize a nation to commit to his evil schemes. The leaders and members of the German Christian Church were strongly complicit in giving support to Adolf Hitler to the point of repeatedly praising him as a man sent by God to lead the German people (Solberg, 2015). The souls of German Jews are still suffering from the terrifying mass murder instigated by or condoned by the Christian majority population (Gershom, 1992).

Every brutal regime throughout history has left a similar trail of broken bodies and scarred soul minds. It is easy to believe that the influential and powerful historical figures behind these regimes were the main cause of suffering in the world because they were an antichrist or were controlled by the Antichrist. The most atrocious evil deeds committed in the world may originate from charismatic but spiritually dead authoritarian leaders, but their evil intentions are perpetrated by their spiritually weak followers. The real culprits in the historical crimes against humanity are the masses of people who always seem so eager and willing to blindly follow leaders who spread lies and social division to further their selfish dreams of power. Evil leaders who think of nothing but self-glorification and self-enrichment have no power except that given to them intentionally by other evil men and unintentionally by too many good men. For the most part, evil leaders simply give orders, and their many willing sycophants do the actual dirty work (Steenkamp, 2023).

Many Christians still await the coming of the Antichrist with dread, believing that the evil leaders of the twentieth century were only a precursor to the real Antichrist, a human incarnation of evil that will bring unbelievable terror and destruction upon mankind on a scale not yet experienced. But the truth is that the spirit of antichrist was in the world long before the time of Jesus, is alive and well in the world today, and will be an active force in the future. The spirit of antichrist, the spirit of rebellion against higher moral and spiritual principles, was in the world even before Amilius first entered the Earth in the form of Adam and was expressed during the time of Adam through the mental attitude and activity of the sons and daughters of Belial. It is the attitude of self-centeredness, self-gratification, self-indulgence, and glorification of the ego that leaves no room for thoughts of spiritual matters or the welfare of other human beings. It lured the descendants of the Adamic group into relationships that weakened their resolve to remain true to their spiritual mission. It prevents the incarnated soul from recognizing that a life devoted to the acquisition of material goods and the satisfaction that comes from power and control over others leads to ruin and suffering in the long run. The spirit of antichrist engulfs every soul that ever held the thought that it could go it alone without God and has lost the sense of the joyful friendship with God that comes from spiritual enlightenment on the path to Christ Consciousness. Antichrist is not an external evil force that manipulates and controls humans, but the corruption of a soul mind and the misuse and abuse of the creative ability of the soul mind to satisfy its selfish desires at the expense of others and to the detriment of its relationship with God.

Mental Illness and Possession

Impaired mental activity in humans can be precipitated by physical damage to the brain, the loss of neurons because of the natural aging processes in the human body, or the presence of a disease that prevents neurons or synaptic junctions from working properly. But what humans call mental illness is not a disease of a "human mind," but a breakdown in the communication between the physical conscious mind of the soul and the neural network of the human body being animated by the soul. Some forms of mental illness are a consequence of behavior during a previous life that contravened spiritual law, leading to causal influences unfolding through the human organism. Even if the person is committed to a mental institution with loss of most rational faculties, the soul retains its full mental faculties but is no longer able to properly manifest its thoughts through the physical body. Some Christians may ascribe certain instances of mental instability and the associated evil, decadent, or strange behavior of the afflicted individual to the action of demonic forces or Satan, but this is not the case. However, under certain conditions, souls in the borderland can communicate with and influence the minds of incarnated souls and cause confusion and mental imbalance that have no physical basis in disease. Neurological dysfunction can create a discontinuity or an opening through which a disincarnated soul in the borderland region can inject itself into the conscious affairs of the individual. Many of these possessed or mentally violated individuals are labeled insane, and the root cause of the insanity may be incorrectly attributed solely to neural deterioration or damage.

Possession can lead to conditions such as schizophrenia and other forms of dementia that cause the individual to hear voices as the conscious mind detects thought interference and is exposed to soul mind influences from the borderland. These psychotically deranged individuals may gain an enhanced awareness of the presence of disincarnate souls, but from the point of view of a human observer focused on the physical world, they appear to have lost their mind (281-24_19; 5753-1_22). Reading 295-8_22 clarifies the statement in Luke 8:2 that Jesus cleansed Mary Magdalene by casting out seven devils (KJV) or seven demons (NIV) by specifying that five of the seven devils were avarice, hate, self-indulgence, hopelessness, and blasphemy. These so-called devils were not spiritual beings that had come to prey on Mary, but were spiritual character flaws of Mary's soul mind that she had allowed to dominate her personality (3175-3_13). They are the same devils that take hold of any person who sinks into selfishness and self-indulgence to the extent that their will becomes the inner drive that prods the conscious mind into unspiritual and unconscionable activity. Mary's behavior was the outward expression of the same inner demons, the same character faults and unloving emotions, that many of us see, experience, and exhibit every day.

The readings warn about the danger of individuals trying to contact deceased relatives and other disincarnate souls. A susceptible person can be mentally compromised or possessed by another soul when it inadvertently allows access to the mind-body connection. The borderland soul may be able to exert control upon the mind and body of the unaware individual in ways that were never intended and can lead the innocent questing soul astray in spiritual matters. In some instances, mental communication or interference from the borderland becomes apparent during dreams, as in the well-documented and interesting case of the soul of a deceased Japanese cook who spoke to Daw Aye Tin in Burma through several dreams to make known his intentions of reincarnating through her. She later had a daughter who, as a child, claimed that she had been a cook in the Japanese army that occupied Burma during WWII and had been killed during a strafing attack by an Allied airplane (Stevenson, 2001). When Daw Aye Tin was interviewed several years later and asked about the dreams, she recalled that she had been friendly with a cook in the Japanese army but did not know if he had survived the war years. Soul-to-soul communication of this type has been recognized and reported across the world. Reincarnation was part of the culture of the Tlingit Indians of southeastern Alaska long before Europeans made first contact with them in the mid-eighteenth century. Older members of the tribe and deceased members alike would make their intentions known as to which woman they wished to be their future mother, usually within the same extended family, and mothers were on the lookout for unusual birthmarks that might verify the previous identity of a newborn child. The persistent and insistent introduction of Christianity and attendant pressure to abandon the belief in reincarnation has all but eliminated this once common belief (Stevenson, 1980).

Reading 1909-3_7 tells us that those who seek answers to spiritual questions by intentionally contacting disincarnate souls run the real risk of opening their inner mind to the ideas and thoughts of another soul that may or may not be attuned to the Mind of God, a soul that may very well want to express its own selfishness through the body of the questioning individual. Not all disincarnate souls have honorable reasons for making contact with an incarnated individual. The reading asks why we would desire to be guided by souls in the borderland when we can have direct access to the Christ Spirit, the spirit of truth, if we will only open our mind to the presence of God and let him commune with us and lead us through the journey of life. Edgar Cayce did not routinely contact disincarnated souls in the borderland to obtain spiritual information. In his purposeful relaxed state, his thoughts could peruse and interpret the memories stored in the Akashic records and the residual radiated energy of activity that was still detectible and accessible in the cosmic realm, and he could access the subconscious minds of individuals that requested his medical advice (364-6_6; 2522-1_3; 3902-2_3; 281-36_11; 294-1_1; 900-22_3). He sometimes warned individuals who sought spiritual guidance through psychic activity to beware of trying to make contact with the borderland region because of the danger of becoming entangled with the mind of a less than altruistic soul.

To summarize, the readings make it clear that the force we call evil is the spirit of soul rebellion against the influences of good, righteousness, and truth and the misapplication of creative forces of good to indulge in rebellious actions (262-52_25). It is the willingness of a soul to misuse its creative ability to generate evil for the selfish benefit of the soul, rather than seeking to be of service to others and to God. Evil can be fed and groomed until it is a prime ingredient of our soul individuality and can be projected into human society through our will and personality. We should never allow our minds to be seized by the fear of demonic possession or the perceived need to ward off disembodied sinister demonic beings that enjoy wreaking havoc on our otherwise innocent lives out of sheer deviltry and diabolical glee. When these self-imposed and imagined fears take root in our minds, they prevent us from growing spiritually or becoming more enlightened through Christ Consciousness. Scripture tells us to fear not, but to trust in God even when it appears that all hope is lost (Mark 5:36), to accept the peace that comes from putting our faith in God (John 14:27), and to fill our heart with the perfect love that drives out fear (1 John 4:18). The trials and temptations we face in life are those that we have caused to befall us by our ignorance or willful neglect of the action of spiritual law and the failure to let love become integral to our subconscious individuality and conscious personality. We are not required to face the consequences of sin that any others have brought upon themselves, including our direct ancestors, unless our soul was incarnated in that ancestor's body and was the perpetrator of the sin. The only evil beings are those souls that have so degraded themselves before God and divorced themselves from God that they are no longer cognizant of their need to take moral responsibility for their thoughts and actions. Their manifested selfishness would come to naught in the society of humans if it were not for the many similar-minded souls or spiritually weak souls that willingly trade their higher consciousness for a baser consciousness that leads to discord, conflict, and wars between contending soul forces.

The ancient battle between right and wrong is not between God and Satan, but between love of the Self and love of God and neighbor, between spiritual purity and material decadence, between moral right and immoral wrong. The battle between the Sons and Daughters of God and the sons and daughters of Belial still plays out on the Earth because souls who are in the wrong believe it is their right to take or destroy what belongs to souls who are in the right. There is evil in the material world, and there is evil in the spiritual borderland realm through which souls pass between incarnations, but it is the evil of unbridled selfish souls that have forsaken their creator. These souls are so blinded by their inflated sense of self-worth that nothing matters except that they get their selfish desires for wealth and power fulfilled even at the expense of the peace and harmony, or even the lives, of others. The gift of free will can be used as a powerful self-serving weapon, and left unchecked can tear apart societies and bring nations to ruin. A spiritually sick and evil soul has the ability to use its God-given mind to create chaos, strife, dissension, and conflict, just as any spiritual and loving soul can create an atmosphere of kindness, generosity, and mercy. The communities that formed and faded into history and the societies that flourish or languish today are conglomerates and composites of souls trying to manifest the love of God and souls hell-bent on serving themselves at the expense of others.

We can harbor a personal devil to which we give sanctuary and obeisance. We can pervert a portion of the goodness that we acquired from God by using our minds and spirit to manifest evil toward fellow souls. We are not pawns of some mythological demonic creature, but we can become pawns of our own unbridled self-centered will and consciousness. The source of evil in the world is not a powerful spiritual being dedicated to tricking and deceiving human beings into committing sins against God and evil actions against fellow souls. It is not a creature created by God that tempts mankind when authorized to do so to test man's resolve to remain faithful to and loyal to God. The readings establish and support the fact that God is not only the creator of all things material and nonmaterial, but that God is the spiritual substance and source essence of all things that have been created. There is nothing that is not God, and there is no place for evil in the omnipresent infinite goodness and love that is God. God does not and cannot create evil. But souls, as free-will agents created in the image of God, have the creative power to misuse spirit for selfish, evil purposes. And they do so in an abundance of selfish creativity that has brought discord and disharmony into the very being of God and caused all manner of spiritual ramifications for souls. The source of evil in the world is not an inherited propensity to sin because of the actions of a long-dead ancestor. The source of evil is us, our willingness to misuse the gift of free will and the incredible power of the mind. As Pogo said, "We have met the enemy and he is us" (Kelly, 1970). Evil is the manifested desire of every soul that acts with selfish intent. The root cause of evil is the will and desire of the soul, and it is transmitted into the words and actions of man through the conscious mind and personality of the incarnated soul. Every evil word and action is preceded by and has its origins in the will and thoughts of a soul mind, the desire of the soul to express itself in ways that are counter to the purpose for which it was created.

The Reality of Consciousness and the Consciousness of Reality

There is the necessity of fitting itself through the experiences of all phases and realms of existence, then; that it, the soul, may not cause disruption in the realm of beauty, harmony, strength of divinity in its companionships with that Creative Force. (Edgar Cayce Reading 805-4_10)

Let's summarize what we have learned about consciousness, reality, and the origin, journey, and destiny of the soul from the Edgar Cayce readings. There is one overarching consciousness in the cosmos; the consciousness of God, the Almighty Creator, Creative Force, and First Cause behind all things, whether animate or inanimate, living or dead, spirit or matter (136-59_4). The inevitable and inescapable conclusion from the readings is that all configurations of reality, all created nonmaterial and material realms, and all forms of life are arrangements and configurations of one Spirit acted upon by the mind of God. The Will of God directs the Creative Force of Mind to bring forth diverse realms of existence that serve the various needs and purposes of God. It determines which of his creative thoughts and ideas will be brought to fruition to create a specific structure within which or upon which consciously directed mental activity, or life, can take place. The source substance of all forms of reality is the unformed eternal Spirit that is the essence of the Omnipresent God. Spirit is reality held in potential waiting to be shaped by the insistence and urging of desire and creative force, the substance from which the various manifested realms of reality are formed or constructed in the cosmic realm and the physical realm. Spirit in the cosmic realm is the analogue of energy in the physical realm. It is the precursor substance of the physical universe, the spirit-energy that manifests in the evolving physical realm as electromagnetic energy and matter.

God creates and sustains various realms of reality by consciously manifesting his desires in diverse ways to fulfill his thoughts, ideas, and purposes. God also creates various forms of consciousness that interface with these realms. Just as forms of reality are variant descendants of the one Spirit of God, so are all variants and forms of consciousness descendants of the Mind of God, the one mind that is the master Creator of all that exists. There is only one mind, one God, but out of that single mind arises many distinct forms of mind and consciousness, each having a definite purpose and each developing according to the nature of the reality it perceives and the manner in which it receives sensory or mental information about that reality. Each mind develops unique characteristics, patterns of thinking, and responses that allow the mind to interact with and integrate with the world in which it is immersed. The nonphysical realm has generally been called the spiritual or cosmic realm herein, but this comprehensive realm includes different regions and dimensions where different levels and types of consciousness are active. Does this imply that God is divided or fractured? On the contrary, it implies a unitary cosmic God that is the wellspring from which issues forth all forms of mental activity, all variants of consciousness, and all configurations of reality. There is a reality of consciousness, a structural reality that pervades the cosmos and creates shape and form, and there is a consciousness of reality, an ongoing perception of that structure in the minds of sentient beings that populate the cosmos, including that portion of the cosmos we call the physical universe.

We have learned that God desired companionship. God is not an uncaring and unfeeling being that exists outside of and beyond his creations. All of his creations are, in one way or another, portions of himself. One of the essential mental and emotional traits of God is love. Love is not simply an aspect of God. Divine love is a fundamental and intrinsic element in the emotional temperament of God. For love to be fulfilled, there must be an object toward which love is directed. God desired to share his creations, his ability to create, and the joy of the creative process with other beings. God wanted like-minded intelligent beings that would fulfill his increasing desire for companionship by consciously receiving, sharing, and conveying his abiding love. These beings would need to have the capacity to feel and express love, but could not be coerced into giving love to their creator. Like all of God's creations, these sentient beings would have to be formed from the Mind and Spirit of God. In the vast cosmic realm where space and time have no meaning, the single consciousness of God released portions of himself, billions of individual points of nascent consciousness, each having the opportunity to develop individualized minds and self-awareness, each with the freedom to make choices that reflect the desires of their independent free wills. The harmonious union and combined activity of will, mind, and spirit would allow these newly aware life forms, these souls, to perceive and manipulate their environment and interact with other souls.

Reality for the soul is created at the intersection of the soul mind and the realm in which it generates activity and has experiences. Each new soul, an immature unit of life created in the image of God, developed its own unique pattern of thinking and its own unique individuality. Factors that affected soul development included the strength and intensity with which they mentally communed with their creator and their interaction and experiences with other souls, especially the way they chose to treat and respond to other souls. Each individual point of evolving consciousness was maturing into a sentient intelligent being with a powerful mind capable of highly advanced analytical skills. The unknown factor was the need for souls to willfully activate their innate desire to emulate the loving and caring attitude of their creator, thereby adding wisdom to their mental skills. Of all the creations made by the Almighty God, souls are the only creations that have the potential to become such a powerful intellectual force in the cosmos. It is the birthright and privilege of every soul to eternally share in the joy of God's creative activities. Souls have been offered the incredible opportunity to become gods, meaning to become as much like God as they desire without actually becoming the entirety of God, but ultimately the choice is up to the soul to accept and embrace that opportunity. As beings formed of spirit, souls are united with the Spirit of God, whether or not they consciously recognize that truth. But souls have used their free will and mind, the factors that coordinate and direct the creative activity of a soul, in ways that have caused them to be mentally separated from God. Souls are the only creations that have the ability to defy their creator. Many souls shone brightly in God consciousness, the awareness of and respect for their creator, but many others became tarnished, dimmed, and diminished as they used their free will to indulge in self-gratification and self-glorification. The desires and thoughts of many souls became far from godly.

Something happened in the mental development of many new soul minds, something that God knew was a possibility, but that he had hoped would not come to pass. Many souls began to abuse the gift of free will so effectively and with such concentrated effort that they forgot their potential and destiny to be eternal companions of God. Nothing can tear a soul away from this spiritual purpose except its own improper and selfish misuse of free will. These errant souls pursued selfish desires at the expense of their well-being and the peace and happiness of other souls, and ignored the need to constrain their creative abilities within the broad confines dictated by spiritual law. Instead of embracing the opportunity to live in glorious communion and companionship with their creator, many souls chose to use their free will to direct their minds to embrace self-indulgence and self-centered egotism. They decided to take the dark path of spiritual rebellion and disobedience, sin against the authority of their creator. Soul selfishness in the noncausal cosmic environment is insidious in that it leads to loss of God awareness without a clear conscious perception of the loss, which feeds into increasing self-centeredness. Because causality is not an intrinsic characteristic of the cosmic realm, rebellious souls found it difficult to recognize and understand the spiritual damage they were inflicting upon themselves by their inappropriate thoughts and behavior. All errant souls must be purged of this tendency to rebel against their creator before they can take their place as companions of God (262-79_11; 262-81_13). The bright future that God set before each point of consciousness, each developing mind, is a wonderful thing that should not be taken lightly.

The quest for new forms of self-indulgence and the incorrect perception that one soul is more important or better than its neighbor are attitudes that can only persist to the detriment of the soul. The minds of these delinquent souls existed in a state of tension between two extremes; the spiritual desire to embrace the innate pattern of the mind that fulfills the purpose of the soul as companion and co-creator with God, and the free-will-driven selfish desire to use the mind to create for selfish gain without regard to God or other souls. On the one hand, God is constantly calling the soul to seek the spiritual state of Christ Consciousness that makes the soul mind cognizant of its oneness with the creator and gives it the strength to fulfill its destiny. On the other hand, the wayward soul is more than willing to be lured by the temptation to use its free will and creative powers to indulge in a range of self-serving pleasures and activities that gratify every desire, feeding its inflated sense of superiority, and detracting the soul mind from its spiritual origins. The freedom of souls to serve the Self without regard for the damage they inflict on other souls or the Whole of God is absolute. When a soul defies its maker, the memory and awareness of its Creator recedes, and the higher consciousness of the soul mind becomes inaccessible. The spiritual nourishment, mental guidance, and outpouring of love that God offers his soul children only makes itself available and useful when the soul intentionally seeks its creator. As the soul looks to God for guidance and spiritual sustenance, the super conscious aspect of the soul mind yields a steady flow of love and support to the soul. The soul mind is the only force that can disrupt this flow of love or destroy the soul's awareness of its intimate relationship with God.

The soul's willingness to ignore or trample on the free will rights of fellow souls as it pursues its own selfish desires severely damages the soul's relationship with God. This sibling disrespect and the tension it causes has been a problem in the spiritual realm since souls gained self-awareness. It eventually brought God to the conclusion that souls would have to face causal spiritual consequences for their actions to help them regain their lost God consciousness. The disharmony among souls in the cosmic realm, the divisiveness it caused, and the disruption of peace and unity within the Whole of God could not be tolerated indefinitely. In essence, because all souls are portions of God, God was warring with and within himself. Rebellious souls are like cancerous cells that are destroying their host body. Souls were not acting for the good and unity of the whole but for their selfish individual interests. God had to act for his own sake as well as for the benefit and survival of his irresponsible and self-indulgent soul children. God perceived the need for an arena where soul minds could personally contend with and correct the spiritual misbehavior that was causing chaos and turmoil within the orderly and peaceful spiritual realm. This was an act of compassion and forgiveness extended to the rebellious souls by a merciful God who would extend every opportunity for errant souls to be redeemed and regain awareness of their Creator.

This new educational facility would encapsulate the ideas expressed in the sayings: "What goes around comes around" and "You reap that which you sow." God decided upon a facility that has three major components: (1) training centers that help restore the mental, emotional, and spiritual balance of the soul mind, and enhance and strengthen the positive godly qualities that souls inherited from God (called the fruits of the spirit in scripture); (2) an associated causal environment of matter and energy where opportunities are made available to the soul to prove it has learned and understood the lessons (the physical universe); and (3) a borderland where souls are active and interact between incarnations and training (called paradise in Scripture). The mental-spiritual training centers are nonmaterial realms of soul activity that help realign the will of the soul to the Will of God. They teach the soul mind the need to respect spiritual law and help cleanse the mind of thoughts and desires that are impediments to the activity of the Christ Spirit, that aspect of God that communes with the soul. The physical universe provides an environment in which souls can periodically demonstrate their understanding of God and spiritual law. When conscious interpersonal activity in space and time is conducted with an attitude of patience and persistent application of spiritual truths, souls can be released from their addiction to selfishness and self-gratification.

The combination of physical causality and spiritual law forces the incarnated soul to face its spiritual misdeeds, its personal sins against God. It provides repeated opportunities for the soul to recognize its failures, repent of its willingness to place the Self before God, and repair its relationship with God. This restoration or salvation process is not easy, and the soul that repeatedly refuses to make the necessary life changes can eventually forfeit its birthright of eternal companionship with God. These repercussions in material experience are not a form of punishment, but arise out of a spiritual law that consistently, repeatedly, and without bias brings new opportunities for delinquent souls to make choices that are aligned with the purpose of soul creation. Through the process of reincarnation, each soul repeats the moral and spiritual lessons it previously failed to learn, until the lessons are absorbed, fully internalized, and become second nature. Each human experience on the Earth is an opportunity for the incarnated soul to glorify God rather than glorify the Self in an environment that enhances its ability to become aware of its separation from God (1602-3_9).

The physical universe that contains the Earth was created out of an enormous one-time injection or encapsulation of spirit-energy that contained everything needed for the energy and matter structures of this physical reality. Its framework and the energy and matter interactions that occur within it are constrained and driven by a passive rule-based form of cosmic consciousness we call universal physical law, a subset of the more comprehensive cosmic law that guides activity in the infinite cosmic realm. Universal physical law defines how a portion of spirit-energy is confined within a realm of spacetime, how raw spirit-energy assumes the physical properties of electromagnetic energy and matter, how energy propagates, and how energy and matter interact within spacetime. All physical matter congeals out of pure energy following the rules embodied in physical law. Matter is at its essence a crystallized expression of the mental desire of a merciful God to create a soul rehabilitation and restoration facility, but matter is sterile and devoid of life as we understand it. God determined that a flourishing biological ecosystem would provide an ideal support system for a particular form of higher-order life that souls could animate while they experienced opportunities for spiritual growth. The biological ecosystem would begin with the fundamental units of life we know as cells, a group of organic molecules given an external injection of spirit and mind to create order, cooperation, and purpose. Without the impetus of this active projection of cosmic consciousness, no matter, not even matter in the form of complex organic molecules, has the capacity for self-directed motion or the ability to think about its current circumstances and plan its future.

Cells were set free to evolve and populate the planet with an amazing diversity of creatures with different ways of perceiving and interacting with their environment, different levels of consciousness, and different approaches to the problem of extracting energy from their environment and protecting the structural integrity of their bodies. Life is the interrelationship between a passive consciousness that gives rise to molecular matter, and an active consciousness that gives life to matter and influences biological evolution. This active consciousness is part of a distributed cosmic consciousness, called Group Mind in the readings, that gives self-identity to otherwise dead groups of organic molecules and gives biological life purpose. It infuses organized matter with the ability to manifest thoughts and instincts that contribute to the formation of a vigorous and dynamic biological ecosystem, intentionally move through the environment, and interact with other similar organisms. The billions of individual biological organisms that inhabit the Earth compete and survive within the framework of an integrated biosphere and evolutionary law. Individual points of plant and animal consciousness develop as portions of Group Mind learn to catalog, resolve, and understand information collected by the sensory organs of each newly forming plant or animal. The level of awareness, capacity to interact with the physical world, and intelligence of each new spark of consciousness depends upon the complexity of the body's sensory organs and neurological system, and the types of experiences it encounters as it leads the body along avenues that will improve its chances of survival.

Evolved human-animals were also directed by Group Mind, but souls interfered with the affairs of these creatures and severely disrupted the natural evolutionary progression of their species. The Group Mind consciousness was co-opted and altered over time to satisfy the curiosity and selfish interests of souls, an event that precipitated the entrance of the soul Amilius and his co-workers to warn the decadent souls of the spiritual danger of their actions and remind them of their original spiritual purpose. The thought-form projections of this Adamic group transformed into physical bodies and became capable of biological reproduction. Their progeny are the primary ancestors of the human bodies that souls animate today. Souls would gradually be required to incarnate only through pure and mixed (with soul-animated human-animals) descendants of the original Adamic group, leaving the naturally evolved human-animal life forms to dwindle and perish from the evolutionary record during the millennia that followed the Adamic group influx. Humans today are entirely animated by soul minds that bear no relation to the Group Mind that controls evolved higher-order animals. Human bodies are still subject to evolutionary laws, but the influence of the soul minds that animate human bodies today profoundly distorts the direction and rate of their natural evolutionary progress.

Most humans do not readily perceive and do not really appreciate that the universe in which we live has an underlying spiritual purpose and is a place where spiritual shortcomings are met with physical, mental, and emotional suffering as souls come face-to-face with unpleasant manifestations of their spiritual rebellion. Societal interaction among incarnated souls is important to the spiritual evolution of soul consciousness. The Earth is sometimes referred to in the readings as the plane of application, the place where humans interact within the various cultures they erect and express their concept of God, primarily through interpersonal relationships. Incarnation is part of a work-study program that gives souls the opportunity to show what they have learned, demonstrate the depth of their understanding of spiritual principles, and receive feedback as needed to correct any misunderstanding. It is where souls feel the full consequences of their propensity to rebel against God. It is not a place where punishment is inflicted on sinners, but is a realm of opportunities designed to correct mental-spiritual deficiencies that lead to the loss of God consciousness that manifests as immoral and ungodly behavior. The expanded awareness of the subconscious mind is reduced to the finite material awareness of a physical conscious mind so that souls can meet and conquer each deficiency in a sequential manner that enhances the probability of rehabilitation success. Human experience, approached properly, repatterns the soul mind to Christ Consciousness. Our human behavior is an expression of our soul's current understanding of God and current state of God consciousness, and determines whether or not we are ready to stand in the presence of God.

Intentional consciousness—the everyday mindfulness of who we are, how we got here, and what we need to do to achieve Christ Consciousness—is necessary to release our souls from the physical realm and end the cycles of incarnation. Any person who diligently seeks to reunite with God in will and purpose through scriptural study, prayer, setting ideals, meditation, and loving service can open his or her mind to the presence of God as the Christ Spirit, even during life's most trying and difficult circumstances. As the mind becomes more receptive to the spirit, the person will begin to detect the influence of the subconscious mind through dreams, intuition, and other unconscious sources of guidance, including spiritual truths studied in the mental-spiritual training centers, thereby glimpsing the infinite in the finite. The incarnated soul instinctively knows its purpose and its creator, but must take the initiative to shift its sphere of awareness to include those aspects of its mind. We can access all that is holy and good within ourselves if we will seek God with our hearts and minds, stay true to the Way taught by Jesus, and imitate the example he provided of a life well lived. The readings declare that ". . . no soul can say that [Jesus the] Christ is come of God SAVE the Holy Spirit convict him of that statement. And should one say such and not live the LIFE that would exemplify that, then such an [sic] one is condemning self already" (262-72_7). The knowledge and understanding that Jesus the Christ is the Son of God comes from an inner awareness and conviction of that truth as verified by the inner prompting of the Holy Spirit, the Christ Spirit. Once an incarnated soul awakens its consciousness to this reality, it cannot act in opposition to his teachings without bringing severe condemnation to itself. It is largely up to us to step out in faith and embrace the ideal of a loving God and loving service toward others. Jesus will help us bear the suffering and burdens we will face during the journey, and God will be merciful to us as we struggle, falter, and even fail to overcome our propensity for selfish thoughts and behavior. Even a sincere effort has spiritual value.

Whereas the mind and consciousness of the Almighty created the reality of a physical universe, the mind of the soul and its consciousness of physical reality give it the opportunity to manifest spiritual truth in a causal realm. The interaction of the physical and spiritual sets up a mental tension in the soul, in which the perception of time, space, and causality in the human experience can bring out the soul's innate sense of spiritual responsibility and lead to attunement with God. The physical law of cause and effect and the analogous spiritual law of sow and reap is in effect whenever a soul animates a human body. This combination governs the physical destiny of the body and the spiritual destiny of the soul. It holds the soul morally and spiritually accountable for its earthly actions and can course correct the wayward soul. Soul growth is intimately bound to human activity. Spiritualized human activity grounded in service moves the incarnated soul away from rebellion and rejection of its Creator and toward eternal loving companionship with its Creator while still retaining its free will and independent identity. The most important lesson an incarnated soul can learn is to balance the needs of the outer material world with the needs of the inner spiritual world by making material choices that honor God and neighbor through the liberal use of love, kindness, generosity, patience, and mercy. An undisciplined soul mind becomes attached to the physical pleasures of self-gratification, the physical desires of power and wealth, and the ability to lord over its siblings. Self-serving desires can be seductive to the conscious mind that is not anchored to the Christ Spirit. Repeated pursuit of those desires can cause the soul mind to wander far from its spiritual roots and interfere with the soul's ability to fulfill its unique and special place in the order of creation, but with the proper guidance from the will, the mind can stop fixating on those experiences. The will of the soul can be attuned to the Will of God and the spiritual purpose of the soul, effectively preventing material addiction and leading the soul to spiritual growth. Properly harnessed, the will is able to suppress and reject inappropriate carnal desires and redirect the soul's attention more toward the creator of the soul.

Soul restoration and redemption is mentally challenging. It involves eliminating habitual patterns of selfish thought, reorienting the soul mind toward God consciousness and spiritual thought patterns, and testifying to those more godly thoughts through service-oriented selfless activity in human society. The incarnated soul must be helpful and generous with time and resources toward more unfortunate fellow souls that are struggling to cope with the trials and temptations brought about by their spiritual rebellion. When the will and mind are harnessed by a spiritually oriented soul, the barriers between God and man begin to break down, and the force of the Christ Spirit will manifest through the soul into the physical world as loving, kind, patient relationships. At first, the manifestation of goodness and godliness will require a conscious effort and frequent willful redirecting of the mind until the new way of thinking and perceiving the world becomes habitual and natural. As the different aspects of the soul mind unify in a common spiritual purpose, a channel or conduit is formed that allows the free flow of the Christ Spirit into our lives to comfort us and aid us in our life struggles. As this force of love radiates outward, it benefits the individuals within our local sphere of influence who are struggling to find their spiritual purpose.

The most important aspect of our humanity, the reality behind the façade of flesh and bones, the full consciousness behind the limited consciousness we mistakenly call human, is our eternal soul. Our innermost consciousness is the most valuable resource we possess, and yet we seldom exercise it or put it to practical use for our spiritual benefit. We rarely lift ourselves above the pursuit of mundane human goals to imagine that our minds run far deeper than the superficial and often inane and selfish expressions of our conscious mind. We seldom envision ourselves as anything greater than smart bipeds among quadrupeds. Why is it that we think so small? It is vitally important that we human beings learn that we are souls first and foremost. Jesus, speaking to the Pharisees at the Jerusalem temple who were ready to stone him for blasphemy, reminded them of the fact that their own scriptures declared that they are gods. The readings affirm the truth of this assertion, but qualify it with the caveat that *we are gods in the making* (262-67_21; 877-21_30). The reality of this amazing proclamation is fulfilled as we learn to apply our soul's mental-spiritual training and consistently project the fruits of the spirit as we serve others in human society. Do we really want to let that promise slip away from us? Is the pursuit of all manner of useless baubles and trinkets or influence, power, and control over our fellow human beings really worth the spiritual cost? What a terrible waste of time, effort, and physical and mental resources. What a waste of life itself. The continued existence of the soul into eternity is inextricably connected with the ability of the soul to remain cognizant of its mental and spiritual connection to God. The soul has a bright future if it will just reject the siren call of sin and rebellion, material self-gratification, and the selfish desire to manipulate, control, and dominate its fellow souls. The soul that succeeds can embrace and experience the glorious reality of communion and companionship with God. The physical universe is designed to cleanse the soul of its evil tendency to rebel against God, but incarnation is only effective to the extent that the soul mind learns to cooperate with God as it faces the challenges and opportunities presented in life. The soul has the potential to be like God, but it takes faith, patience, and perseverance to reach out and grasp that possibility.

Much of the physical pain and agony, emotional depression and anxiety, and mental sorrow and anguish that we experience during human incarnations is self-created. It is a direct consequence of willful selfish activity that rebels against God or violates spiritual law, causing us to lose awareness of his presence and block our ability to feel his boundless love. The illnesses that wrack human bodies are largely a result of our inability or reduced ability to receive the flow of love and life force that God, as the Christ Spirit, desires to bestow upon us. The hateful rhetoric that tears apart families, the civil chaos that divides nations, and the economic and military conflicts that pit nation against nation are driven by the inability of people to embrace the concepts of cooperation and love thy neighbor as thyself. These human tragedies are naturally eliminated in the mindset of Christ Consciousness as we open ourselves to the Christ Spirit for aid, sustenance, support, and strength. We can begin this spiritual transformation at any moment during any life situation we face. Souls that honor God will be glorified to God's service as the soul mind gains a restored consciousness of his presence. The soul is redeemed, forgiven, and saved, to use the parlance of traditional Christianity, as it regains conscious awareness of its creator and embraces the original purpose of its creation. It is the culmination of the long journey that leads wayward souls from spiritual rebellion to material incarnation to companionship with God. It takes many lifetimes and focused intentional desire, dedication, and serious work before a soul can naturally and consistently express the love of God to every neighbor in a way that is totally selfless, but that is the measure by which God assesses our worthiness to reside with him for eternity in the cosmic realm. We do not go to heaven, but we grow toward heaven in consciousness as we learn to spiritually, mentally, and emotionally embrace a loving God as our creator and virtuously apply the fruits of the spirit in our lives (2505-1_17).

References

Agranoff, B. W., and others, 1999, Invertebrate Learning and Memory, In: Siegel, G.J., et al., editors. Basic Neurochemistry: Molecular, Cellular and Medical Aspects, 6th edition, Philadelphia: Lippincott-Raven; 1999. <https://www.ncbi.nlm.nih.gov/books/NBK28212/>

Avalon, Arthur, 1974, The Serpent Power: The Secrets of Tantric and Shaktic Yoga: Dover Publications.

Boston, P. J., 2008, Encyclopedia of Ecology: Elsevier B.V., Amsterdam, The Netherlands, pages 1727–1731. <https://courses.seas.harvard.edu/climate/eli/Courses/EPS281r/Sources/Gaia/Gaia-hypothesis-wikipedia.pdf >

Bro, Harmon H., 2011, Edgar Cayce - A Seer Out of Season; The Life of History's Greatest Psychic: A.R.E. Press, Virginia Beach, Virginia.

Cayce, Edgar, and Van Auken, John, 2007, Toward a Deeper Meditation: A.R.E. Press, Virginia Beach, Virginia.

Davies, Brian, and Evans, G. R., (ed.), 2008, Why God Became Man; Anselm of Canterbury, The Major Works: Oxford, Oxford University Press.

Enns, Peter, 2012, Evolution of Adam; What the Bible Does and Doesn't Say about Human Origins: Brazos Press, Grand Rapids, Michigan.

Fu, Q., Hajdinjak, M., Moldovan, O., et al., 2015, An Early Modern Human From Romania with a Recent Neanderthal Ancestor: Nature 524, 216–219. <https://www.nature.com/articles/nature14558>

Furst, Jeffrey, 1976, Edgar Cayce's Story of Jesus: Berkley Books.

Gershom, Yonassan, 1992, Beyond the Ashes: Cases of Reincarnation from the Holocaust: A.R.E. Press, Virginia Beach, Virginia.

Goff, Phillip, 2017, The Case For Panpsychism: Philosophy Now: A Magazine of Ideas, London, United Kingdom. <https://philosophynow.org/issues/121/The_Case_For_Panpsychism>

Greene, Brian, 2005, The Fabric of the Cosmos: Space, Time, and the Texture Of Reality: Random House Inc., New York, New York.

Hazen, R. M. and others, 2008, Mineral Evolution: American Mineralogist, Vol. 93, 1693–1720. Summary Article - Carnegie Institution, 2008, Mineral Kingdom Has Co-evolved With Life, Scientists Find: Science Daily, Nov 14, 2008. <https://www.sciencedaily.com/releases/2008/11/081113181035.htm>

Imes, Jeffrey, 2021, The Essenes and the Advent of Jesus: BookBaby Publishers, p. 79.

Imes, J.L., 2022, The Spiritual Purpose of the Physical Universe, BookBaby Publishers.

Iyengar, B. K. S., 1979, Light on Yoga: Revised Edition, Shocken Books, New York, NY.

Jabr, F., 2012, How brainless slime molds redefine intelligence: Nature. <https://www.nature.com/articles/nature.2012.11811>

Jung, C. G., 1971, The Portable Jung: Edited by Joseph Campbell, The Viking Portable Library, Viking press, New York.

Jung, C. G., 1989, Memories, Dreams, Reflections: Edited by Aniela Jaffe, Translated by Richard and Clara Winston, Vintage Books, Penguin Random House, New York, New York.

Kelly, Walt, 1970, We Have Met the Enemy and He Is Us: Walt Kelly coined the phrase for an anti-pollution Earth Day poster in 1970. <https://library.osu.edu/site/40stories/2020/01/05/we-have-met-the-enemy/>

Kandel, E. R., 2006, In Search of Memory; The Emergence of a New Science of Mind: W. W Norton and Company, New York, New York.

Kirkpatrick, S. D., 2001, Edgar Cayce - An American Prophet: Riverhead Books.

Larsen, C. S., 2019, Our Origins: W. W. Norton & Company, New York, New York.

Latty, Tanya and Beekman, Madeleine, 2011, Irrational Decision-Making in an Amoeboid Organism: Transitivity and Context-Dependent Preferences: Proc. R. Soc. B.278307–312 <https://royalsocietypublishing.org/doi/full/10.1098/rspb.2010.1045>

Leininger, B., Leininger, A., and Gross, K., 2010, Soul Survivor: The Reincarnation of a World War II Fighter Pilot: Grand Central Publishing, New York, NY.

Levitsky, Steven, and Ziblatt, Daniel, 2019, How Democracies Die; What History Reveals About Our Future: Crown Publishing Group, New York

Levitsky, Steven, and Ziblatt, Daniel, 2023, Tyranny of the Minority; Why American Democracy Reached the Breaking Point: Crown Publishing Group, New York

Lovelock, James, 1995, The Ages of Gaia; A Biography of Our Living Earth: 2nd edition. Oxford, Oxford University Press

Margulis, Lynn and Sagan, Dorion, 1997, Microcosmos, Four Billion years of Microbial Evolution: University of California Press, Berkeley, California.

Martin, Malachi, 1981, The Decline and Fall of the Roman Church: G. P. Putnam's Sons, New York, New York.

Millard, Joseph, 2007, Edgar Cayce: Mystery Man of Miracles: A.R.E. Press, Virginia Beach, Virginia.

Newberg, Andrew, 2012, The Spiritual Brain; Science and Religious Experience: The Teaching Company, The Great Courses, No. 1682, Chantilly, Virginia

Ouspensky, P. D., 2022, Tertium Organum (Annotated): The Third Canon of Thought: A Key To The Enigmas Of The World: Introduction by Jeff Carreira, Emergence Education.

Pasricha, S. K., Keil, J., Tucker, J. B., and Stevenson, I., 2005, Some Bodily Malformations Attributed to Previous Lives: Journal of Scientific Exploration, 19, 359–383.

Pepperberg, I. M., 2009, Alex and Me; How a Scientist and a Parrot Discovered a Hidden World of Animal Intelligence - and Formed a Deep Bond in the Process: Harper Perennial; Illustrated edition. <https://youtu.be/7yGOgs_UlEc> <https://youtu.be/cO6XuVlcEO4>

Plato, 2008, Timaeus and Critias: Penguin Classics, Penguin Random House, New York, New York.

Puryear, Herbert, 1992, Meditation and the Mind of Man: A.R.E. Press, Virginia Beach, Virginia.

Reid C. R., Latty T., 2016, Collective Behaviour and Swarm Intelligence in Slime Moulds: FEMS Microbiol Rev. 2016 Nov 1;40(6):798–806. <https://pubmed.ncbi.nlm.nih.gov/28204482/>

Reich, David, 2018, Ancient DNA and the New Science of the Human Past: Evolution Matters Lecture Series, Harvard Museum of Natural History. <https://youtu.bewww/990052wQywM>

Rosenblum, Bruce and Kuttner, Fred, 2011, Quantum Enigma: Physics Encounters Consciousness 2nd Edition: Oxford University Press, Oxford, United Kingdom.

Salzberg, S. L., 2018, Open Questions: How Many Genes Do We Have? BMC Biol 16, 94 (2018). <https://doi.org/10.1186/s12915-018-0564-x> <https://bmcbiol.biomedcentral.com/articles/10.1186/s12915-018-0564-x>

Sanderfur, Glenn, 1988, Lives of the Master; The Rest of the Jesus Story: A.R.E. Press, Virginia Beach, Virginia.

Schaff, Philip and Wace, Henry, eds., 1900, Second Council of Constantinople: Translated by Henry Percival. From Nicene and Post-Nicene Fathers, Second Series, Vol. 14, Buffalo, NY: Christian Literature Publishing Co., 1900. Revised and edited for New Advent by Kevin Knight. <http://www.newadvent.org/fathers/3812.htm>

Serres, M. H., Gopal, S, Nahum, L. A., Liang, P., Gaasterland, T., Riley, M., 2001, A Functional Update of the Escherichia coli K-12 Genome: Genome Biol. 2001;2(9):RESEARCH0035. doi: 10.1186/gb-2001-2-9-research0035. <https://pubmed.ncbi.nlm.nih.gov/11574054/>

Shambaugh, D. E. and Puryear, H. B., 1981, Day by Day; Steps to a New Life: A.R.E. Press, Virginia Beach, Virginia.

Skrbina, David, 2017, Panpsychism in the West: Revised edition, MIT Press, Cambridge, Massachusetts.

Solberg, M. M., 2015, A Church Undone; Documents from the German Christian Faith Movement 1932–1940: Fortress Press, Minneapolis, Minnesota.

Study Group #1, 2019, A Search for God: Book I: Association for Research and Enlightenment, A.R.E. Press, Virginia Beach, Virginia, 61st Printing.

Study Group #1, 2016, A Search for God: Book II: Association for Research and Enlightenment, A.R.E. Press, Virginia Beach, Virginia, 35th Printing.

Steenkamp, Jan-Benedict, 2023, The Top-10 Most Evil Men of the 20th Century and Cautionary Lessons We Can Draw From Their Success. <https://medium.com/@jbs_78429>

Stevenson, Ian, 1980, Twenty Cases Suggestive of Reincarnation: University of Virginia Press, Charlottesville, Virginia.

Stevenson, Ian, 1983, American Children Who Claim to Remember Previous Lives: The Journal of Nervous and Mental Disease 171(12):p 742–748, December 1983. <https://med.virginia.edu/perceptual-studies/wp-content/uploads/sites/360/2016/12/STE17.pdf>

Stevenson, Ian, 1997, Where Reincarnation and Biology Intersect: Praeger Publishers, Westport, Connecticut.

Stevenson, Ian, 2001, Children Who Remember Previous Lives: A Question of Reincarnation: McFarland and Company, Inc., North Carolina

Sugrue, Thomas, 1997, There is a River: A.R.E. Press, Virginia Beach, Virginia.

Tucker, J. B., 2007, Children Who Claim to Remember Previous Lives: Past, Present, and Future Research: Journal of Scientific Exploration, Vol. 21, No. 3, pp. 543–552. <https://med.virginia.edu/perceptual-studies/wp-content/uploads/sites/360/2015/11/REI35.pdf>

Tucker, J. B., 2008, Ian Stevenson and Cases of the Reincarnation Type: Journal of Scientific Exploration, Vol. 22, No. 1, pp. 36–43. <https://med.virginia.edu/perceptual-studies/wp-content/uploads/sites/360/2016/12/REI36Tucker-1.pdf>

Todeschi, K. J., 2007, Edgar Cayce on the Akashic Records: A.R.E. Press, Virginia Beach, Virginia.

Todeschi, K. J., 2010, Edgar Cayce's Twelve Lessons in Personal Spirituality: Yazdan Publishing. Virginia Beach, Virginia.

Todeschi, K. J., 2011, Edgar Cayce on Reincarnation and Family Karma: Yazdan Publishing. Virginia Beach, Virginia.

Thurston, Mark, 1976, Experiments in a Search for God: The Edgar Cayce Path of Application: A.R.E. Press, Virginia Beach, Virginia.

Thurston, M. A., 1989, How to Interpret Your Dreams: Practical Techniques Based on the Edgar Cayce Readings: A.R.E. Press, Virginia Beach, Virginia.

Thurston, M. A., 1996, The Inner Power of Silence: A Universal Way of Meditation: A.R.E. Press, Virginia Beach, Virginia.

United Nations, 2022, World Population Prospects 2022: Summary of Results. <https://www.un.org/development/desa/pd/sites/www.un.org.development.desa.pd/files/wpp2022_summary_of_results.pdf>

Walter, B. F., 2023, How Civil Wars Start: And How to Stop Them: Crown Publishing Group, a division of Penguin Random House, New York, New York.

Whittle, M., 2008, Cosmology; The History and Nature of Our Universe: The Teaching Company, The Great Courses, no. 1830, Chantilly, Virginia.

Acknowledgements

I would like to thank the several friends and acquaintances who have taken the time to give thoughtful comments about the conceptual idea and structure of this book, and those who have expended the energy to carefully review the manuscript. I greatly appreciate their constructive ideas and gently given criticisms. My thanks go to Joseph Taylor and Patrick Belisle for their thoughts on the book manuscript in its earlier draft. I appreciate the ideas and comments of my good friend K.M. King, who has been very supportive and encouraging of my efforts to write about the Edgar Cayce readings. I extend heartfelt thanks to Marisa Tusha for her detailed and comprehensive review of the manuscript. Her deep knowledge of the readings was readily apparent in her incisive comments, which prompted me to improve the flow of the text, forced me to rethink and revise some of the original wording, and caused me to think more critically about some aspects of the readings. Any errors and omissions herein are entirely mine.

Edgar Cayce and the A.R.E.

The Edgar Cayce readings are housed at the Association for Research and Enlightenment (A.R.E.) located in Virginia Beach, Virginia. The A.R.E. not only archives the readings and associated correspondence to and from the people who requested readings but also publishes, teaches, and explores the concepts presented in the readings. The topics of investigation include holistic health, meditation and prayer, the origin and nature of the soul and man, the relationship between man and God, intuition and dream interpretation, psychic phenomena, and reincarnation. Many of the readings offer insights into an ancient history of the human race that extends one hundred thousand years into the past, and document mankind's long struggle to find its way back to God. The A.R.E. actively promotes research into various topics of the readings and organizes conferences and webinars to disseminate information from the readings and related topics. The affiliated Atlantic University offers courses in transpersonal psychology and mindfulness using concepts from the readings to study the interrelationships among body, mind, and spirit. The university stresses the importance of service to humanity and the need for each individual to contribute to the spiritual advancement of humankind.

The reader is encouraged to seek out and explore the readings and apply the information therein to their daily lives in conjunction with their traditional religious beliefs. The two books *A Search for God: Book I* and *A Search for God: Book II*, or one of the excellent biographical sketches of Cayce referenced herein, are a good place to start. The guiding principle of the Association for Research and Enlightenment, as suggested in readings taken in reference to the creation of the organization, is that research must come before enlightenment. There are many books that cover various aspects of the readings that offer a way to begin understanding the readings without diving into the original documentation. The subjects contained in the readings are wide-ranging in scope, intellectually challenging in their depth and complexity, and the structure and grammar can be a bit intimidating. One can spend a lifetime unraveling and deciphering the various themes that thread their way through them, but the journey will be well worth the effort. The information held in trust at the Association for Research and Enlightenment can be used as a springboard to a lifetime of rewarding and fulfilling study on the nature of the soul and the purpose for material incarnation. It can give meaning and reason to what often seems like random life events within a greater society that often seems to be heading nowhere fast. To discover more about the A.R.E. visit the website https://edgarcayce.org/.

About the Author

Jeffrey Imes is a retired PhD physicist. His career included working with a private geophysics firm to locate oil reservoirs in Libya and Tunisia, for the US Geological Survey (USGS) to search for offshore oil reservoirs in the Gulf of Mexico, and with the USGS to develop computer simulations of groundwater flow through the aquifers of southern Missouri. He also studied the aquifers of Abu Dhabi Emirate, worked with the US Navy and USAID to identify promising locations for village water wells in Kenya and Djibouti, and worked with the World Health Organization to study aquifer production and arsenic contamination in Bangladesh. His interests range from cosmology to archaeology to spirituality. He has studied the Edgar Cayce readings for about forty-five years and appreciates the natural way in which the philosophy of the readings integrate science, Christianity, and certain aspects of Eastern religious thought in a coherent nondogmatic manner. He has published two other books that explore Christianity and the nature of the soul from the perspective of the Edgar Cayce Readings: *The Spiritual Purpose of the Physical Universe (2022)*, and *The Essenes and the Advent of Jesus (2021)*. Learn more at jeffreyimes-author.com.

www.ingramcontent.com/pod-product-compliance
Lightning Source LLC
Chambersburg PA
CBHW030906120626
46554CB00001B/32